ENGLISH KEYBOARD MUSIC *before the Nineteenth Century*

John Caldwell

Dover Publications, Inc.
New York

Published in Canada by General Publishing Company,
Ltd., 30 Lesmill Road, Don Mills, Toronto, Ontario.
Published in the United Kingdom by Constable and
Company, Ltd., 10 Orange Street, London WC2H 7EG.

This Dover edition, first published in 1985, is an unabridged republication of the work first published by
Praeger Publishers, New York, in 1973 (original English
publisher: Basil Blackwell, Oxford, 1973). The present edition is published by special arrangement with Basil Blackwell Ltd., 108 Cowley Road, Oxford OX4 1JF, England.

Manufactured in the United States of America
Dover Publications, Inc., 31 East 2nd Street, Mineola,
N.Y. 11501

Library of Congress Cataloging in Publication Data

Caldwell, John, 1938–
    English keyboard music before the nineteenth century.

    Reprint. Originally published: New York : Praeger,
1973.
    Bibliography: p.
    Includes index.
    1. Harpsichord music—History and criticism.   2.
Organ music—History and criticism.   3. Music—En-
gland—History and criticism.   I. Title.
ML728.C3   1985   786'.0942   84-21211
ISBN 0-486-24851-8

TO MY WIFE

Contents

Tables in Text

Preface

The intention of this book is to provide a summary of the development of English keyboard art during five centuries, and at the same time to offer to the student who wishes to investigate its details more thoroughly the bulk of the bibliographical and other material in a handy form. The author's own research was initially directed at the music of the earlier periods; but he eventually came to the conclusion that, while earlier studies such as that of van den Borren have tended to concentrate quite justifiably on the greatest phase of English keyboard music (that of the so-called 'virginalists'), the time had come to place the latter in its historical context, and to continue the story at least until the emergence of the pianoforte and the beginning of the English organ's protracted passage from insular independence to something approaching continental normality. The choice of the terminal date 1800 has been dictated largely by bibliographical convenience, though it will be seen that something has been said about the early nineteenth century—a period which has recently attracted some long overdue attention—in an informal way. If domestic keyboard music alone had been under consideration, it might have been possible to call a halt at 1720, the publication date of Handel's *Pièces de Clavecin*, before the flood-tide of popular arrangements begins to make nonsense of the ideal of bibliographical completeness; the history of church organ music, on the other hand, is a continuing process after 1660, in which the year 1837, marking the death of Samuel Wesley and the accession of Victoria, represents the only realistic dividing line. The deliberate vagueness of the expression 'before the nineteenth century' is thus the outcome of a necessary compromise, made the more inevitable by the overlapping of styles and media.

It is clear that a study such as this could not have been attempted except with the aid of a large number of scholarly editions and works of reference. Serious re-publication of our national treasures began in 1899 with Barclay Squire and Fuller-

Maitland's edition of the Fitzwilliam Virginal Book; subsequent editions of important manuscript sources in their entirety include Hilda Andrews' edition of *My Ladye Nevells Booke*, of the Mulliner Book by Denis Stevens (*Musica Britannica*, i), and of the Dublin Virginal Manuscript by John Ward. Later volumes of *Musica Britannica* have been devoted to the complete keyboard works of Thomas Tomkins, John Bull, Orlando Gibbons, Giles and Richard Farnaby, and William Byrd: the debt of scholarship to this monumental enterprise cannot be overestimated. Three smaller series in particular have contributed in making this music available to a wider public and in exploring that of later periods: Stainer and Bell's keyboard series, Hinrichsen's *Tallis to Wesley*, and Novello's *Early Organ Music*. Details of these editions in so far as they are relevant, together with those of such other modern editions as can be recommended on the grounds of scholarship in editing or the uniqueness of the music made available, can be found in the Bibliography.

As to works of reference, the most important have been the Hughes-Hughes catalogue of British Museum manuscripts (now supplemented by a handlist by Pamela Willetts published in 1970) and the *British Union-Catalogue of Early Music*. To these must be added the cataloguing labours of Arkwright, Barclay Squire, Fuller-Maitland, E. H. Fellowes, W. C. Smith and others, both printed and manuscript; the more significant of these have been enumerated in the Bibliography. It is fortunate that one of the volumes of the *Répertoire International des Sources Musicales* already in print should be that devoted to eighteenth-century collective publications; to the contents of the *British Union-Catalogue* it adds works found only in foreign sources, and foreign locations for works already listed there; it also names the composers who contributed to such publications, though without specifying the individual pieces. It would be too much to hope that the appendices of this book incorporate all the relevant material which the printed catalogues have to offer; nevertheless the latter have valuably supplemented my own necessarily incomplete assembly of sources from manuscript catalogues in the libraries themselves.

Apart from *Grove's Dictionary*, useful material has been

extracted from Eitner's *Quellen-Lexicon*, which apart from its own contribution summarises very adequately what can be gleaned from earlier authors, and from *Die Musik in Geschichte und Gegenwart*, especially in its later volumes. As to the history of the instruments themselves, which is not the main concern of this study, I have relied very heavily, as can be seen, on the standard works of Russell, Sumner, and Clutton and Niland. Treatment of this subject has been confined to that thought necessary in order to illuminate the development of keyboard style.

Oxford,
April 1972

Acknowledgements

My first thanks must go to Dr F. W. Sternfeld, who suggested the writing of this book and who has been a constant source of encouragement and friendly advice at every stage of its production. I also wish to thank Miss J. C. Pistor; Mr R. Langley; Dr H. D. Johnstone, who has kindly allowed me to make use of his work on Maurice Greene; and Mr B. A. R. Cooper, who has read the proofs and enabled me to incorporate a number of improvements in matters of detail. Most of all I wish to thank my wife, who has typed the book (much of it twice), read the proofs and generally expedited its production.

Most of the musical examples are transcribed from the original sources. But it has been a convenience to make use of the standard texts published in the series *Musica Britannica*. I therefore wish to thank the Royal Musical Association for permission to quote directly from the following volumes of *Musica Britannica*: vols. v (Exx. 87–92), xiv (42, 51, 53–59), xv (75c), xvii (146), xix (64–65, 69, 73, 86), xx (44, 46, 71), xxiv (76), xxvii (63, 81), and xxviii (40, 41a, 60a, 61–62). I also wish to thank the Trustees of the British Museum for permission to reproduce the page from the Robertsbridge Codex.

Author's Note

1. MSS are referred to in the order: Town, Library (see List of Abbreviations), Collection, Number.

Certain frequently mentioned MSS have acquired nicknames, which are retained: the Mulliner Book, Dublin Virginal Manuscript, Fitzwilliam Virginal Book, etc. The shelf-marks of these are quoted on their first appearance (for which see Index). When the names are italicised the reference is more specifically to the modern printed edition (see Bibliography). The editorial numberings of pieces have generally been quoted in preference to the folio or page numbers of the original MSS.

In general, titles of volumes are italicised while individual items are placed within quotation marks; italics have been retained, however, for all titles in foreign languages.

2. In the notation of pitches, the system of Helmholtz is adopted, thus:

This is used even in descriptions of organ compass, although organ-builders still employ an archaic notation.

In addition octave-notation by pipe-length is adopted for all keyboard instruments (eight-foot tone = sounding at written pitch; four-foot tone = sounding an octave higher; sixteen-foot tone = sounding an octave lower). Thus C_1 (eight-foot tone understood) = C sixteen-foot tone; c = C four-foot tone.

The compass of keyboard instruments is defined according to the lowest manual note; but it is not always possible to determine with certainty whether such a note is to be regarded (for example) as c eight-foot or C four-foot. The deciding factor would be its relationship to written music; but this evidence is not always available, and in any case the relationship might change, even on the same instrument and with the same player, according to circumstances.

The pitch-standards of earlier times did not differ from present-day standards sufficiently to affect octave-notation. Extremes of high and low pitch were respectively above and below that of today in the sixteenth and seventeenth centuries. Thus the lowest note of the Worcester Cathedral Organ (1614), sounding approximately A_1 flat in modern terms, can be described as F_1 in terms of their choir pitch (which was high), or as C in terms of their organ pitch (which was low).

List of Abbreviations

1. *Libraries*

Bib. du Cons.	Bibliothèque du Conservatoire (Paris, Brussels)
Bib. Nat.	Bibliothèque Nationale (Paris)
Bod. Lib.	Bodleian Library (Oxford)
Brit. Mus.	British Museum (London)
Ch. Ch.	Christ Church (Oxford)
Coll.	College
Fitz. Mus.	Fitzwilliam Museum (Cambridge)
Lib.	Library
Nat. Bib.	National Bibliothek (Vienna)
Nat. Lib.	National Library (Edinburgh)
P.R.O.	Public Record Office (London)
Pub. Lib.	Public Library (New York)
R.C.M.	Royal College of Music (London)
R.C.O.	Royal College of Organists (London)
Staatsbib.	Staatsbibliothek (Berlin)
Univ. Lib.	University Library (Cambridge, Liège, Uppsala)

2. *Printed Sources*

BC1-5	*Bland's Collection (ca.* 1790–4)
CC	*A Choice Collection* (1700)
CL	*A Collection of Lessons* (1702)
CSEL	*A Collection of Six Easy Lessons (ca.* 1780)
CV1-4	*A Collection of Voluntaries* (1777) and subsequent volumes in the same series (see Appendix I)
HM	*The Harpsicord Master* (1697)
2HM	*The Second Book of the Harpsicord Master* (1700)
3HM	*The Third Book of the Harpsicord Master* (1702)
HMI(1)	*The Harpsicord Master Improved* (1711)
HMI(2)	*The Harpsicord Master Improved* (1718)
HP	*The Harpsichord Preceptor (ca.* 1785)
HSM	*The Harpsichord or Spinnet Miscellany (ca.* 1765)
LB	*The Ladys Banquet* (1704)

2LB	*The Second Book of the Ladys Banquet* (1706)
LB1, LB2	*The Lady's Banquet, 1st (2d) Book* (1730–1733)
LBC1–10	*Longman and Broderip's Collection* (ca. 1795)
LE, LE2	*The Lady's Entertainment* (1708)
LT	*The Leaves of Terpsichore* (ca. 1795)
M	*Melothesia* (1673)
MH/1–2	*Musicks Hand-maide* (1663, ca. 1668)
MH/3	*Musicks Hand-maid* (1678)
2MH	*The Second Part of Musick's Hand-maid* (1689)
MM	*Musical Miscellanies* (1784)
MM1–7	*Mercurius Musicus* (1708–1709)
NA	*A New Assistant* (ca. 1790)
P	*Parthenia* (ca. 1612)
PeL1–4	*Periodical Lessons* (ca. 1790)
PH	*Playing the Harpsichord* (ca. 1775)
PI	*Parthenia In-Violata* (ca. 1625)
PM1–16	*The Piano-Forte Magazine* (1797–1802)
PrL1–2	*Progressive Lessons* (ca. 1795)
SC1–2	*Storace's Collection* (1787–1789)
SCL	*Suits of the most Celebrated Lessons* (1717)
SCP1–8	*Select Concert Pieces* (1785)
SHSL	*Suits of Harpsichord and Spinnet Lessons* (ca. 1715)
SS	*Six Sonattas* (ca. 1770)
SV	*Six Voluntaries* (ca. 1775)
TV	*Ten Voluntarys* (1767)
TwV	*Twelve Voluntaries* (ca. 1780)

3. *Journals and Modern editions, etc.*

AMO	*Archives des Maîtres de l'Orgue*
BUCEM	*British Union-Catalogue of Early Music*
CEKM	*Corpus of Early Keyboard Music*
CM	*Clavichord Music of the Seventeenth Century*
CP	*Contemporaries of Purcell*
DDT	*Denkmäler Deutscher Tonkunst*
DVM	*The Dublin Virginal Manuscript*
EECM	*Early English Church Music*
EEH	*Early English Harmony*

EEOM	*Early English Organ Music*
EKM	*Early Keyboard Music*
EOM	*Early Organ Music*
FWVB	*Fitzwilliam Virginal Book*
HAM	*Historical Anthology of Music*
IMG	*International Musik-Gesellschaft*
JAMS	*Journal of the American Musicological Society*
MA	*Musica Antiqua*
MB	*Musica Britannica*
MGG	*Die Musik in Geschichte und Gegenwart*
ML	*Music and Letters*
MLNB	*My Ladye Nevells Booke*
MMN	*Monumenta Musica Neerlandica*
MQ	*Musical Quarterly*
MR	*Music Review*
MT	*Musical Times*
NOHM	*New Oxford History of Music*
OEOM	*Old English Organ Music*
PBVB	*Priscilla Bunbury's Virginal Book*
PRMA	*Proceedings of the Royal Musical Association*
PSMS	*Penn State Music Series*
RISM	*Répertoire International des Sources Musicales*
RRMBE	*Recent Researches in Music of the Baroque Era*
SBK	Stainer and Bell, Keyboard series
TCM	*Tudor Church Music*
TW	*Tallis to Wesley*

A small roman numeral indicates the volume number within a series (e.g. *MB*, v). References to articles are given in abbreviated form: e.g. Dart, *ML* (1959) 279. Reference to the Bibliography will elicit the full title.

London, Brit. Mus. Add 28550 (The 'Robertsbridge Codex'), ff. 43v–44r

The Middle Ages:
The Robertsbridge Codex

The development of keyboard instruments in the British Isles during the middle ages was certainly no slower than on the continent: in some respects, indeed, it seems to have been British craftsmen who provided models for the rest of the world. The oldest of these instruments by a very long way was the organ. Invented during the third century B.C., apparently by one Ktesibios of Alexandria, the organ in its hydraulic form enjoyed enormous popularity throughout the classical world. As a pneumatic instrument, blown by bellows rather than a pump, it was adopted by the Emperors of the East to enhance their out-door ceremonies of acclamation; and it was in this form, as a present from Constantine Copronymus to Pepin III, that it was re-introduced to the Western world in 756 or 757.

So at least runs the conventional account. Beside it must be placed the undoubted fact that St. Aldhelm (640–709) knew the organ in its pneumatic form; his verse not only demonstrates that he was familiar with its appearance and mechanics, but also implies that it could be used in worship.[1] There is also the less well-documented statement that St. Mailduf (d. *ca.* 675), an Irish monk who founded Malmesbury Abbey in Wiltshire, built or at any rate patronised the building of organs.[2] It is conceivable that St. Aldhelm, who became abbot of Malmesbury, obtained his knowledge of the instrument from British examples, and that the craft was first developed in the Christian west by Irish scholars,

---

[1] *De Laudibus Virginum* and *Enigmata XIII*. The relevant passages are quoted by J. Perrot, *L'Orgue*, p. 400 (French translations on pp. 288–9). The description of a bellow-organ by Bede (d. 735), on the other hand, is copied from Cassiodorus' commentary on Ps. 150 (Perrot, *op. cit.*, p. 385).

[2] Sumner, *The Organ*, p. 35.

whose passion at this date for travel and curious learning is well known. There is evidence that an organ in the church at Clogher was destroyed by fire in 814.[3]

It is certain that in the two centuries following the 'official' introduction of the organ to the West, British interest did not decline. It would seem in the main to have centred around the monastic communities. During the tenth century the abbeys at Malmesbury, Abingdon, Glastonbury and Ramsey were provided with organs.[4] Most famous of all was the organ built at Winchester Cathedral during the bishopric of Elphege II, who reigned from 984 to 1005. The monastic rule had been established there in 964, one year after St. Ethelwold, who is said to have built the organ at Abingdon 'with his own hands', had become bishop.[5] The Winchester organ was exceptional for its size: 400 pipes arranged in ten ranks. It required 70 blowers and two players, of whom the latter were required to be 'brethren of concordant spirit'. Each 'managed his own alphabet', which may be interpreted to mean that they played polyphonically, each covering the same range of 20 notes (in all probability a diatonic scale with the addition of B flats). The combination of their 'free' *organum* with the parallel *organum* produced by the ten ranks of pipes would have resulted in an extraordinary noise, and the monk Wulstan's reference to a sound 'like thunder' may not be the exaggeration which it is commonly taken to be.[6]

During the next four centuries records of the organ in Britain are scarce, but they are sufficient to show that there was no decline in their use. From the second half of the fourteenth century the organ used for choir services was normally placed in

[3] F. E. Warren, *The Liturgy and Ritual of the Celtic Church*, Oxford, 1881, p. 126. But see Perrot, *op. cit.*, pp. 295–6.

[4] The organ at Malmesbury was given by St. Dunstan (*ca.* 909–988), who was himself a musician, and dedicated to St. Aldhelm. The organ at Ramsey was presented by the Count Ailwyn in time for the dedication of the Abbey in November 991.

[5] He had been Abbot of Abingdon from 954. On the dating of the Winchester organ, which may have been preceded by a smaller instrument under Ethelwold, see A. Holschneider, *Die Organa von Winchester*, Hildesheim, 1968, pp. 76–8.

[6] See also Holschneider, *op. cit.*, pp. 139–42, and Perrot, *op. cit.*, pp. 305–8, 406–7.

the *pulpitum* or choir-screen[7] in secular churches, a practice which reflects both the tendency towards smaller instruments and a change in their use, namely the accompaniment of solo singers who were also placed on the screen. The larger monastic establishments, including cathedrals under monastic rule, originally employed the screen for the purpose of separating the monastic part of the church from that open to the laity, but they may have anticipated the secular churches in using them to bear the organ.

The English were also in the forefront in the development of an instrument which can hardly be anything but the harpsichord. The *eschaquier d' Engleterre* is mentioned by Machaut (*ca.* 1300– 77) in his *Prise d'Alexandrie* and *Li temps pastour*, and in 1360 Edward III gave an 'echiquier' to his captive, King John of France.[8] It is difficult to know how the term 'chessboard' came to be applied to a musical instrument, unless it referred simply to its external decoration. The instrument is no doubt the same as the *Schachbrett* mentioned in Eberhard Cersne von Minden's *Minneregeln* (1404). According to Curt Sachs[9] the word *Schach* is equivalent to *Schacht,* a Dutch word meaning 'spring' or 'quill', and the Western European terms are a mistranslation of the German. There is a chronological difficulty here, inasmuch as the term *eschaquier* precedes the earliest known appearance of *Schachbrett* or *Schachtbrett*. It is quite conceivable, however, that it was in use for 50 years or so before the *Minneregeln*. This theory postulates a Germanic origin for the instrument; but there is no doubt of its close association with England, where it was also known as 'chekker'.[10]

It is to England, finally, that the distinction belongs of having harboured the earliest known keyboard music. The fragment consists of two leaves (ff. 43 and 44) bound up with an old register from Robertsbridge Abbey (London, Brit. Mus., MS Add. 28550): hence the expression 'Robertsbridge Codex', which cannot properly refer to the musical fragment alone. Its

[7] Harrison, *Music in Medieval Britain*, pp. 202–5.

[8] Reese, *Music in the Middle Ages*, p. 483.

[9] Sachs, *Sammelbände der IMG* (1912) 485–6, cited by Panum, *Stringed Instruments*, pp. 492–3.

[10] In 1392–3. See Hayes, *NOHM*, iii. 483.

present location, indeed, hardly throws much light on its ultimate provenance. The date is usually given as *ca.* 1325, although it could be up to 25 years later. The manuscript contains three *estampies* (dances in several sections), of which the first is incomplete, and three motet transcriptions, the third incomplete.[11] The first two of these transcriptions can be identified as motets from the *Roman de Fauvel*, a French satirical poem copied, with musical interpolations, by Chaillou de Pesstain in 1316.[12]

The *estampies* beginning on f. 43 are not so called in the manuscript, but belong to the formal pattern of this medieval dance. Each of the two complete pieces consists of several *puncti* or sections, each repeated and provided with 'first and second time bars', indicated by the French terms *ouert* and *clos*. In both cases the second and succeeding *puncti* recapitulate substantial portions of the first, so that the same *ouert* and *clos* sections serve for each *punctus*. In the first piece the recapitulations are all from the same point, and are marked in the score by the English word 'return' or an abbreviation thereof; in the second they are from different points in the first *punctus* and are mostly implied by the context. The following diagram of the first piece will make its formal structure clear:

Punctus 1 (7) retn. (32) *ouert* (7) [*Punctus* 1 (7) retn. (32)] *clos* (7)
Punctus 2 (16) [retn. (32) *ouert* (7) *Punctus* 2 (16) retn. (32) *clos* (7)]
Punctus 3 (20) [retn. (32) *ouert* (7) *Punctus* 3 (20) retn. (32) *clos* (7)]
Punctus 4 (25) [retn. (32) *ouert* (7) *Punctus* 4 (25) retn. (32) *clos* (7)]

Here the symbol 'retn.' means the recapitulation from the point so indicated in the first *punctus*, and square brackets refer to music intended to be played but not actually written down. Figures in brackets represent numbers of bars in modern notation. The second piece differs only in having five *puncti* and in that the returns are made from varying points in the first *punctus*.

The incomplete piece at the beginning must have been written out in full, if indeed it was an *estampie* at all, since it ends with the indications of *ouert* and *clos* which in the two complete pieces needed only to be written after the first *punctus*.

---

[11] Complete edition in *CEKM*, i. Facsimile in *EEH*, i.
[12] Paris, Bib. Nat., MS fonds fr. 146.

The style of these pieces appears to be Italian rather than French, in spite of the use of French terminology. There is a very strong link between them and the monophonic Italian dances of about the same date from London, Brit. Mus., MS Add. 29987, as the following examples will show:

These dances are mostly *estampies*, although they bear a variety of titles. It has been conjectured[13] that the Robertsbridge dances were also originally monophonic, and that their notation (a row of letters beneath the single staff) stems from the fact that they are arrangements. There are two objections to this: the argument could not apply to the motets, presently to be described; and certain hocket-like passages, such as the following, could hardly have been conceived monophonically:

The motets are, of course, arrangements, but of polyphonic works, all the voices of which are represented in the transcription. Their appearance in the manuscript is somewhat confusing, for a verbal text, for the most part that of the top part of the motet in question, is intermingled with the letter-notation here used to represent the lowest voice. The following example will

[13] Handschin, *Acta Musicologica* (1938) 29.

illustrate the relation between the first motet, *Firmissime/Adesto/ Alleluia Benedictus*, and its transcription:[14]

The second motet, *Tribum quem/Merito/Quoniam* is treated in a similar manner, except that it is transposed up a tone, and that the solo opening of the original is given an accompaniment:

[14] The transcription of pairs of semibreves in the vocal version as equal notes is uncertain, but is retained here (in the form of equal semiquavers) to show the literal reading of the source. See Apel, *The Notation of Polyphonic Music*, p. 330. Facsimile of the vocal version on p. 329.

The third, incomplete piece, *Flos vernalis*, cannot be traced anywhere else, although it is obviously an arrangement like the others since the text of the original is underlaid throughout. It is in a different metre and apparently more floridly ornamented than its companions:

The notation of the manuscript is of interest. Its most significant feature, the combination of a single staff with a row of letters indicating pitches, was later to be used in German keyboard music, the earliest documents of which are from the early fifteenth century. But the gap in dates is too great for a German origin for the manuscript to be inferred from this, and the true source of this aspect of the notation is unknown.

It is the notation of the upper parts which affords the greatest fascination. They are written in a primitive form of Italian *ars nova* notation; so primitive, indeed, that it might be interpreted as representing the transition between the universally recognised notation of the late thirteenth century (*ars antiqua*) and the nationally divided (French or Italian) notation of the early fourteenth century (*ars nova*).[15] The main unit of time, the breve, represents the beat, not the bar as in later French and Italian music. Another transitional document is the *Roman de Fauvel* itself, from which the two complete Robertsbridge motets are transcribed. The significant point about the *Roman de Fauvel* is the addition to certain semibreves in a later hand of downward stems, signifying greater length compared with unmarked semibreves. It is precisely this feature of the Robertsbridge manuscript which is considered so decisively Italian; but the additions to the *Roman de Fauvel* show that, for a short time at least, the downward stem was a notational device known in France. It soon dropped out of the French system completely, while becoming indispensable in the Italian. The whole point of this discussion is to demonstrate that the Robertsbridge notation in its essentials would have been understood all over Western Europe in the early fourteenth century, and is not inconsistent with the view that these fragments may have been written down by an Englishman.

The motets, though French and not Italian in style, are written in the same notation as the *estampies*. They make much more frequent use of smaller note-values such as the minim, however, which was only very tentatively introduced into the *Roman de Fauvel*.[16] The hypothesis of an English scribe remains the most plausible, and the use of the word 'return' in the *estampies* would seem to clinch the matter. There is no problem about an Englishman having access to Italian and French music: such contacts were frequent in the fourteenth century.

A few scribal peculiarities remain to be discussed. Prolongation of the breve is expressed, not by the use of the long but by repeating the breve once or twice in outline, thus: ▪ □   or ▪ □ □ . A small circle or semi-circle above some notes may

---

[15] For a full discussion of the relevant notation, see Apel, *op. cit.*, pp. 37–40, 310–84; Parrish, *The Notation of Medieval Music*, pp. 108–86; and *NOHM*, iii 2–6, 48–52.

[16] In the first motet only, and by a later scribe. Apel, *op. cit.*, pp. 325–6.

indicate an ornament such as ✢ . The most pressing problem is the inscription at the head of the third *estampie*, which has been variously transcribed as 'Petrone' and 'Retrove'. The first might be the name of the composer, while the second might be an indication to return to the beginning, presumably after the *ouert* ending of the first *punctus*.

Are the Robertsbridge pieces genuine keyboard music (allowing for the fact that the motets, at least, are transcriptions)? The notation forbids any idea of a performance by instruments playing single parts, and in some places the scribe even indicates that the left hand has to play the top part.[17] But there remains the possibility of performance on the psaltery plucked with the fingers. The harpsichord in its essentials is of course nothing but a psaltery provided with quills and keys, so that the question is not as fundamentally important as might be supposed. On the whole, the highly decorative nature of the writing would suggest the presence of a keyboard mechanism. The existence of the *echiquier* at this early date, while not proved, is at least highly probable, and it may well have been the instrument for which the *estampies* were intended. They could also have been played on a small organ: not the tiny portative which was limited to monophonic music,[18] but the smaller kind of fixed, or positive, organ so often depicted. The church organ is the most likely instrument for the motets, although performance on an instrument of the harpsichord type cannot be ruled out. Numerous documents of the thirteenth and fourteenth centuries attest to the use of the organ in church services, especially during the Mass. In these motet arrangements we may perhaps find the answer, so often difficult to provide, as to the kind of music which was actually played on such occasions in fourteenth-century England.

[17] See Plate I. The method of indication is a small circle round the note or notes in question, as in f. 43v, line 8 and f. 44r, line 5. The circles in *Flos vernalis* merely draw attention to miscopied passages which are corrected by the letter-notation.

[18] The player's free hand operated the bellows.

II

The Fifteenth Century

No fifteenth-century English keyboard music has survived. It is true that one fragmentary document has been cited in this connection, but its credentials are not strong.[1] Nevertheless, the fifteenth century saw considerable advances both in the construction of instruments and in keyboard technique.

During this period the organ gradually became ubiquitous in cathedrals, abbeys and the larger parish churches. We have already noted its migration to the choir-screen in the cathedral and abbeys (pp. 2–3). This screen, made of stone and properly called the *pulpitum*, was normally built across the eastern arch of the transept in the secular cathedrals and across the western arch, or still further west, in monastic churches (including the monastic cathedrals). There were exceptions to this rule, but the object in all cases was to separate the community which governed the building from the laity, who were allowed to enter only the nave, or the nave and transept, as the case might be. Collegiate churches adopted a similar practice, as did college chapels, which were without a nave. Parish churches were content at first with an open wooden screen.

In the secular cathedrals, collegiate churches and college chapels, the *pulpitum* was used for the singing of the Epistle, Gradual, *Alleluia* and Gospel at Mass, and for the lessons, and apparently the responds which followed them, at Matins. The practice of singing the responsorial items, including the Gradual and *Alleluia*, in polyphony may have led to the placing of the organ on the screen to assist the solo singers, and in the course of time no doubt this method of performance would have come to be used for the musical successors of the respond, namely the

---

[1] Dart, *ML* (1954) 201. But see Ex. 7 below. Oxford, Bod. Lib., MS Douce 381, f. 23. Facsimile in *Early Bodleian Music*, i, pl. 25.

clausula and motet.[2] The monastic churches to a certain extent followed these liturgical customs, and during the fifteenth century most of the larger abbeys and cathedrals had an organ on the *pulpitum*. Finally the larger parish churches extended their screens by the addition of a rood-loft which was large enough to accommodate an organ and the singers of polyphony.

The basis of the later medieval arrangement was that every altar at which the polyphonic services were performed should be provided with an organ, usually in a raised position at the west end of the 'chapel'. In the case of services performed at the high altar this normally meant the main screen of the church. The next most important services were the votive masses of the Blessed Virgin Mary, performed in Her chapel. Since the *pulpitum* was not needed for ritual purposes at Lady-masses, the organ must frequently have been placed on the floor of the chapel. Nevertheless, the Lady-chapel was provided with a *pulpitum* at the collegiate churches of Ripon and Ottery St. Mary.

Shortly before the Reformation the personalised cult of Jesus began to rival that of Mary and so 'Jesus-altars', 'Jesus-chapels' and 'Jesus-masses' came into being. In some places, for example at Westminster Abbey and Durham Cathedral, the cult involved the use of a separate organ. At Durham, the Jesus-altar was in effect the nave altar. It was placed immediately in front of the rood-screen which, as in most monastic churches, was added west of the stone *pulpitum*. The organ was not placed, as one might have expected, on the rood-screen itself, but, faithful to the principal of having the organ west of the altar, in a loft between the two pillars of the second bay on the north side of the nave. At Ottery St. Mary, on the other hand, where the monastic arrangement of screens was adopted, the nave altar was provided with an organ placed on the rood-screen immediately behind and above it.

It is at Durham that the most complete known arrangement of organs existed before the Reformation. The Lady-chapel was placed at the west end of the church in the 'Galilee' and provided with its organ. The Jesus-altar and its organ have already been described. A third organ, its pipes 'all of most fine wood' was

2 See Harrison, *Music in Medieval Britain*, pp. 122–6.

placed on the stone *pulpitum*, but this was used only for 'principal feasts'. Two further organs were placed respectively on the north and south side of the choir (in a raised position above the choir-stalls), the former for use on Sundays and festivals which were not principal feasts, and the latter 'at ordinary service'. In most churches, however, a single organ would have sufficed for the choir services.[3]

Consideration of these liturgical factors is necessary for an understanding of medieval English organ building and organ music. It also helps to explain some curious facts. It explains, for example, the multiplication of organs in churches without any evidence that they were ever used in combination. It also accounts for the violence of Puritan objections in the sixteenth and seventeenth centuries, for these instruments were intimately bound up with the hated ritual of the medieval church, often enacted behind a screen through which the laity were refused admittance.

The fifteenth-century English organ was usually a small and simple instrument. There is no evidence that it ever included a pedal-board or more than one manual. The compass may have been that of the medieval theoretical scale known as the gamut ($G-e''$), or less, and some instruments may not even have been fully chromatic. Individual ranks of pipes could not be separated (this innovation apparently belongs to the sixteenth century and will be considered in the next chapter), and so the organ, once built, retained its individual characteristics of dynamics and *timbre*. No doubt these were decided upon in the first instance in connection with the liturgical function of the organ, the size of the church and its position therein. There is some evidence, however, that tonal *finesse* was rated more highly than mere volume. The organ did not have to fill the entire building with its sound, as it had at Winchester in the tenth century. The principal organ at Durham had wooden pipes only and was 'one of the fairest paire of the 3' choir organs: 'there was but 2 paire more of them in all England of the same makinge, one paire in Yorke and another in Paules'.[4] Wooden pipes, then, being a

[3] See *Rites of Durham*. The account just given draws largely on Harrison, *Music in Medieval Britain*, pp. 210–13.

[4] *Rites of Durham*, cited *ibid.*, p. 212.

rarity, we may suppose metal (tin or lead) to have been the usual material.[5]

The music played on these unpretentious instruments was closely bound up with the liturgy. Before about 1450, one of the functions of the organ may well have been to sustain the tenor line in motets, and music in motet style sung by soloists. From at least the beginning of the century, however,[6] it was also used for a different and more significant purpose, the replacement of some or all of the plainsong of certain liturgical items. The organ in this case fulfilled the functions of either one side of the choir or of a solo singer, or indeed of each in turn. It may also have alternated with choral polyphony when the latter became established after the middle of the century; but there is no evidence that the organ was ever used to accompany the choir.

The normal pattern for the use of the organ in the liturgy, therefore, was in alternation with plainsong, even though the latter may at times have been restricted to a mere intonation, followed by an organ piece of considerable length. Such at least was the case in the written Offertories of the sixteenth century. The origin of the practice is unclear, but it is said to have been introduced in order to relieve the monotony of the long services in choir. The earliest English reference, however, is to a ceremonial performance of the *Te Deum*, where perhaps the text was sufficiently well known for every other verse to be transferred to the organ alone.[7] In all probability the principle, once introduced, was extended gradually to many of the items of the Mass and Office, although the practice of performing the *Te Deum* ceremonially in this way still continued.[8] A Leicester Abbey inventory of *ca.* 1493 indicates the organist's repertory in a large monastic establishment at the end of the century: antiphons, hymns, responds, *Te Deum*, *Magnificat* for the offices; settings of

---

[5] For details of organ construction in the fifteenth century see Hopkins and Rimbault, *The Organ, Its History and Construction*, part i, 'The History of the Organ', pp. 46–52; Hopkins, *The English Medieval Church Organ*; Sumner, *The Organ*.

[6] The earliest known references to *alternatim* performance in England is from the year 1396 in connection with the *Te Deum*. See Harrison, *op. cit.*, p. 206.

[7] See footnote 6.

[8] Harrison, *op. cit.*, p. 216.

the *Kyrie, Sanctus, Agnus, Alleluia* and Sequence for the Mass.[9] This will be compared in the following chapter with the sixteenth-century repertory as it has come down to us.

It has been suggested that the organist originally played only the single notes of the plainsong allotted to him, and that this practice continued in the monasteries during the fifteenth century, at least where unskilled players were employed.[10] But there can be little doubt that from the beginning of the century if not before, organists began to transfer their knowledge of improvised vocal descant to the organ. In vocal descant, one performer sang the plainsong in even note-values while the other improvised a part above, below or 'against' it (i.e. in the same range), according to a set of rules determined by the range of his voice. Such music was rarely written down, for there was no need to do so. One of the few exceptions, copied *ca.* 1420, is the fragment referred to in the first paragraph of this chapter; and it is possible that it illustrates the current style of organ as well as of vocal descant:

The flowing 6/8 rhythm is typical of the music of the period, and we may expect that the organists followed the changing stylistic fashions as the century proceeded. Gradually, too, they would have freed themselves from the fetters of vocal range and technique. They may have imitated the technique of faburden, in which two parts were added below the plainsong (the latter

[9] Harrison, *loc. cit.*
[10] Harrison, *op. cit.*, pp. 206, 214.

transposed up an octave if necessary).[11] They may also have
been the first to treat the faburden of the chant (the lowest part)
as a separate entity, improvising upon it instead of on the chant
itself.[12] There is abundant evidence that boys were taught descant
at the organ from *ca.* 1475, although this may have occurred
much earlier. There are no separate treatises on the subject, but
in some of those dealing with vocal descant there are passing
references to the organ.[13]

A piece written down in the early sixteenth century may
indicate the stage which improvised organ descant had reached
by the end of the fifteenth century. It is considerably more
florid than the previous example, and the additional part is
successively above and below the *cantus firmus*. The latter is not a
plainsong, but a monophonic, measured melody called a 'square'
and associated particularly with the celebration of the Lady-mass
(*EECM*, x, No. 3):

Although none has survived, organ music was certainly written down before the end of the century. Originally the organist
was simply provided with an antiphonal and gradual from which
to improvise. But the items listed above as having been performed
at Leicester Abbey were written 'in duobus libris ordinatis

[11] Originally the *cantus firmus* was in the middle voice: see Trowell,
Musica Disciplina (1959) 43.

[12] Harrison, *Musica Disciplina* (1962) 11.

[13] E.g. London, Brit. Mus., Add. MS 21455, f. 9v.

tantum pro organis', which taken together with the mixed nature of their contents strongly suggests organ polyphony. One must be careful in interpreting medieval inventories, for such terms as 'organ book' and *organista* may mean no more than a collection of vocal polyphony and a singer of polyphony respectively. The 'Libri organici' in a Fotheringay inventory certainly refer to vocal polyphony; but the 'Organ book bounde' in a Warwick inventory of 1465 may well have contained organ music, since it is distinguished from volumes of 'pricksong'.[14]

We are far less well informed about keyboard instruments other than the organ and the music played on them. The name *eschaquier* mentioned in Chapter I disappeared in the fifteenth century, but its harpsichord principle (if our interpretation is correct) was retained. The earliest known appearance of the instrument in its standard 'wing' shape is in a woodcarving at Manchester Cathedral.[15]

It was the clavichord which, perhaps because of its novelty and simplicity, was the more popular instrument during this period. It is true that too much reliance cannot be placed on the appearance of the mere name 'clavichord' in English documents, for in France, Italy and Spain and even Scotland the name given to this instrument was normally some variant of 'manichord', while, in Spain at least, 'clavichord' meant the harpsichord.[16] Nevertheless, the primitive carving in St. Mary's, Shrewsbury (fifteenth century, reproduced by Galpin)[17] is almost certainly a clavichord, and is indeed the earliest known pictorial representation of the instrument anywhere. Cersne von Minden, whose *Minneregeln* (1404) was cited in Chapter I, distinguishes between the *Schachtbrett* and the *Clavichordium*, and it seems likely that the latter was a genuine clavichord and that in England the Germanic usage prevailed.

The clavichord is named many times in fifteenth-century

[14] London, P.R.O., K.R. Inventories (E 154) 1/44 (Fotheringay), 1/46 (Warwick).

[15] Galpin, *Old English Instruments of Music*, p. 123.

[16] Hayes, *NOHM*, iii. 484.

[17] Galpin, *loc. cit.*

documents. One literary reference is in Caxton's translation of Geoffry de la Tours' *Romance* (1483). It is sometimes mentioned in contexts which imply that it was used by budding organists as a practice instrument: when William Horwood was appointed instructor of the choristers at Lincoln Cathedral in 1477 he was ordered to teach them 'in playing the organ and especially those whom he shall find apt to learn the clavychordes'.[18] Further references of this kind occur in documents of the early sixteenth century, and there can be little doubt that the clavichord was used as a substitute for the organ from about 1450 to the Reformation.

But we are utterly ignorant of the music proper to the clavichord or harpsichord at this time. One hypothesis will be mentioned here for what it is worth. The basis of sacred keyboard art was improvisation against a plainsong. The secular equivalent of this was the *basse dance*, which has been defined by Gombosi as 'a *cantus firmus* dance'.[19] The dance was normally improvised by two instrumentalists, and a continental example of this kind of polyphony has, by some rare chance, survived.[20] There seems no reason why English keyboard players should not have adapted such an art to their own needs, just as the organists had adapted vocal improvisation. Three melodies, written in a primitive stroke notation, are found in a Bodleian manuscript of the third quarter of the fifteenth century, the first two of which may be dance *cantus firmi*.[21] The first of them, 'Quene note', is provided with a counterpoint on a separate stave. Like the *Felix namque* quoted in Ex. 7 it may be regarded as an example of what a keyboard player could do at the time, even though it is not keyboard music as it stands in the manuscript. It is transcribed in full as Ex. 9.

---

[18] Harrison, *Music in Medieval Britain*, p. 177.

[19] *The Capirola Lute Book*, p. xxxvi.

[20] Bukofzer, *Studies in Medieval and Renaissance Music*, pp. 195–200.

[21] Oxford, Bod. Lib., MS Digby 167, f. 31v. Facsimile in *Early Bodleian Music*, i, pl. 98. The third tune is the faburden of the plainsong hymn *Aeterne Rex Altissime*. Further *cantus firmi* of this kind occur in London, Brit. Mus., Cotton MS Titus A. xxvi, ff. 5, 7, 8. A two-part composition based on the tenor of Binchois' chanson *Votre très douce regard*, and apparently a *basse dance*, is in 'Ritson's MS', Brit. Mus., Add. 5665, f. 144v.

III

The Early Sixteenth Century: Liturgical Organ Music

The placing, function, and essential mechanism of the church organ did not change with the new century. There was perhaps a tendency towards an increase in size, as is shown by the cost of building and installing an organ at Exeter Cathedral in 1513–14: £164. 15s. 7¼d. But this seems to have been exceptional and a small organ for a Lady-chapel could be valued at as little as 10s.[1]

One very important advance, however, can be assigned to the early sixteenth century: the device for shutting off one or more ranks of pipes. The very English word 'stop', so different from the French *jeu* or German *Register*, illustrates its origin very vividly: a stop was a mechanism for 'stopping' part of the organ from sounding, not for making it sound. The terminology has been retained in the English-speaking world, even though the word quickly came to be virtually synonymous with 'rank'. At St. Laurence, Reading, in 1513, 11d. was paid for 'ij lokks . . . one for the stopps and the other for the keyes'.[2] Later, in 1531, 2d. was spent on 'mendying the stoppes of the grete organs'.[3] In 1526 John Howe and John Clymmowe built an organ at Holy Trinity, Coventry, 'with vii stops and xxvii pleyn keyes'.[4]

A reference to '27 plain keys' also occurs in the earliest extant specification for an English organ, a contract between the churchwardens of All Hallows, Barking, and Anthony Duddyngton, dated 1519. This is a document of such importance that a substantial extract must be quoted:[5]

---

1 Harrison, *Music in Medieval Britain*, pp. 209, 210.
2 Sumner, *The Organ*, p. 107.   3 Harrison, *op. cit.*, p. 214.
4 Sumner, *op. cit.*, p. 109. See also the discussion of the chamber organ in the following chapter.
5 Printed in full in Hopkins and Rimbault, *The Organ*, part i, pp. 55–6.

This endenture . . . Witnesseth that Anthony Duddyngton, Citezen of London, Organ-Maker, hath made a full bargayn, . . . to make an instrument, that is to say a payer of organs for the forsed churche, of dowble Ce-fa-ut that ys to saye, xxvij. playne keyes, and the pryncipale to conteyn the length of v foote, so folowing with Bassys called Diapason to the same, conteyning length of x foot or more: And to be dowble pryncipalls thoroweout the said instrument, so that the pyppes with inforth shall be as fyne metall and stuff as the utter parts, that is to say of pure Tyn, with as fewe stops as may be convenient.

Starting from Peter F. Williams' valuable explanation of 'principal' as 'a Blockwerk, the indivisible Mixture which constituted the . . . basis . . . of major church organs',[6] the phrase 'dowble pryncipalls thoroweout' can be interpreted as meaning: 'all the ranks in the principal division are carried to the lowest note of the instrument'. The lowest of these ranks was what we would call a 5-foot stop, and, one octave below, a diapason rank[7] descended to 'x foot or more'. Possibly these lengths may indicate a pitch a major third or so below that of the present day; alternatively, they may include the foot of the pipe, below its sounding length. Be that as it may, the terminology suggests that the diapason was originally introduced as what we should call a 16-foot stop, rather than as providing the standard pitch-level of the instrument. By a curious process not paralleled on the continent, the 'principal' came to mean an octave-higher rank, perhaps owing to a gradual shift in English pitch-standards. The transition is illustrated in the early sixteenth century by some pieces having the compass *c–g'''*. One or two of these are marked to be played '8 notes lower', and it becomes apparent that all such pieces were played an octave lower but without the diapason rank.

This brings us directly to the compass of Duddyngton's instrument. The '27 plain keys' are usually interpreted, surely correctly, as the 'white notes' of the instrument. With a short

[6] Williams, *MT* (1965) 463.

[7] The word 'diapason' was used by Greek and medieval Latin authors for the interval of an octave.

octave (in which the five lowest notes, which look like *E*, *F*, *F#*, *G* and *G#*, sound respectively *C*, *F*, *D*, *G* and *E*, and in which the notes *C#*, *D#*, *F#* and *G#* are thus not available) this gives a four-octave compass of *C–c'''*; otherwise the compass would be *C–a'''*, a total of 27 diatonic notes as on the modern pianoforte. I favour the latter interpretation for two reasons: some pieces appear to require the low *F#* and *G#*; and the compass *C–a''* is sufficient for the entire extant repertory (no pieces going higher than *a''* descend below *c*).[8]

The only manuscript which appears to have been compiled expressly for liturgical use is London, Brit. Mus., Add. 29996. This large composite manuscript, which later belonged to Thomas Tomkins and was finally indexed by Nathaniel Tomkins, contains three sections devoted to liturgical organ music. The first (ff. 6–48) was probably written *ca.* 1548, apart from two later pieces at the end of the section. The second section (ff. 49–67) is devoted entirely to the music of Thomas Preston, and may have been written during the reign of Mary. The same or a similar hand wrote the third section (ff. 158–178v), devoted to a series of anonymous hymn-settings based on the faburden of the chant. These may also be by Preston.

The dating of the first part of this manuscript is helped by the reference on f. 28v to Philip ap Rhys as being 'Off Saynt poulls in london', as it is known that he went there from St. Mary-at-Hill on the death of Redford in 1547. Its repertory on the other hand is so uniformly archaic that it could hardly have been compiled after the introduction of the first Prayer Book in 1549. The composers represented are John Redford, Kyrton, E. Strowger, Richard Wynslate, Avery Burton, Philip ap Rhys, John Thorne, Thomas Preston and Robert Coxsun; Kyrton, Strowger and Coxsun are names known only from this manuscript, which in addition contains the only surviving music of Wynslate and ap Rhys. Ff. 6v–28r are devoted to the Office, ff. 28v–47v to the Mass. A series of fourteen *Miserere* settings is followed by fifteen hymns, four antiphons, two settings of the *Te Deum* and one *Magnificat*. There follows the Ordinary of the

8 For the detailed argument, see Caldwell, *MT* (1967) 254, and *ML* (1970) 156.

Mass by Philip ap Rhys, with blank staves ruled for the *Credo* but including the Offertory for the feast of the Trinity. Ten Offertories follow, including four settings of *Felix namque*. The last of these, and the last liturgical item in the section, is a *Felix namque* by Preston, written in a hand resembling that of the scribe of the second section, into whose possession the first section had doubtless come. He also added a non-liturgical piece, 'Uppon la mi re', on f. 48r; this may very well be by Preston too.

The second section, devoted entirely to Preston, begins with nine Offertories, the last seven being settings of *Felix namque*, a series intended possibly for the daily Lady-mass. The antiphon *Beatus Laurentius* is followed by the Offertory *Confessio et pulchritudo*, both for the feast of St. Laurence. Finally there is his Proper of the Mass for Easter Day, which breaks off in the middle of the Sequence *Fulgens praeclara* at the bottom of f. 67v: evidently some pages are missing here. The third section contains a cycle of hymns in the order of the breviary, breaking off in *Ecce tempus idoneum* for Vespers on the first Sunday of Lent. There are no pages missing here, however, for the scribe simply stopped writing: his ruled staves continue until f. 182r and were partly used by Thomas Tomkins for later pieces.[9]

The picture of the repertory contained in this manuscript, while very nearly complete, can be rounded out with a few scattered items from other sources. The first of a pair of manuscripts loosely associated with the West Country (London, Brit. Mus., Roy. App. 56 and 58) contains a few anonymous liturgical items amongst its very miscellaneous contents: the date is *ca.* 1530 and the musical style rather removed from that of the main repertory. London, Brit. Mus., Add. 15233, on the other hand, is devoted to John Redford and includes a complete *Te Deum*; it also contains his *Play of Wit and Science* and poems by him, John Thorne and others. Still more interesting is the Mulliner Book (London, Brit. Mus., Add. 30513),[10] written 1560–75 but including liturgical works by Redford as well as by later composers such as Tallis and Blitheman. Finally (apart from two or three quite marginal sources mostly of later date)[11] we

---

[9] These three sections will be referred to henceforth as Add. 29996/i, etc.
[10] *MB*, i, ed. Denis Stevens.   [11] *EECM*, vi. 137; *EECM*, x. 119.

may mention Oxford, Christ Church, MS 371, an attractive little oblong volume written on printed music paper *ca.* 1560, and again including some liturgical pieces by Redford.

While the evidence is far from complete, there is enough to attempt a broad chronological picture of stylistic development. The pieces from Roy. App. 56 are very archaic, and even if they are not actually the earliest we possess, they are sufficiently far removed from the main line of development to require separate treatment. A *Felix namque*, the first piece in the manuscript, incorporates such oddities as quintuple metre and, later, 8:3 proportion:[12]

[12] *Altenglische Orgelmusik*, p. 3; *EECM*, x, No. 10. In the numerical ratios the two figures denote the numbers of notes of the same face-value to be performed in the same unit of time, either successively or simultaneously. Usually the notes represented by the first figure were blackened. Thus 8:3 might mean 'eight (black) minims are to be performed in the time previously taken by three (white) minims'. But English scribes were not always careful to compare notes of equal face-value, and modern transcriptions frequently obscure the original ratios. In this book numerical ratios always refer to the original notation, comparing notes of equal denomination. Blackening is denoted by broken brackets ⌐ ¬. *Sesquialtera* = 3:2; *sesquitertia* = 4:3. Further on proportions see Morley, *A Plain and Easy Introduction*, pp. 42–88, 126–37.

The fragmentary conclusion of a second *Felix namque* exhibits a primitive style of four-part writing:

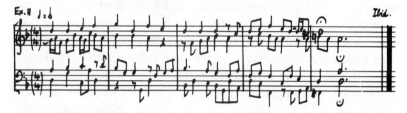

while a third is some form of duet. The plainsong is written out separately at the end of the piece, but must be played simultaneously with it by a second performer, either at the same keyboard or on a separate instrument. The player must transpose the plainsong an octave higher than it is written in order to avoid false dissonances and a generally confusing texture, a solution which favours the hypothesis of a keyboard duet:

The other liturgical pieces in this manuscript are a Communion, *Beata viscera*, a *Miserere* and the *Kyrie* quoted in the previous chapter as Ex. 8. There are also some fragments which are not readily identifiable as liturgical compositions, and an extract (two voices only in keyboard score) from Taverner's Mass *The Western Wind*. The general impression is of a rather odd collection of pieces, hastily scribbled down to serve the needs of the moment.[13] One technical feature of the plainsong settings

[13] Liturgical contents printed *EECM*, x, Nos. 2, 10, 11, 29; App. II, 1. The MS also includes Magnificat faburdens in measured monophony and the even-numbered verses of the *Te Deum*, apparently for alternation with organ. For the faburdens, see Harrison, *Musica Disciplina* (1962) 11.

may be noted: the *cantus firmi* are heard in virtually unornamented form.

From the main repertory as preserved in our remaining sources the oldest pieces are a *Te Deum* by Avery Burton (*EECM*, x, No. 1), whose name disappears from the records of the Chapel Royal after 1542, and some anonymous pieces in a similar style. Of the latter, a setting of the hymn *Salvator mundi* (*EECM*, vi, No. 53) includes a verse in four parts, the primitive nature of which recalls Ex. 11:

The plainsong is transposed down a tone and is presented as an ornamented faburden (see Chapter II, pp. 14–15) in the top voice. A second setting (*EECM*, vi, No. 54), transposing the plainsong down a fifth, begins with a lively dotted figure. It also illustrates the early habit of beginning an organ hymn with the first line intoned by a cantor: the second and subsequent lines of the tune are treated as a faburden in the bass:

The dotted figure, coupled with transposition down a tone, recurs in Burton's *Te Deum*:

Transposition of the plainsong seems to have been employed in organ settings in order to ensure that the singing of the alternate verses could take place at a comfortable pitch. This is borne out by its frequent application to melodies with a high *tessitura*, especially those of the seventh and eighth mode. Transposition down a fifth is the commonest, but transposition down a tone is also found, not only in these early pieces but in as late a work as Blitheman's *Te Deum*.[14] Both of Redford's *Te Deum* settings transpose the plainsong down a fifth.[15]

John Redford (d. 1547), the almoner of St. Paul's Cathedral who acted as its organist with such resounding fame, is the great early master of liturgical organ composition. He wrote examples in most forms and practised nearly every style, and his music is found in more manuscripts than that of any other composer. The openings of three successive verses of a hymn, *Deus Creator omnium* (*EECM*, vi, No. 42) will illustrate three styles in which he excelled:

14 *MB*, i, No. 77.

15 *EECM*, vi, Nos. 2 and 3. For a theory concerning different transpositions applied to the *Te Deum* and other melodies see Caldwell, *ML* (1970) 156. Fragments of two more settings of the *Te Deum*, both employing transposition down a tone, have turned up at Oxford, Brasenose Coll.

The second verse shows the unornamented form of the plainsong (though it is lightly ornamented later on in the verse) in the middle voice: in the other two verses it is in the bass. The basic principle of the ornamentation is that each note of the plainsong is allotted the same time-value, within which framework the ornamentation (except at final cadences) is rigidly confined. The time-value chosen for all three verses in this case is a semibreve (minim in the transcription).[16]

An essential distinction will be found between the styles of the second and third verses of Ex. 16. That of the second has its roots in vocal descant, originally 'composed by setting a "counter" . . . below the monorhythmic tenor and adding a mean (medius) above it'.[17] In the third verse it is the middle part which is the 'mean', and which characteristically wanders from hand to hand. The plainsong is usually in the bass and all parts are similar

[16] See the discussion by Thomas Morley in *A Plain and Easy Introduction*, pp. 177–9.
[17] Harrison, *NOHM*, iii. 97.

in rhythmic movement. The total range of the three parts together is often considerable, resulting in a lean, spare texture. Originally, as here, such pieces were written on a single staff of twelve or more lines, the middle part being distinguished clearly from the other two by being written in black notation. Mulliner, copying such pieces after about 1560, redistributed the parts on two staves but retained the black notation and nearly always used the phrase 'with a mean'. The cultivation of this 'mean' style was perhaps Redford's most distinctive contribution to organ literature.

Certain other technical features can conveniently be illustrated from his work: *sesquialtera* proportion, faburden, four-part writing and the use of larger or smaller note-values to carry the plainsong. The first of these involved the settings of three black semibreves against two normal (white) semibreves, and is here illustrated in connection with the three-part descant texture, though it was perhaps commoner in two-part writing (*EECM*, vi, No. 28):

Such pieces are, however, more conveniently transcribed in 6/8 time: the 'triplet' notation used here affords a readier comparison with the other examples. His only two examples of four-part writing are settings of the Compline antiphon *Lucem tuam*: both are in the Mulliner Book, and the second also illustrates the use of the breve (original notation) for the *cantus firmus* (*MB*, i, No. 39):

One final example of his work, a *Te Deum* verse (*EECM*, vi, No. 3), will illustrate both faburden and the use of smaller note-values (minims in the original) to represent the *cantus firmus*:

The editorial triple metre derives not from the *cantus firmus* but from the rhythmic pattern of the upper part.

Several anonymous compositions can tentatively be ascribed to Redford on stylistic grounds, one of the finest being the elaborate *Magnificat* from Add. 29996/i (*EECM*, vi, No. 4). It is entitled simply 'The viij tune in C faut'—a hint that the plainsong has been transposed down a fifth—and the first two verses are marked to be played an octave lower (see above, p. 20).

Of Redford's immediate contemporaries little need be said. The solitary settings of the *Miserere* antiphon by Kyrton and E. Strowger[18] do nothing to rescue their composers from the decent obscurity in which they lie buried. Philip ap Rhys owes his fame to the largely accidental fact that he wrote the only surviving Organ Mass (i.e. Ordinary of the Mass) by an English composer. He set the *Kyrie*-trope *Deus Creator omnium, Gloria, Sanctus* and *Agnus*; as we have seen the staves for the *Credo* were left blank, but the Offertory for Trinity Sunday, *Benedictus sit*, was thrown in for good measure. He may have been an organist of distinction but as a composer, so far from being a 'star of the first magnitude',[19] he possessed only a meagre talent. Richard Wynslate, organist and master of the choristers at Winchester Cathedral, 1540–1572, was a much more original figure, as appears from a charming *Lucem tuam*.[20] Coxsun, known only from two pieces in Add. 29996/i, was the possessor of a gift for the bizarre, as is shown in parts of his Offertory *Veritas mea* (*EECM*, x, No. 28):

[18] *EECM*, vi, Nos. 18, 22.

[19] Rokseth, *NOHM*, iii. 458. The Mass is in *EECM*, x, No. 1 and *Altenglische Orgelmusik*, pp. 24–35.

[20] *EECM*, vi, No. 9.

John Thorne, organist at York Minster until his death in 1573, wrote a colourless Offertory, *Exsultabunt Sancti*.[21]

So far we have considered at least three composers who out-lived Redford by many years (Philip ap Rhys was still organist at St. Paul's in 1559).[22] Their organ music survives, however, only in Add. 29996/i, a collection which almost certainly dates from before 1549. A further striking fact emerges about Wynslate, Thorne and ap Rhys. They were all at some time employed at St. Mary-at-Hill in London: ap Rhys as organist for the daily Lady-mass until 1547; Wynslate as a singer at various times from 1537 to 1540; and Thorne as a singer in 1540. All three

21 *EECM*, x, No. 9.
22 Baillie, *ML* (1955) 55.

subsequently became cathedral organists. It is practically certain that Add. 29996/i was written down by someone closely associated with this church around 1540 and who subsequently left London—possibly even Wynslate himself. It was not Thorne, who would not have needed to have described himself (on f. 38) as 'of York', and by the same token it was not ap Rhys, who is referred to on f. 28v as being 'Off Saynt poulls in london', nor anyone who needed to describe the location of St. Paul's. Wynslate, however, leaving London for Winchester in 1540, might well have taken with him copies of the art of Redford and his school, and subsequently made a fair copy for his own use. His name at the end of his *Lucem tuam*, and that of Robert Coxsun on its two appearances, are the only ones in the manuscript which could conceivably be interpreted as signatures: all the other names are ruled out in this connection by the prefix 'Mr.' or some other evidence.

A fourth cathedral organist of this generation, William Shelbye, organist at Canterbury for six years from 1547,[23] survives through two pieces in the Mulliner Book,[24] neither of which shows him to have been more than a mechanician, a deployer of *cantus firmi*. It is difficult to say whether these compositions represent Henrician or Marian art.

Far more significant than any of these, and indeed the biggest figure with whom we have to deal in this chapter, is Thomas Preston. A *Reges Tharsis* (Offertory for the Epiphany) by 'Master prestun' is included in Add. 29996/i, and this may very well be our composer, although a John Preston was organist of St. Dunstan-in-the-West in 1544–5. At all events it is in the style of the 1540s—the 'mean' style, in fact—and could easily be accepted as an early work of this great composer. A Preston whose first name is unrecorded was organist and master of the choristers at Magdalen College, Oxford, in 1543, and the name recurs in the records of Windsor Chapel for 1558–9.[25] This latter is almost certainly the Thomas Preston who composed the organ music

---

[23] West, *Cathedral Organists*, p. 10, states that he died in 1570.
[24] *MB*, i, Nos. 34, 41.
[25] Harrison, *Music in Medieval Britain*, p. 192; Fellowes, *Windsor Organists*, pp. 22–3.

and a few other pieces such as an *In nomine* for strings.[26] The style and the evidence of the manuscript sources suggest a composer active during the reign of Mary.

The bulk of Thomas Preston's authenticated organ music is for the Mass. As we have seen the copyist of his music acquired Add. 29996/i and wrote in a *Felix namque* by him towards the end (45v–47v). His own two collections (Add. 29996/ii and iii) have been transmitted together with that section ever since. This *Felix namque* is an imposing piece of enormous difficulty.[27] The intonation is set[28] as a majestic introduction in duple time. Thereafter the plainsong, transposed down a fourth and in the bass, is laid out in dotted semibreves (original notation), above which are woven two contrapuntal parts which gradually increase in speed as the piece proceeds.

Passing over 'Uppon la mi re' we reach Add. 29996/ii, the first item of which, *Diffusa est gratia*, is an Offertory markedly similar to the *Felix namque*. Here, however, the plainsong is in the top voice and the accompanying parts are confined to the left hand. A few extracts will demonstrate some of the formidable technical problems of the piece (*EECM*, x, No. 8):

26 Oxford, Bod. Lib., MSS Mus. Sch. d. 212–16. The MS also contains an *In nomine* by Thorne.

27 *EECM*, x, No. 12; *Altenglische Orgelmusik*, pp. 6–9.

28 As also in the *Felix namque* by Philip ap Rhys (*EECM*, x, No. 22).

The next ten works show a different side of Preston's musical character. Here the emphasis is on melodic and contrapuntal interest. The Offertory *Benedictus sit*[29] and the first four of the seven settings of *Felix namque* are in four parts with the *cantus firmus* in breves. We have seen (Ex. 18) that Redford had attempted this technique, but Preston was much more skilled. *Benedictus sit* is an enormously long piece (166 bars) with its plain *cantus firmus* in the top voice; but owing to Preston's consistent use of imitation the interest never flags:

The first four settings of *Felix namque* present the *cantus firmus* respectively in the treble, bass, alto and tenor at varying pitches. The last three are only half the length, the *cantus firmus* in semibreves and ornamented. The remaining two of these ten items, the antiphon and Offertory of St. Laurence,[30] revert to the manner of the first five.

[29] *Ibid.*, No. 6 (called 'Benedicta' in the MS). The seven settings of *Felix namque* printed *ibid.*, Nos. 13–19.

[30] *Beatus Laurentius* and *Confessio et pulchritudo*. EECM, vi, No. 5 and x, No. 7.

The fullest expression of Preston's fiery genius is to be found in his Proper for Easter Day (*EECM*, x, No. 1). The Introit, *Resurrexi*, is in two, three and four parts successively:

The first two sections recall Redford's style as illustrated in Ex. 16 (a) and (b) though the first ultimately exceeds it in rhythmic

complexity. The third section achieves a suavity never approached by Redford in four parts. The Gradual, *Haec dies*, setting the
soloists' portion of the chant, reaches heights of rhythmic
complexity:

In the *Alleluia* he transposed the plainsong down a fourth,
involving himself in key-signatures of one and even two sharps;
yet the actual style here is prosaic, the three-part 'descant' and
'mean' styles being used for the verses *Pascha nostrum* and
Epulemur respectively. The short alternate verses of the Sequence,
Fulgens praeclara, are on the other hand a microcosm of different
styles and techniques. A short quotation will illustrate *sesquitertia*
proportion (four black against three white semibreves) in connection with 'descant' style:

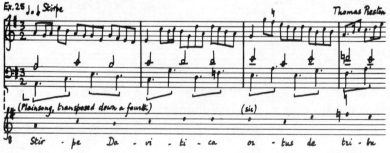

Yet the piece breaks off in the middle of the verse *Redemptori*, a makeshift cadence having been supplied in a later hand, and we shall never know if Preston completed his Proper with an Offertory and Communion.[31]

The faburden hymns of Add. 29996/iii, if they are not by Preston, are by at least as great a composer, steeped in the same tradition. It is chiefly the Preston of the Easter Mass which is apparent here: all the styles and textures found there are reproduced. The use of the faburden, nearly always ornamented in some degree, raises the composer's achievement to a still higher level of sophistication, and his dependence on the plainsong is no longer an audible factor. His finest work is to be found in some of the four-part verses, where the *cantus firmus* is usually in the bass. This and the other parts are so carefully unified in material that no stylistic discrepancy occurs (*EECM*, vi, No. 24):

It remains to consider those composers—other than Shelbye—whose liturgical organ music is found only in the Mulliner Book. Of these Nicholas Carleton (the elder), Alwood, Farrant and Heath can be dismissed as mere names in this connection, though some of them achieved distinction in other fields. Tallis and Blitheman on the other hand deserve attention. Tallis was leading an active professional life for many years before 1549, his recorded posts at this time being organist of Dover Priory (1532); conduct (singer) at St. Mary-at-Hill (1537); a post at Waltham Abbey, dissolved in 1540; lay clerk at Canterbury (1541); and gentleman of the Chapel Royal (*ca.* 1542). It is

---

[31] See D. Stevens, *JAMS* (1956) 1.

perhaps strange, in view of the theory outlined above, that none of his organ music survives in Add. 29996/i. What we have in the Mulliner Book looks Marian in style, with the possible exception of the very brief *Natus est nobis* (No. 9). Without being his best work it none the less has a quiet distinction.

Blitheman's recorded career on the other hand is purely Elizabethan (he died in 1591) and his liturgical organ music must be Marian. It includes a *Felix namque* in 'mean' style (No. 32), a *Te Deum* (No. 77) which embodies the same scheme of transposition as that by Avery Burton (see above, pp. 25–6) and four verses for the hymn *Aeterne rerum Conditor* (Nos. 49–52). The style is somewhat derivative in all three works, although in the last two there is a hint of the virtuosity which was to be put to such fruitful use in his six settings of *Gloria tibi Trinitas* (see Chapter V).

Liturgical organ music in England, after its brief revival under the reign of Mary, came to an abrupt end with the Elizabethan Act of Uniformity in 1559; but some of its techniques were retained and developed in the plainsong settings and fugal forms of the succeeding epoch. In addition, the virtuosity attained by Preston, Blitheman and, as we shall see, Tallis, was a necessary element in the evolution of English keyboard music as a whole.

IV

The Early Sixteenth Century: Secular Music

The list of musical instruments belonging to Henry VIII, extracted from an inventory dated 1547,[1] has often been discussed; but a summary of its contents insofar as they relate to keyboard instruments will still afford the best idea of the nature and scope of the resources available to players and composers at this time.

Of the 'Stuffe and Implements at Grenewiche' there were 'In the Kynges priuey Chambre' 'One paier of Regalles with the case' (f. 54), 'In the Kynges Withdrawing Chambre' 'One faire Instrument being Regalles and Virgynalles' (f. 56) and 'In the Kynges Gallery' 'A paier of Virgynalles' (f. 57v).

A whole section, beginning at f. 200, is devoted to 'Instruments at Westminster in the charge of Philipp Van Wilder'. (Van Wilder was 'Keeper of the Instruments' at the court of Henry VIII.) Under the heading 'Double Regalles' we have 'Firste a paire of double Regalles with twoo Stoppes of pipes. . . . Item. A paire of double Regalles with twoo Stoppes of pipes. . . . Item. A paire of double Regalles of latten with iii Stoppes of pipes . . . standinge upon a foote of wainscott painted in Rabeske woorke wherein liethe the Bellowes. Item. A paire of double Regalles with viii halfe Stoppes and one hole stoppe of pipes . . . standinge upon a foote of woode beinge painted wherein liethe the Bellowes. Item. A paire of double Regalles with iii stoppes of pipes . . . standinge upon a foote of wainscott . . . wherein liethe the Bellowes: the same hath but twoo stoppes of pipes and thother stoppe is but a Cimball'.

[1] London, Brit. Mus., MS Harl. 1419. Printed in Galpin, *Old English Instruments of Music*, pp. 292–300; Russell, *The Harpsichord and Clavichord*, pp. 155–60.

There follow the 'Single Regalles: Item. One paire of single Regalles with iii stoppes of pipes . . . it hathe but one Stoppe pipe of tinne one Regall of Tinne and a Cimball. Item. One paire of single Regalles with twoo Stoppes of pipes . . . it hathe but one Stoppe of pipes of woode with a Cimball of Tinne and the Regall of papire. Item. Twoo paire of single Regalles euerie of them with vi halfe stoppes of brase pipes. . . . Item. V small single Regalles. . . . Item. One paire of single Regalles with twoo Stoppes of pipes of timbre and one Stoppe of pipes of Tinne . . . the same hathe but one Stoppe of pipes of woode the Regall of papire and hathe a Cimball.[2] Item. One paire of single Regalles with iiii Stoppes of pipes . . . it hathe but one Stoppe of pipes of woode a Cimball of Tinne and a Regall.[3] Item. One paire of single Regalles with twoo stoppes of pipes . . . standinge uppon a foote of wainscott painted grene with the Bellowes liinge in the same havinge a Cimball. Item. One paire of single Regalles with vii halfe Stoppes of pipes . . . with a foot of wainscott unpainted wherein liethe the Bellowes: the saide vii stoppes are but vii Registers diuided in three Stoppes with a Cimball'.

The 'Virgynalles' follow: 'Item. An Instrumente with a single Virgynall and single Regall withe a Stoppe of timbre pipes. . . . Item. An Instrumente with a double Virgynall and a double Regall with iii Stoppes of pipes. . . . Item. An Instrument that goethe with a whele without playinge uppon. . . .' Then come details of four pairs of 'double Virgynalles' and nine pairs of 'single Virgynalles', one of the latter having 'pipes underneth'. Under 'Instruments of Soundrie Kindes' come first two pairs of 'Claricordes'.

A fresh start is made on f. 204v with 'Fyrste one newe paire of double Virginalles. . . . Item. Another newe paire of double Virginalles. . . . Item. A little paire of Virginalles single. . . . Item. Twoo faire paire of newe longe Virginalles made harpe fasshion . . . .' 'At Hampton Courte', 'In the Privey Chambre' were 'One payre of portatives with the Kynges and Quene Janes Armes' (f. 243v) and 'In the next bed chambre' 'A paire of Virgynalles the case covered with blacke Lether' (f. 245v). 'In

[2] Possibly the stop of wooden pipes was divided.
[3] See footnote 2.

the long Galorie' were 'A paire of Regalles . . .', 'Seven paires of Virginalles . . .' and 'A paire of Virginalles facioned like a harp' (f. 247); 'In another Chambre', 'One paire of portatives . . .' (f. 248); and 'In the Quenes Galorie' a 'Paire of Regalles in a case of lether' (f. 249v). 'At Wynsore' was 'One doble Regall with doble pipes . . .' (f. 315); 'at the More' the 'Soundrie parcelles' included 'One olde paire of Regalles broken in peces' (f. 340) and 'Two paires of olde Virginalles' (f. 340v). 'At Newhall' were 'A paire of faire greate Organes in the Chappell . . .' and 'A paire of Virginalles verye olde and broken' (f. 362); 'at Notyngham Castell' was 'an olde paire of Organes' (f. 367). Finally 'At Saynt James House' 'A paire of Organes standinge in the Chapple' (f. 445).

Many of these instruments were sumptuously decorated, the descriptions having been omitted from this summary for the sake of brevity. The terms 'pair', 'single', and 'double' have all been explained correctly by Galpin. The word 'pair' was originally applied to the organ, known in Latin as *organa* or *par organorum*, each pipe being an *organum* or single instrument, and *par* meaning a matching set. The word 'paire' can equally well bear the same meaning in English. Its application to the virginals and clavichord came about by analogy, although if the derivation of 'virginals' from *virga* or *virgula* be correct there is some logic in applying the term to the row of jacks on that instrument. 'Single' and 'double' are derived from the habit of writing notes below G^4 as double letters. A 'single' instrument descended to c or G, and a 'double' one to C or G_1.

We may now consider the regal, virginals and clavichord in turn. It seems quite evident that by this time regal and portative were synonymous, both being small organs, with or without a reed stop, which could be moved from place to place but not necessarily, like the earlier portative, played while carried on the arm or blown by the player. There was no essential difference between the chamber organ and the smaller kind of church instrument used in Lady-chapels and elsewhere. Sumner quotes an agreement, dated 1536, between Richard Charpyngton, organ-builder of South Molton, Devon, and twelve members of the parish of

4 This note itself was written as Γ (gamma); hence the 'gamut'.

St. Olave, Exeter, to keep the organ in repair during his lifetime: 'Condition that whereas the above named Thomas Walys etc. of late have bought of abovbound Richard, a new pair of portavys which now stand in the parish church of St. Olav in the city of Exeter, if the abovebound Richard from henceforth as often as need shall require without any delay at his own proper cost & charges during the life of the said Richard, do repair, sustain, maintain and amend and keep in tune as well the pipes of the said portatyves as the bellows and all other instraments now being in the said portatyves except the stop off Regals in the same instrament which must be tuned by the player thereof . . .' (etc.).[5] This description of course bears a striking resemblance to that of some of Henry VIII's own instruments. We may perhaps deduce that the term regal, orginally meaning (as in Germany) a reed stop, came to be applied to the instrument which bore it, whether this were the only rank of pipes or no, and ultimately to any small organ; but it still retained its earlier meanings. (Reed stops, of the 'beating' type, though known to classical organ makers, were re-introduced in Europe around 1460.[6]) According to Galpin the word is derived from the Latin *regula* and the original purpose of the instrument was to 'rule' the choir and its plainsong;[7] in which case it might have first been applied to a single pipe blown with the mouth in order to set the pitch.

We are rather better informed as to the construction of chamber organs in the early sixteenth century than in the case of the 'great' organs in churches. We learn of wood, tin and brass as materials for pipework, and even paper in the case of reed stops. The number of 'stops' varies from two to nine, one of which was normally the reed or 'regal' itself. Sometimes the stops were only 'half-stops', i.e. applied to half the keyboard (upper or lower) so that a melody might be accompanied by a softer stop. This would have an obvious advantage if a *cantus firmus* were employed, whether sacred or secular. The word 'stop' generally carries exactly the same meaning as at the present day, i.e. any division

---

5 Sumner, *The Organ*, p. 108.
6 Galpin, *op. cit.*, p. 225.
7 *Ibid.*, p. 230.

of the organ brought into action by a single knob or lever. There is some confusion, however, in connection with the last of the single regals belonging to Henry VIII at Westminster, of which we read that 'the saide vii stoppes are but vii Registers diuided in three Stoppes with a Cimball'. Here 'stop', as used the second time, means a 'rank of pipes', and 'register' means 'stop-mechanism'; the obvious sense of the passage is that three ranks of pipes are divided into six half-stops. The 'cimball' was probably a small mixture combining the twelfth and fifteenth. A typical specification probably consisted of stopped diapason, principal, cimball and the regal itself.

Several instruments described in the Inventory were combinations of regal and virginals. Probably a single manual could be connected to either mechanism. Turning to the virginals proper, we find examples of both 'single' and 'double' range. Particularly interesting are the 'longe Virginalles made harpe fasshion', implying that the majority of instruments were not yet constructed in 'wing' shape; although, as we have seen (Chapter II), this shape was already known in the fifteenth century. Without going into the etymology of the word, one may note that it was even at this early date applied to harpsichords of all shapes and sizes, and not only to the small rectangular instruments. Finally, Russell quotes (p. 67) from the Privy Purse expenses for 1530 'ij payer of virginalles in one coffer with iiij stoppes': a clear reference to a two-manual harpsichord.

The 'clarichords' were the poor relations of the other 'secular' keyboard instruments, fit to be listed only with 'instruments of sundry kinds'. The word is simply a mis-spelling of clavichord and interchangeable with it. The instrument was still used for training organists, and no doubt was in demand whenever its small tone and ready portability were an advantage. It continued in use down to the end of the seventeenth century,[8] but never underwent the renaissance and late flowering which it enjoyed in Germany.

[8] It cannot be shown to have been made in England in the eighteenth century, but examples were imported from Germany. The authenticity of the instrument inscribed *Peter Hicks Fecit*, and assigned by Galpin (*op. cit.*, p. 118 and pl. XXII) to *ca.* 1700, is uncertain. See Russell, *op. cit.*, pp. 87–8. The instrument is in the Victoria and Albert Museum.

Not only these instruments but also their names survived for surprisingly long. In 1673 Henry Purcell was appointed as John Hingston's assistant as 'keeper, maker, mender, repayrer and tuner of the regalls, organs, virginalls . . .',[9] and the terminology was retained when he succeeded Hingston on the latter's death in December 1683. Although there is no mention of the clavichord, in 1666 Hingston himself was paid for mending a 'claricon'; this term probably arose by analogy with 'harpsicon', a word which was now preferred by musicians to 'virginals' even though the latter had not as yet been ousted from common parlance.[10] That the regal was no miniature is shown by the magnificent example by John Loosemore dated 1650 and now preserved in Blair Atholl castle: it has five divided stops including a trumpet.[11]

Unlike the liturgical organ music of the early sixteenth century the secular repertory is preserved only in scattered sources. One would expect the basis of such a repertory to consist of dance and song arrangements, but while such things do exist there are numerous pieces which seem to defy categorisation. Another difficulty concerns dating, as it is often hard to say whether pieces in such manuscripts as the Mulliner Book and Oxford, Ch. Ch. 371 are Elizabethan or earlier. The music discussed in this chapter is all, as far as we know, pre-Elizabethan, but it is not always possible to be certain.

Some of the most ill-defined pieces are the non-liturgical items from London, Brit. Mus., Roy. App. 56. It is difficult to know whether an untitled, anonymous piece like the following bears a hidden *cantus firmus* or is mere aimless wandering:

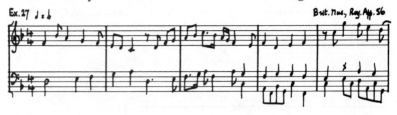

Ex. 27   ♩ = ♪   Brit. Mus., Roy. App. 56

[9] Lafontaine, *The King's Musick*, p. 225.   [10] Galpin, *op. cit.*, pp. 118–19.

[11] *Ibid.*, p. 232 and pl. XLVII. Its specification (Stop Diapason, Principal, Twelfth, Fifteenth, Trumpet) probably differed little from that of Henry VIII's larger instruments, except for the separation of the twelfth and fifteenth. See above, p. 43.

However, there is in existence one piece which though untitled in the manuscript truly deserves the name of fantasia in that it is a reasonably consistent treatment of original material in something approaching contrapuntal style. It is ascribed to one John Ambrose and survives in a curious manuscript of *ca.* 1570 (Oxford, Ch. Ch. 1034A) which looks elegant but in fact contains innumerable errors in the placing of the notes. The opening is a piece of genuine four-part imitative writing in spite of the curious notation:

The bulk of the writing is in fewer than four parts, and the counterpoint is suggested rather than explicit. It ends with a burst of virtuosity:

The only other works in the manuscript are the second half of an Offertory, *Tui sunt caeli*, by Redford, and an incomplete version of another freely composed piece by Tallis which will be considered in the next chapter. Of Ambrose himself we know virtually nothing: there is a wordless canon in London, Brit. Mus., Roy. App. 58, f. 16v, and an 'Ambros' was clerk at King's College, 1481–2. At all events a Henrician date seems indicated.

Arrangements of secular part-songs are never more than strict (but often incompetent) transcriptions, and can scarcely be considered as keyboard music at all. More interest attaches to some of the dance arrangements, in that the originals have all disappeared. Six pieces from Roy. App. 58 appear to allude to the visit of Charles V to England in 1522: they include 'The emperorse pavyn', 'The kyngs pavin' (later annotated 'kyng harry viijth pavyn' and also found in a much better text in Phalèse's *Liber Primus Leviorum Carminum*, Louvain, 1571, with the title 'Pavane Lesquecarde') and 'The kyngs marke' (= maske?).[12] More interesting still are the three genuinely keyboard pieces from this manuscript: 'A hornepype' by 'hughe aston', 'My lady careys dompe' and 'The short mesure off my lady wynkfylds rownde'. Sir Richard Wyngfeld and Sir Nicholas Carew were prominent members of the King's retinue at this time,[13] and

---

[12] London, Brit. Mus., MS Roy. App. 58, printed in *EKM*, i.

[13] See the account of Charles V's visit in Hall's *Chronicle*. The 'dump' has been interpreted as the equivalent of the *déploration* or *tombeau*, and was frequently based on a simple harmonic ground. See Ward, *JAMS* (1951) 111.

there can be little doubt that this music was intended for performance at the court of Henry VIII. Its real value for us is that it shows the first beginnings of a true harpsichord style. Apart from one or two quite fragmentary pieces nothing else of the kind before the age of Elizabeth has survived.

The 'hornepype' is the most astonishing of the three works, and for its period it is a really remarkable achievement. It is based on a ground, but not the mere melodic ground which was to satisfy English composers for so long; instead, it is based on a harmonic progression of the simplest kind—dominant, tonic—which may be varied but is never totally absent. Such a technique was known in Italy in the early sixteenth century, and a more complex bass with implied harmonies was employed for the *passamezzo*. Aston's piece begins with two bars of dominant harmony treated as an anacrusis: the notes in brackets may have been omitted by the copyist and are supplied editorially:

It continues in this way while the tension caused by the constant repetition of the harmonies mounts up. Half-way through it suddenly changes to a quicker tempo:

It ends with great *panache* on the tonic chord on a 'strong' bar:

The second piece, a 'dompe', is also based on an alternation of tonic and dominant harmony, but it begins on the strong beat and the left-hand pattern is never varied. Over it is woven a rhapsodic melody, which eventually leads back to a repeat of the whole composition (repeat-signs, and the second-time bar, are editorial):

The third piece has an irregular metrical structure: a nine-bar phrase, repeated, is answered by a ten-bar phrase, also repeated, and then the entire composition is repeated in full with only minor variants:

A persistent feature of all this music is the idiomatic layout of the left-hand part with its broken chords and lack of strict part-writing. The right hand, with momentary exceptions, carries a single melodic line of great fluidity and agility.

It has sometimes been suggested that Aston composed all three pieces, and although the manuscript provides no confirmation of this the hypothesis cannot be ruled out on stylistic grounds. It is practically certain that he is to be identified with the composer of two masses and several antiphons[14] and with the 'Hugo Haston' who supplicated for the B.Mus. degree at Oxford in 1510 and the 'Hugo Asseton' who was *magister choristarum* at Newarke College, Leicester, 1525–1548. It is not at all improbable that such a man should have been active in London between 1510 and 1525 and composed keyboard music during that period.

The three works just described are the sole remnant of an art which was in great repute at the court of Henry VIII. It may have been sparked off by the arrival of Fra Dionisius Memo, organist of St. Mark's, Venice, in 1516. This virtuoso became a favourite of the King almost immediately. Reports of his successes are preserved in the despatches of the Venetian ambassador and the letters of the latter's secretary, Sagudino. One concert is said to have lasted four hours. Another foreigner, Benedictus de Opitiis, formerly organist at Antwerp, arrived in the same year 'to waite opon the kinge in his chambre'.[15] The great English player of the time was John Heywood: gentleman, playwright, poet and musician. He was described as a 'singer' in 1520 but soon established a reputation as a keyboard player. He remained in the service of Queen Mary, fleeing abroad at her death and dying eventually at Malines in 1587. Before he left he had become acquainted with Thomas Mulliner, whose manuscript, considered in the next two chapters, bears the inscription 'Sum liber thomae mullineri, iohanne heywoode teste'. These were professionals, but the amateur cult was led by Henry himself (Sagudino also played). Numerous accounts are given of his prowess, and the art became a recognised courtly accomplishment. Not that it was a novelty to the court of Henry VIII: in 1503, during the progress of Princess Margaret to Scotland, both she and her future husband, James IV, are recorded as having played the 'clarycordes'.[16]

One last indisputably pre-Elizabethan piece must be discussed before this chapter closes: the anonymous 'Uppon la mi re'

14 *TCM*, x. Much of the biographical information given there is untrustworthy.

15 J. Stevens, *Music and Poetry at the Early Tudor Court*, p. 266.

16 *Ibid.*, p. 269. In Scotland the instrument was generally known as 'monocordis', a term similar to the French and Spanish words but virtually unknown in England.

already noted in the previous chapter as having been copied at the end of Add. 29996/i by the scribe of the second and third sections of that manuscript. For this reason it may possibly be by Thomas Preston. It is based on an unusual ground consisting of the three notes of the hexachord which give the piece its title, treated in close canon. Above this there is a winding melodic line not very dissimilar to that of 'My lady careys dompe'—in fact its opening is almost identical (*cf.* Ex. 33):

Towards the end it changes to a flowing *sesquialtera*:

The d-clef in which the lower part is written is ambiguous. D. Stevens[17] has assumed that the note specified by the clef is *d'*, but it cannot logically mean this note because it stands in a space, whereas the clef stands clearly on a line. It might therefore refer to *d* or *d''*. If the latter is the case, the parts will overlap, and if the former, the total range (*D—d'''*) will exceed that assumed to be normal for instruments of the time. The solution must surely be that the work was intended for an organ with divided stops, a claviorgan, or a two-manual harpsichord (see above, p. 43). Whether the left-hand part was played on a '4-foot' stop and the right-hand part on an '8-foot' stop, or vice versa, cannot

[17] *Altenglische Orgelmusik*, pp. 13–15. For this clef, see also *DVM*, No. 10 (facsimile on p. xvi) where the lower octave (*d*) is clearly intended. This piece must be a duet: see Chapter VI, p. 113.

be determined with any certainty. In the examples above, the latter method is assumed, but the piece does not really suffer either way. It is a charming and imaginative work, and a precious relic of the all but forgotten art of its day.

V

The Elizabethan and Jacobean Period: Plainsong Settings and Fugal Forms

With the final abandonment of the Latin rite in 1559 the clear distinction between sacred and secular keyboard music vanishes. There was at first no clearly-defined use to which the church organ could be put; and even when, in the course of time, a tradition of performing voluntaries at specified points of the service arose, the liturgy did not impose a particular form or style upon the player. From this point onwards, therefore, if a division has to be drawn, it is better to do so according to form rather than according to function. The forms discussed in this chapter, with the exception of the double voluntary, could be used for both sacred and secular purposes; those discussed in the following chapter, however, relate purely to secular use. In the following pages it will be necessary to discuss not only the church organ and its liturgical function but also the secular instruments and their uses before turning to the music itself.

The church organ suffered a period of neglect and apathy during the reign of Elizabeth. After the death of the London organ-builder John Howe in 1571 few parish churches cared to keep their instruments in playing order, and even in the cathedrals they were looked upon as an encumbrance. In the early years of the seventeenth century there was a revival, and the typical large church instrument came to possess two manuals and a dozen or more stops. Its popularity increased until the Civil War and Commonwealth brought the destruction of many instruments. The organ built at Worcester Cathedral in 1613 or 1614 by Thomas Dallam may be taken as a typical, though comparatively early, example. It is described in the Treasurer's Accounts in the Cathedral Library.[1] Translated into modern

[1] MS d. 248. Transcribed in Sumner, *The Organ*, pp. 117–18. Another

terms the specification was as follows. Great organ: 2 open diapasons (8'); 2 principals (4'); 2 fifteenths (2'); one twelfth (2⅔'); one recorder (8', stopped). 'Chaire organ': one principal (4'); one [stopped] diapason (8'); one flute (4'); one fifteenth (2'); one twenty-second (1'). The length and pitch of the lowest diapason pipes, however, are stated to be: 'CC fa ut a pipe of 10 foot long'. This, if the length refers to the actual speaking part of the pipe, indicates a pitch something like a major third below that of the present day.

In a copy belonging to St. Michael's College, Tenbury, of the *Pars organica* of Tomkins' posthumous *Musica Deo Sacra* (1668) are given two instructions, apparently added at the last moment in the printing, one governing the speed and the other the pitch of the music. The latter states that the written note *f* should be the sound produced by an open pipe 2½ feet long. This gives in modern terms approximately the note *a* flat, about a minor third higher. The apparent paradox has puzzled even experts.[2] The explanation is that in the first half of the seventeenth century (and probably ever since the Reformation), 'choir pitch' was a fifth higher than 'organ pitch'. When accompanying a choir in those days, the organist was expected to transpose his part up a fifth, which could easily be done by mentally substituting a C clef for an F clef and a G clef for a C clef. Both transposed and untransposed organ-parts survive today. By the time *Musica Deo Sacra* was printed choir and organ pitch had reached conformity once more and the instruction refers to the pitch of the music as a whole.

This solution of the problem is strikingly corroborated by a famous letter of Nathanial Tomkins to John Sayer, dated 22 May 1665. Quoting the specification of the Worcester organ, he begins with '2 open diapasons of pure and massy mettall, double F fa ut of the quire pitch & according to Guido Aretines scale (or as some term it double C fa ut according to the keys &

description, substantially the same, is contained in a letter from Nathaniel Tomkins to John Sayer dated 22 May 1665. Oxford, Bod. Lib., Add. MS C 304a, ff. 141–2. See below, pp. 53–4.

[2] For example in *MB*, xx. But see P. Le Huray, *Music and the Reformation in England*, pp. 112–15.

musiks) an open pipe of ten foot long . . .'. This permits of only one interpretation: the bottom note (sounding A_1 flat according to modern pitch) looked like C on the keyboard and corresponded to written C in music, but was in fact F_1 in terms of choir pitch. If it be objected that 'double F fa ut' ought to mean F rather than F_1, it must be remembered that a pipe $2\frac{1}{2}$ feet long was supposed to yield f, and that therefore a pipe four times the length could only give F_1, not F.[3]

This situation may be regarded as standard in the early seventeenth century and can be summarised as follows: organ pitch a fifth lower than choir pitch; the former a major third lower, the latter a minor third higher, than that of today. We have seen that both untransposed and transposed organ parts to anthems and services exist. However, other transpositions are also found. A transposition up a fourth indicates a closer relationship between choir and organ pitch; but whether the organ were higher or the choir lower, or a combination of the two, cannot be determined. Transpositions down a fourth or fifth are the equivalent of those up a fifth and fourth respectively, and were intended for use without the diapason stops. Equally they may have been destined for instruments lacking the 10-foot diapason, or, to put it another way, descending only to tenor c, a restriction applying not only to small organs but also, at times, to the 'chair organ' of a two-manual instrument.[4]

As to the function of the organ in the English liturgy, we are reasonably well informed. A note in Clifford's *The Divine Services and Anthems usually sung in His Majesties Chappell* (1663 and 1664) suggests that voluntaries were played between the psalms and the first lesson at Matins and Evensong for some time before the

[3] See footnote 1. Nathaniel's letter to Sayer contains interesting evidence that he was the editor of *Musica Deo Sacra* and hence of the remark on pitch contained in it. This evidence takes the form of a request to Sayer to secure from William Godbid (the publisher of *Musica Deo Sacra*) what look like certain proof-sheets of the volume.

[4] *Cf.* the terms 'tenor' and 'base', 'single' and 'double', for the two manuals in MSS of the period. For a general comment on transposition by organists, see Morley, 'A Plain and Easy Introduction', p. 261. The whole question of organ pitch and transposition at this time is dealt with in Caldwell, *ML* (1970) 156.

Civil War. The Rev. James Clifford, canon of St. Paul's, was intent, like others of his day, upon restoring the routine of the pre-Commonwealth services. Other sources, such as the Check Book of the Chapel Royal, indicate that the Offertory was considered a suitable point for organ playing; and it must be remembered that in Elizabethan and Jacobean times the sung part of the Communion service normally ended after the Creed. Finally there is evidence that an organ prelude was sometimes prefixed to the anthem: a piece by Edward Gibbons in one of Tudway's retrospective volumes of church music[5] has the title 'A Prelude upon the Organ, as was then usual before the Anthem'.

Only a brief discussion of the secular keyboard instruments is necessary. The regal and harpsichord (under its generic name of virginals) continued to be popular, while the clavichord sank into relative obscurity. While the regal was often made by English craftsmen,[6] harpsichords were frequently imported, particularly those of the Antwerp firm of Ruckers. Netherlands instrument-makers also settled in England, notably Ludowicus Theewes, by whom a combined harpsichord and organ, dated 1579, has survived.[7] (The earliest surviving harpsichord by an English maker—not in playing order—is an instrument by John Haward dated 1622.[8]) The Ruckers single manual harpsichord had a compass of four octaves from C, short octave, with one 8-foot and one 4-foot stop; their double manual model was intended purely for transposing purposes.[9] Some English harpsichord music of the early seventeenth century, especially by Gibbons, descends to A_1, and it may be this that accounts for the unsatisfactory reception accorded to a Ruckers instrument intended for the use of Charles I.[10]

[5] London, Brit. Mus., MS Harl. 7340 (early eighteenth century). The place of the voluntary is discussed in Le Huray, *op. cit.*, pp. 163–70.

[6] William Treasorer was 'Regall Maker' to Edward VI and Elizabeth. Sumner, *The Organ*, p. 112. See also the list of makers given by Russell, *The Harpsichord and Clavichord*, p. 65.

[7] *Ibid.*, p. 65 and plates 53 and 54.

[8] *Ibid.*, pp. 65–6 and plates 55 and 56.

[9] *Ibid.*, pp. 44–6, and plates 33–5.

[10] *Ibid.*, pp. 161–2.

The virginals proper (though in England the term was used to denote any keyboard instrument with plucked strings) was an oblong instrument with one manual and 8-foot tone only, usually portable and placed on a table. Only towards the end of the seventeenth century was there any real attempt made at a terminological distinction between harpsichord and virginals, and by this time the latter was being superseded by the spinet, a small wing-shaped harpsichord.[11]

We may now turn to the study of the actual music of this period, discussing the chronological development of each of the main forms in turn.

The free fugal forms were virtually an innovation of the Reformation, although we have examined a striking precursor by John Ambrose in the preceding chapter. Their immediate ancestors are perhaps those plainsong settings in which the *cantus firmus* is so freely decorated that it becomes indistinguishable in style from the other parts (see Ex. 26). In the same manuscript as the Ambrose piece is an untitled work by Tallis beginning with a fugal exposition. In Oxford, Christ Church, MS 371, it is provided with an introduction in which the bass line closely resembles a *cantus firmus*: the intonation to an Offertory, perhaps? But in default of any identification the piece must be regarded as freely fugal:[12]

[11] English virginals generally had the keyboard to the left, which meant that the strings were plucked close to the nut, giving a bright tone. Early spinets retained this characteristic, though the larger eighteenth-century instruments were less incisive in tone. Russell, *op. cit.*, pp. 69, 72–3.

[12] Printed in Tallis, *Complete Keyboard Works*, pp. 8–9, with the title 'Fantasy'.

\# ms has g for e

Alwood's famous 'Voluntary' from the Mulliner Book[13] may be regarded in the same light, for its bass line is set apart from the other fugal entries by its more deliberate motion. Closer analysis shows that the first set of entries is based on two separate ideas, the alto part being a subtle fusion of the two:

It is in fact a carefully wrought and charming piece altogether, with a purely musical value quite independent of its status as the earliest example of a 'voluntary'.

The only other work in this manuscript with this title is a little snippet by Farrant in the old 'mean' style, like the 'Meane' by Redford (No. 67); both are probably extracts from lost liturgical works. More relevant to the present discussion are six short fragments called 'Point', and three pieces by Sheppard called 'Versus'. Four of the 'Points' are anonymous (Nos. 64, 65, 68 and 69). Pfatteicher[14] ascribed them to Redford; quite unjustifiably, for they bear no resemblance to his authentic style. They may be extracts from vocal works, or simply brief exercises by Mulliner himself. No. 33, ascribed to Sheppard, is very similar, and suggests a possible authorship for the other four. No. 103 is assigned to Tallis and is more extended (13 bars) with a very personal cadence:

13 *MB*, i, No. 17.
14 Pfatteicher, *John Redford*.

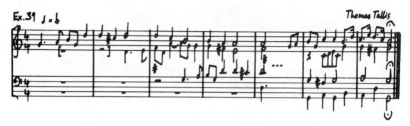

Of the three 'versus' by Sheppard (Nos. 55–7) the first is a point of ten bars, the second is a more extended point with a repeated section, while the third is largely chordal. Finally the title 'Fansye' does appear once in the Mulliner Book: it is a semi-fugal piece by Newman (No. 10), an arrangement of a work for lute.[15]

The three terms 'voluntary', 'verse', and 'fancy' or 'fantasia' were henceforth used largely interchangeably for the next hundred years or so, mainly carrying a fugal connotation but occasionally implying the more improvisatory style upon which organists thrive. However, whereas 'voluntary' and 'verse' were virtually restricted to church organ music, 'fantasia' was also used in a secular context and was not, indeed, restricted to the keyboard at all. The word 'verse' has obvious liturgical associations and was in common use even at a time when it does not appear in the manuscripts at all frequently: in 1624, when the French ambassadors were shown Westminster Abbey, 'the organ was touched by the best finger of that age, Mr. Orlando Gibbons . . . and while a verse was played, the Lord Keeper presented the ambassadors and the rest of the noblest quality of their nation with [the] liturgy as it spake to them in their own language'.[16] While the 'verse' and 'voluntary' reappeared with the Restoration, the 'fantasia' as a keyboard form did not survive the Commonwealth.

The fantasia and its cousins probably owed much of their vitality to the influence of the string repertory of such pieces. Springing partly from the instrumental performance of Latin

[15] *An Anthology of English Lute Music*, No. 23. The same composer's 'Pavyon' (*MB*, i, No. 116) is also in the Dallis Lute-Book (Dublin, Trinity Coll. Lib., MS D. 3. 30, bound with the Dublin Virginal Manuscript).

[16] Le Huray, *op. cit.*, p. 166.

motets and partly from the Italian *ricercare*, this vigorous growth reached early maturity during the reign of Elizabeth. The fantasias of Byrd were probably all written before the 1590s and one of them, a canonic essay in five parts, reappears as 'A Lesson of Voluntarie' in *My Ladye Nevells Booke* (No. 29), copied in 1591.[17] It is more of a re-working than a mere arrangement, its contrapuntal parts being fully reconciled to the demands of the two hands. At the beginning the canonic writing in the upper two voices is completely disguised by the fugal entries which have preceded it:

After a triple-time section with a delightful lilt, there is a return to the original metre but with a good deal more contrapuntal activity. To round off the work, Byrd revised and shortened the ending of the string version, no doubt because its sustained tones would be less effective on the keyboard:

---

[17] Ed. H. Andrews (*MLNB*). Also in *MB*, xxvii, No. 26.

The survival of the string version in various keyboard arrangements, apparently for the purposes of accompaniment, shows clearly the difference between a mere transcription and a vital re-working.[18]

This early use of the word 'lesson', later to be applied to almost any kind of short keyboard piece, is matched by a curious 'Lesson: Two Parts in One', ascribed in one manuscript (London, Brit. Mus., Add. 30485, where it is incomplete) to Tallis and in another (Add. 31403) to Bull. The canon is clearly distinguished in rhythm and pitch from its accompanying bass, and practically the only interest of this absurd piece is its appalling difficulty, both digital and mental.[19] In the circumstances it seems hardly worth while trying to settle its authorship.

To return to Byrd, this great composer wrote numerous fantasias and related pieces of varying quality. The little 'Verse of two parts' copied out by Tomkins[20] is hardly more than a student exercise, and even more mature pieces like the Fantasia in A minor,[21] though delightfully inventive, are apt to be somewhat sectionalised and not fully integrated. But to compensate for such deficiencies as these we have such splendid achievements as the Voluntary already discussed and another piece from the same manuscript, also called 'A Voluntarie'; the sub-title 'for my ladye nevell' again makes it unlikely that it was ever intended for church organ.[22] The fugal section is heralded by a short, solemn introduction; the polyphony is imaginative, vigorous and aptly laid out for the keyboard; and the whole gracefully proportioned work is rounded off by a little flourish of scales.

[18] *Ibid.*, where all the sources are discussed.
[19] Tallis, *Complete Keyboard Works*, p. 35; *MB*, xiv, No. 51.
[20] Paris, Bib. du Cons., MS Rés. 1122, p. 38. *MB*, xxvii, No. 28.
[21] *Ibid.*, No. 13.
[22] *MLNB*, No. 26; *MB*, xxviii, No. 61.

The fantasias of John Bull are remarkably individual works. They are all published in *Musica Britannica*, xiv, the numbering of which is adopted in the following discussion.[23] Most of them were probably written after his flight to the continent in 1613, and betray the influence of Sweelinck. Of the others, two (10 and 11) are *bicinia* in the manner of the Byrd 'Verse' just mentioned; a third (No. 15) is a featureless piece of three-part counterpoint. No. 12 is an elaborate work of great rhythmic ingenuity in the English tradition. It is found only in Ben Cosyn's Virginal Book, (London, Brit. Mus., R.M. 23.l.4), and the editor of *Musica Britannica*, xix (the second volume of Bull's keyboard music) is inclined to attribute it to Cosyn himself—which does not explain why the latter should have ascribed it to Bull.

The remaining fantasias of Bull are found only in continental sources (except for the Prelude belonging to No. 2 which is found also in an English manuscript). These sources are Vienna, Nat. Bib., MS 17771, a small manuscript in tablature; and London, Brit. Mus., Add. 23623, copied after Bull's death by Gulielmus à Messaus. Messaus was evidently an admirer of Bull and tended to ascribe to him works by other composers, both English and continental. An ascription by Messaus is very far from being a guarantee of authenticity, and even when it cannot be questioned there can be no certainty that such a work was composed after 1613. However, in the case of the fantasias being discussed there is usually some other evidence, of style or of borrowed material, in favour of continental origin. Four of Bull's fantasias are preceded by a prelude in the sources: Nos. 1, 2, 6, 14; but of these the first prelude is incomplete and the last two are really by Byrd and Gibbons respectively.[24] Two fantasias on Palestrina's famous madrigal *Vestiva i colli* illustrate one form which the genre could take: the free adaptation of a vocal piece. Others are based merely on a single thematic fragment, his own or someone else's: to the former category belong Nos. 2 ('sopra sol ut ʄ mi fa sol la') and 14 ('sopra re re re sol ut mi fa sol'); and to the latter, Nos. 3 ('op de fuge van La Guamina',

[23] The fantasias are placed first in the volume, so fantasia number equals volume number.

[24] They were printed in *Parthenia*, Nos. 1 and 21.

from a canzona by Gioseffo Guami), 4 (on a theme by Sweelinck) and possibly 7 ('sopra A Leona'). The treatment of No. 14 has led to the suggestion[25] that the work is in fact by Sweelinck, for after a long series of statements in the original note-values it is treated first in simple and then in double diminution. It is true that genuine works of Sweelinck have been attributed to Bull (for instance the *Fantasia Chromatica*, No. 1 of the Seiffert edition) in some sources; and also that Sweelinck does use this device of diminution. But Sweelinck's initial treatment of the theme is usually more genuinely fugal than in this piece, and he can rarely resist the temptation of treating the theme in augmentation as well. Another work (No. 13) has been tentatively assigned to Pieter Cornet on stylistic grounds. Of the indisputably authentic works, few are finer than No. 4, on a theme of Swee-linck, dated 15 December 1621. The free treatment of the sombre theme contrasts strongly with the schematic layout favoured by Sweelinck himself; diminution is already present in the second entry:

Ex. 42   John Bull

Soon the inevitable semiquavers appear, but there is a return to the quiet mood of the opening.

Peter Philips, like Bull, spent much of his life abroad, leaving England in 1582 and settling down as court organist in Brussels from 1597 until his death in 1628. His intabulations of vocal pieces are fairly strict and are not called fantasias. Of the two works in the Fitzwilliam Virginal Book (Cambridge, Fitz. Mus., 32. g. 29) which bear this title, one[26] is dated 1582 and may have just preceded his departure from England; the other[27] is more ambitious and treats the theme first in its original note-values, then in diminution, then in augmentation and finally in diminu-

[25] *MB*, xix, p. 223.   [26] *FWVB*, No. 88.
[27] *Ibid.*, No. 84.

tion once more. The scribe, Francis Tregian (see p. 129), con-
scientiously numbers the entries of the theme: 39 in all.[28]

Giles Farnaby was another composer favoured by Tregian in
the Fitzwilliam Virginal Book:[29] his fantasias are close to those of
Bull in style. One of them (*Musica Britannica*, xxiv, No. 11) is
simply a transcription of one of his canzonets, 'Ay me, poor
heart'; and others may have a vocal origin as yet unidentified.
For the rest, his fantasias have invention, but they tend to be
disjointed and over-elaborate.

It was in the hands of Orlando Gibbons that the form reached
the highest peak of its development. Only he seems to have had
the strength of purpose to subordinate his technical virtuosity to
the demands of a closely-knit polyphonic structure. He wrote
alike for harpsichord and organ: in the *Musica Britannica* edition
of his keyboard works (vol. xx), No. 12 is from *Parthenia or the
Maydenhead of the first musicke that ever was printed for the Virginalls*,
while No. 7 is 'A Fancy for a double Orgaine'. Most of them can
be played on either instrument. Except in two very short
examples (Nos. 5 and 6: the first is no more than a single 'point')
and in an uncharacteristic piece like No. 10 he eschews the dry
monothematicism of the Netherlanders and constructs his
fantasias like a motet, based on several points of imitation in
turn. Generally he avoids both scale-passages (No. 10 is again an
exception) and dance-like interludes as sometimes found in
Byrd (e.g. *My Ladye Nevells Booke*, No. 41); the contrapuntal
style is maintained throughout. The lack of thematic unity
makes his achievement in imparting a coherent sense of structure
to works of considerable length all the more striking. The
Parthenia piece is a good example. There are at least seven different themes in succession but they are so skilfully woven into the
counterpoint that the effect is of continuous development. The
following example summarises the course of events:

[28] Keyboard music by Philips is also contained in two related MSS from
the Spanish Netherlands: Liège, Univ. Lib. MS 153, *olim* 888 ('Liber Fratrum
Cruciferorum') and the former Berlin, Staatsbib., MS 40316 (destroyed in
World War II; photographic copy at Harvard, Isham Memorial Library).

[29] All but one of his surviving keyboard works are contained in it. A
complete edition is printed as *MB*, xxiv, the introduction of which gives a
balanced view of the composer's merits.

Ex. 43

Orlando Gibbons

The 'Fancy in Gamut flatt' (No. 9) is almost better, the diminished fourth of its first theme lending it something of the character of a Frescobaldi *ricercare*:

This interval is exploited harmonically in a later passage where a wonderful modulation is carried along by the persistent application of a single motive:

The title is Cosyn's, and is found only in the index of his virginal book; but it does illustrate a wakening attitude to the concept of tonality, meaning neither more nor less than G minor.

The 'Fancy for a double Orgaine' (No. 7) has a different kind of importance, being the earliest extant example of the 'double voluntary' as such pieces later came to be called. Cosyn is again the only source and he uses the terms 'ten[or]' and 'base' to distinguish the manuals.[30] Towards the end he gets confused and his markings do not make perfect sense.[31] He also tried to make a double voluntary out of the 'Fancy in gamut flatt', which it clearly is not. The present work, however, is certainly a genuine example of the genre, with its rhetorical passages for left-hand solo:

The right hand is never given a solo, but towards the end both hands are evidently intended to play on the great organ.

Only four other pre-Restoration double voluntaries are known —one by Portman and three by Lugge—and they will be discussed in Chapter VII.

The fantasia could incorporate various styles: chordal, scalic and contrapuntal, separately or in combination, though the last of these prevailed. Mention must not be omitted of such oddities as John Mundy's programmatic effort in the Fitzwilliam Virginal Book (No. 3), beginning with 'Faire Wether' and continuing with 'Lightning', 'Thunder', 'Calme Wether', etc., and finally 'A cleare Day'. A composer might set out to write a fantasia with Morley's famous description in mind,[32] but he would not restrict himself to the idiom demanded by a consort of viols. It must be stressed that nomenclature and form do not always correspond in Elizabethan and Jacobean music, and copyists were a law unto themselves as regards terminology. The result is that almost any kind of piece based on newly-invented material (except for the dance) could be called a 'fantasia'; and we have

[30] See footnote 4 above.

[31] Emendations have been attempted in *MB*, xx, which includes a facsimile of the complete piece. Another edition: *TW*, ix.

[32] '. . . the Fantasy, that is when a musician taketh a point at his pleasure and wresteth and turneth it as he list, making either much or little of it according as shall seem best in his own conceit'. *A Plain and Easy Introduction*, p. 296.

seen that even the basic principle of an original idea was occasionally discarded.

This last remark vividly illustrates the difficulties inherent in trying to classify the musical forms of this period. When a composer 'taketh a point at his pleasure' it makes no musical difference as to whether the point is his own or someone else's; but there is a real distinction between a purely fugal type of treatment and the method which approaches that of a ground. This second method has already been found in certain fantasias by Bull and Philips, but never to the entire exclusion of fugal treatment. The ground as a musical form will be dealt with at the beginning of the next chapter, but first it is necessary to approach the same evolutionary point from a different angle, that of the plainsong or *cantus firmus* setting.

Cantus firmus settings were never (so far as I am aware) called fantasias in England, but both they and the fugal forms stem from the work of the pre-Reformation organists. The latter, as we have seen, are derived from the polyphonic style of highly ornamented plainsong settings in four parts, where the *cantus firmus* and the other parts are indistinguishable in style. The former take as their point of departure the *cantus firmus* itself. The term 'plainsong', in this context, means any theme of non-mensural origin presented in even note-values. The genre therefore includes hexachord settings and pieces based on other schematic melodies, whether heard once or several times. The crucial distinction between these and the grounds lies in the mensural character of the latter. It might be thought that plainsong settings are closer to the liturgical background than the fugal forms, but in reality this is not so: the former preserve and develop a technique, the latter a style. There was a tendency in post-Reformation keyboard music, not very marked at first but gradually more and more so as time went on, to differentiate strongly between the two genres by presenting a *cantus firmus* in plain rather than ornamented form; in seventeenth-century settings they are usually very sparsely embellished if at all. Even in early Elizabethan times, the ornamentation of a plainsong was usually confined to pieces in two parts only, thus largely avoiding confusion with the free voluntary.

The setting of a liturgical plainsong was too deeply ingrained a habit for the English composer to throw it away lightly at the Reformation.[33] Two settings of the Marian Offertory *Felix namque* of Tallis will illustrate both the debt to the liturgical tradition and the extent to which it has been discarded. Both are in the Fitzwilliam Virginal Book (Nos. 109 and 110), dated respectively 1562 and 1564. (The second is also in a number of other manuscripts, sometimes without the introductory intonation.) In both works Tallis sets both the intonation and the final *Alleluia*, both normally but not invariably omitted in liturgical settings (most pre-Reformation settings were apparently intended for use in Lent, when the *Alleluia* was not sung). It is clear that Tallis's main purpose was to find as long a plainsong as possible to accompany his overflowingly inventive figuration. The first setting transposes the plainsong (*finalis* D) to G, the second to A: there is pre-Reformation precedent for both. In the first, the intonation is heard in the tenor in semibreves (original notation) without any fugal preamble; the main part of the melody is heard in the top voice in doubled semibreves after a fugal introduction:

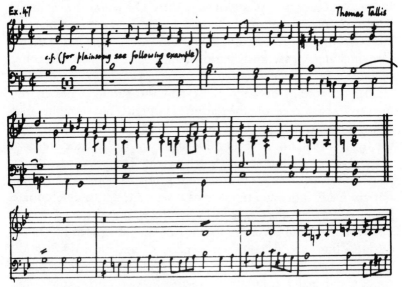

Ex. 47   Thomas Tallis

c.f. (for plainsong see following example)

33 See Caldwell, *Musica Disciplina* (1965) 129.

In the second setting, the procedure is reversed: after a fugal introduction the intonation is presented in the treble in semibreves, while the *cantus firmus* in the main section starts immediately in the middle voice in doubled semibreves:

The use of repeated semibreves rather than single breves for the *cantus firmus* strongly suggests the harpsichord rather than the organ.[34]

In both pieces the accompaniment is very elaborate, though it is imposed on the *cantus firmus* rather than derived from it, and figurative rather than contrapuntal. The proportions 3:2 and 9:4 are used, the latter being a speciality of the English keyboard composers. It is basically a triplet of triplets. Tallis's second piece is the more coherently constructed of the two, passing first to 3:2, then to 9:4 and finally back to duple metre. The following example shows the transitions, the last extract being a setting of the final note of the plainsong:[35]

---

[34] The repeat signs in *FWVB* are incorrect, owing to the editors' misunderstanding of the double-bar signs of the original. See Ferguson, *ML* (1962) 345. On the sources of this work see D. Stevens, *MT* (1952) 303.

[35] In Tallis, *Complete Keyboard Works*, note-values are halved, except, illogically, in the final section.

No other post-Reformation settings of this plainsong are known,[36] but the influence of Tallis's pieces, especially that of the second, was enormous. They provided a pattern for this kind of setting which was followed particularly closely by Bull and even Tomkins. Furthermore a Fantasia by Byrd already discussed (*Musica Britannica*, xxvii, No. 13) follows exactly the metrical scheme of the second setting, its final section being precisely the same length as Tallis's. Tomkins was probably thinking of it in his 'Offertory' (1637), a long and elaborate piece based on a phrase strikingly similar to the *Felix namque* intonation: it too drags in the 9:4 proportion.[37]

If the *Felix namque* was ideally long for some purposes, then the *Miserere* was admirably short for others. A Compline-

[36] *FWVB*, No. 111, is, however, a very primitive setting of the *Alleluia* only of *Felix namque*; it is in three parts and uses only notes of a single shape: black notes without stems. It is perhaps a sketch for a complete composition.

[37] *MB*, v, No. 21.

antiphon frequently set by Redford and his contemporaries, its twenty-six notes made it a suitable length for the display of canonic and other skills on a small scale. London, Brit. Mus., MS Add. 29996 contains a set of twenty in canon by one Thomas Woodson,[38] but they are scarcely in a keyboard idiom at all; on the other hand the tradition handed on by Bull to Tomkins respects the character of the instrument.

Of the other liturgical plainsongs set after the Reformation, the antiphon *Clarifica me Pater* provides a nice problem. To begin with, no scribe succeeded in getting the title right. The Mulliner Book includes three settings by Tallis, all without title, and presumably intended for liturgical use. While the first of them uses the usual form of the chant as found in the Sarum antiphonal,[39] the second and third use a modified form not only incorporating the optional final *Alleluia*, but also making minor changes in the rest of the melody. All later settings use this modified form of the chant, though Byrd's third setting adds a further gloss of its own. Byrd's three settings occur consecutively in London, Brit. Mus., MS Add. 30485, where they are called '2 partes', 'upon a playn songe' and 'In nomine' respectively. The second and third are also in the Fitzwilliam Virginal Book (Nos. 176 and 177—properly 175 and 176),[40] both called 'Miserere'; finally a setting by Tomkins is given the title 'glorifica me pater'.

Other popular melodies were those of hymns: *Aeterne rerum Conditor, Aurora lucis rutilat, Christe Redemptor omnium, Salvator mundi Domine, Veni Redemptor gentium* and others.

But it was the *Gloria tibi Trinitas* melody which really caught the imagination of the English composers and called forth the best and most numerous of their plainsong settings. It was one of the five psalm-antiphons for first Vespers on the feast of the Trinity, and was used also for the *Quicunque vult* at Prime. It can be shown almost conclusively that it was never used liturgically by the organists: settings of its four companion antiphons at

[38] London, Brit. Mus., Add. 29996, ff. 184v-189r. A selection printed in Miller, *JAMS* (1955) 14.

[39] *Antiphonale Sarisburiense*, pl. 201.

[40] The numbering after 95 is editorial. The editors missed out the number 171 by mistake, but compensated by repeating the number 182. The three settings are in *MB*, xxviii, Nos. 47–9.

Vespers are totally lacking, and the organ was virtually never used at Prime.[41] What then was the cause of its popularity with sixteenth- and seventeenth-century composers of keyboard and chamber music?

The Elizabethans were immensely fond of selecting and transcribing passages of discarded masses and motets of the past, often for improbable forces. One of the extracts treated in this way was the *in nomine* section of the *Sanctus* of Taverner's six-part Mass *Gloria tibi Trinitas*: hence the frequently-found title *In nomine*. In this four-part section the plainsong was stated in breves in the second voice. It is a passage of singular beauty:

Of the extant arrangements, two are for voices with English words, one is for voice and lute, two are for strings (one with a fifth part added) and two are for keyboard.[42] The two keyboard

---

[41] Two hymn-verses for *Iam lucis orto sidere*, the hymn at Prime, are found in the Mulliner Book (*MB*, i, Nos. 75 and 86). Two settings are also assigned to Bull (*MB*, xiv, No. 45). *Iam lucis* had no tune of its own, but was sung to various tunes associated with other hymns according to the season.

[42] London, Brit. Mus., Add. MS 15166, f. 88v (vocal four-part, 'In trouble and adversitye'). Top voice only in this source, but printed by Day, *Certaine Notes* (1560, 1565); Add. MS 30480–4 (vocal four-part, 'O give thanks unto the Lord'); Oxford, Bod. Lib., Mus. Sch. d. 212–16, No. 2 (strings four-

arrangements are in the Mulliner Book and in Oxford, Christ Church, MS 371. Mulliner at least probably copied his version from string parts, since his book includes two arrangements of *In nomines* originally for strings (by Johnson and White). The Christ Church version is lightly embellished and there is no evidence as to its immediate origin. It should be remembered that no arrangement can be shown to date from before the reign of Elizabeth, and the popularity of the work probably derives from its revival in Marian times (it was composed before 1530).

It is probable that the independent cult of the *In nomine* by Elizabethan composers began in the sphere of chamber music. Taverner's original words served as the title of their settings of the plainsong, and they often began with a direct quotation from the model. Preston, Thorne and Tallis all wrote *In nomines* for consort, but of these only Tallis also set the melody for keyboard. However, the earliest keyboard settings cannot have lagged far behind. Composers initially had a clear choice of styles: either they could copy the smooth polyphony of the consort settings, or else they could adopt a more idiomatic style, generally in two parts with the plainsong in the bass. Mulliner provided a clear prototype for the former in his transcriptions of Taverner, Johnson and White, followed by Alwood in his two settings.[43] The earliest examples of the latter are settings by Tallis and Strowgers in Christ Church 371 and the six by Blitheman in the Mulliner Book.[44] These last are really remarkable works, a coherent set of greatly varying mood.

Byrd's only original setting follows Tallis in being in two parts and having the ornamented plainsong in the bass.[45] Bull is

---

part); London, Brit. Mus., Add. MS 31390, f. 101 (strings five-part); Add. 4900, f. 61v (top part only; the lute accompaniment has been lost); Add. 29246, f. 54v (the three lower parts arranged for lute).

[43] London, Brit. Mus., Add. 30485, ff. 48v, 55v; *EEOM*, Nos. 24, 25. The *In nomine* by Alwood in *MB*, i, No. 23, is based not on *Gloria tibi Trinitas* but on the five-note ostinato from his Mass 'Praise him Praiseworthy' (*EECM*, i, No. 1).

[44] Tallis, *Complete Keyboard Works*, p. 32; one by Strowgers in *Altenglische Orgelmusik*, p. 11; Blitheman in *MB*, i, Nos 91–6.

[45] Byrd, *The Collected Works*, xx. 135; Byrd, *Forty-five Pieces*, No. 3; *MB*, xxviii, No. 50.

the direct successor of Blitheman, though he also profited from the more elaborate works of Preston and Tallis. His twelve *In nomines*, all published in *Musica Britannica*, xiv, are a goldmine of scholastic devices. Such brilliance is out of fashion nowadays, but it may be closer to the ideal of the time than music with a more direct appeal. The work in 11/4 time (No. 9), though possibly not the best of the set, illustrates the extreme to which the pursuit of the ideal could lead. Pre-Reformation composers had already achieved quintuple metre by laying out the plainsong in notes of five minims in length (expressed as breve plus minim); to give each note the value of eleven crotchets is only an extension of the same idea. Similarly *sesquialtera* (3:2) was an old device; after 46 notes of the *cantus firmus* in 11/4 Bull applies it and produces bars of 33/8 to last exactly the same length of time:

It is easy enough to work out these matters on paper, but the connoisseurs of the day could no doubt appreciate the subtlety in performance. It was after all an age in which, to borrow Morley's slightly overdrawn account, it was considered good fun on a country walk to descant upon plainsongs, wrangling with one's companions to bring in the hardest proportions and the jolliest folk-tunes.[46]

The *In nomines* of Carleton the younger, Tomkins and Lugge will be discussed in Chapter VII.

A few examples survive of settings by English composers of plainsongs which, though Gregorian, do not follow the Sarum text. To this category belong the two settings of *Salve Regina* by Bull. There was no tradition of setting this melody for keyboard in England, and it is clear that Bull's pieces were intended for liturgical use on the continent. They follow a line that can be

---

[46] *A Plain and Easy Introduction*, pp. 213, 214.

traced back to the Buxheim manuscript of *ca.* 1470, and treat the plainsong much more freely than English custom permitted. Bull's second setting, with only two 'verses', is obviously incomplete as it stands.

There are also instances of settings of unidentified *cantus firmi*, some of which are obviously not Gregorian and are fairly clearly made up by the composers themselves. The authorship of one particularly interesting example of this type has never been satisfactorily settled. It is assigned in Cosyn's MS, in Oxford, Christ Church, MS 1113 and in London, Brit. Mus., MS Add. 36661 to Gibbons; but Tomkins listed it in the index of his manuscript (Paris, Bib. Nat., fonds du Cons., Rés. 1122) with the *In nomines* of Bull and it certainly resembles his style more closely than any undisputed work of Gibbons. Tomkins' title, given with the piece itself, is *Kyrie Eleyson*, which is inexplicable; Cosyn calls it *In nomine*, which it is not. There is a resemblance to the plainsong *Victimae paschali* in the first few notes,[47] but it extends no further than that.

Some plainsongs were short enough to be repeated during the course of a piece. The *Miserere* was treated in this way by Bull, Cosyn, Tomkins and others. Bull's three-fold setting (*Musica Britannica*, xiv, No. 34) is a good example, the figuration becoming more elaborate with each repetition. It is clear that in works of this type variation form is approached. Bull also did this with the slightly longer melody of the hymn *Salvator mundi Domine*. Here the figuration does not merely change with each repetition, but also during the course of the melody itself, giving the effect of continuous development. Such a piece begins to look very like a Sweelinck chorale or Genevan psalm setting; but Bull's piece, found only in English sources and based on a Sarum chant, must surely have been composed before 1613, and it is very likely that Sweelinck was influenced by Bull in such matters rather than the reverse.

Consideration of non-Gregorian *cantus firmi*, as also of two-fold and three-fold settings of plainsongs, brings us straight to the subject of pieces based on the hexachord and other schematic melodies. The essential factor here is their non-mensural char-

[47] D. Stevens, *JAMS* (1956) 1.

acter, resulting in a row of notes of equal value in the setting. It is, admittedly, sometimes difficult to draw the dividing line. Bull's third 'Ut re mi fa sol la'[48] is a fugal fantasia on those notes, while his 'God save the King' (based on Ut sol fa mi), discussed at the end of this chapter, might equally well be considered a ground according to our definition. However, the majority of examples fall clearly enough into the 'plainsong' category.

The earliest and most primitive example of a hexachord setting is one by 'Mr. Whight' (presumably Robert White) in Christ Church MS 371. It consists only of a single statement up and down and is short enough to be quoted complete:

A piece by Strowgers in the same manuscript bears the heading 'upon ut re my fa soul la ij longe'. The *cantus firmus* is not written out but must be supplied in notes two semibreves in length, starting on *c″*. It can only be played by a second performer, probably at the same keyboard. A piece of the same kind by Byrd has survived in the Tomkins holograph (Paris, Bib. Nat., fonds du Cons., Réserve 1122). Here the hexachord is written out separately and annotated 'The playne song Briefs To be played by a Second person—playe This Ut re mee Fa Sol la: For the grownd of this lesson'.

We have just seen that Bull's third hexachord setting is in fugal style. His first is an interesting essay in chromaticism. Taking the ascending and descending form in semibreves he

[48] *MB*, xiv, No. 19.

begins in the top voice on *g* and starts the succeeding entries a tone higher in turn: *a, b, d'* flat, *e'* flat, *f'*. At this point, omitting any entry on *g'*, he transfers the *cantus firmus* to the bass and gives a set of entries on *A* flat, *B* flat, *c, d, e* (at which point it becomes the tenor), *f* sharp and *g*. The last four entries are in the treble on *g'*. The work requires a system of temperament in which all keys are available, such as sixteenth- and seventeenth-century composers are not generally thought to have possessed.[49] Bull's scheme, adventurous though it is, does not rival that of Alfonso Ferrabosco in a pair of pieces originally intended for strings.[50] In the first of these the ascending hexachord is presented on successively higher semitones from *c'* to *g'*; in the second the descending hexachord is given in reverse order. These pieces are preserved in a keyboard score by Thomas Tomkins (London, Brit. Mus., Add. 29996), but this may have been intended for accompaniment rather than for solo performance.

Bull's second hexachord setting follows what may be called the standard pattern. The plainsong remains in the treble at the same pitch, beginning on *g'*, throughout. As neither *The Fitzwilliam Virginal Book* (*FWVB*) nor the *Musica Britannica* edition (*MB*) give a clear picture of the complex metrical structure of this work a full analysis is desirable. After a six-bar introduction the *cantus firmus* enters in two-part counterpoint:

Ex. 53   *John Bull*

This continues for some time, though the accompaniment becomes ever more elaborate. Just before the start of the eighth

[49] The question is discussed in Curtis, *Sweelinck's Keyboard Music*, pp. 143–7, where he suggests that one of the varieties of mean-tone temperament then in use could have coped with most of the chromaticism used at the time.

[50] Original version *a 4* in Oxford, Christ Church, MSS 2, 397–400, 473–8, 517–20; Bod. Lib., Mus. Sch. e. 437–42, 568–9; Dublin, Marsh's Lib., MS Z3. 4. 7–12. For strings *a 5*: Christ Church MSS 2, 403–8; London, R.C.M., MS 1145. For keyboard: Christ Church MS 436; London, Brit. Mus., Add. MS 29996, f. 189v–192r.

statement 3:2 proportion[51] and three-part counterpoint are ushered in simultaneously (*MB* halves the values but gives the correct ratio):

Ex. 54   John Bull

Again the figuration is intensified. A quotation of statement 12 shows (a) the stage which this process eventually reaches, (b) a transitional passage combining the *sesquialtera* with the original values, (c) the break into 9:4 proportion and (d) the introduction of a fourth part:

Ex. 55   John Bull

While four-part writing prevails, the rhythmic temperature drops first to *sesquialtera* (bar 163 in *MB*) and then to the original note-values (bar 181). Here the texture is simplified to three-part

[51] Called 6:1 in the MS. I give the mathematically correct ratio.

chords in the right hand accompanied by semiquavers in the left. This continues down to the end of statement 17. So far the notes of the plainsong have been presented only as semibreves. Now we are suddenly jolted out of our complacency as the time-value of these is shortened by one crotchet. But there is no proportional change: the crotchets move at identical speed and the ratio suggested in *MB* must be ignored. Ex. 56 shows the transition:

At bar 223 (*MB*), the crotchets are subdivided into triplets. With statement 21 the notes of the hexachord are again shortened by a crotchet and the ratio given in *MB* should once more be ignored.[52] Ex. 57 shows the transition:

This triplet accompaniment remains, while at bar 271 (statement 23) the notes of the plainsong are suddenly doubled to their original length. Half-way through this final statement the triplets become duplets once more and the original metre is restored to bring the piece to a triumphant conclusion:

[52] If the editors' instructions are followed throughout, bars 247-end will be played at half the correct speed.

To illustrate the use of schematic plainsongs other than the hexachord, Bull's 'God save the King' may be mentioned. It will also serve as an example of a really knotty problem of attribution and textual criticism. The basic situation is that there are (or were) three manuscripts containing two pieces, each based on the notes C G F E (ut sol fa mi). The work first appeared in William Kitchiner's *The Loyal and National Songs of England* (1823) in a transcription by Edward Jones from a manuscript written by Gulielmus à Messaus which once belonged to Pepusch (MS 18, i) and is now irretrievably lost. In that manuscript the work was attributed to Bull and dated 1616. This is the version printed in *Musica Britannica*, xiv (No. 32). Another source (Berlin, Staatsbib., MS Lynar A1) attributes it to Sweelinck, calls it 'Phantasia Ut sol fa mi' and gives it a variant ending (from bar 111). This is the version printed by Max Seiffert in *Werken voor Orgel en Clavecimbel*, No. 12. This ending, or rather the last eight bars of it, is also used as the conclusion of a quite different composition found anonymously in a tablature from Lüneburg. This is given as No. 13 in Seiffert's edition. There is no need to connect this second work with Bull, but it certainly links up with Sweelinck by virtue of its ending. The solution may be that the Pepusch manuscript preserved a genuine work of Bull and the Lüneburg manuscript a genuine (though anonymous) work of Sweelinck. The scribe of Lynar A1 has transmitted an amalgam of the two (but including nine bars not found in the other sources) and ascribed it to Sweelinck. He may have been in possession of a copy containing the Bull setting followed by the Sweelinck, but with some pages missing. The inexplicable transition from bar 110 of Bull's work to the conclusion of Sweelinck's could have caused him to supply nine bars of his own as a link between the two, and the (correct) ascription to Sweelinck at the end of the second piece he naturally took to refer to the whole lot. At all events this process probably occurred at *some* stage in the transmission of the work.[53]

Bull's composition (the Pepusch version as given in *Musica Britannica*), though austere, is typical of his concern for continuous development. After the opening the theme is heard only in the top voice. The first statement gives the theme as four semibreves, but thereafter the first note is always modified to a minim, preceded by a minim rest. In the following quotation, Kitchiner's text is emended from the Lynar source:

Ex. 59   John Bull

* g' in Pepusch source   † rhythm ♩ ♩ in Pepusch source

As we have said, this work is virtually a ground according to the classification adopted for our purposes. With the mensural ground we move right away from forms which can be related to the ecclesiastical background, and towards those which have exclusively secular connotations. A consideration of these forms will be the main concern of our next chapter.

[53] But see Curtis, *op. cit.*, pp. 61–4.

VI

The Elizabethan and Jacobean Period: Secular Variations and the Dance

There is nothing intrinsically secular about the form or style of the ground, but it may conveniently be discussed between plainsong settings and variations on avowedly secular melodies. There are really two distinct classes of ground. One is always a bass and carries harmonic implications: this kind will be discussed later. The other had purely melodic significance and may appear in any part of the texture. There are also examples which do not clearly fall into either category. Such a piece is 'The second grownde' by Byrd from *My Ladye Nevells Booke* (No. 30):[1] to begin with the theme appears in the bass and dominates the harmonic structure; but from variation 11 (Nevell numbering) it appears in a modified form in the treble. Even so, the two-bar echo which concludes each strain remains in the bass, sometimes so ornamented as to be almost unrecognisable. Since the modification of the tune in the treble involves the substitution of a 'leading-note' in bar 3 for the 'dominant', the basic impression is of a harmonically rather than melodically controlled structure, even though melodic elements are undeniably present in the ground.

A good example of the purely melodic type of ground is one by Thomas Tomkins in the Fitzwilliam Virginal Book (No. 130): it is therefore an early work and falls well within the period under discussion.[2] A simple melody, it consists of four bars only of 3/4 time, first stated in the treble without accompaniment. Its polyphonic treatment follows the expected course of gradually increasing complexity. It occurs mainly in the treble and bass, sometimes lightly embellished, but also at times in the middle of the texture. It is never transposed. When it occurs in the bass the

[1] *MB*, xxvii, No. 42. It is based on a tune called 'Goodnight'. Cf. *DVM*, No. 10, and Ward's notes on this piece. [2] *MB*, v, No. 39.

harmonies it generates are incidental, not vital to the conception of the work.

From this kind of piece it is only a short step, from the point of view of classification, to the set of variations on a melody of avowedly secular association. Such works are interesting not only for their own sake, but also because they often present the best, or the only, surviving versions of a song popular in those days. The essence of the variation technique in these works is the preservation of the melody throughout; it may become highly decorated, and it may pass to any voice of the texture, but only rarely will it be abandoned in favour of its purely harmonic implications.

The technique of variation in this sense is inherent in the very act of 'setting' a tune for keyboard, lute or consort. The mere harmonisation of a melody represents a polyphonic variant which is already at one remove from the original. So it is that Elizabethan scribes number the variations from the very beginning of the piece; the melody on which it is based exists only as a Platonic 'idea' in the mind of the hearer. Its first appearance may not even be the simplest and the entire set of variations needs to be studied to discover the 'ideal' form of the tune. This is quite different from the eighteenth-century concept of a 'theme' (such as the *Aria* of Bach's 'Goldberg Variations'), self-sufficient with melody, bass and harmonies, as a subject for future variations. The sixteenth-century notion, as we shall see, applied also to standard basses with implied harmonies, the very first presentation of which already involves an interpretation. In this book the term 'melodic variation' is used to mean 'variation in which the melody (however embellished) is the constant factor', and 'harmonic variation' to mean 'variation in which the general harmonic sense is the constant factor'.

Elizabethan and Jacobean settings of well-known tunes, apart from the mere single statement, could extend from two to thirty or more presentations. A simple piece with only two statements of the theme occurs in the Mulliner Book as a later addition to the manuscript (No. 1 in *Musica Britannica*, i).[3] It is clear that a

[3] This is actually the second piece in the MS. 'No. o' is not incomplete at the beginning. See *DVM*, p. xii.

certain amount of embellishment is already present at the first statement, and the second hardly involves any intensification of the texture. The theme on which it is based can be identified from a setting by William Byrd entitled 'The Maidens Songe' (*My Ladye Nevells Booke*, No. 28; *Musica Britannica*, xxviii, No. 82). Byrd, however, always repeats the first four-bar strain, making the twelve-bar tune into a sixteen-bar tune. A comparison of the Mulliner initial statement with that of Byrd will illustrate the incomparably greater sophistication of the latter:

The second statement in Mulliner can achieve only a purely decorative embellishment while Byrd by his eighth and last statement has reached the heights of contrapuntal eloquence:

Note also the faultless anticipation (by means of canon) of the theme's anacrusis. In the Mulliner Book the last two bars of Ex. 60 are followed by a metrically superfluous up-beat.

Indeed, if in the period 1560–1625 Gibbons is the great master of fugue and Bull of *cantus firmus*, then to Byrd must belong the distinction of excelling in variation form. His mature keyboard style is perfectly adapted to the suggestion of counterpoint where a literal presentation becomes impracticable. He is constantly jumping from the explicit to the implicit, and the style can encompass the plainest of harmony and the most complex counterpoint. It is this mastery of keyboard polyphony which can render his variations on the simplest of themes such an ennobling musical experience. The Variations on 'Sellingers Rownde' (*My Ladye Nevells Booke*, No. 37; *Musica Britannica*, xxviii, No. 84) subject the theme to every possible polyphonic treatment without ever causing it to lose its basic identity. 'Will yow walke the woods soe wylde' owes its success to the composer's respect for the simplicity of the naïve tune. So clearly is its outline impressed on our minds that Byrd for once abandons the melodic outline of the theme in statements 8–11, only to reaffirm it in the concluding variation:

The tiny coda is just what is needed to reinforce the G tonality. Compared with this, the setting by Gibbons[4] appears over-elaborate and inconsistent with the character of the tune, and its coda merely commonplace.

Byrd's frequent use of a coda is typical of his concern for the large-scale organisation of his variations. Another manifestation of this concern is found in the not unusual ternary structure of his sets, often characterised by a middle section in triplets. A common trait is the unison opening phrase ('Maiden's Song', 'Walsingham', 'Carman's Whistle') and, allied to this, a feeling for the dialogue possibilities of the original melody. Both 'Will you walk' and 'The Maiden's song' open with a pair of statements suggesting by their pitch-level a dialogue between a man and a woman. Even the titles (at least as given in *My Ladye Nevells Booke*) are often more complete than in the works of other composers, suggesting a concern for the implications of the original text and sometimes hinting to the modern scholar an otherwise unknown version of the poem.

'Have with yow to Walsingame' (*My Ladye Nevells Booke*, No. 31)[5] illustrates most of these characteristics, and provides an illuminating comparison with the great setting by Bull, chosen by Tregian to commence his monumental collection.[6]

4 *MB*, xx, No. 29. The Byrd setting is in *MB*, xxviii, No. 85 (*MLNB*, No. 27, *FWVB*, No. 67); it is dated 1590.

5 *MB*, xxvii, No. 8; *FWVB*, No. 68.

6 *MB*, xix, No. 85; *FWVB*, No. 1.

Byrd's title deserves initial consideration. In *My Ladye Nevells Booke*, the source closest to Byrd himself, it is as already given; in two other sources (Will Forster's Book, London, Brit. Mus., R.M. 24. d. 3, and London, Brit. Mus., Add. 30486) it is 'As I went to Walsingham', and in the Fitzwilliam Virginal Book it is simply 'Walsingham'. This last is also the title of Bull's set in three sources (including the Fitzwilliam Virginal Book), while its title in Cosyn's MS is again 'As I went to Walsingham'.

A poem by Walter Raleigh, 'As you came from the holy land/Of Walsingham', survives in four sources, though in only one (Oxford, Bod. Lib., MS Rawl. Poet. 85, f. 123) is it subscribed 'Sr W.R.'.[7] In this source, also, the first stanza exists as a correction of one originally beginning 'As you went to Walsingham'. This is clearly nearer to the popular ballad 'As I went to Walsingham' from which Raleigh must have worked, and which survives in a Pepysian manuscript as well as in the musical sources noted above. The Pepysian version begins 'As I went to Walsingham/To the shrine with speed',[8] indicating a closer connection with the great medieval pilgrimage centre than in Raleigh's poem. Byrd's title in *My Ladye Nevells Booke*, 'Have with yow to Walsingame', appears to be unique and may indicate a further genuine variant of the popular poem. In this version, if Byrd's initial statement is to be trusted, a dialogue already occurs within the first stanza, not merely from stanza to stanza as in Raleigh:

Ex. 63   William Byrd

[7] F. W. Sternfeld, *ML* (1964) 108; A. M. C. Latham, *Poems of Ralegh*, 2nd edn. (1951), pp. 22–3, 120–2.

[8] W. Chappell, *Popular Music of the Olden Time*, London, 1859, i. 122–3 (reprinted New York, 1965, with an Introduction by F. W. Sternfeld).

No such hint of dialogue is to be found in Bull's setting: indeed throughout his entire composition the melody is found at the same pitch in the top voice. He does follow Byrd, however, in beginning with a unison phrase:

Two characteristic features of the tune are the downward drop of a fourth in bars 2 and 6 and the turn to the major in bar 7. In Byrd's setting the downward fourth is sometimes apparently modified to a downward second (major or minor), as it is also in lute settings by Collard and Cutting, although at times the original interval is present elsewhere in the texture. At any rate the second should not necessarily be regarded as representing the original version of the tune, any more than any of the numerous other modifications introduced during the course of both sets for purely musical reasons.

Bull's composition, possibly written with the intention of rivalling that of Byrd, differs from it in many ways. Pitching the tune a tone higher, its aim is evidently to dazzle the listener with the brilliance of its harpsichord writing. Trills, repeated semi-quavers, rushing scale-passages, left-hand arpeggios, even the crossing of hands, are all present. Passages like the following have an incredibly modern look about them:

Following Byrd, he introduces *sesquialtera* and triplets for a
'middle section' (statements 20–4); with the twenty-fifth variant
he returns to duple time, concluding with an immensely grandiose statement (No. 30) to round off the whole work.

Byrd, by contrast, employs purely 'musical' (to be tendentious)
devices. His theme appears in all voices of the texture, and the
interest of the accompaniment is contrapuntal rather than
technical. He prefers to introduce *sesquialtera* half-way through a
variation (No. 15). Generally he uses longer note-values than
Bull and the theme does not have to be slowed down to quite the
same extent. Finally there is a short coda in duple time, serving
to relieve the tension in a way which Bull's final statement cannot
achieve.

Byrd is equally a master of 'harmonic' variation, though here
his monopoly of excellence is not so complete. We have already
seen that the distinction between the melodically and harmonically conceived ground is sometimes difficult to draw. In the example discussed above (p. 83) the transference of the ground to
the treble (albeit with a significant difference) provided evidence
of its melodic nature. Where the ground is confined entirely to
the bass, the distinction becomes even finer. In 'My Ladye
Nevels Grownde' and 'Hughe Ashtons Grownde' (*My Ladye
Nevells Booke*, Nos. 1, 35) the almost complete respect for the
original bass is matched by an equal concern to preserve its
harmonic implications. 'Hughe Ashtons Grownde' is called
'Treg. Ground' in the Fitzwilliam Virginal Book,[9] which has
been widely interpreted as 'Tregian's Ground'. *My Ladye
Nevells Booke* is correct, since the ground is that of 'Hugh
Ashtons Maske', a four-part piece in Oxford, Ch. Ch. 979–83,

9 No. 20. Also in Will Forster's Book (London, Brit. Mus., R.M. 24. d. 3),
p. 390; Add. 30485, f. 61. *MB*, xxvii, No. 20.

which appears to be by William Whytbrooke. 'Qui passe' or 'Kapasse'[10] is based ultimately on a *Villotta alla Padoana* by Filippo Azzaiuolo, *Chi passa per questa strada* (1557); the tune became incredibly popular all over Europe, but by the time Byrd composed his setting only its very simple harmonic basis remained as a constant factor. Two settings, respectively for gittern and cittern, are preserved in the Mulliner Book, without the vital bass-line, and an early keyboard version occurs in the Dublin Virginal Book, (Dublin, Trinity Coll., Marsh's Lib., D. 3. 30) to which we shall return.[11]

Nearly all of Byrd's ground *basses* appear to be in some measure harmonically conceived. A final example, his early 'Hornpipe',[12] demonstrates one major influence. The resemblance to Aston's famous piece is very close, at least superficially. A section in 3/2, based on a four-bar ground, is followed by a 6/4 section in which the ground is compressed into two bars. However, whereas Aston's piece is so strongly harmonic that his dominant-tonic progressions give the impression of weak-strong accentuation, this element is not so prominent in Byrd. His ground (C D C C, in which D can be replaced by G) does not carry this stress-pattern but, if anything, the reverse. Moreover, while Aston's last (weak–strong) progression in 3/2 is incomplete, its last two bars being compressed into the first 6/4 bar, Byrd completes his four-bar progression in 3/2 and then starts a rather different chordal pattern in 6/4. Here he takes the opportunity of reversing his (strong–weak) dominant–tonic progression to one of tonic–dominant. Byrd later achieved a far finer version of the first part of this ground, compressed to a single bar, in 'The Bells'.[13]

But it was to the realm of dance-music that the 'harmonic' style of variation really belonged; and Aston's 'Hornepype', on which Byrd's composition was rather unsuccessfully based, provided an early and primitive instance of its application. In

[10] *MLNB*, No. 2; *MB*, xxvii, No. 19.
[11] D. Stevens, *The Mulliner Book, A Commentary*, Appendix, Nos. 3, 7; *DVM*, No. 30.
[12] *MB*, xxvii, No. 39.
[13] *Ibid.*, No. 38.

order to understand how this connection arose, it is necessary to discuss briefly the history of the Renaissance dance.

We have already referred (Chapter II) to the *basse dance*. In the second half of the fifteenth century this was danced all over civilised Europe to improvised polyphony over a *cantus firmus*. In Italy four measures could be danced to the same *cantus firmus*: the *bassadanza* proper, the *quaternaria* (or *saltarello tedesca*), the *saltarello* and the *piva*, to progress from the slowest to the fastest.[14] The *quaternaria* and *piva*, however, were not considered 'courtly' dances. In France and Burgundy only two measures were adopted: the *basse dance* itself, and the *pas de Brabant*, the latter being the equivalent of the *saltarello*. Italy also possessed the *ballo*, a dramatic or pantomimic dance made of a variety of dance steps, its melodies being notated in rhythmic form at treble pitch.

By about 1500, however, the old courtly dances were falling into decay, and were superseded by newer measures. In France, the numerous choreographies of the old *basse dances*, now known as *incommunes*, were replaced by the single choreography of the *basse dance commune*.[15] Musically, in place of the old *cantus firmus*, usually adapted from the tenor of the old-style *chanson*, the superius of the newer kind of *chanson* cultivated by Sermisy and others provided the basis of the dance. This, of course, meant a good deal of actual rewriting of music. In Italy a different solution was largely adopted. In place of the *cantus firmus* there arose basses with clear harmonic implications: the *folia*, *romanesca*, *passamezzo* and so on. The effect in both countries was similar: the irregular phrase-lengths of the *basse dance* tenors were replaced by short phrases of regular length which could be repeated as necessary. But the Italian system, soon to be imitated in France and elsewhere, permitted greater flexibility and allowed any number of instrumentalists to improvise simultaneously. The process really indicates the beginning of modern harmony.

It must not be thought that this system grew up overnight.

---

[14] The length of each note of the *cantus firmus* was determined by the measure to be danced, thus: ♩. ♩ ♩.(*bassadanza*), ♩ ♩ (*quaternaria*), ♩. (*saltarello*) and ○. (*piva*). Gombosi, *MQ* (1941) 289.

[15] Heartz, *Annales Musicologiques* (1958–63) 287.

On the contrary, there was a period of transition, and indeed the idea of a rigid repertory of dances was never recaptured. For a time old and new names co-existed: Joanambrosio Dalza's *Intabulatura de lauto* of 1508 follows its new *pavane* (*padoane* or dances from Padua) with *saltarelli* or *pive*. The pavans are duple-time dances (occasionally, in other sources, triple) over very simple harmonies which are designated by the terms 'a la venetiana' or 'a la ferrarese' and partly repeated in the *saltarelli* and *pive*. The *piva* may well be the ancestor of the English hornpipe, although Aston's example seems to incorporate both measures. The galliard also seems to have originated in northern Italy,[16] though it does not occur in early Italian musical sources. Musically, if not choreographically, it was similar to the *saltarello*.

The earliest hint of the bass later to be called *passamezzo antico* occurs in a *Padoana ala francese* from the Capirola lute-book of 1517.[17] Both this and the *romanesca* are the basis of several *basses dances*, *pavanes* and *gaillardes* in Attaingnant's *Dix-huit basses dances* for lute (1530). From this it can be seen that these basses, like the older *cantus firmi*, were capable of being adapted to a variety of dance measures. The term 'passo e mezzo' is found in an Italian keyboard manuscript of *ca.* 1520,[18] once in connection with the 'Venetian' bass and once in connection with the true *passamezzo* bass. Later it received the epithet *antico* to distinguish it from a major-key version known as *moderno*. In England, both the *antico* and *moderno* basses were largely bound up with the pavan and galliard, while the *romanesca*, a similar bass, virtually disappeared from keyboard music after about 1560. The Dublin Virginal Book, dating from about that time, is the earliest source of such compositions, although contemporary and earlier lute sources have survived.[19]

We now give the *passamezzo antico* and *romanesca* basses, choosing the note values most commonly associated with them:

Ex. 66

16 *Preludes, Chansons and Dances for Lute*, ed. Heartz, p. lii.
17 *The Capirola Lute Book*, No. 28. See especially the last eight bars (p. 83).
18 *Balli Antichi Veneziani*, Nos. 4, 19.
19 For the details see *DVM*, pp. 40, 42–4, and Table 1.

TABLE 1. *Italian Grounds*

	English keyboard music	English works for other media, and continental keyboard works
Passamezzo antico and variants	*DVM*, Nos. 1, 2 (Pavan and Galliard). Byrd: Pavan and Galliard (*MB*, xxvii, No. 2). Phillips: Pavan and Galliard (*FWVB*, Nos. 76–7). Gibbons: Ground (*MB*, xx, No. 26). Farnaby: 'Quodling's Delight' (*MB*, xxiv, No. 42; *FWVB*, No. 114). Variations on 'Fortune my Foe' by Tomkins (*MB*, v, No. 64) and Byrd (*MB*, xxvii, No. 6). See also *Folia*.	Lute pieces from London, Brit. Mus., Roy. App. 58, printed Ward, *JAMS* (1960) 117, exx. 5, 7; the first = 'Queen Maries Dump', the second = 'Pastime with good company' (original version in *MB*, xviii, Nos. 7, 7a). 2 further versions of 'Queen Maries Dump' (see Ward, *JAMS* (1951) 111). London, Brit. Mus., Stowe 389, f. 123 (printed *DVM*, 40). London, Brit. Mus., Roy. App. 74, f. 38 (single treble part only). 'Greensleeves' in Ballet MS (Dublin, Trinity Coll., D. 1. 21). See also *Romanesca*. 3 lute pieces in Washington D.C., Folger Shakespeare Lib., MS v. a. 1. 59. London, Brit. Mus., Add. 30513, Nos. 4, 6, 8b of the cittern and gittern pieces (printed in Stevens, D., *The Mulliner Book*, *A Commentary*[1]). 2 lute pieces from Le Roy, *A Briefe and Easy Instruction*, London, 1568.

Table 1 (*contd.*)

	English keyboard music	English works for other media, and continental keyboard works
		Philips, Pavan *a 6* (*MB*, ix, No. 90; not *FWVB*, No. 76). Anon., 'Passo e mezzo', *ca.* 1520 (Jeppesen, *Balli*, No. 19). Anon., *Passamezzo antico* I, II, III, 1551 (*SBK*, xxiii). A. Gabrieli, 'Pass' e mezzo antico' (Torchi, *L'Arte Musicale in Italia*, iii. 71). S. Scheidt, *Passamezzo* (*DDT*, i. 40). 'Fortune my Foe' by Scheidt (*DDT*, i. 126) and Sweelinck, *Werken*, i, No. 64. London, Brit. Mus., Stowe 389, ff. 120v–121r (3 lute settings, printed *DVM*, 42–43). Lute setting in Le Roy, *op. cit.* London, Brit. Mus., Add. 30513, No. 5 of the cittern and gittern pieces (printed in Stevens, D., *Op. cit.*). This is merely a fragment.[1] 'Grien Slivis' for 2 lutes, Washington D.C., Folger Shakespeare Lib., MS 1610. 1, f. 5 (printed Ward, *JAMS* (1957) 157).
Romanesca	*DVM*, No. 9. 'Q:M: Dumpe', Paris, Bib. Nat., fonds du Cons., Rés. 1186, f. 93; printed *DVM*, 43. 'J. W. Dumpe', New York, Pub. Lib., Drexel 5609, p. 156 (see Ward, *JAMS* (1951) 111).	

Table 1 (*contd.*)

	English keyboard music	English works for other media, and continental keyboard works
La Folia	Settings of 'What if a Day': Anon: Paris, Bib. Nat., fonds du Cons., Res. 1186, f. 15 (see Greer, article cited opposite); Tomkins: *MB*, v, No. 64. See also 'Fortune my Foe', s.v. *Passamezzo antico*.	Frescobaldi, *Orgel- und Klavierwerke*, ed. Pidoux, Bärenreiter: Kassel and Basel, 1954, iii. 46. For non-keyboard settings of 'What if a Day' see Greer, *ML* (1962) 304. 'Blame not my lute' (See Chapter VII, footnote 56).
Passamezzo moderno and variants	Byrd: 'Quadran' Pavan and Galliard (*FWVB*, Nos. 133–4). Bull: 'Quadran' Pavan and Galliard (*MB*, xix, No. 127a–f). Morley: 'Quadran' Pavan and Galliard (*SBK*, xii). Settings of 'John come kiss me now' by Byrd (*FWVB*, No. 10) and John Tomkins (*EKM*, iv, No. 7).	London, Brit. Mus., Add. 30153, Nos. 1, 2 of the cittern and gittern pieces (ed. Stevens, D., *op. cit.*). Richard Allison, 'Quadro' Pavan for lute (ed. Lumsden, *Anthology*, No. 15). *Passamezzo nuovo* I, II, III, 1551 (*SBK*, xxiii). Sweelinck, *Werken*, i, No. 67.
Bergamasca	Bull: 'Dr. Bull's Ground (I)' and *Het nieu Bergomasco* (*MB*, xix, Nos. 102a, 124).	2 dumps for lute, one[1] by John Johnson. See Ward, *JAMS* (1957) 151.

[1] In the list printed in the 2nd edn. of *MB*, i, the numbering has been revised so that the fragment, No. 5, is unnumbered, and the two separate pieces originally numbered 8 have become 7 and 8.

The first two items in the Dublin Virginal Book are a Pavan and Galliard on the *passamezzo antico*, using a form of the bass in which *g* is substituted for *b* flat as the fifth note. Transposing the bass down a fifth, the chord on the note *c* is always major rather than minor, either by design or owing to the copyist's omission of E flat from the key-signature. The Pavan and Galliard each incorporate four variations. The ninth piece in the manuscript is a *romanesca*, untransposed. Of its ten variations, Nos. 1 and 3 bear a remarkable resemblance to a piece in Paris, Bib. Nat., fonds du Cons., MS Rés. 1186, compiled in the 1630s by Robert Creyghton, entitled 'Q[ueen] M[aries] Dumpe'. Indeed, the early dump also made use of the *passamezzo antico* as well as the *romanesca* bass and the simple tonic–dominant progression noted in Chapter III.[20]

The Dublin manuscript is a fascinating and vital source for the interrelation between popular and art-music in the cloudy years at the beginning of Elizabeth's reign. Nevertheless we must now leave it and pursue the later history of the *passamezzo* in England. Byrd, as usual, marks a tremendous advance over his predecessors. His *passamezzo* Pavan and Galliard[21] are mature works without any sign of experimentation, based on the normal form of the *passamezzo antico* as quoted above. With six and nine variations respectively, they make a bow to the conventional tripartite division of these dances. His 'Quadran' Pavan and Galliard employ the passamezzo with the '*b quadratum*', i.e. the *passamezzo moderno* in G major (*Musica Britannica*, xxviii, No. 70):

Ex. 67   Passamezzo moderno

To this bass, which we may call section A, he adds a second strain of half the length (b):

Ex. 68   Ibid.

[20] Ward, *JAMS*, (1951) 111.
[21] *MB*, xxvii, No. 2; *MLNB*, Nos. 24–5; *FWVB*, Nos. 56–7.

This addition appears to be exclusively English in origin: an early example is provided by the second of the cittern pieces in the Mulliner Book. Since each section is subject to immediate repetition the form of the Pavan is:

$$A_1 \ A_2 \ b_1 \ b_2 \ A_3 \ A_4 \ b_3 \ b_4$$

The Galliard is longer by one third:

$$A_1 \ A_2 \ b_1 \ b_2 \ A_3 \ A_4 \ b_3 \ b_4 \ A_5 \ A_6 \ b_5 \ b_6$$

Bull wrote no setting of the *passamezzo antico*, but his 'Quadran' Pavan and Galliard are evidently modelled on Byrd's. In all sources except the Fitzwilliam Virginal Book Byrd's structure is followed exactly in both movements. This is the music printed in *Musica Britannica*, xix, as 'The Quadran Pavan, II and III', and 'The Quadran Galliard, I–III' (i.e. Nos. 127b–127f) and in *The Fitzwilliam Virginal Book* as Nos. 32 and 33. In the latter, however, the Pavan is preceded by another, simpler version (No. 31), and the Pavan of the other sources is labelled 'Variatio'. While the simple version or the Variatio might be omitted, or either or both played without the Galliard, there is no justification for chopping up the Variatio or the Galliard into separate pieces, as the *Musica Britannica* numbering suggests: the Fitzwilliam divisions here give a better idea of the composer's structure. If the whole piece is played right through, the Galliard is inclined to be an anti-climax, but the Pavan with its variation is one of the most monumental examples of continuously developing variation in the entire virginalist repertory. Bull neither aims at nor achieves Byrd's euphonious counterpoint: his concern is to amaze, and he does this by a variety of technical effects which even by his standards are outstandingly inventive:

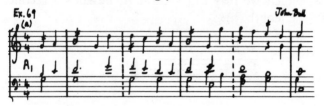

But the technique of harmonic variation was not confined to
the writing of variations on these specific basses. It was an
important factor in the composition of almost all dance music for
keyboard. Even where an embellished repetition of a section is
not written out, an improvised one can often be assumed. Moreover, a galliard was sometimes a variation of the preceding
pavan, the resulting pair being a 'variation suite'. The most
thoroughgoing application of this technique known to me is the
'Long' Pavan and Galliard by the Scottish composer William
Kinloch.[22] Here the customary three sections of the Pavan are
each followed by a varied repetition, and then the entire scheme
is repeated in varied form. Finally the Galliard is a variation (in
quicker time) of the whole Pavan. The 'Pavana-Variatio-
Galiarda-Variation' by Ferdinando Richardson, *alias* Heybourne
(*The Fitzwilliam Virginal Book*, Nos. 4–7) represents a commoner
type, inasmuch as the Galliard, while it refers to the melodic
material of the Pavan, does not provide a complete variation of it.
This procedure is also found in pavan-galliard pairs in which the
component dances are not each provided with their own com-

22 *SBK*, xv, Nos. 3, 4.

plete variation. In fact, the relationship of galliard to pavan in English keyboard music varies from complete subservience to complete independence in all respects except tonality and basic form.

The pavan-galliard pair in England came to assume the same sort of importance in the context of the dance generally as the *bassadanza-saltarello* (*basse dance-pas de Brabant*) had done in fifteenth-century Italy and France. Not since then had such stability existed in dance convention. That the English forms, though highly stylised versions of the dances concerned, were no mere archaic survival is shown by contemporary publications of pavans and galliards for consorts of instruments, presumably intended for actual dancing.[23]

An important new element in the technique of 'harmonic' variation as applied to the ordinary pavan and galliard is the melodic factor. When a dance-section is repeated in embellished form, it is varied in its totality of melody, bass and harmony. In other words, we have almost arrived at the 'Goldberg Variations' stage (referred to above) though the technique is not yet, and will not be for a long time, applied to sets of variations in the ordinary sense. We have already discovered hints of this state of affairs in both 'melodic' and 'harmonic' variation techniques. In Byrd's variations on 'Will you walk the woods so wild', the harmonic implications of the tune were the only constant factor for several variations in succession. On the other hand the *passamezzo* and *romanesca* basses were loosely associated with certain melodic ideas,[24] which have not been mentioned above because they seem to have been largely ignored by English composers.[25] Be that as it may, the concept of a closely related melody, harmony and bass as an entity for variation is fully developed in English dance music for keyboard.

The earliest pavans and galliards written idiomatically for the keyboard are a number of untitled movements in the Dublin

[23] E.g. A. Holborne, *Pauans, Galliards . . .*, 1599.

[24] The *romanesca* bass, for example, is closely associated with the Spanish song *Guardame las vacas*. See *HAM*, i, No. 124.

[25] However, the English songs 'Greensleeves' and 'Quodling's Delight' do have a close connection with the *passamezzo antico*. See Table 1.

Virginal Book (3–4, 5–6, 7–8, 17, 21–2, 23, 26–7: all are pavan-galliard pairs except for 17 and 23, which are separate galliards). There is also a Pavan by Newman in the Mulliner Book (No. 116) which has four instead of the usual three sections. The Dublin pieces are identifiable from their rhythm and tripartite structure, though it is sometimes difficult, as the editor remarks, to distinguish between a pavan and an alman. It may be remarked in passing that several pieces in the manuscript have been identified as almans and *branles* from their tunes as found in continental sources.

No. 3 in the book is ascribed to one 'Mastyre Taylere', who cannot be identified with any certainty; and No. 4 can be assigned to him on grounds of musical similarity. The pair form a tiny Pavan and Galliard, each with three repeated four-bar phrases. The first two phrases of the Pavan, though written out in full, are virtually unchanged. In the Galliard, all the phrases are varied on repetition. It is no slavish imitator of the Pavan, but it does follow its general melodic and harmonic outline. Ex. 70 shows the first strain of each piece:

It is a far cry from these simple and rather amateurish pieces to the great pavans and galliards of Byrd: yet as usual there is no evidence of a transitional phase. Byrd leaps into full maturity with 'the first t[hat] ever hee m[ade]' as Tregian put it (*The Fitzwilliam Virginal Book*, No. 167). Since this piece is 'The firste pavian' in *My Ladye Nevells Booke*, the latter's numbering may well carry great authority. Of the ten pavans, the seventh and eighth are without a galliard, the ninth is the *passamezzo*, already discussed, while the tenth is headed 'Mr. W. Peter' (Sr. Wm. Peter in *Parthenia*). William Petre, Junior, born in 1575, was knighted in 1603; Byrd's Pavan and Galliard must have been written by the summer of 1591,[26] but probably not long before. The sixth Pavan and Galliard are inscribed 'Kinbrugh Goodd'; Kinborough Good was the daughter of Dr. James Good of Malden, Surrey, and she married before 1589.[27] The pavans and galliards in *My Ladye Nevells Booke*, though far from being all he wrote, form an almost complete picture of his work in this form. Only one other pair, the 'Earl of Salisbury' can be dated any later with confidence: Robert Cecil was created Earl of Salisbury in 1605 and died on 24 May 1612, and the works by Byrd and Gibbons in his honour (or in his memory?) were published in *Parthenia* in 1612 or 1613.

That first Pavan, in the key of C minor with two flats, is already imbued with the intense gravity which was to become a hall-mark of the genre. The dancing rhythms of the Galliard, complete with the characteristic alternation of 3/2 and 6/4, scarcely dispel the elegiac note. The kinship of the two move-ments is a subtle matter of mood and style, for they are not overtly related except by key and basic structure. Though Byrd often drew level with this achievement later on he can scarcely be said to have surpassed it.

The 'Earl of Salisbury' Pavan and Galliard are very different: so much so that they are scarcely recognisable as the work of the same man. Both are in two short strains, each of which is re-peated without variation. Though they are the work of an old man, too tired perhaps to write at greater length, they are never-theless from the pen of one who was incapable of writing a melody without charm. However, the really great work in-scribed to Lord Salisbury is Gibbons' Pavan and Galliard, also printed in *Parthenia*. Gibbons, a much younger man than Byrd, really takes on his mantle in the early years of the seventeenth

---

[26] *My Ladye Nevells Booke* was finished on 11 September 1591. See *MB*, xxvii. 170, 172.

[27] *Ibid.*, p. 178.

century. Curiously enough, 'Lord Salisbury' is his only authenticated pavan-galliard pair, although a number of separate
movements survive. Here the comparatively slow pace of the
Galliard contributes greatly to the overall breadth of the work.
Elsewhere, Gibbons slowed down the pavan itself. The following
example has to be barred in 4/4 even though it is really only the
equivalent of an eight-bar strain in 4/2. It is a good example of
his sense of melodic line:[28]

Ex. 71   Orlando Gibbons

The pavans and galliards of Bull are of a different kind. Gravity
was not part of his make-up. He was quite capable of being
'melancholy', 'fantastic', or simply 'chromatic', to quote from
some of his own titles; but these moods were masks to be assumed when appropriate. At his most natural, as in 'Lord
Lumley's Pavan and Galliard',[29] he is brilliant and quite cool.
The tempo of the Pavan is slower than ever, but the ornamentation includes extended passages in demisemiquavers, and Bull's
4/4 is hardly faster than Byrd's 4/2. The first two strains are of

[28] *MB*, xx, No. 15.
[29] *MB*, xix, No. 129.

eleven bars each. The Galliard, by comparison, sounds per-
functory.

A good deal of unsuspected charm emerges from Bull's
almans, corantos and other light pieces. Both the alman and
coranto are effectively present in the Dublin Virginal Book,
since the *branles gays* of this source (to use Attaingnant's terminology) are quick dances in 6/4 time. No. 12 was known on the
continent as 'Branle Hoboken', and No. 13 as 'Alman Guerre guerre
gay'.[30] The latter has the form AAB and was sung in England to
the words 'Was not good King Solomon'.[31] Nos. 15 and 16 are
an interesting pair, a setting of the continental 'Almande du
Prince', followed by its *reprise* (variation) in the rhythm of a
galliard:[32]

The mature alman of the Elizabethans was a slower dance but
in the same 4/2 time. Rhythmically it was similar to the pavan,
but it generally had two strains rather than three. Each was
subject to immediate varied repetition, and in the case of Byrd
the whole scheme might then be repeated with further variations,

[30] S. Vreedman, *Carminum quae Cythara pulsantur Liber Secundus*, Louvain,
1569.

[31] *Cf.* D. Stevens, *The Mulliner Book, A Commentary*, Appendix No. 8 (first
ten bars). The following setting of the *passamezzo antico* is mistakenly transcribed as part of the same piece; but the error is rectified in the second
edition of *MB*, i, the two pieces being now numbered 7 and 8 respectively.
(The former No. 5, a fragment, is omitted from the revised numbering.)

[32] Also in Vreedman, *op. cit.* See *DVM*, pp. 49–50.

either once or twice (see *Musica Britannica*, xxvii, Nos. 10 and 11). His 'Monsieurs Alman' with its 'Variatio' (*The Fitzwilliam Virginal Book*, Nos. 61 and 62) represent a particularly elaborate arrangement, for the usual pattern $A_1 A_2 B_1 B_2$ is heard twice in the original piece and three times in the 'Variatio', making a total of five versions in all. It is the 'Variatio' alone that is given as 'Munsers Almaine' in *My Ladye Nevells Booke* (No. 38), and no doubt this is the piece as Byrd wished to preserve it.

In Bull, the 4/2 measure is usually slow enough to warrant modern barring in 4/4 (or at least 2/2). A 'Germain's Alman', 'French Alman' and 'English Toy', all in A minor,[33] are examples of the two-strain alman, and the last of them reminds us that a dance-measure may easily lie concealed beneath a descriptive title. There is no noticeable difference in style between these three pieces. Another pair in the unusual key of D major[34] have an indefinably wistful character, illustrated well in the following cadence:

Ex. 73   John Bull

The corantos have an equally individual flavour. To the same category belongs that appealing group of pieces entitled 'My Self', 'My Grief', 'My Choice' and 'My Jewel'.[35] 'My Grief' and 'My Jewel' are considerably slower, but they have the same rhythmic character. 'My Self' has three repeated sections, with a variation of the whole. 'My Jewel' follows the same plan, though without the variation. In a later version of this piece, dedicated to Jacques Champion and dated 1621,[36] 'The Woods so wild' is introduced (once only) as a fourth section.

We have now discussed the main forms cultivated by the

[33] *MB*, xix, Nos. 94–6.
[34] *Ibid.*, Nos. 114, 115.
[35] *Ibid.*, Nos. 138–41.
[36] See Dart, *ML* (1959) 279, for the identification of the dedicatee with Jacques Champion.

Elizabethan and Jacobean composers. But the feast includes an abundance of side-dishes: medleys, programme music, transcriptions, stage music, duets, and so on. These categories are not mutually exclusive, nor are they entirely separate from the forms just described; but they deserve independent treatment by virtue of some special characteristic which is not part and parcel of those forms.

Perhaps the finest example of a medley is Byrd's 'The Barelye Breake' (*My Ladye Nevells Booke*, No. 6). The title is explained by the editor of the source, Miss H. Andrews, as 'a country game and dance which could be accompanied by some sort of musical medley'.[37] Thirteen tunes, long and short, some of them identifiable and others not, are quoted in disconcerting profusion. Each is followed by a variation. The only unity about the work, apart from that of Byrd's mature personal style, is tonal, and even this does not apply to each tune individually. 'Johnson's Medley' is a lute piece which survives in three keyboard versions, by Byrd (in Will Forster's Virginal Book, p. 188), Randall (in Tisdale's Virginal Book, Cambridge, Fitz. Mus., 52. d. 25, f. 74v) and anonymously in the Fitzwilliam Virginal Book. This last source ascribes the original more precisely to one Edward Johnson. There are six sections, each with its varied repeat, and a short coda. A short piece by Giles Farnaby, 'His Humour',[38] belongs to this category. The first section is a simple melody, the second is an exercise in chromaticism, the third is a lively dance ending on the dominant, and the fourth is an ascending and descending hexachord. Only the first section is marked to be repeated.

The title of this last piece brings it close to the realm of programme music, the simplest kind of which is represented by pieces with titles describing moods, objects or actions. 'His Humour' is preceded in the Fitzwilliam Book by 'Giles Farnaby's Dreame' and 'His Rest'.[39] The former is in the style and construction of a pavan, and the latter is actually called 'Galiard';

[37] *MLNB*, p. xxxix. Also printed in *MB*, xxviii, No. 92. *Cf.* also *FWVB*, No. 173.

[38] *MB*, xxiv, No. 53 (*FWVB*, No. 196).

[39] *Cf* also the pieces by Bull mentioned above, p. 106.

but they are not related by key. 'His Conceit' occurs later on in the same manuscript (No. 273). Immediately before it come two pieces by Martin Peerson with more concrete connotations: 'The Primrose' and 'The Fall of the Leafe'. The latter is genuinely descriptive, capturing as it does the delicate fluttering of the leaf before it comes to rest:

Ex. 74   Martin Peerson

John Mundy's Fantasia beginning with 'Faire Wether' (see above, p. 66) aims higher but achieves less. Neither musically nor descriptively is it a success: in style it is very disjointed, and the fair weather, lightning and thunder sequence is repeated several times with alarming rapidity.

The doyen of Elizabethan programmatic pieces is undoubtedly Byrd's 'The Battell'. To us it may seem naïve, but to Byrd it was of sufficient importance to be included in *My Ladye Nevells Booke* (No. 4). It is divided into nine short sections, with three additions (possibly not authentic) from other sources. Part of its interest now lies in the reproduction of the military music of his day. It is preceded by 'The Marche before the Battell' (found independently in the Fitzwilliam Virginal Book, No. 259, as 'The Earle of Oxfords Marche') and followed by 'The Galliarde for the Victorie'. These two splendid pieces greatly enhance the work as a whole, and have the effect of enclosing the C major kernel of the 'Battell' itself within a G major shell (*Musica Britannica*, xxviii, Nos. 93–5).

Byrd was not the only composer to write battle music, for the Paris manuscript, Rés. 1185, contains several anonymous pieces of this kind. Since this manuscript is thought to be partly in the hand of Bull, there is some probability that the anonymous pieces which it contains are by him.[40] A 'Battle paven' and 'Galyard' are followed by 'A Battle, and no Battle: frigian musique' and

---

[40] See also Chapter VII, p. 127.

'Almaine. Ionicke, and frigian musique'.[41] The 'Battle and no Battle' is a duet and will be discussed below; the terms 'phrygian' and 'ionic' must refer to the mood rather than the mode of the piece, like the various pieces from the same manuscript (and also anonymous) inscribed 'Dorick musique'.[42]

Transcriptions of all kinds of music fill the pages of the anthologists of the time. To begin with vocal music, the Mulliner Book includes plain transcriptions of Latin motet extracts, English anthems and secular part-songs. Sometimes, as with such masterpieces as the anonymous 'Rejoice in the Lord alway' and 'In going to my naked bed' (possibly by the author of the poem, Richard Edwards), Mulliner preserves the only extant complete text. By way of contrast the elaborate intabulations by Peter Philips of chansons and madrigals, which are preserved in the Fitzwilliam Virginal Book, seem to owe much to Italian practice.

Transcriptions of music composed for other instrumental *media* were even more popular, although we must not overlook the fact that plain transcriptions of viol consorts from about 1580 on were probably intended as accompaniments rather than for independent performance. However, this would not apply to Mulliner's transcriptions of *In nomines* by Robert Johnson (the elder) and Robert White. Byrd's arrangement of a famous five-part *In nomine* by Robert Parsons is more ambitious.[43] Dance music was not neglected: Dowland's 'Lachrymae Pavan' was set by Byrd, Cosyn, Morley, Randall and Giles Farnaby (and also by Sweelinck), and his 'Piper's Galliard' by Bull.[44] An anonymous Scottish piece, 'Prince Edward's Pavan', occurs in an arrangement (also probably by a Scot) under the title 'The Queine of

[41] *MB*, xix, Nos. 109a, 109b, 108, 110.
[42] *MB*, xiv, Nos. 57, 58, 59; *cf.* also Nos. 58a, 60, 61, and Critical Commentary to all works.
[43] *FWVB*, No. 140; *MB*, xxviii, No. 51.
[44] 'Lachrymae', arr. Byrd: *MB*, xxviii, No. 54; *FWVB*, No. 121; Farnaby: *ibid.*, No. 290 (*MB*, xxiv, No. 16); Morley: *FWVB*, No. 153 (*SBK*, xii, No. 5); Randall: *SBK*, xxiv, No. 9; Sweelinck, *Werken voor Orgel en Clavecimbel*, No. 66. The original version for voice and lute was published in Dowland's *The Second Book of Songs or Ayres* (1600). For 'Piper's Galliard' see Chapter VII, footnote 31.

Ingland's Lessoune'.[45] This is an elaborate affair, each section
having its varied repetition and the whole scheme then under-
going a further variation. Here is the first strain of the original in
four different versions:

[45] *SBK*, xv, No. 5; *MB*, xv, No. 76. This piece derives from a setting of
Wyatt's poem 'Heaven and Earth', found in the following sources: London,
Brit. Mus., Roy. App. 58, f. 52, printed in Ward, *JAMS* (1960) 120 (for lute);
FWVB, No. 105 (a keyboard elaboration). For a fuller list, see Ward, *JAMS*
(1957) 179, note 101.

The Johnson family, if they were a family, provided a rich source of material for the virginalists. They included an Edward, a John and a Robert (II), this last not to be confused with the elder Robert mentioned above. A Pavan and Galliard, 'Delight', by Edward Johnson was set by Byrd (*The Fitzwilliam Virginal Book*, Nos. 277–8; also in Forster's Book, p. 276) and (?) Kinloch; but only the Fitzwilliam Virginal Book specifies Edward as the composer; the other sources, including those of the original lute piece, ascribe it variously to John, Robert, or simply to 'Johnson'.[46] A 'Flat Pavan' by John Johnson was set by Giles Farnaby, who also arranged a pavan and an alman by Robert Johnson.[47] Two almans by the latter in the Fitzwilliam Virginal

[46] For the version which may be by Kinloch, see *SBK*, xv, No. 1. The lute original is in *An Anthology of English Lute Music*, ed. D. Lumsden, which includes details of sources.

[47] *MB*, xxiv, Nos. 15, 14, 23.

Book (Nos. 145, 146) may also be arrangements by an unknown hand.

Stage music was also transcribed for keyboard; indeed some of the music just mentioned may have been intended originally for the stage. The term 'Mask' nearly always indicates the origin of the piece as a dance or a song in a masque. Sometimes we are fortunate enough to be able to identify the name of the composer and the masque for which it was intended. Farnaby arranged a tune by John Coperario which was probably used in Beaumont's 'The Masque of the Inner Temple' (1613).[48] Gibbons has a 'Lincoln's Inn Mask' and 'The Temple Mask', the titles of which sufficiently indicate their place of origin,[49] while the tune of another[50] is identifiable from other keyboard arrangements as a 'Gray's Inn Mask' with the title 'The fairest nymphs the valleys or mountains ever bred'. The musical interest of such arrangements usually resides in the provision of varied repeats by a composer of repute. Great confusion has reigned over an alman by William Lawes which survives in arrangements by Cosyn and Gibbons.[51] The former is preserved in Paris, MS Rés. 1185, in Cosyn's hand with the ascription to Lawes and 'Finis B.C.' at the end. It alone has varied repeats. The editor of the *Musica Britannica* volume of Gibbons' keyboard music says 'Since Lawes is known to have rewritten and expanded other composers' music, it is likely that this version is Lawes' own setting of an alman by Gibbons'. It would have been more logical to conclude that 'since Lawes is known to have composed for the theatre and cannot be proved to have written any original keyboard music, the version in Cosyn's hand with varied repeats is his own arrangement of an Alman by Lawes which also survives in arrangements (without varied repeats) by Gibbons'. The latter are known variously as 'A Toy' or 'An Aire', while one anonymous version of the tune[52] actually gives the title 'A Maske'. Another manuscript preserving the tune anonymously (Oxford, Christ Church, MS 92) was evidently some sort of repository of

[48] *MB*, xxiv, No. 33 and p. 142.   [49] *MB*, xx, Nos. 44, 45.
[50] *Ibid.*, No. 43. See also Boston, *ML* (1955) 368–9.
[51] *MB*, xx, No. 34. See p. 100.
[52] *PBVB*, f. [9]. See Boston, *op. cit.*

theatrical transcriptions, for it also includes an inept version of a dance thought by Cutts to have been composed specially by Robert Johnson for 'Macbeth'.[53]

The keyboard duet was in its infancy in the sixteenth century, and was confined to the *cantus firmus* and ground forms. We have discussed a *Felix namque* of pre-Reformation date (Chapter III, p. 24), and settings of 'Ut re mi fa sol la' by Nicholas Strowgers and Byrd (Chapter V, p. 77). Performance by two persons in these cases is unquestionable, but we cannot be certain that they were both intended to play at the same keyboard, or indeed that the *cantus firmus* was to be played on a keyboard at all. One can only say that the disposition of the parts in no case makes keyboard duet performance impossible (allowing for octave transposition in the case of the *Felix namque*: see p. 24). There is much less uncertainty about 'A Battle and no Battle', probably by John Bull (see above, p. 108). Here the ground is in the bass, ruling out most instruments other than the keyboard: even a bass viol would be unsatisfactory unless it were doubled on the keyboard, and a bass wind instrument seems unthinkable. The ground, consisting of four bars of 3/2 time, is written out only once, after the end of the piece, and it must be drastically modified if it is to fit the conclusion. The piece is an interesting curiosity, but no more. It also seems certain that the Dublin Virginal Manuscript, No. 10, is a duet, the ground bass being played by a second performer.

In the seventeenth century the duet form, unequivocally labelled as such in the sources, was to be expanded and made to serve new purposes by Thomas Tomkins and his friend Nicholas Carleton: these works will be described in Chapter VIII. In the meantime, Giles Farnaby had produced the first piece for two virginals, in the form of an alman.[54] Incidentally, this is the only occasion on which an instrument is actually named in the Fitzwilliam Virginal Book. A quotation of the first strain of this tiny piece will indicate the manner in which the second player elaborates simultaneously the simple tune as it occurs in the first part:

[53] Both versions in *Musique de la Troupe de Shakespeare* (Paris, 1959), Nos. 8, 8a.
[54] *MB*, xx, No. 25; *FWVB*, No. 55.

VII

The Elizabethan and Jacobean Period: The Development of the Style

The preceding discussion of the formal procedures of the Elizabethan and Jacobean composers has not allowed us to consider the chronological development of the style as a whole, its dependence on foreign models and its subsequent influence on continental composers. Into the account which it is now proposed to give may be interwoven such information about the composers and sources as is necessary to an understanding of the subject.

The origin of the Elizabethan style lies in the subtle fusion of native and foreign influences from the reigns of Henry VIII, Edward VI and Mary. These were sufficient to ensure the vitality of English keyboard music until about 1600 without much further infiltration of foreign elements. After then, composers became increasingly under continental domination once more. It must be added that in the field of vocal music the influence, especially of Italy, was much stronger and was renewed at an earlier date. Though this current did not directly affect keyboard music, it was bound to have an indirect effect on its style.

The native element of the English style is found in the liturgical organ repertory, just as what is specifically English in Byrd's vocal polyphony stems from Fayrfax and Taverner. Its characteristics were a close adherence to the plainsong and the systematic application of its polyphonic accompaniment in a fixed number of voice-parts. The continental element is a more complex matter.

At the court of Henry VIII, French and Italian influences were mingled in about equal measure. The former were a backward-looking feature of the culture of the day, the latter the more modern and up to date. Though Italian influence had been present in English music and poetry in the fourteenth century, this source had largely dried up during the fifteenth and was once again something of a novelty in the early sixteenth. French influence, however, had been a traditional feature of English culture since the time of the Norman conquest. This particular strand was soon to be relinquished, but not before it had had time to be a decisive element in the Elizabethan artistic make-up. It is to be seen in the barbarous Norman-French of the early Tudor song-books:

> Sy fortune mace bien purchase enuers amors que tant mon detenu non bien mamour on soit tous mes a puis si me semble il que rennan obtenu puisque de vous aprouchez Je ne puis.[1]

It is present in Robert Coplande's *Maner of Dauncing base daunces* (1521) and in the *basse dance* choreographies which have survived in English sources.[2] In a more subtle way it can be observed in much of the poetic diction and musical style of the time. The French element was naturally extended to include that of Burgundy and the Netherlands, and so it is that music by Isaac, Busnois and van Ghizeghem as well as Compère and Févin was included in the musical repertory of the Henrician court.[3] All this was very much a matter of the 'declining middle ages': required by the conventions of the day but not the most vital force for the artistic development of the future.

The Italian contribution is seen in the Petrarchan and other imitations of Sir Thomas Wyatt, and in music in the enthusiastic reception accorded to Memo, the organist of St. Mark's, Venice (see Chapter IV, p. 49). Nor is there much doubt that Italian harpsichords and chamber organs were imported at that time.[4] We have seen the Italian side of simple harmonic grounds in the keyboard music of Aston and his contemporaries, and this must certainly have been the style of playing adopted by John Heywood, who became virginalist to Queen Mary. It is difficult

---

[1] J. Stevens, *Music and Poetry in the Early Tudor Court*, p. 404 (textual repetitions removed). In *MB*, xviii, No. 46, an emended text is underlaid.

[2] Heartz, *Annales Musicologiques* (1958–63) 287.

[3] Printed in *MB*, xviii.

[4] Russell, *The Harpsichord and Clavichord*, p. 67.

to believe that a 'Q[ueen] M[aries] Dumpe', preserved in a much later source but found in prototype in a set of variations on the *romanesca* bass in the Dublin Virginal Book of 1560–70, does not hand down to us something of the character of his music.[5]

Of the three main sources dating from the first dozen years or so of Elizabeth's reign, the Dublin Virginal Book, compiled in London, is the most important in helping us to bridge the stylistic gap between Aston and Byrd. It contains both Italian and French elements, the latter mainly in a debased form through the dance publications of the Netherlanders: Phalèse, Susato, Vreedman and so on. On the whole it was the Italianate strain which was to prove the more lasting in its effect on later English keyboard music. This itself must partly have been transmitted through French sources; and it is this older, inextricable mixture of the two which has given English keyboard music its involvement with the harmonic ground and the pavangalliard pair. The *passamezzo moderno* and the *Chi passa* are merely later additions to an existing substratum.

Only one composer is mentioned in the Dublin Virginal Book: a 'Mastyre Taylere' who may, as Ward has suggested, be 'the John Taylor who was master of the singing children of the hospital of St Mary's, Woolnoth, in 1557 and, between 1561–1568, master of "the children of the grammer schoole in the colledge of Westminster"'.[6] He was also organist of Westminster Abbey, 1562–1570. His activity during the vital decade 1560–1570 and in Westminster makes him a very likely candidate as contributor to a cosmopolitan collection of this kind. The title 'mastyre' forbids one to suppose that he was himself the copyist; the collection looks as though it was made by an amateur anxious to preserve for himself the fashionable keyboard art of his day.

The Mulliner Book preserves a rather different repertory, and is altogether more insular in tone. It is not necessary to believe that it was started before about 1560, although it is certainly retrospective, containing as it does liturgical music by Redford, Tallis and Blitheman. What is clear, however, is that Mulliner

[5] See Chapter VI, p. 97. *DVM*, No. 9, and pp. 43–4 ('Q:M: Dumpe').
[6] *DVM*, p. xi.

himself did not collect this music for liturgical use; probably he intended it for his own private amusement. Whenever it was started, the copying certainly continued until 1570 or 1575, which is the probable date of the music for cittern and gittern at the end and of some of the keyboard pieces tacked on to the beginning (Nos. 0–4). The former exhibit many of the strands present in the Dublin Virginal Book: there are pieces based on the *passamezzo antico* (Nos. 4, 5, 8), *romanesca* (fragment on f. 121v) and *Chi passa* (Nos. 3, 6); and there is a setting of the *Alman Guerre guerre gay* with its English title of 'Was not good King Solomon' (No. 7).[7] There are also a 'French Galliard' and a 'Venetian Galliard' (Nos. 10 and 11),[8] while the 'Pavan' (No. 2) is already clearly based on the quadran ground complete with its 'English' appendage (see Exx. 67 and 68). Of the pieces added at the beginning of the anthology, Nos. 3 and 4 are a *Gloria tibi Trinitas* and an *Audi benigne Conditor*, the latter copied from an imperfect source, by Nicholas Carleton the elder. Nos. 0–2 concern the development of the secular style at a stage practically identical with that represented in the Dublin manuscript. No. 0 is not in fact incomplete at the beginning, as the editor believed; entitled 'O ye happy dames', it is identical with a piece called 'My hearte is lenid on the lande' in Raphe Bowle's lute manuscript (London, Brit. Mus., Stowe 389, f. 120).[9] No. 1 ('The Maiden's Song') has been discussed earlier (p. 85); No. 2, evidently in the rhythm of a galliard, is the most interesting of the entire group. Like so many of its type, it is based on a simple harmonic ground. This is in two eight-bar sections, the second differing from the first only in the substitution of dominant for tonic harmony in the first complete bar. Each section is subject to immediate varied repetition, and the entire scheme is gone over three times:

$$(A_1\ A_2\ B_1\ B_2) \times 3$$

The example shows the two strains in their simplest form, with the beginning of each reprise:

[7] *Cf. DVM*, No. 13.

[8] *Cf. The Capirola Lute Book*, Nos. 9, 28 ('Padoana Francese' I and II) and 17 ('Padoana [alla venetiana]'). For a discussion of parallel material see *ibid.*, pp. lxiv-lxxii.

[9] *DVM*, p. xii.

A third manuscript of this date, Oxford, Christ Church, MS 371, is very similar to the earlier part of the Mulliner Book in date and repertory. It too includes liturgical music by Redford and others, arrangements of English and foreign part-songs, a version of the Taverner *In nomine*, post-Reformation plainsong settings, etc. It is much smaller (25 leaves in its present state) and was copied on to printed music-paper. It is particularly interesting for its inclusion of *In nomines* and a hexachord setting by Strowgers and pieces by Tallis and Byrd. Not much is at present known about Strowgers, but the composer of these pieces is certainly the Nicholas Strogers who wrote *In nomines* for strings, consort songs, lute music and Latin motets.[10] This is all consistent with a composer working in the fifth and sixth decades of the century. He is not to be confused with the earlier 'E. Strowger'

10 There is also a Fantasia by Strogers in *FWVB*, No. 89.

of London, Brit. Mus., Add. 29996, the composer of a *Miserere* about whom nothing else is known.

The pieces by Tallis from Oxford, Christ Church, MS 371, have already been mentioned. It is also the earliest source of keyboard music by Byrd. The *Miserere* on f. 15 is indeed primitive and could easily be the work of a boy in his teens. It is preceded in the manuscript by another *Miserere*,[11] copied in such a way as to leave no room for a composer's name at the end. It is my belief that the two works belong together and that both are by Byrd. They are complementary in technique, the first being in two voices with the plainsong ornamented in the lower, and the second in three with the plainsong unornamented in the upper:

---

[11] Printed in Caldwell, *Musica Disciplina* (1965) 148–9. Both pieces now in *MB*, xxviii, Nos. 66–7.

The next source of English keyboard music, apart from a few fragments of minimal value, is none other than *My Ladye Nevells Booke*, completed in 1591 and devoted entirely to Byrd. Moreover, it contains scarcely anything by him which is not a mature masterpiece. For a study of his earlier keyboard music one must have recourse to the compilations of Forster (London, Brit. Mus., R.M. 24. d. 3) and Tomkins (Paris, Bib. Nat., fonds du Cons., Rés. 1122). Both evidently had access to loose papers of Byrd, and Forster in particular (whose enormous Virginal Book is dated 1624) was evidently at some pains to preserve as much as he could.[12] Tregian (in the Fitzwilliam Virginal Book) and the compiler of London, Brit. Mus., MS Add. 30485 also copied some early works as well as numerous examples of his mature style.

What is quite evident is that the renaissance of keyboard music in the 1580s is almost entirely due to the single-handed efforts of Byrd himself. Without him the plainsong setting and, to a certain extent, the fugal style would have remained, ultimately to become debased and wither away; but the secular variation and dance, the conveyors of all that is most characteristic of the virginalist style, would have scarcely begun to live. Practically everything that we regard as typical of the English manner can be

---

[12] About half the eighty pieces in it are by Byrd.

found in its simplest and purest form in the music of William Byrd. It is therefore appropriate to give a brief account of his early life and musical development.

He was born in 1543, probably the son of one Thomas Byrd, a member of the Chapel Royal in the reigns of Edward VI and Mary. At least one work ascribed to 'Byrd', the *Similis illis fiant* which is part of a composite ritual psalm setting by Sheppard, Byrd and William Mundy,[13] is likely to be by the father, Thomas, since it was included in a manuscript intended for the Sarum liturgy and therefore probably compiled before 1559.[14] It is a fluent piece of work, rather too assured in its older style to be the work of a fifteen-year-old, however gifted. It is probable that around 1560 he was composing exercises like the *Miserere* settings quoted above (Ex. 78) and the twenty or so consort settings of plainsong melodies which have survived.[15] It has been never proved that he was a formal pupil of Tallis, but he could scarcely have avoided his influence in the milieu of the Chapel Royal.

From 1563 to 1572 Byrd was organist of Lincoln Cathedral,[16] though we are not to imagine that he lived in isolation from London. In fact he became a gentleman of the Chapel Royal on 22 February 1570 (n.s.). Lincoln is not far from Newark-on-Trent, where Robert Parsons, Byrd's predecessor at the Chapel Royal, was tragically drowned on 25 January 1570. It is difficult not to believe that Byrd and Parsons were well acquainted during those Lincoln days, and that Parsons helped in the furtherance of his career and the formation of his style. Some of Byrd's consort music can probably be dated from this time, and one five-part *In nomine* of his seems directly dependent on Parsons' very famous and only surviving five-part *In nomine*. The two works are found consecutively in numerous sources.[17] At this time too can

13 *TCM*, ix. 298.

14 London, Brit. Mus., Add. MSS 17802–5 (the 'Gyffard' part-books). A recent study of this MS, however, suggests a compilation over a period of time extending beyond 1559: Bray, *Research Chronicle*, vii. 31.

15 A full list printed by Oliver Neighbour, *MT* (1967) 506.

16 See Watkins Shaw, *ML* (1967) 52.

17 Amongst others, Oxford, Christ Church MSS 984–8. Byrd's elaborated version for keyboard of the Parsons work is in *FWVB*, No. 140 and in Will

probably be dated some of the less mature works which were to be included in the Tallis—Byrd *Cantiones Sacrae* of 1575, such as a setting of the respond *Libera me de morte aeterna* which again bears a striking resemblance to one by Parsons.[18] But this publication itself affords clear proof of Byrd's full maturity in the superb *Emendemus in melius,* with which he chose to open his contribution to the volume. Though Byrd was often later to publish works with an archaic flavour about them, they may probably be dated before 1575. This year marks a watershed in his development, the point at which earlier experiment gave way to the full flow of his creative imagination.

It is not difficult to fit the keyboard music into this scheme. The early works include the plainsong settings, the Hornpipe based on Aston's work (see Chapter VI, p. 91), the two-part 'Verse' copied by Tomkins (see Chapter V, p. 60) and the Fantasia incorporating the rhythmic scheme of Tallis' second *Felix namque* (Chapter V, pp. 60, 71). There is also a three-part Fantasia which must be comparatively early, of which the latter part has found its way into *My Ladye Nevells Booke,* probably as a space-filler.[19] Other works could probably be adduced, not all of them accepted as authentic by modern scholarship; but the bulk of what remains is mature work.

A close study of Byrd's mature style reveals very little of the direct influence of Tallis as a writer of keyboard music. The specifically keyboard idioms in his work are derived from Aston and his unknown contemporaries and successors. One of these is a left-hand accompanimental figure which survives with a re-markable persistence:

Ex. 79

Forster's Book (London, Brit. Mus., R.M. 24 d. 3), f. 137v (printed in *MB*, xxviii, No. 51).

[18] Byrd: *TCM*, ix. 81–85; Parsons: the section *Dies Illa* from his setting, erroneously attributed to Byrd, *ibid.*, 303–4.

[19] No. 42, 'A Voluntarie'. The complete piece is in London, R.C.M., MS 2093, p. 31 ('Fantasia'): *MB*, xxvii, No. 27.

For the rest, he seems to have applied his experience in writing vocal and instrumental polyphony to the keyboard. Here, of course, the indirect influence of Tallis and Parsons is clear, though it is by no means the only one. The scholastic polyphony of the *cantus firmus* responds and the *In nomines* for strings was superseded, we may suppose, by early attempts at purely imitative polyphony. The majority of his contributions to the 1575 publication are of this kind, and the technique is found also in several early fantasias for strings. It left its mark on the mature keyboard style in a few transcriptions and reworkings of such pieces, as well as in some completely new compositions. But complete polyphonic liberation is achieved when neither a *cantus firmus* nor a rigid system of imitative entries is necessary for the composer to express his feelings, as the opening of *Emendemus in melius* very clearly shows:

The equivalent of this in terms of the keyboard can be seen in passages such as the following second strain from a pavan found only in the Fitzwilliam Virginal Book (No. 165)[20] and which I suspect to be a comparatively early work:

[20] *MB*, xxvii, No. 4a.

Here the 'free-voiced' texture, the spare but telling use of ornamentation, and the hint of the old left-hand figure (see Ex. 79) in the last bar form a natural counterpart to the 'floating' polyphony, its stillness gently disturbed at the cadences, of *Emendemus*. We might mention in passing that the unusual key of B flat, found in *Tribue Domine* and *Gloria Patri* in the 1575 *Cantiones Sacrae,* occurs also in a splendid Pavan and Galliard which again did not find a place in the scheme of *My Ladye Nevells Booke*.[21]

Byrd's colossal achievement in the field of keyboard music, then, is largely the result of his own imagination in applying the lessons learnt from his experiments in ensemble and vocal polyphony to this medium. His subsequent influence was enormous, and none of his younger contemporaries of real repute was unaffected by it; not even John Bull, whose main artistic ancestry can be traced back in a line including Blitheman, Tallis, Preston and Redford. This is the second main stream to flow into the broad river of the English keyboard style, the 'native' element referred to above (p. 115), and it must now be examined in greater detail.

Redford had largely cultivated a simple melodic style, but such mechanical features as were inherent in it were seized upon by Preston and became a salient constituent of his writing. This, added to his formidable virtuosity, resulted in passages of the kind quoted in Ex. 21. It is this aspect of Preston's work which predominates in the work of Blitheman. One may instance a passage from Blitheman's second *Gloria tibi Trinitas*:[22]

[21] *Ibid.*, No. 23. There is also a Pavan and Galliard in B flat by Thomas Warrock in *FWVB*, Nos. 97–8.

[22] *MB*, i, No. 92.

Also present are the cross-rhythms:

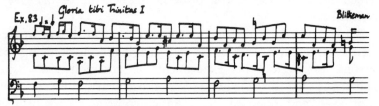

and rhythmic differentiation amongst the voices, of the earlier style:

However, as the sixth *Gloria tibi Trinitas* shows, he was also capable of smooth counterpoint over a *cantus firmus*.

None of these mannerisms were lost on John Bull, whom Blitheman's epitaph shows to have been his scholar.[23] His second hexachord setting, from which several quotations have been given above (Chapter V, Exx. 53–8) exhibits them in profusion. He was also capable of the quieter style, if the ascriptions of several hymn settings copied down by Messaus are correct.

[23] See *MB*, xiv, p. xxi.

There is some doubt about this as Messaus, compiling his manuscript (London, Brit. Mus., Add. 23623) shortly after Bull's death, from his papers, tended to ascribe everything he found to him indiscriminately. A *Veni Redemptor gentium* so ascribed is attributed to Tallis in the Mulliner Book,[24] and there can be no doubt that Mulliner was right. In that case, Messaus may have been wrong in other instances also. Four verses of the nine-verse hymn *Vexilla regis prodeunt*[25] look suspiciously like an *alternatim* setting intended for a liturgy which was obsolete before Bull was born.[26]

Bull undoubtedly learnt from Tallis also, and much of the figuration of the twelve *In nomines* can be traced back to the two great settings of *Felix namque* by the older master. It seems clear that he venerated Tallis and Blitheman for the link which they afforded him with the generation represented by Preston, and for their connection with the old religion and its musical requirements. Two hymn-verses from the 'faburden' section of Add. 29996 survive in his hand, or at least in a volume which belonged to him (Paris, Bib. Nat., fonds du Cons., Rés. 1185).

This manuscript, now in Paris, is of the greatest interest and importance. The main reason for believing the principal part of it to be in the hand of Bull himself is that it preserves a great deal of his music anonymously and in excellent texts.[27] The music is arranged according to key and has all the appearance of a fair copy. It is quite likely that many of the pieces which are unique to this source are also by Bull, and the more probable ones have been incorporated into the *Musica Britannica* edition. My impression is that Bull, preparing for his flight to Brussels (which took place about September 1613), made a copy of the music he wished to preserve and left it in the hands of his friend Ben Cosyn. Interspersed amongst the original contents are additions in the hand of Cosyn (known from his famous Virginal Book in the Royal Music Library), who also provided an index dated 1652.

[24] *MB*, i, 102; ascribed to Bull in London, Brit. Mus., Add. 23623, f. 167.
[25] *MB*, xiv, No. 44.
[26] Caldwell, *Musica Disciplina* (1965) 150.
[27] *MB*, xix, p. xviii.

This manuscript affords a clear picture of the stature of John Bull before he became virtually a Netherlands composer. It is not a style devoid of continental traits, however, for Bull had travelled extensively in 1601, when he may have become acquainted with Jacques Champion, 'sieur de La Chappelle' (the father of Jacques Champion de Chambonnières), Sweelinck and others. The fruits of this journey are to be seen in such pieces as the Galliard composed for Charlotte de la Haye (i.e. 'of the Hague'),[28] the 'French' Alman and Coranto,[29] and the 'Germans Alman' perhaps intended for a courtier to Henri IV known as M. de St Germain.[30] But the English manner predominates even in these works, and it is explicit in the two 'Piper's Galliards', which are settings of a well-known song by Dowland.[31] For the rest, the only possible model for his secular style was that of William Byrd, and a work like the 'Walsingham' variations is clearly written in straightforward emulation of the older master. To this style he adds his own contribution of spiky brilliance, with a consequent loss of emotional depth, and a genuine melodic gift of a somewhat popular but very charming nature.

Of Orlando Gibbons, Bull's near contemporary, little can be added to the account already given (pp. 63–6, 103–4). The danger lies perhaps in assuming him to be too nearly the antithesis in temperament of his great rival. Like Bull, he possessed a formidable keyboard technique, and on occasion this can be felt to be an intrusion on the deeper musical meaning of a passage. Some of the sets of variations are disfigured in this way. A particular prelude of his,[32] a fine exercise in finger-technique, enjoyed greater popularity, right into the eighteenth century, than any other example of the genre. Like Bull, he slowed down the tempo of the pavan and galliard: particularly in the case of the latter. But unlike Bull there is not a trace of the old *cantus firmus* mentality in his artistic make-up. In tonality, too, he is perhaps more modern: there is a definite fondness for the major

28 *MB*, xix, No. 73: see p. 228.

29 *Ibid.*, Nos. 95, 105.

30 *Ibid.*, No. 94: see p. 232.

31 *Ibid.*, Nos. 89a, 89b. The song is 'If my complaints could passions move', (*MB*, vi, No. 4), also found in eight sources for lute solo.

32 *MB*, xx, No. 2.

mode, and his treatment of the minor is usually direct and forceful. Much more than Bull, he is the direct recipient of the inheritance of Byrd.

The final summing-up of all that was characteristic of the Elizabethan and Jacobean virginalists was to be left to Thomas Tomkins, whose work is discussed in the following chapter. In the meantime, something must be said of the work of lesser composers, who for the sake of clarity have been omitted from the preceding account. They include men of the stature of Farnaby, Philips and Cosyn, who in a less brilliant company would have shone with greater splendour. Except for Cosyn, these and many others can conveniently be studied through the Fitzwilliam Virginal Book.

This monumental collection, with 297 pieces, is certainly the largest of the contemporary anthologies. It was edited in 1899 by Fuller-Maitland and Barclay Squire, whose theory that the manuscript was compiled by the younger Francis Tregian during his imprisonment in the Fleet for recusancy from 1609 until his death in 1619 has since been confirmed by comparison with other manuscript collections which are undoubtedly in his hand. Tregian was educated at the college of Douai and would have had ample opportunity during his residence abroad to collect the works by Peter Philips and Sweelinck which are included in the manuscript. Otherwise the main composers represented are Byrd and Bull, both Roman Catholics, and Farnaby, who was a disciple of Bull. Works like William Tisdall's 'Pavan Chromatica: Mrs. Katherin Tregians Paven', betray a still closer association with the compiler. Tregian's orginal copies were of gseatly varying value, and he was not a critical editor of the music. During the course of copying he took to adding redundant final chords of a breve in value to pieces which did not end with a note of this denomination, by false analogy with other pieces which did. It is a great mistake to play these. (It might be added here that the editors frequently mistook Tregian's thickly dotted double-bar as a sign of repetition, and that most of the repeats in the edition can safely be ignored; they should be observed only when this is structurally necessary.[33])

[33] See above, Chapter V, footnote 34.

The range covered by the book is astonishing: the earliest dated piece is the first *Felix namque* by Tallis (No. 109: 1562) and the latest an 'Ut re mi fa sol la' by Sweelinck (No. 118: 1612); Tregian was not confined to music collected during his liberty. It includes some of the greatest masterpieces of Byrd and Bull, and it illuminates many an obscure corner of English popular and ephemeral music. Some of the composers represented are known only from this manuscript, and not all can be dismissed as easily as 'M.S.', an abbreviation for 'Mal Sims' (see No. 281), the popular tune of which the so-called 'Pavana' (No. 16) is a setting. As to the identity of 'El. Kiderminster', the reputed composer of a wretched 'Praeludium' (No. 23), we are not likely to be curious; but what of Thomas Oldfield, Galeazzo and Jehan Ostermayre? The foreigners, apart from Sweelinck, also included Giovanni Pichi, an important Italian composer of dance music for keyboard who is not adequately represented by the rather eccentric 'Toccata' (No. 95), even discounting the obvious corruption of the text. The older English composers represented include Strogers and Blitheman as well as Tallis. Ferdinando Richardson was the *nom de guerre* of Sir Ferdinando Heybourne, an amateur composer who died in 1618. William Tisdall may possibly be the Tisdale who probably compiled another collection which is also now housed in the Fitzwilliam Museum, Cambridge,[34] and which once belonged to Bull. It contains twenty-one pieces. Tregian himself is mentioned as arranger or dedicatee in several cases. Of many others, including Morley, John Mundy, Martin Peerson, Edmund Hooper and lesser-known figures, nothing more need be said: but Farnaby and Philips deserve some attention.

The Fitzwilliam Virginal Book contains virtually the whole of Giles Farnaby's output, as well as all that is known of that of his son Richard.[35] He was at best an outstandingly gifted amateur, destined at first for the joiner's trade. He may have been involved in the making of keyboard instruments, like his relative Nicholas.[36] He obtained the Oxford B.Mus. in 1592, and contributed

[34] MS 52. d. 25. Printed *SBK*, xxiv.
[35] Printed complete in *MB*, xxiv.
[36] *Ibid.*, pp. xix, xxii, where an account of his life is given.

to Este's Psalter, published in that year. His *Canzonets to fowre voyces* were published in 1598 and dedicated to Heybourne. (It has been noticed that some passages in Heybourne's keyboard music are similar to that of Farnaby in style.) He died (probably) as late as 1640, but virtually all his surviving keyboard music must have been composed by the time of Tregian's death in 1619.

The predominant impression created by this music is of considerable technical difficulty of a somewhat unrewarding nature, combined with a rather eccentric musical personality, which is not, however, without its own quaint charm. His Ground (No. 2)[37] is of the purely melodic type, a row of eleven semibreves treated in rigid contrapuntal fashion. Of his eleven fantasias, one (No. 11) is a transcription of one of his canzonets, 'Ay me, poor heart', and others may be based on vocal models so far unidentified (see above, p. 63). He was an inveterate arranger, and transcriptions survive of dances by Robert and John Johnson, Dowland (the 'Lachrymae Pavan'), Byrd (or Morley), Bull, Rosseter and Coperario.[38] Nearly always the feeling of the original is obscured by excessive ornamentation. More attractive are the lighter dances and the sets of variations. These latter are often similar to the dances in construction, each strain being followed immediately by its varied reprise before the whole scheme is subjected to variation. In the case of 'The New Sa-hoo' (No. 45) Farnaby is content with the reprise of each strain and the result is indistinguishable from an alman or 'toy'. This tune was known on the continent as *Est-ce Mars* and was treated at great length by both Sweelinck and Scheidt.[39] It illustrates Farnaby's preoccupation with the newest fashions, for although he used some material in common with Bull he did not share his and Gibbons' fascination with the older melodies favoured by Byrd. 'Quodling's Delight', however, is based on the *passamezzo antico*, and Farnaby's version (No. 42) is therefore none other than a set of variations on that well-tried formula.[40] Above all influences, that of Bull predominates; but although he often

---

[37] The numbering is that of *MB*, xxiv.   [38] For details see *ibid.*
[39] Sweelinck, *Werken voor Orgel en Clavecimbel*, No. 58. Scheidt: *DDT*, i. 65.
[40] *Cf.* Richard Farnaby's 'Fain Would I Wed' (*MB*, xxiv, No. 57), based on an Ayre by Campian.

wrote at considerable length, Bull's sense of large-scale design completely escaped him.

Peter Philips was a much more commanding figure, whose interest and importance for the history of English music is only gradually coming to be appreciated. Born probably in London in 1560 or 1561, he left England permanently in 1582 for the sake of religion. He soon found himself at Rome, and from 1585 to 1590 was in the service of Lord Thomas Paget. From 1590 to 1597 he taught at Antwerp, and from then until his death in 1628 he was the first organist at the archducal chapel in Brussels. Here he would have met John Bull in 1613 on the latter's first arrival from England. The bulk of his output consists of Latin motets and Italian madrigals, but his two dozen or more surviving keyboard works form a not insignificant contribution to his *œuvre*. Nineteen of them were included in the Fitzwilliam Book (Nos. 70–88), and while a critical edition based on all the sources is most urgently needed, Tregian's selection will do very well as a basis for discussion. Some of the pieces are dated, and the dates range from 1580 to 1605. The work of 1580 is a 'Pavana' (No. 85) and is annotated 'The first one Philips made'. It is an amazingly confident work for a twenty-year-old, in the Byrd tradition but with an individual touch in the semibreve theme of the third section. Philips certainly took this composition abroad with him, for Sweelinck, whom he met in 1593, elaborated it in his own way.[41] It has already been mentioned that the Fantasia dated 1582 (No. 88) was probably composed before he left England; the other (No. 84) looks like a later piece and shows the influence of Sweelinck, though the subject on which it is based was also used by Byrd.[42] The splendid 'Pavana Pagget' with its 'Galiarda' (Nos. 74, 75) evidently relates to his period of service with Thomas Paget, 1585–1590; possibly it was composed as a memorial on his death in 1590, but the connection with Paget's younger brother Charles suggested in the Düben Tablature of 1641 seems unfounded.[43] The *passamezzo* Pavan and Galliard

[41] Sweelinck, *Werken voor Orgel en Clavecimbel*, No. 69.

[42] *FWVB*, No. 261. Byrd does not use the Sweelinckian device of augmentation in this work, however.

[43] The original version for five-part ensemble is printed in *MB*, ix, Nos. 71–2.

(Nos. 76, 77) are dated 1592;[44] the magnificent 'Pavana dolorosa' (No. 80) with its Galliard (No. 81) was composed during a short period of imprisonment on a trumped-up charge in 1593. It shows great familiarity with the 'short-octave' system, as the following passage shows:

Ex. 85   Peter Philips

Here and in the Galliard, Philips makes full use of the sonorities which the system allows, the low *C*, *D* and *E* being obtained by depressing keys in the position of *E*, *F#*, and *G#* respectively. Elsewhere the presence of the *G#* itself in the music shows that Philips was writing for an instrument with split *F#* and *G#* keys. In this system the raised back half of these two keys gives their apparent pitch; their front halves give *D* and *E* respectively.[45] The music of English composers who did not travel abroad never shows any awareness of the short-octave system, much less of split keys. It seems likely that the short octave was first adopted by English makers with the extension of the compass down to A_1 (as required by Gibbons), the *C#* and *D#* keys sounding A_1 and B_1 respectively.[46]

The works of Philips dated 1595 and later are all intabulations of madrigals and chansons by Caccini and Lasso. The most ambitious similar settings, the 'Tirsi', with 'Freno' and 'Così moriro' by Luca Marenzio (Nos. 70-2)[47] are undated but are probably from the same period, unless indeed the set dates from his stay in Italy. These arrangements do not have the same

[44] The date, though attached to the Pavan only, is surely intended to apply to both movements. Note the *Saltarella* section at the end of the Galliard. The six-part 'Passamezzo Pavan' in *MB*, ix, No. 90, is a different work.

[45] Curtis, *Sweelinck's Keyboard Music*, pp. 28–31.

[46] This also applies to the downward extension of organ compass to G_1 or F_1 at the Restoration. See Chapter IX, p. 157.

[47] *Tirsi morir volea*, ed. A. Einstein, Luca Marenzio, *Sämtliche Werke*, i, in *Publikationen älterer Musik*, Jahrg. IVi (1929), No. 12.

interest as the original compositions, but they are vastly superior to Farnaby's efforts in this sphere, the ornamentation being consistent and even expressive.

It is not so easy to obtain a representative picture of Ben Cosyn. Even the details of his life are obscure. Born around 1570, he became organist of Dulwich College in 1623, and of Charterhouse in 1626. The index of his Virginal Book,[48] a major source of the keyboard works of Gibbons, Bull and himself, is dated 1620; the index of the 'Bull' manuscript (Paris, Bib. du Cons., Rés. 1185) which came into his possession (see above, p. 127) is dated 1652. An elaborate three-fold setting of the *Miserere* melody[49] betrays the strong influence of Bull, and other works are so obviously based on existing models of his that they have been mistakenly attributed to him: 'The King's Hunt', 'Lord Lumley's Pavan and Galliard', 'My Self' and so on. He also supplied an alternative Galliard to Bull's 'Fantastic Pavan', attributed by Tregian to Bull himself (*The Fitzwilliam Virginal Book*, No. 48).[50] Several untitled pieces bearing the initials 'B.C.' in Oxford, Christ Church, MS 1113 may illustrate the style of his organ voluntaries.[51] They seem to exhibit a later style, comparable with that of Lugge, and, in his organ music, Tomkins.

This book is not the place for a discussion of the lute and its music;[52] but its repertory and that of related instruments to a certain extent parallels that of the keyboard instruments and can occasionally throw light on the latter. One may hazard the guess that it was the emergence of the lute, the most intimate and easiest to learn of all the truly artistic instruments, which threw the clavichord into comparative obscurity. The tablature indicating finger-placement made a knowledge of the staff and its notation unnecessary, and the beginner's chief difficulty was rhythmic.

[48] London, Brit. Mus., R.M. 24.l.4.

[49] *Ibid.*, f. 35v.

[50] See *MB*, xix, p. 221, for incipits and sources of these works.

[51] *EOM*, xiv.

[52] The definitive work on this subject is the unpublished thesis (Cambridge) by D. Lumsden, *The sources of English Lute Music*. His *Anthology of English Lute Music* is a useful collection. On the Ballet and Dallis lute books in Dublin see Ward, *Lute Society Journal* (1967–8).

The earliest known English music for lute is contained in the MS London, Brit. Mus., Royal Appendix 58.[53] If John Ward's theory that the 'dump' is a memorial for a dead person is correct, then the first piece, 'The Duke of Somersettes Dompe' will not have been composed before 1552. (The lute music in this manuscript is in any case obviously a later addition to the main part, which dates from *ca.* 1530, being fitted into odd spaces between ff. 51v and 55r, with a diagram of lute tuning and notation on f. 56r.) This dump and various others, also mostly for lute, bear out the impression created by 'My lady careys dompe' (see above, p. 48) that a distinguishing feature of the form is its use of standard harmonic grounds, ranging from a simple alternation of tonic and dominant to the *passamezzo antico, romanesca,* and *bergamasca.*[54] The fourth lute piece of this manuscript, 'Heven & earth', is obviously related to Wyatt's poem of that title, though it is unlikely that the music was in existence when Wyatt wrote his lyric.[55] Its rhythm is defective, but a more correct rhythm is found in an otherwise inept version in the Fitzwilliam Virginal Book (No. 105) ascribed to 'Fre'. It also assumed the form of a pavan, the 'Prince Edward's Pavan' and its keyboard derivative (Chapter VI, p. 110).

Another early musical setting for lute of a Wyatt poem, 'Blame not my lute', is based on the *folia* (the first chord is probably missing).[56] The fifth piece of Roy. App. 58 uses a modified form of the *passamezzo antico* (fifth note *g* instead of *b* flat) found also in the Dublin Virginal Manuscript (Nos. 1 and 2). It is evidently an accompaniment to a missing melody. Something of the same sort of thing is found in a version of 'Grien slivis' for two lutes in the Folger Shakespeare Library, MS 1610.1, f. 5.[57] The second lute plays the harmonies, in this case using the *romanesca* bass,

---

[53] Printed, with facsimiles, in Ward, *JAMS* (1960) 117.

[54] Ward, *JAMS* (1951) 111.

[55] *Collected Poems of Sir Thomas Wyatt*, ed. K. Muir, No. 73. See J. Stevens, *Music and Poetry at the Early Tudor Court*, pp. 135–6. See Chapter VI, footnote 45.

[56] Washington, D.C., Folger Shakespeare Lib., MS 448. 16, f. 4v. Printed in J. Stevens, *op. cit.*, p. 137. Further on this piece, see Ward, *JAMS* (1957) 179, note 101.

[57] Printed in Ward, *op. cit.*, p. 157.

while the first lute plays a duple-time version of the tune which evidently preceded the more familiar triple-time version as the latter does not quite fit the bass.[58] (It has already been mentioned that 'Quodling's Delight' is based on the *passamezzo antico*, and it might be added that 'John come kiss me now' is based on a version of the *passamezzo moderno* and that 'What if a day' is related to the *folia*.[59]) John Ward has printed Raphe Bowles' versions of the *passamezzo antico* and *romanesca* harmonies,[60] and the relevance of the cittern and gittern music in the Mulliner Book to this subject has already been noted.

A dance for solo lute was no more intended for actual dancing than a dance for keyboard. Dowland's 'Piper's Galliard', for example, exists in eight sources for solo lute; it was printed in *The First Booke of Songs* (1597) to the words 'If my complaints could passions move'; it was included in *Lachrimae* (1604); and it exists as a keyboard arrangement with varied reprises and one further complete variation by John Bull.[61] A similar situation exists with regard to 'The Earl of Essex's Galliard' ('Can she excuse my wrongs') and the 'Frog Galliard' ('Now, oh now I needs must part'), though the latter was not included in *Lachrimae*.[62] It is difficult to know which of these versions was the original in many cases, except that the keyboard versions, indicating by their titles whether they are derived from an instrumental or vocal form, are always arrangements.

It remains to consider the international aspects of English keyboard music at the turn of the century. This involves two factors: the borrowing of actual musical material (popular songs and dances), and stylistic influences. In the latter case, two kinds of evidence are available to explain the musical facts: the known

[58] In the Ballet lute-book (Dublin, Trinity Coll. Lib., MS D. 1. 21), the tune is fitted to the *passamezzo antico*, which the composer is forced to modify for the refrain. Ward, *op. cit.*

[59] Greer, *ML* (1962) 311. For the ramifications of the *passamezzo moderno* see Ward, *op. cit.*

[60] *DVM*, pp. 40–1, 42–3, after London, Brit. Mus., Stowe MS 389.

[61] *MB*, xix, Nos. 89a, 89b.

[62] The four-part vocal versions, with or without lute, are printed in *MB*, vi, Nos. 5, 6. Keyboard arrangements of the former are in *FWVB*, No. [188] and *SBK*, xxiv, No. 7 (both anonymous), and of the latter in *PBVB*, No. 15 (by Robert Hall).

movements of the composers concerned and the existence of manuscripts of English music copied abroad and of foreign music copied in England. Such evidence does not illuminate the international currency of popular tunes to anything like the same extent, for as Ward observes, these 'can be transported by a whistling sailor'. Even here, however, documentary evidence can be of some value. We begin by considering popular music.

Though the direct influence of contemporary continental style upon English keyboard music virtually ceased with the death of Henry, the interchange of popular music did not. This interchange worked in both directions. The 'Heaven and Earth/ Prince Edward's Pavan' material was published in Paris by Gervaise in 1555,[63] while a tune associated with the dance known as 'Essex Measures' was included by Jean Estrée in his *Tiers Livre de Danseries* (Paris, 1559) with the title 'Tintelore d'Angleterre'.[64] The Dublin Virginal Manuscript on the other hand also contains numerous settings of tunes which appear to be continental in origin: the branles *Hoboken* and *L'homme armé* and the almans *Guerre guerre gay, du Prince, Le pied de cheval* and *Bruynsmedelyn*. Most of these are first encountered in Sebastian Vreedman's *Carminum quae Cythara pulsantur Liber Secundus* (Louvain, 1569).[65] At the end of the century, Susanne van Soldt's manuscript of keyboard music (1599)[66] provides valuable further evidence of the passage of material from England to the Netherlands, including some which actually originated on the continent.[67]

We have already noted early examples of Italian standard basses in England, and to these should be added the *bergamasca*. It is utilised in two dumps for lute (one by John Johnson),[68] and

---

[63] Ward, *op. cit.*, p. 179.

[64] *DVM*, No. 11 and notes on pp. 46–7. Earlier, 'The kyngs pavin' from London, Brit. Mus., Roy. App. 58 had been transmitted (or re-transmitted), to the continent, finally to appear in Louvain in 1571. See above, Chapter IV, p. 46.

[65] *Ibid.*, Nos. 12, 20, 13, 15, 18, 19 and notes thereto.

[66] London, Brit. Mus., Add. MS 29485, ed. *MMN*, iii.

[67] E.g. 'Pavane d'Anvers', f. 17, originating in an Italian song, 'Gentil madonna del mio cor patrona', and known in England as 'Turkeylony'. *DVM*, pp. 55–6 and No. 25.

[68] Ward, *JAMS* (1957) 151.

consists of a simple I IV V I pattern in the major key. It occurs again in 'Dr Bull's Ground (I)' and in his *Het nieu Bergomasco*.[69] As to popular tunes, *Est-ce Mars* was not alone in finding its way to England. A particular favourite was the one sometimes known as *More palatino*. It was treated by Frescobaldi (*Aria detto Balletto* from the second book of toccatas), Sweelinck (*More palatino*), Bull (*Revenant*) and Gibbons ('The Italian Ground').[70] In the opposite direction, 'Fortune my foe', set by Byrd and later by Tomkins, exists in versions by Sweelinck and Scheidt.[71] It is worth noting the similarity of this tune to 'What if a day', which also turns up in Dutch song-books and was set for keyboard in England.[72]

Matters of style are less tangible than actual tunes and it is not always easy to assess priority. The evidence suggests that it was the English who influenced the Netherlanders (especially Sweelinck, and through him the Germans including Scheidt), and that it was only later in the seventeenth century that English keyboard music again came under continental sway, and then mainly through French and Italian sources (see below, pp. 151–2). The isolated appearance of music by Sweelinck in the Fitzwilliam Virginal Book would not have had any appreciable effect on English style, and reflects only Tregian's continued access to continental music even after his imprisonment. It is true that Bull was influenced by Sweelinck in his later years, and that Philips took his cuc for the elaboration of chansons and madrigals from the techniques of Merulo, Andrea Gabrieli and Frescobaldi; but in neither case did these composers any longer represent the main English stream. On the other hand their own influence on the continental style is indubitable and their widespread representation in continental manuscripts provides the documentary evidence to support the hypothesis.[73] It is not too much to say

[69] *MB*, xix, Nos. 102a, 124.

[70] Frescobaldi, *Orgel- und Klavierwerke*, iv, p. 82; Sweelinck, *Werken voor Orgel en Clavecimbel*, No. 61; Bull, *MB*, xix, No. 100; Gibbons, *MB*, xx, No. 27.

[71] Byrd, *MB*, xxvii, No. 6; Tomkins, *MB*, v, No. 61; Sweelinck, *op. cit.*, No. 64; Scheidt, *DDT*, i. 126.

[72] Greer, *op. cit.* To his list of settings of the tune must be added the set of variations by Thomas Tomkins (*MB*, v, No. 64).

[73] Peter Philips in Liège, Univ. Lib., MS 153 (*olim* 888) and Berlin, Staats-

that English techniques of variation represent a major strand in the stylistic web of baroque keyboard music until the time of Bach.

Sweelinck's keyboard style was fundamentally Italian by derivation. The *ricercare* provided the foundation of his fugal mastery in the fantasias, and the *toccata* was another major constituent. The occasional chromaticism and the use of echo-effects are also Italian in origin. To this was added a specifically English quality in his figuration and passage-work. His meeting with Philips in 1593 might have been the starting point for this development, and he actually wrote a 'Pavana Philippi' (see above, p. 132). John Bull may have met him in 1601. His use of 'Lachrymae' provides another point of contact, and his setting of the *passamezzo moderno* may have been inspired by English custom, though it lacks the 'English' second section.[74]

In the field of secular variation his tone is often English without the benefit of an English tune. *Mein junges Leben hat ein End*[75] is a good example, with its imaginative polyphony, sparing but telling ornamentation of the melody and elaborate passage-work. It is true that a few mannerisms, such as the repeated notes and the left-hand arpeggios, could have been picked up by Bull from Sweelinck in 1601, but the general impression is of English methods and most of the technical devices derive ultimately from Preston, Tallis and Blitheman. The connection can be demonstrated only by extensive quotation:

Ex. 86

bib., MS 40316 (see Chapter V, footnote 28); and Bull in Berlin, Staatsbib., MS Lynar A1, Vienna, Nat. Bib., MS 17771 and Uppsala, Univ. Lib., MS 408.

[74] Sweelinck, *Werken voor Orgel en Clavecimbel*, No. 67.   [75] *Ibid.*, No. 60.

English methods were put to even more significant use in the sacred variations. The traditional techniques of *cantus firmus* were easily adopted to the solemn melodies of the Lutheran chorale and Calvinist psalm. It was Sweelinck who established the tradition of setting these melodies (he also set plainsong hymns), though only the chorale was destined to survive.

Apart from Sweelinck, Philips probably influenced the Catholic organ school led by Pieter Cornet, while a few works of Jacques Champion survive to demonstrate the very strong influence of Bull.[76] But in neither case was a tradition established.

[76] See Dart, *ML* (1959) 279. It has recently been suggested that the large collection of Catholic organ music in Oxford, Christ Church, MS 89 was formed by Richard Deering, and that its anonymous pieces (the bulk of the collection) are by Deering himself. See Dart, *ML* (1971) 27. Deering was organist at the convent of English nuns in Brussels, *ca.* 1617-*ca.* 1625, and at Queen Henrietta Maria's chapel at Somerset House from *ca.* 1625 until his death in 1630.

VIII

The Transition, 1625–1660

The era of Charles Í and the Commonwealth, from our point of view, was one of stylistic conflict. To begin with, the conservatives included the greatest composer then living, Thomas Tomkins, and a number of other lesser figures such as Lugge, Nicholas Carleton and Arthur Phillips. Widening the field to include those who wrote no solo keyboard music, the names of Childe and John Jenkins immediately spring to mind. Amongst the progressives, the most important name is that of William Lawes, the epitome of Caroline culture, who also probably wrote no original keyboard music; but Matthew Locke and those who contributed to his *Melothesia* (published in 1673) must have been active during the Commonwealth if not before. Their transformation of the older dance-forms and their evolving of the keyboard suite are achievements marking the culmination of a process which can be traced back to commonplace books of the 1630s.

The career of Thomas Tomkins curiously resembles that of J. S. Bach. He was by no means a conservative at the outset of his career, and his *Songs of 3, 4, 5 and 6 Parts* (published in 1622) bear the marks of full maturity. Tomkins was nearly fifty at the time, but from the point of view of his life-span as a whole they stand in much the same relation to the rest of his output as do (say) the Brandenburg Concertos in the case of Bach. From that point on the development of each composer took the form of a refining of his personal idiom while the rest of the musical world moved on. There is a kind of loneliness about the position of such men in later life, all the more so for Tomkins owing to the death of his friends and the changes in the political and religious life of the country. For everything one reads about Tomkins reinforces the impression of one of the kindliest of great composers. The separate dedications of each item of the 1622 *Songs* to his musician friends are a revealing feature. He was a royalist and a traditional churchman, and the loss of his post at Worcester Cathedral with the surrender of the city in July 1646 was more than a financial matter to him. There is something curiously moving about the penning of 'A Sad Pavan: for these distracted times' two weeks after the execution of Charles I, and in the composition (in increasingly shaky handwriting) of *In nomines* and *Misereres* in the 1650s.

We are fortunate in possessing the manuscript (Paris, Bib. Nat., fonds du Cons., Rés. 1122) in which Tomkins, having made copies of several works by Byrd and Bull, wrote down by far the greater part of his keyboard music which has come down to us. His entire keyboard works have been edited in exemplary fashion by Stephen Tuttle,[1] together with a full description of the holograph. A list of 'Lessons of worthe' includes a great many by Byrd and Bull (several no longer extant), revealing the main influences on Tomkins' keyboard style. Indeed it may be described as a perfect amalgam of the two traditions which those composers represent. A secondary influence was that of Tallis, whose 'offertori' (almost certainly his second *Felix namque*) heads the list. Nor must it be forgotten that he had a performer's acquaintance with the old liturgical repertory of London, Brit. Mus., Add. 29996, as his annotations and emendations prove; though the latter also demonstrate his ignorance of the true nature of faburden.

Tomkins wrote in all the main forms: fugal (under the titles of 'voluntary', 'fancy' and 'verse') *cantus firmus* (including the hexachord), ground and secular variation, and the dance. There are also preludes and a few genre pieces. They cover a long period of his life. The five pieces in the Fitzwilliam Virginal Book must have been composed by 1615 at the latest, and they bear the marks of early, though not immature, work. 'Robin Hood', included anonymously in Will Forster's book and assigned to the composer on the grounds of the inclusion of this title in 'Lessons of worthe', was composed by 1624, and most of the pieces included in manuscripts other than the holograph must have been written

[1] *MB*, v.

during the course of the next two decades. The great 'Offertory' is dated 1637, and the Pavan 'Lord Canterbury', incomplete in the manuscript (Add. 29996) owing to the loss of a page, is dated 1647. About half the works in the holograph are dated, and the dates range from 1646 to 1654, two years before his death. If in some respects a comparison with Bach is suggested, the rejuvenation apparent in the work of his last decade is strongly reminiscent of Verdi.

One feature of the virginalists is absent from Tomkins: the harmonic ground. There is no *passamezzo* or quadran pavan, though he praised the Quadran Pavan and Galliard of Byrd 'for matter' and that of Bull 'for the hand'. However, the varied repeats in some of the dances show his ability in this direction and his sets of variations are harmonically rather than contrapuntally conceived. His early work is remarkable for the virtuosity it demands of the player. It is revealing to compare the extremes of 'Barafostus' Dream', from the Fitzwilliam Virginal Book,[2] with the altogether more moderate demands of 'Fortune my Foe', completed on 4 July 1654.[3] A favourite device of the earlier work is the leap of two octaves in the left hand:

Towards the end, the compression of a cadence in 3/4 to 4/4 time initiates a passage of *sesquitertia* (4:3) which is not very successfully handled: indeed the composer's intentions are not at all easy to follow:

[2] *Ibid.*, No. 62.   [3] *Ibid.*, No. 61.

The 'Offertory' of 1637[4] is also enormously difficult, and the lengthy 'Ut re mi fa sol la' and 'Ut mi re' from the same manuscript[5] are probably of similar date. They rather interfere with the picture of a composer gradually arriving at serenity in old age (he was 64 in 1637), but one can only suppose that he retained his vigour longer than most. The 'Offertory', based on a phrase resembling the intonation of *Felix namque*, is a sort of fantasia and ground combined,[6] and the copyist numbered the 'ways' rather erratically, up to 64. *Fermata* occur at various points, possibly to indicate suitable stopping-places, or else indicating the stages in which Tomkins composed the work. *Sesquialtera* and 9:4 make their inevitable appearance, as they do indeed in 'Ut re mi fa sol la'. The obvious model for this piece is Bull's second setting (see above, p. 78), and while he does not succeed in being more difficult than Bull he is a good deal more musical. The work survives in two different forms, with a different number and selection of variations in each; but as the Paris version decrees 'Use as many or as few as you will of these many wayes upon this playnesong' the precise structure cannot be a matter of great concern.

The works of the final decade include fancies, plainsong settings, pavans and galliards, and variations. The fancies are exquisitely moulded, their free-voiced counterpoint being skilfully handled. If there is a fault, it is a tendency to overdo a single phrase, as in the work dated 8 July 1647,[7] which might have deserved the title of another, undated piece: 'A substantiall verse; mayntayning the poynte.'[8] Most of the pieces of this kind may be allotted a late date. It is perhaps surprising, in view of the potentialities of the Worcester organ, not to find a double voluntary amongst even the earlier works. One curiosity is the famous 'Fancy for two to play',[9] a keyboard duet evidently

4 *MB*, v, No. 21.

5 *Ibid.*, Nos. 35, 38. The MS (Oxford, Bod. Lib., Mus. Sch. c. 93) is a miscellaneous collection of leaves copied by Tomkins and his circle. No. 35 is also in Paris, Rés. 1122.

6 *Cf.* the Fantasia by Peter Philips mentioned in Chapter VII, footnote 42.

7 *MB*, v, No. 23.

8 *Ibid.*, No. 31.

9 *Ibid.*, No. 32. Also in *Two Elizabethan Keyboard Duets*, No. 2.

written in imitation of the piece immediately preceding it in the manuscript,[10] which is an *In nomine* duet by Carleton. Carleton died in 1630, but it is difficult to assign a date to Tomkins' piece, which may be much later. It has the great merit of belonging entirely to the medium for which it was composed, being full of delightful echo effects which could not be achieved by a single player.

The plainsong settings are a remarkable achievement. A *Clarifica me pater*, six *In nomines* and four of the eight *Misereres* were composed between 1647 and 1652. The four undated *Misereres* almost certainly belong to the same period: at any rate they are indistinguishable in style. The influence of Bull is clear in a three-fold setting of *Miserere* dated 3–4 February 1652; the use of repeated semiquavers and the mechanical nature of some of the counterpoint indicate the source, and yet there is a greater freedom here than Bull would have permitted himself. The *In nomines*, the first and fifth of which exist in two versions, are further removed from the model. The second[11] shows great mastery in its introduction of the *cantus firmus*, which is so completely anticipated that its entry passes virtually unnoticed:

The final cadence, with its fine disregard of metre, also deserves quotation:

---

[10] London, Brit. Mus., Add. 29996. *Two Elizabethan Keyboard Duets*, No. 1.
[11] *MB*, v, No. 7.

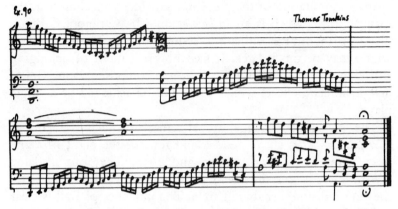

All but one of the surviving pavan-galliard pairs, and all but
one of the single pavans, are dated and were composed during
the final decade. The Pavan and Galliard 'of 3 parts' (Nos.
49–50) can also be assigned to a late date on the grounds of style
and inclusion in Rés. 1122. On the other hand the single rather
chromatic pavan from the Fitzwilliam Virginal Book (No. 123),
which is a version of a piece originally for strings, must be an
early work.[12] (Curiously enough, all the separate galliards are
early: 'The Hunting Galliard' is in the Fitzwilliam Virginal
Book; 'The Lady Folliott's Galliard', in two sections only, bears
the marks of an early style and descends to low A_1, frequent in
the early works but absent from the later; while the third separate
galliard is found in Ben Cosyn's book, dated 1620, with an
ascription to Gibbons which is almost certainly correct.[13])

All in all, the finest of the late pavans and galliards is probably
the 'Earl Stafford' pair in its long version. A short version,
without varied repeats, is dated 29 September 1647. The long
version (1–2 October 1647) does more than merely provide
varied repetitions, for the plain final breves which conclude each
strain in the short version are here ornamented even on their
first appearance. There is a nobility in this work about the
harmony and modulations which raise it above the common

12 *MB*, v, No. 56. The original version for five-part ensemble is printed
in *MB*, ix, No. 73.
13 *Ibid.*, Nos. 58–60. The last ascribed to Gibbons also in Add. 36661, but
to Tomkins in New York, Pub. Lib., Drexel 5612.

level. The latter may be illustrated by the unexpected close of the second strain of the Pavan:

The Galliard demonstrates cross-rhythms, not only on the 3/2:6/4 level, but also on the 3/4:6/8, in its third strain (values are halved in the edition):

Tomkins follows Morley's prescription[14] exactly by making each strain of his Pavan four groups of four semibreves, and each strain of his Galliard four groups of six minims, in length. The same applies to the Pavan of April 1650 and its Galliard of 1 October 1650.[15] So far into the future did the principles of *bassadanza* and *saltarello* cast their shadow. The 'Short Pavan' of 19 July 1654 is still composed in groups of four semibreves, although Bull had abandoned the principle long before.

'Fortune my Foe', dated 4 July 1654,[16] is the ultimate expression of traditional English variation technique. Seven statements of the theme are followed by a short coda, and this is the version

---

[14] *A Plain and Easy Introduction*, p. 297.

[15] *MB*, v, Nos. 45–6.

[16] *Ibid.*, No. 61.

dated by Tomkins. Later an eighth statement was added, but it begins as a close variant of the seventh and should be considered as an alternative rather than an addition. It too has its own rather more elaborate coda. A fragment of a ninth setting survives, and it looks as though Tomkins intended to return to the work and give it a definitive shape at some stage. His last dated piece is called 'The Perpetual Round' and was finished on 8 September 1654.[17] It is a curious exercise in canon and sequence, with a 'division'.

It is not easy to define the character of Tomkins' later music. Structurally his model is usually Byrd (except in *cantus firmus* settings), while much of the external figuration derives from Bull. The latter's brilliance, however, is softened and the passage-work is put to a more expressive use. The years 1646–1650 saw the climax of his creative life, after which his work begins to suffer from an understandable irresolution. The year 1654 marks both his cessation (as far as we know) from composition and his final departure from Worcester to the near-by village of Martin Hussingtree, where he died in June 1656.

Of Tomkins' immediate family, only John Tomkins, his younger half-brother (*ca.* 1586–1638) survives as a composer of keyboard music. His variations on 'John come kiss me now'[18] were written into Add. 29996 by two scribes who also contributed to Oxford, Bod. Lib., Mus. Sch. c.93. (Both manuscripts show signs of having been compiled by various members of the Tomkins circle, and pieces were frequently interrupted in the middle and resumed in another hand.) This set rivals that of Byrd in resourcefulness and structural ingenuity.

An even more obscure member of the circle was Arthur Phillips (1605–1695), organist first of Bristol Cathedral and then of Magdalen College, Oxford. A 'Ground' by him is preserved in Add. 29996,[19] but it is attributed to Thomas Tomkins in the index, which is in the hand of Thomas's son, Nathaniel. The list of 'lessons of worthe' in Rés. 1122 includes 'Tomkins on these notes [followed by the notes of the Phillips Ground] in the Redish

17 *MB*, v, No. 66.
18 *EKM*, iv, No. 7.
19 *Ibid.*, No. 2; *MB*, v, No. 40.

Clasped Booke'. It has been conjectured that this book was Add. 29996; but the hypothesis cannot be proved, and Tomkins may have written a different piece on the same ground. The question of authorship therefore remains open. It is a fine piece, if a little disjointed.

More of a distinct personality emerges from the music of Nicholas Carleton, who died in 1630. It is all in Add. 29996 and consists of two duets (one incomplete) and two other pieces. The first duet is an *In nomine*, entitled 'A verse for two to play on one virginall or organs', and betrays no sign of experimentation.[20] The second duet is a 'Praeludium' of which only the lower part was copied into the manuscript; blank staves appear on the right-hand page, but the piece has been published as a self-sufficient entity.[21] The 'Verse of four parts' is a remarkable essay in modulation.[22] The main key is C minor, but the music cadences in such keys as G sharp minor and B flat minor: the remotest chords are F sharp major and D flat major. Not the least noteworthy feature, however, is the long drawn-out final cadence, in which tonal equilibrium is gradually restored. Such music, like Bull's first 'Ut re mi fa sol la' (see Chapter VI, p. 77), requires a tuning approaching equal temperament if it is to sound at all satisfactory, and experiments of this kind were not pursued after the Restoration. There was, however, quite a vogue for them in the early seventeenth century. The aim was to produce smooth modulations, or, more simply, to write in outlandish keys, rather than to achieve the 'affective' devices of the Italian baroque. The younger Alfonso Ferrabosco (who was born, lived and died in England) had demonstrated perfect mastery of the entire tonal gamut in his hexachord settings, and in a four-part fancy.[23] These works are, of course, for strings, but they may well have been accompanied by a keyboard instrument, and the hexachord settings survive in short scores by Tomkins.[24] John Wilson,

[20] *Two Elizabethan Keyboard Duets*, No. 1.
[21] *EKM*, iv, No. 3.
[22] *Ibid.*, No. 4.
[23] Copied in score by Tomkins, London, Brit. Mus., Add. 29996, ff. 94v-97r.
[24] See above, Chapter VI, footnote 50.

Professor of Music at Oxford University, wrote pieces for lute in all the keys.[25]

Carleton's 'Verse' is a good example of the modulatory type, while his last piece, 'Upon the sharpe' is simply a piece in C minor written one semitone higher. The aim can only have been to demonstrate mastery of notation (not very complete) or a system of tuning.

The conservative element in English keyboard music at this time is also found in the work of John Lugge, organist of Exeter Cathedral from 1602 (or earlier) to 1645 (or later). His choirmaster from 1608 was Edward Gibbons, by whom a Prelude has survived,[26] and in 1638 Matthew Locke was in his choir. From him, Locke must first have heard the art of the double voluntary which he himself was later to transform. Lugge's keyboard music consists of several plainsong settings, three double voluntaries, a 'Jigg' and two 'Toys'. The plainsong settings have not been published, although they are splendidly resourceful examples of their type.[27] The double voluntaries, which have been edited in modern times,[28] are even more valuable, being amongst the few surviving pre-Commonwealth examples of the genre. He wrote, it would seem, for an instrument in which the choir organ descended to the full compass (see Voluntary I, bars 60–1). The right hand is never given a solo, but each piece ends, as did that of Gibbons, with both hands on the great organ. The only other piece of the kind which remains is a voluntary by Richard Portman (pupil of Orlando Gibbons and organist of Westminster Abbey from 1633 to the Civil War).[29] More clearly than in the works of Lugge, it anticipates the style of the Restoration.

The outbreak of Civil War and the subsequent Commonwealth effectively impeded the development of an idiomatic organ style. Organists were relieved of their duties and in most cases the instruments were actually destroyed. After the Restoration, it was some years before the majority of cathedrals and large

[25] Duckles, *JAMS* (1954) 103.

[26] See above; Chapter V, p. 55 and footnote 5.

[27] Caldwell, *Musica Disciplina* (1965) 129.

[28] Lugge, *Three Voluntaries*.

[29] MS at Wimborne Minster, Dorset, f. 3v. See Le Huray, *Music and the Reformation in England*, pp. 168–9.

churches were again provided with satisfactory organs. The voluntaries published in *Melothesia* (1673) therefore represent a fresh start rather than the culmination of a continuous process. It was quite otherwise in the case of 'secular' keyboard music.

After 1625, England was once again receptive to continental styles, both Italian and French. The former for a long time remained a somewhat specialised taste. Italian monody and recitative were known to England perhaps as early as 1617,[30] and Walter Porter may have studied with Monteverdi; various English collections of Italian monody have survived.[31] A manuscript which has been mistakenly supposed to be in the hand of William Ellis, but which may be dated as early as 1620,[32] includes music by Frescobaldi and is the earliest in England to mention—quite fortuitously, as it happens—the use of organ pedals. But the style of the Italian baroque, with few exceptions, did not really begin to penetrate instrumental music—and certainly not keyboard music—until after the Restoration. The decisive factor here was French.

In this respect keyboard music took its cue from the dances of the Stuart masque, and from such dance styles as were fashionable at court. The influence was not so much the dramatic or pantomimic dance, such as was also employed in the 'straight' theatre, but the ordinary social dance, whether it occurred in a 'normal' social context or as the climax to a masque.[33] In the Jacobean era, it was still possible for such dances to be composed for 'whole consort', the main repertory consisting of pavans, galliards, almans and corantos. In Caroline times, a more exciting instrumentation, and newer dance forms, were demanded. When collected together, they were arranged in suites according to their key. The principle purveyor of such music at the highest social level was William Lawes (1602–1645).

[30] In the music by Lanier for Ben Jonson's masque 'Lovers made Men'. The reference to recitative, however, occurs only in the edition of 1640: see Emslie, *ML* (1960) 13.

[31] See especially, Willetts, *ML* (1962) 329.

[32] Oxford, Christ Church, MS 1113. The identity of 'W.E.', whose initials are stamped on the binding and attached to one of the pieces, is unknown.

[33] Many examples printed in A. J. Sabol, *Songs and Dances for the Stuart Masque*, Providence, Rhode Island, 1959.

The points which emerge from a study of Lawes' dance music[34] are: the comparative rarity of the pavan; the emergence of the saraband and the confusion of identity between it and the galliard;[35] and the slowing down of the alman and coranto. It was the alman, coranto and saraband which were to form the basis of the new keyboard style. This was also the order of dances frequently adopted, under French influence, in Lawes' consort dances: the first 'Harp' consort consists of an alman, two corantos and a saraband.

The French element can be seen at first hand in certain English manuscripts of the mid-seventeenth century which include pieces by such composers as Tresure, La Barre (spelt as 'Labar' or 'Beare'), Chambonnières, Mercure and Du Fault. Pierre de La Barre (1592-1656), organist to Louis XIII from 1630 until his death, is represented in Oxford, Christ Church, MS 1236 (compiled by Ellis); New York, Pub. Lib., Drexel MS 5611; London, Brit. Mus., Add. 10337 (see below); and Oxford, Christ Church, MS 1177, a post-Restoration source which also contains a saraband by Richard Portman.[36] Jacques Champion de Chambonnières (*ca.* 1601-*ca.* 1671) was of course the son of the Jacques Champion who was a friend of Bull. He and the others are all represented in Ellis's manuscript, which also includes dances by English composers: Bryan, Loosemore, Coleman, John Ferrabosco, Rogers, and Ellis himself. Thomas Heardson's anthology of *ca.* 1650 (New York, Pub. Lib., Drexel MS 5611) contains a similar repertory.

One of the most interesting collections of the time is 'Elizabeth Rogers hir Virginall Booke, Februarye the 27, 1656' (? 1657, n.s.).[37] This is often described as the last of the virginal

---

[34] *MB*, xxi. See also Appendix II, Part i, s.v. Lawes. A small amount of keyboard music attributed to Lawes has survived, most of it printed in *Musicks Hand-maide* (1663). It is probable that these pieces are simply arrangements of consort works.

[35] Originally the galliard was related musically to the *saltarello* and was in C (6/2) time with a half-bar anacrusis and an element of cross-rhythm (6/2: 3/1). In Lawes and his contemporaries the galliard becomes a simple triple-time dance akin to the saraband.

[36] On f. 1v. Incipit in *MB*, xx, No. 52.

[37] London, Brit. Mus., Add. MS 10337.

books, although post-Restoration sources frequently contain copies of the old repertory. Its 79 keyboard pieces (eight are in a later hand) range from Byrd's 'The Battle' (composed before 1591) to almans, corantos and sarabands in the current style.

The most significant feature of this source is its grouping of dance movements together in what may be termed primitive suites. There are two alman-coranto pairs by one Thomas Strengthfeild (Nos. 14-15, 17-18),[38] an alman-coranto-saraband group of which the coranto is attributed to him (63-65), and a pair, of which the second is a saraband, assigned to 'T.S.' (70-71). Nos. 20-1 is a coranto-saraband pair by La Barre, while Nos. 73 and 76 may be a suite by Mercure. There are various other groups by unnamed composers, one of which (Nos. 29-30) has been included in *EKM*, v. It is just possible that the following movement (No. 31, 'A Maske') also belongs to the set.[39] Nos. 50-3 in D minor may be a four-movement suite: Alman-Coranto-Saraband-'My Delyght'.

In the newer kind of alman (or 'almaygne') as represented in this source, the tempo has slowed down considerably, and the upbeat is now regularly found. The coranto or 'corrant', though slower than its Elizabethan/Jacobean predecessor, retained its tendency to cross-rhythm (6/4 against 3/2), and generally began with an upbeat. The saraband ('selebrand') always began on the first beat of the bar, generally with a series of three crotchets at the same pitch. Cross-rhythms are normally avoided, although the barring in the sources is usually 6/4 rather than 3/4. The suite, Nos. 63-5 of Add. 10337, illustrates these features. Although only the second movement is ascribed to Strengthfeild, there can be little doubt that the whole work is by him:

Ex. 93 Almaygne   Thomas Strengthfeild?

---

[38] The numbering is that of Hughes-Hughes, *Catalogue of Manuscript Music*.
[39] *EKM*, v, Nos. 6, 7, 8.

Corrant   Thomas Strengthfeild

Selebrand   Thomas Strengthfeild?

A noteworthy feature is the use of the sign ᷆ side by side with the traditional double stroke through the stem. It is not clear whether the former sign has its traditional continental meaning of *Pralltriller* (French *tremblement*) or whether it has the later English meaning of 'beat' (i.e. mordent).

Other interesting sources for the pre-Restoration suite are Oxford, Christ Church, MS 1236, and Playford's *Musicks Hand-maide* (1663, reprinted with additions *ca.* 1668, and with further additions in 1678).[40] The first edition of the latter included suites by Benjamin Sandley, William Lawes and Benjamin Rogers. The suites by Lawes are probably transcriptions, but the actual music dates from before the composer's death in 1645. Sandley's Suite, though its first three movements are technically anonymous, has the distinction of being the earliest known four-movement suite by a named composer. This first edition also included two pieces by Matthew Locke, to which six more were added in 1678. Of these latter, 'The Simerons Dance' belonged to the incidental music for *The History of Sir Francis Drake*, staged in 1658, while four pieces were taken from the masque *Cupid and Death*,[41] revived with Locke's music in 1656. But it is not certain that the arrangements themselves date from the same period, or even that they are by Locke himself.

More interesting is a group of pieces by Locke, forming a three-movement suite, found in New York, Pub. Lib., Drexel MS 5611, a mid-century source (pp. 139–41).[42] Even if these pieces are a later addition to the manuscript, the writing displays archaic features, such as the use of the old ornament signs, (double and single strokes through the stem), which seem to place it in the pre-Restoration era. The music itself, however, is startlingly modern for such a date. To begin with it is in the key of D major, with its key-signature of two sharps.[43] The Alman (untitled in the source) is slower than ever, approaching the speed of those of the suites in *Melothesia*. The Coranto surprises

---

[40] *SBK*, xxviii. See also Chapter IX, p. 175.

[41] *SBK*, vi, Nos. 24, 27, 29. For the original versions, see *MB*, ii.

[42] *SBK*, vi, Nos. 33–5.

[43] It is possible, however, that a Suite by John Ferrabosco in this key (Oxford, Christ Church, MS 1236) pre-dates Locke's Suite.

with a fermata in the second bar; otherwise it is normal. The Saraband has dispensed with the three repeated crotchets at the beginning, but it has varied repeats, an archaic feature not retained in the mature suite.

This work, like the primitive suites of the Elizabeth Rogers manuscript, shows more promise than achievement, although the composer cannot be blamed for the poor text as transmitted by the manuscript. The notation, indeed, shows distinct signs of the strain imposed on it by a new style. It provides dramatic evidence of the struggle generated at the birth of new forms of art. Locke's own hand was clear and purposeful, as his autograph score of *Cupid and Death* clearly shows, but we do not know how he himself first coped with the broken chords and ornaments of idiomatic keyboard music in the new style. The emergence of the new ornament system (described in the next chapter) is shrouded in mystery, but it is fundamentally a haphazard adaptation of the French system to English convention.[44]

The optimism generated by the Restoration was favourable to the development of the new art-form, as also to the growth of new styles of organ music. But progress was gradual, and from this point to the end of the century the story is one of steady improvement rather than of a spectacular renaissance.

[44] For a new and careful discussion see Harley, *MR* (1970) 177.

IX

Sacred and Secular Forms, 1660–1700

With the Restoration of the monarchy, a tremendous revival of
the traditions and forms of church worship immediately began.
The immediate aim was to revive the pre-Commonwealth services, as certain publications make clear. Clifford's *Divine
Services* (1663) recalled the customs of the Chapel Royal. Church
choirs were re-formed, but one difficulty was the lack of trained
boys. This was quickly remedied, but in the meantime cornetts
were resorted to as a substitute. Much of what we know about
the revival of church music centres around the activities of the
Chapel Royal, and it must not be supposed that the revival was so
prompt, or the musical results so elaborate, in provincial cathedrals. However, there was a genuine restoration of the old
musical traditions in most parts of the country, and the Puritan-
ism prevalent in many places before the Civil War was now much
less in evidence.

A prominent feature of the revival was the building of new
organs. In many cases, however, old instruments were patched
up, either temporarily or permanently, as at York, where the old
instrument survived many rebuildings until the fire of 1829. At
Exeter, John Loosemore's new organ was ready in 1665. The
compass of the open diapason was now generally extended down
to G_1, but it was more a difference of nomenclature than of
actual pitch. The Exeter organ, uniquely, was provided with
double diapasons, and the speaking length of the largest of these
was said to be 20′ 6″, almost exactly double the length of the
largest Worcester pipe in 1614. This would put the organ
approximately a semitone above present-day pitch; but we cannot suppose that complete uniformity of pitch existed throughout the country, and elsewhere organs may have approached the

pitch of the present day or even a semitone lower.[1] At the same time choir pitch was generally lowered to bring it in conformity with that of the instruments, and the double standard no longer applied; hence the instruction in *Musica Deo Sacra* (see pp. 53-4).

The famous double diapasons at Exeter were fourteen in number, which, allowing for the short octave, would give them a compass of a twelfth from G_2–C_1. Opinion was divided as to their usefulness, but it was agreed that their effect was good only at a distance and with the full organ. Elsewhere builders were content with an '8-foot' stop as the lowest sounding rank, and this is adequate for the performance of the surviving organ music. On modern instruments, the occasional A_1 or G_1, usually confined to cadences, can be discreetly supplied by a pedal stop at 16-foot pitch.

Specifications, even of new instruments, remained at first much as they were before the Civil War. Occasionally one reads of a tierce (seventeenth) or nineteenth rank. Important advances were made by Bernard Smith, now thought to have been an Englishman who had emigrated, probably to Holland, during the Commonwealth. Apart from a somewhat unsatisfactory instrument built for the Chapel Royal in 1662, his career as an organ-builder dates from 1671, when he supplied a single-manual organ for the Sheldonian Theatre, Oxford. It seems to have been Smith who introduced the cornet to England. This was a powerful solo stop, of four or five ranks of (unison), octave, twelfth, fifteenth and seventeenth pitch, from c' or $c'\#$ upwards. The sesquialtera was a similar stop extending throughout the keyboard, though without the unison and octave ranks: 'sexquialtera bass' became a popular registration for left-hand solos. Smith even included the seventeenth in his mixtures, thus initiating a peculiarly English custom. Renatus Harris, on the contrary, whose recorded career dates from *ca.* 1674, tended to omit the seventeenth even from the cornet and sesquialtera. Both Smith and Harris added an 'echo organ' to the now customary

[1] On the Exeter organ see Sumner, *The Organ*, pp. 122–3. The organ commissioned for Wells in 1662 from Robert Taunton had diapasons of $12\frac{1}{2}$ feet and principals of six feet. This of course indicates a lower pitch, but the manual compass may have been to F_1. *Ibid.*, p. 129.

great and chair in their largest instruments, placed in a permanently closed box. The earliest example is Smith's organ for the Temple Church, built in 1683. On chamber organs there was a tendency to exploit novel tone-colours.[2]

Harpsichords of the late seventeenth century retained their characteristic features, the compass being frequently extended to G_1 from the A_1 which was in common use in the early seventeenth century. The oblong small virginal became very rare and was replaced as a domestic instrument by the small wing-shaped spinet, which had a brighter tone. The clavichord was virtually obsolete, although there is a record of payment to John Hingston for tuning a 'claricon' (see above, p. 44). As to nomenclature, 'virginal' or 'virginals' was retained in some contexts as a generic term for instruments of the harpsichord type; but like the old English word 'recorder' it fell into disuse amongst practising musicians and was replaced by 'harpsicon' or 'harpsichord' for the large instrument and 'spinet' (a word long used on the continent) for the small.

The earliest voluntaries to appear in the new era were the seven by Matthew Locke printed in *Melothesia* (1673). Four of them (Nos. 1, 4, 5 and 6 in the original edition)[3] are short pieces of less than twenty bars. The first, cadencing on to a chord of E major, is quite archaic in its tonality, emphasising the subdominant in a manner resembling the 'quartus tonus' of continental composers. Nos. 5 and 6 are plainly in G major and A minor respectively, while No. 4 is little more than a piece of two-part counterpoint in D minor. The other three have more of interest to offer. No. 7 is 'For a Double Organ', and here we notice a great increase in the resourcefulness of the writing compared with earlier composers. There are solos for right hand as well as left, and after both hands have joined together on the great organ there is an antiphonal passage between it and the chair organ. Nos. 2 and 3 are examples of an introduction—purely chordal in the case of

[2] A Loosemore organ of 1665 included a 'flute', 'recorde', 'flagilett', 'trumpett' and 'shaking stopp'. Sumner, *op. cit.*, p. 123. On the later seventeenth-century organ see Clutton and Niland, *The British Organ*, pp. 62–81.

[3] *SBK*, vii. The numbering of this edition is changed from the original for the purposes of avoiding page-turns, and the ornament-signs modernised. The original order and ornament-signs are retained in *TW*, vi.

the former—and fugal allegro, a form which was to remain the basis of the larger English voluntary for a century and a half.

So much for the purely external features of these works. We may well ask what is the background to a style so different from that of English organ music in the early seventeenth century. The answer is that French and Italian elements are both present, remembering that the latter could have been derived in part from French sources. Pelham Humfrey, of course, had travelled in France and Italy between 1664 and 1667; but we are not dependent on his visit for evidence of continental influence. We have seen that the toccatas of Frescobaldi had been copied in the 1620s, and extracts from two of them were to appear submerged in voluntaries by Blow.[4] Works attributed to Purcell by English copyists have turned out to be by Nicolas Lebègue and Michelangelo Rossi.[5] The nature of the ornamentation and its use in connection with slow fugal writing and with what is called the *style brisé* is purely French, having been adapted to the keyboard from the idioms of the lute. On the other hand the free toccata-like writing and the quick, canzona-like fugato are fundamentally Italian in character. These features may be illustrated from the third voluntary of *Melothesia*, the best of the seven. The opening fugue is of fundamentally French inspiration:

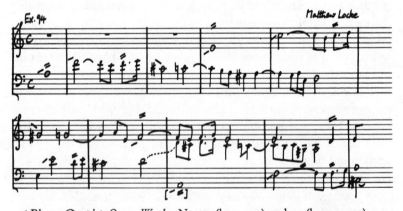

[4] Blow, *Complete Organ Works*, Nos. 2 (bars 1–9) and 29 (bars 45–57).

[5] Purcell, *The Organ Works*, No. 1 (omitted from 2nd edn.) and the Toccata in A (London, Brit. Mus., Add. 34695) excluded from this edition. Music by Froberger has been found in an English source: see Dart, *ML* (1969) 470. On the Toccata in A see G. Rose, *Acta Musicologica* (1968) 203, where Rossi's authorship is questioned.

The curiously ambivalent tonality allows the first note of the subject to be construed as either its tonic or its dominant. The fourth entry begins on *b'* and leads the music into E minor; the next two are on *F#* and *f'#* in stretto and there is a cadence in B minor. A closer stretto with entries on *e'* and *A* respectively brings the music round to an imperfect cadence in A minor. The music plunges into a more lively fugato:

The treatment here is much freer, and soon there is little left of the theme beyond the rhythm and tonal direction of its first three notes. The music then dissolves into free toccata-like figuration based, in part, upon a new idea:

heard later in diminution:

TABLE 2. *Ornaments in English Keyboard Music*[1]

	Forefall	Backfall	Shake	Beat	(Forefall-and-Beat)	Plain note and shake	Shake turned	Turn	Battery		
Before 1150[2]											
1550–1660			etc.[4]	(Add. 10337)						(Ch. Ch. 1236)	Occurs once in Purcell, *A Choice Collection of Lessons*
1660–1720[6]	Fore-fall	Back-fall	Shake	Beat (or — or even — ?)	— or — ?	Plain note and shake	Shake turned	Turn	Battery		
1720–1800	Re-placed by small note	Re-placed by small note		Re-placed by small note[7]					Numerous interpretations of (and possible		Beat [8][9][10]

The whole of this second section (from bar 22) is a mixture of the Italian canzona and toccata styles such as one encounters in the music of Michelangelo Rossi and Bernardo Pasquini. The specifically English and personal element in the work is the concentration of style, the economy in the use of the material and the boldness of the modulations. What one lacks is a sense of spaciousness, particularly in the canzona section. This is to be a recurrent complaint in English music in the Italian style before about 1700. Purcell disarms criticism by his sheer inventiveness; but in the lesser composers the inability to develop the music on a satisfactory time-scale is a serious disadvantage.

The ornaments used in *Melothesia* are the Forefall, Backfall, Shake, Beat, and Forefall-and-shake. The first four correspond to the French *port-de-voix*, *coulé*, *tremblement* and *pincé*. The traditional English double stroke, now above the note instead of through the stem, was retained for the shake, and the French *tremblement* sign was transferred to the beat. Later sources add the Shake turned, Forefall-and-beat, Backfall-and-shake, Turn, Slur and Battery, the Forefall-and-shake being dispensed with. The earliest extant explanations of these ornaments occur in the third edition of 1699 (possibly also the lost second edition of 1697) of Purcell's posthumous *A Choice Collection of Lessons*, and in Young's *A Choice Collection of Ayres* (1700) and Walsh's *The Second Book of the Harpsicord Master* (1700). Their interpretation is summarised in the accompanying table. I have made use of Howard Ferguson's ingenious emendation, according to which the explanation of the Forefall-and-beat became attached to the name and sign of the Beat, the name and sign of the former and the explanation of the latter having been erroneously omitted. This fails to account for the subsequent verbal explanation in the Purcell volume: 'Observe that you always *shake* from the note above, and *beat* from the note or half note below, according to the key you play in'; but the gloss may be merely an unthinking explanation based on the already miscopied table. The French antecedents strongly support Ferguson's contention. As to Purcell's supposed connection with the table,[6] it is obvious that

6 The lost *The Harpsicord Master* (Walsh, 1699) contained 'plain and easy instructions for learners on the Spinnet or Harpsichord; written by the late

he was not responsible for the form in which it appeared in print.

Apart from the question of ornaments it is clear that English performance was to a certain extent affected by French conventions of inequality and double dotting. The evidence for this exists in different copies and editions of the same pieces. On the whole it is the later sources which are the more accurately notated. For example, in a Saraband for harpsichord by John Blow, first printed in *The Second Part of Musick's Hand-maid* (1689), the rhythms ♩. ♪♩ and ♫ ♫ are given as ♩. ♪♩ and ♫. ♫. in the 1704 edition of Blow's *A Choice Collection of Lessons*. In the case of Purcell, the differences between manuscript and printed versions of the same piece may be examined in the Ferguson edition of the eight Suites. In general the use of a slur over a pair of notes seems to imply 'reversed inequality' (short–long). On the whole the available evidence relates to harpsichord and spinet music rather than to organ music; but a careful consideration of the contexts involved will often reveal its appropriateness in the latter.

John Blow succeeded Albert Bryan as organist of Westminster Abbey in December 1668 at the age of nineteen. In 1679 he was followed by Henry Purcell, but resumed the post on the latter's death in 1695. Most of his organ music survives only in late seventeenth- or early eighteenth-century copies, but this is no argument for a late date of composition. The only hint we have of any sort of date concerns the Voluntary on the 'Old Hundredth', which was described in one manuscript as by 'Mr. Blow'; from this Stafford Smith, whose transcript in *Musica Antiqua* (1812) is now the only record of the source, deduced that it was composed before Blow took his doctorate in 1677.[7]

famous Mr. H. Purcell', and it is virtually certain that these were identical with the 'Rules' found in the surviving second and third books of that publication (1700, 1702). These in turn are similar to those found in the third edition of Purcell's *A Choice Collection* (1699) and presumably in the lost second edition of 1697 (the first edition, 1696, contained no instructions, but they were advertised for the second edition in 1697). Ferguson suggests that both sets derived from an inaccurate copy of Purcell's original manuscript. Blow, *Six Suites*, p. 18. See, however, Harley, *MR* (1970) 177.

[7] This was a Lambeth doctorate, reputedly the first to be awarded (*Grove's Dictionary*, s.v. Blow).

As this work is ascribed to Purcell in another manuscript it presents special problems of attribution and will be considered separately. With one or two exceptions, Blow's organ music lacks polish and assurance and is best considered before Purcell's. With about thirty extant works, however, he ranks as the most prolific of the major composers for the instrument at this time.

The great majority of these works are fugues of some kind (often now so-called in the sources) and even when the form is that of an introduction and allegro, the first section as well as the second is normally fugal. Amongst the exceptions, No. 2[8] begins with a direct quotation from Frescobaldi's twelfth Toccata (Book I); the others are Nos. 8 and 23. The fugues may be divided into (a) slow (b) quick, in the Italian style and (c) both in succession. Amongst the slow pieces, No. 15 may be regarded as typical of the quieter style:

Double counterpoint may be used, as in No. 17:

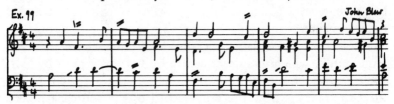

Even triple counterpoint of a kind occurs, although in the following case a vital part has to be continued editorially (No. 7):

---

[8] The references are to the *Complete Organ Works*, ed. Watkins Shaw. Another work is printed in *TW*, xxi, and another two in *EOM*, xxiii.

But the 'slow' fugue is not always quiet: it can include spectacular passages in demisemiquavers (No. 20) or employ a harsh chromaticism as in the splendid No. 18, where the chromatic subject generates a wealth of countersubjects and episodes.

The quick fugues are generally less successful, lacking the consistency which the canzona style demands. No. 14 in A major is too obviously experimental, even allowing for the possible corruption of the text, to be wholly convincing, as the rather lame conclusion shows:[9]

No. 3 in G is a good deal more satisfactory, and although the key of the supertonic (apparently a favourite of Restoration organists) is emphasised too late in the fugue for comfort, it is both approached and quitted without difficulty:

[9] Shaw's emendation seems unconvincing. I propose *E B e* for *G d g*. The work is followed by a second movement in London, Brit. Mus., Add. 31446, where it is found anonymously.

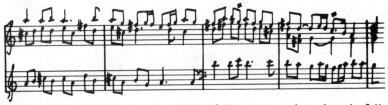

No. 24 is a double fugue of Handelian pretention, but it falls short of the ideal.

Only two works (Nos. 10 and 16) are clearly in two sections. No. 10 is curious in that it ends with an imperfect cadence; it can hardly be considered to be in the mixolydian mode, for the rest of it is in a thoroughly orthodox G major. Indeed it is one of the most assured works, tonally, that he wrote, and may well belong to the early eighteenth century. One can only suppose that it was designed to lead into a third movement, now lost, or into some piece of music at a service. The two movements of No. 16 are agreeable, but hardly seem to belong together and indeed survive separately in some sources.

There are five double voluntaries, not counting the 'Old Hundredth', making Blow the most prolific seventeenth-century composer for this medium. All three forms are represented. No. 25 is really in two sections, the second starting at bar 28, though the join is well concealed:

No. 26 is a straightforward work in C major of the canzona type. No. 27 is 'slow', with plenty of brilliant passage-work and a long free coda. No. 28 is 'for the Cornett and Single Organ'. Since the cornet operated only from *c'* or *c'#*, the solos in this voluntary are confined to the right hand.[10] It is an extended piece (86 bars), but the main thematic material is abandoned after bar 37 and the

10 See above, p. 158. The second work in *EOM*, xxiii, utilises the cornet, sesquialtera, and echo organ.

writing becomes somewhat aimless. The twenty-ninth voluntary is in some ways the best of all, in spite of another chunk of Frescobaldi in the middle.[11] Here, both fugues are of the canzona type. The first resolves on to a long dominant pedal, followed by the Frescobaldi passage on the chair organ:

*-✦ *cf. Frescobaldi, Toccata VIII, Book I, bars 18-24*

The second fugue follows on a subject of great brilliance which is heard only on the great organ, both as a solo in each hand in turn, and later with both hands on the great. A massive plagal cadence over 5½ bars brings the work to a satisfying conclusion.

The organ works of Henry Purcell may be numerically insignificant in the context of his output as a whole, but as his most recent editor remarks, 'There is no such wealth of seventeenth-century organ music that they can be dismissed as relatively unimportant by organists'.[12] Unfortunately his edition must be reduced still further as the work ascribed to 'H. Purcell' in Ch. Ch. MS 1179, p. 36, has been identified as being by Lebègue.[13]

[11] See above, footnote 4.
[12] *The Organ Works*, ed. McLean.
[13] See above, footnote 5.

This makes one suspect the authenticity of the indifferent
voluntary in C on p. 38 of the same manuscript. The 'Verse' in F
is a short fugal piece of no particular distinction. The Voluntary
in D minor on the other hand, especially in its version for double
organ, is a masterpiece. The first nineteen bars of the two are
essentially the same, after which the version for single organ
continues to utilise the same fugue-subject, followed by a coda
based on new but ill-defined material. The two-manual version
grows out of the same point at which, this time in the form of a
left-hand solo, the fugue-subject is transformed into a wild
rushing passage in which harmony stands frozen in suspense:

Thereafter the main theme is treated considerably more spaciously
than in the first version, always as a solo for right or left hand.
At last, after a half-close, a new theme is hinted at in a fantasia-
like passage of some length:

The music turns towards F major, and after an imperfect cadence in *that* key the final canzona-section begins:

Ex. 107   Henry Purcell

Great organ both hands

The fugal treatment is not maintained for long, but the tonality settles down again to D minor, a dominant pedal and the final cadence. The novelty of the design, the subtlety of the tonal argument, and the fiery brilliance of the writing, combine to make this a uniquely fascinating work of its period.

The Voluntary in G is wholly Italian in inspiration. The slow, non-fugal introduction, with its sustained dissonances, its chromaticism, its occasional outbreaks of ornamentation, and its use of 'Lombardic' rhythm (♫.) recalls strongly the toccatas of Frescobaldi and Rossi; while the subsequent fugue is a canzona of the most up-to-date kind. It is here, perhaps, that the criticism of inordinate brevity might be made; but the tonal scheme is comparably restricted and there is no undue lack of balance.

And so to the Voluntary on the 'Old Hundredth'. This survives in two sources: John Stafford Smith's *Musica Antiqua* (1812), based on a manuscript now lost in which the work was ascribed to 'Mr. Blow'; and an early eighteenth-century manuscript in the hand of one Nicholas Harrison (London, Brit. Mus., Add. 34695) in which it is ascribed to 'Mr. Henry Purcell'. The former is printed in Blow's *Complete Organ Works*, ed. Watkins Shaw, and the latter in Purcell's *Organ Works*, ed. Hugh McLean, but with Smith's variant readings. The two versions differ in several respects. It is not clear to what extent Smith's transcription can be trusted. The numerous G naturals in his version (the piece is in A major) may represent a genuine variant in his source, or an editorial dislike of doubled leading notes and so on. He certainly misunderstood the repeat convention of the manuscript, as his ludicrous first- and second-time bars show.[14]

[14] Quoted literally in McLean's commentary. Shaw's emendation is unsatisfactory (Blow, *Complete Organ Works*, No. 30).

However, this cannot explain all the differences. The Harrison
text does not merely represent an adaptation for a single organ
with divided stops; it incorporates radical improvements in
numerous places. Compare, for example, bars 45–51 (McLean's
numbering) in both versions:

It is not certain that the Smith version was intended for a two-
manual instrument; all one can say is that the layout for the
hands suggests that it may have been. Harrison's copy calls for a
'half stop' in the lower register for the first part and a 'cornet' for
the second. In the following passage, the half-stop would have to
be drawn quickly between bars 16 and 17 and would reinforce
the stops already drawn in order to bring out the theme clearly:

In the second half, the cornet stop was presumably intended to sound alone. The necessity for keeping the left hand below *c'#* partly accounts for the differences shown in Ex. 108; but we have seen that it was a musical improvement as well. The changes at the end, however, are dictated by purely musical considerations:[15]

The left-hand *c'* ♮ in bar 66 is of course the highest note possible without straying into the register of the cornet, and its use may have been suggested by the limitations of the instrument.

Whether the work is by Blow or Purcell, or a revision by Purcell of a piece by Blow, it is in its single-manual form one of the most striking and imaginative organ works of its time. Both composers were organists of Westminster Abbey at different times, and it is possible that the single-manual version was made for the small organ used to supplement the large instrument at the coronations of James II and William III.[16] The rarity of the form, a type of chorale-prelude, in English keyboard music (the only known example of earlier date is the *Psalmus* 'O Lord turn

[15] The interlude in the version by Blow is one bar shorter than in Purcell's.
[16] Westrup, *Henry Purcell*, pp. 53, 62.

TABLE 3. *Contents of* 'Melothesia' (*1673*)

No.[1]	Title and Ascription[2]	No.[1]	Title and Ascription[2]
*1[3]	Prelude/M.L. (C major)	†33	Saraband/W.G. (D minor)
*2	Saraband/M.L. (C major)	*34	Horne Pipe/M.L. [sic] (D minor)
*3	Prelude/M.L. (C major)		
*4	Almain/M.L. (C major)	35	Almaine/W.G. (D major)
*5	Corant/M.L. (C major)	36	Corant/W.G. (D major)
*6	Gavott[3] (C major)	37	Gavott/W.G. (D major)
*7	Country Dance / M.L. (C. major)	38	An Ayre (A minor)
		39	Saraband (A minor)
*8	Almain/M.L. (G minor)	40	— (A minor)
*9	Saraband/M.L. (G minor)	41	A Jigge (A minor)
*10	Virago/M.L. (G minor)	†42	Corant/Mr. Will Hall (G major)
*11	Roundo/M.L. (G minor)		
*12	Prelude/M.L. (C major)	†43	—/Mr. Rob. Smith (G major)
*13	Almain/M.L. (C major)		
*14	Corant/M.L. (C major)	†44	—/R.S. (G major)
*15	Saraband/M.L. (C major)	†45	—/R.S. (G major)
*16	Jig/M.L. (C major)	†46	An Ayre (C major)
*17	Prelude/M.L. (D major)	†47	Gavott (C major)
*18	Almain/M.L. (D major)	†48	—/Mr. John Banister (C major)
*19	Corant/M.L. (D major)		
*20	Saraband/M.L. (D major)	†49	— (D minor)
*21	Rant/M.L. (D major)	†50	— (D minor)
†22	Prelude/Mr. Chr. Preston (G major)	†51	Charity (D minor)
		†52	— (D minor)
†23	Almain/C.P. (G major)	53	— (C major)
†24	Corant/C.P. (G major)	†54	Almain / Mr. J. Moss (F major)
†25	Saraband/C.P. (G major)		
†26	Prelude/Mr. John Roberts (E minor)	†55	Corant/J. M. (F major)
		†56	Saraband[5] (F major)
†27	Almain/J.R. (E minor)	†57	A Jig-Almain/J.M. (F major)
†28	Corant/J.R.[4] (E minor)	†58	Almain/Mr. G. Diesner (C major)
†29	Corant/J.R. (E minor)		
†30	Saraband/J.R. (E minor)	†59	Jigg/G.D. (C major)
†31	Almain/W.G. (D minor)	60	Horn Pipe/C.P. (D minor)
†32	Corant/Mr. Will Gregorie (D minor)	61	Horn-Pipe/C.P. (D minor)
		*62	For the Organ/M.L. (E

Table 3 (*contd.*)

No.[1]	Title and Ascription[2]	No.[1]	Title and Ascription[2]
	phrygian)	*66	For the Organ/M.L. (G major)
*63	For the Organ/M.L. (F major)		
*64	For the Organ/M.L. (A minor)	*67	For the Organ/M.L. (A minor)
*65	For the Organ/M.L. (D minor)	*68	For a Double Organ/M.L. (D minor)

* Printed in *SBK*, vi-vii; organ pieces also in *TW*, vi.

† Printed in *PSMS*, xvi.

[1] Not in source.

[2] Stroke separates title at beginning of piece from ascription at end. Pieces unsigned are by Thatcher (see Locke's Preface) except probably for Nos. 6 and 56.

[3] Probably by Locke.   [4] With varied repeats.   [5] Probably by Moss.

not away' in the Mulliner Book) certainly suggests that it might have been intended for a special occasion.

Another possibility is that such works were often improvised but rarely written down. It is, after all, easier to improvise on a *cantus firmus* than to play a fugue extempore. For the professional organist, of course, the latter was also an essential part of his equipment, and the surviving repertory reflects more the needs of amateurs and pupils than the urge to set down in written form what could be just as conveniently improvised.

This was also true of secular keyboard music; but the amateur market was much greater and it was for this that the surviving printed editions were prepared. John Playford entered the field with *Musicks Hand-maide* (1663); further editions appeared *ca.* 1668 and, much enlarged, in 1678. In the meantime *Melothesia*, a treatise on playing a thorough-bass, with harpsichord and organ music, edited by Locke, had been published (1673). *The Second Part of Musick's Hand-maid* followed in 1689 (reprinted 1705).[17]

[17] *Musicks Hand-maide* reprinted *SBK*, xxviii; *The Second Part of Musick's Handmaid*, *SBK*, x. Extracts from *Melothesia* in *SBK*, vi, vii; *PSMS,* xvi. Full contents of *Melothesia* in Table 3. There is also 'An Entry' for keyboard in Locke's *The Present Practice of Musick Vindicated*, London, 1673, p. 10.

Purcell's suites and a few separate pieces were published post-humously in 1696. Blow's own *Choice Collection* appeared in 1698, while various anthologies printed from 1700 on included seventeenth-century music.[18]

The main form was the suite, the kernel of which was usually the alman-coranto-saraband sequence. It could also incorporate the prelude, other dances, and theatre tunes (which themselves were often dances of some kind). Movements found separately in some sources occur in the context of a suite in others. Certain suites in *Melothesia* are not even the work of a single composer. The best plan will be to deal with each form in turn, followed by a consideration of the suite as a whole. Again the music of Locke, Blow and Purcell furnishes virtually a complete guide to the forms and styles of the day.

The alman (almain, almand) had slowed down by 1660 to such an extent that the quaver was now definitely the beat. In Locke this is still rather a fast quaver, and there is always a quaver upbeat which should almost certainly be given its full value in performance. The alman-type can be recognised in many pieces, such as 'ayres', which are not explicitly so called. In the following named example, from his fourth suite, the continuation proves that in the deceptively slow opening, the crotchet must not be taken for the beat:

Ex. III   Matthew Locke

In Purcell and Blow, the quaver beat is usually much slower. The Almand 'Bell-barr' from Purcell's seventh Suite is actually marked 'very slow'. But there is also found a type in which a crotchet is substituted for a quaver beat, though the time-signature remains ₵. This may be recognised in Purcell's second and fifth suites. (The almand from his first Suite I prefer to regard as having a fast quaver beat; this can be demonstrated from the fact that if inequality were to be applied, it would be to pairs of semiquavers rather than to pairs of quavers). The upbeat is now frequently a half-beat, and the context frequently suggests that in performance this should be shortened still further to a quarter-beat.[19] The Almand from Blow's sixth Suite lacks any upbeat at all, though its second section has one.

The coranto (corant, etc.) follows the alman as surely as the galliard once followed the pavan. Its upbeat-convention follows that of the alman very closely. The beat is the crotchet, the metrical scheme being an alternation between 2 × 3/4 and 3/2. Barring in the sources and in modern editions varies from three to six crotchets according to the prevalence of either rhythm. In Locke's first and third suites (the second has no coranto) the basic 3/2 metre is preserved even at cadences; in his fourth Suite, however, the later convention is observed:

Ex. 112   Matthew Locke

[19] See *SBK*, xxi. 27.

The main modifications in Blow and Purcell are an increase in the tendency towards dotted rhythms and the preponderance of 3/4 over 3/2.

The saraband was always in a straightforward 3/4 time, without upbeat. Originally it began with three successive crotchets at the same pitch, a convention which was later modified so as to permit other pitches and other rhythms (such as ♩♩♫ and ♩♩.♪). Even so, the idea of repeated notes was not altogether abandoned. The Saraband from Locke's fourth Suite may be quoted in its entirety:

Ex. 113

The rather aimless syncopations towards the end were to become a not altogether pleasing mannerism in Purcell: the Saraband from his fifth Suite contains very little else.

It is a constant feature in the history of the dance that as old dances become slower in performance their place is taken by newer dances designed for the sprightlier measures thus left vacant. Old and new often persist side by side for many a generation. Thus in the present instance the place of the alman is taken by the gavott and rigadoon, that of the coranto by the jigg, and that of the saraband by the minuet. Except for the last of these, name and style are not always in conformity, however. The Gavott from Locke's first Suite has a moderate crotchet beat with sharply dotted rhythms, with no upbeat, and the piece entitled 'Virago' from the second Suite has much the same characteristics. For Blow the term implied a quick 2/2 with crotchet upbeat, as is shown by the Gavott from his fourth Suite in C and the 'Gavot in

Gamut' from *The Second Part of Musick's Hand-maid*, No. 10. These are very close to two rigadoons by Purcell,[20] though the first of these is without upbeat.

There is a similar confusion between 'jigg' and 'hornpipe'. There are really two distinct measures involved: the quick 6/4 and the moderate 3/2 or 3/4. The Jig from Locke's third Suite belongs to the latter category, and is by later standards a pure hornpipe. The modern time-signature would be 3/2. Similarly, the Jigg from Blow's third Suite is in a moderate 3/4. What one might be tempted to call the 'true jig' in 6/4 is given such names as 'Country Dance', 'Roundo' and 'Rant' by Locke, the second title referring specifically to its Da Capo form.[21] Blow does give the name 'Jigg' to a piece in 6/4: it is the fourth movement of his first Suite, and has something of what Dryden called 'the rude sweetness of a Scotch tune'.[22] The piece was originally printed as No. 2 of *The Second Part of Musick's Hand-maid*.

With Purcell, modern terminology is established. His eight suites include one Hornpipe so called (the last movement of the seventh Suite), and another without title is the last movement of the sixth Suite. The Jigg which concludes the 'Suite of Lessons' in *The Second Part of Musick's Hand-maid*[23] is in quick 3/8 time with dotted rhythms alternating between long-short and short-long:

Ex. 114   Henry Purcell

[20] *SBK*, xxii, Nos. 11, 44.

[21] *Cf.* the 'Round O' transcribed from Purcell's 'Abdelazar'; *ibid.*, No. 38.

[22] *SBK*, v, No. 4.

[23] See below, p. 183, for further discussion of this suite.

A study of its harmonic rhythm reveals that its true metre is an alternation between 9/8 and 6/8 (the original time-signature is 8/6). Altogether it is one of the most interesting products, rhythmically, of late seventeenth-century England.

The same publication includes four minuets by Purcell, one of them without title. This (No. 14) and No. 12 ('New Minuet') are fairly lively short pieces in Da Capo form. The other two (Nos. 15 and 29) are in binary form, the latter being a transcription of a ritornello from 'Raise the voice' (Z. 334/6). The Minuet from the eighth Suite is also a transcription, this time from the incidental music which he composed for Congreve's 'The Double Dealer' (Z. 592/3). The last movement of the first Suite is also usually regarded as a minuet, although it could equally well be thought of as a saraband.

The extant sources abound in untitled pieces and 'ayres' which conform in some measure to the various dances just described. The same may be said of many of the 'theatre tunes', some of which carry the title of a dance in their original form. Trumpet tunes and marches again are often of a dance-like character and in some cases are also transcriptions. Then there are song transcriptions, settings of popular tunes (such as 'Lilliburlero'), chaconnes and grounds, preludes, and such oddities as 'Motley's Maggot' (by Richard Motley, a very obscure composer). Except for the preludes, which are quite distinctive in character, these forms overlap to such an extent that any rigid classification is impossible. 'A New Ground' by Purcell from *The Second Part of Musick's Hand-maid* (No. 17) is an example of a ground which is also a transcription (from the Ode for St. Cecilia's Day, 'Welcome to all the pleasures'). The keyboard version should certainly not be ignored: the distinctive ornamentation applied to the original alto solo (transposed an octave higher), quite transforms its character. The treatment of the bass when the voice is silent also provides an authentic specimen of the composer's ideas of continuo realisation:

Ex. 115   Henry Purcell

This sort of thing must have been very characteristic, for it recurs in other grounds by Purcell.

When one begins to investigate the repertory of popular song-settings and theatre transcriptions, one is immediately plunged into a labyrinth of cross-references from which escape is all but impossible. There was a particular fondness for Scotch and Irish tunes, which of course had to be harmonised. There was also a market, which Purcell helped to satisfy, for the sophisticated imitation of such things, both for the voice and on the keyboard. For the historian of popular song and of the theatre, the keyboard collections are a minor but indispensable aid.

The prelude had of course been cultivated by the Elizabethan and Jacobean harpsichordists. For Locke and Purcell it was normally used as an introduction to a complete suite. From the rather rambling models provided by Locke, Purcell developed a more coherent style, although even he did not always succeed in resolving the conflict between material and form. We may distinguish between the purely rhapsodic and the imitative types. Locke had tried out the latter in an independent Prelude in A minor,[24] although he did not achieve real consistency of style. Purcell in his second Suite wrote what is virtually a three-part fugue as a Prelude, although it degenerates into *arpeggiando* passage-work towards the end. The Prelude to the fifth Suite, with its vigorous rhythmic movement and quasi-orchestral style is by far the most successful of these early efforts; and while the subject disappears before the end, the music continues to be based on one of its salient rhythmic motives:

[24] *Keyboard Suites*, No. 32. This work may have been intended for the organ.

The suite in England did not, by the end of the seventeenth century, reach that degree of formal and stylistic perfection which we find in Froberger, Chambonnières and d'Anglebert. It usually incorporated the almand, corant and saraband, though the last is far from invariable. In Purcell it is generally replaced, rather than followed, by some such movement as minuet or hornpipe. Locke's design is more variable, generally with more, though shorter, movements than in Purcell or Blow. It is in

TABLE 4. *Contents of* 'A Choice Collection of Ayres' (*1700*)

No.[1]	Title and Ascription	Page
	A sett by Dr. Blow (D minor)	
†*1	Almand	1
†*2	Corant	2
†*3	Minuett	3
†4	Saraband by Mr. Crofts (D minor)[2]	3
†5	Iigg (A major)	4
	A set by Mr. Frn. Piggett (C major)	
†6	Prelude	4
†7	Almand	5
†8	Corant	6
†9	Sarabrand	7
†10	Iigg	8
†11	A March[3]	9
12	Minuet	9
13	A Trumpett Minnuett by Mr. Clarke (C major)[4]	10
14	A march by Mr. Clarke (C major)	11
†15	An Ayre by Mr. Clarke (C major)	11
16	The Emperour of Germanys March by Mr. Clarke (D major)[5]	12
17	The Serenade by Mr. Clarke (D major)	12
18	The Prince of Denmark's March by Mr. Clarke (D major)	13
	A set of Ayers by Mr. John Barrett (A major)	
†19	Almand	14
†20	Corant	14
†21	Sarabrand[6]	15
†22	The St. Catherine	15
	A set by Mr. Wm. Croft (C minor)	

Table 4 (*contd.*)

No.[1]	Title and Ascription	
†23	Almand[7]	16
†24	Sarabrand	16
†25	Corant	17
†26	Aire	17
	A set by Mr. Wm. Croft (E minor)	
†27	Almand	18
†28	Corant	18
†29	Sarabrand	19
†30	—	19

* Printed in *SBK*, v.
† Printed in *CP*.
[1] Not in source.
[2] In *CP*, iv. 13, in C minor after London, Brit. Mus., Add. 31467.
[3] In 2HM, No. 13.
[4] Nos. 13–15 in 2HM, Nos. 10–12.
[5] Nos. 16–18 in 2HM, Nos. 7–9.
[6] Nos. 21–2 in 2HM, Nos. 18–19.
[7] Nos. 23, 25–6 in 2HM, Nos. 23–5.

Melothesia, however (though not in connection with Locke himself) that we find the extraordinary anomaly of a single suite by more than one composer.[25] Blow and Purcell incorporated transcriptions to make up their suites, although in Purcell's case this may have been done posthumously.[26] Several of Purcell's suites exist in different versions. An extraordinary example is the relationship between the 'Suit of Lessons' from *The Second Part of Musick's Hand-maid* (1689) and the fifth suite from the *Choice Collection* (1696). The Corant and Saraband are identical in the two works, but the 'Almond' of 1689 is replaced by a similar

[25] The last movement of Locke's first suite (*SBK*, vi, No. 7) is unsigned, which according to the preface signifies a piece by William Thatcher; but the whole of the section in which this movement appears is devoted to Locke, and the absence of his initials is probably accidental. Nevertheless there are several instances of composite authorship elsewhere in *Melothesia*.

[26] By Purcell's widow or her advisers. The *Choice Collection* first appeared in 1696.

TABLE 5. *Contents of* 'The Second Book of the Harpsicord Master' *(1700)*

No.[1]	Title and Ascription
*1	Almand by Dr. Blow (G minor)
*2	Sarabrand by Dr. Blow (G minor)
*3	Aire by Dr. Blow (G minor)
4	Almand by Mr. Courtivil (C major)
5	Corrant by Mr. Courtivill (C major)
6	Aire by Mr. Courtivill (C major)
7	The Emperour of Germany's March by Mr. Clark (D major)[2]
8	Serenade by Mr. Clark (D major)
9	The Prince of Denmark's March by Mr. Clark (D major)
10	A Trumpett Minuett by Mr. Clark (C major)[3]
11	A March by Mr. Clark (C major)
12	Aire Mr. Clark (C major)
13	A March (C major)[4]
14	Almand Mr. Barrett (B minor)
15	Corant Mr. Barrett (B minor)
16	Sarabrand Mr. Barrett (B minor)
17	Minuett (B minor; probably by Barrett)
18	Sarabrand (A major)[5]
19	The Catherine A Country Dance (A major)
20	Aire Mr. Barratt (B minor)
21	Aire Mr. Barratt (B minor)
22	Jigg Mr. Barrett (B minor)
23	Almand Mr. Crofts (C minor)[6]
24	Corant Mr. Crofts (C minor)
25	Aire Mr. Crofts (C minor)
26	Mr. Crofts (C minor)

* Printed in *SBK*, v.
[1] Not in source.
[2] Nos. 7–9 in CC, Nos. 16–18.
[3] Nos. 10–12 in CC, Nos. 13–15.
[4] In CC, No. 11.
[5] Nos. 18–19 in CC, Nos. 21–2, where Barrett's authorship is implied.
[6] Nos. 23–5 in CC Nos. 23, 25–6.

though more finely-wrought movement, and the Prelude already discussed is added in the version of 1696. But it is rather curious that the excellent Jigg of 1689 (see Ex. 114) should be dropped, unless it were that Mrs. Purcell was prejudiced against suites of more than four movements. At any rate a most satisfactory composite work could be formed from the 1696 Suite followed by the 1689 Jigg.

The six suites of Blow, which were published in 1698 and 1700,[27] are more varied and, on the whole, more ambitious than those of Purcell. But there is the same element of compilation (three movements had previously appeared in *The Second Part of Musick's Hand-maid*), and there are never more than four movements. A few distinctive features stand out. In the first section of the Almand of the first Suite, in D minor, the melodic line undergoes a striking ascent from the sombre opening on d' to an octave and a fifth higher. The rhythm of the second movement shows a striking departure from that of the usual corant (if indeed this untitled piece is intended as such) in its insistence on the upbeat rhythm. The same rhythm characterises the rondo-form second movement of the second Suite. The first movement of that work is not an almand but a 'Ground' of unusual construction: $A_1 A_2 B_1 B_2 A_3 A_4 B_3 B_4 B_4$. In general, good use is made of the sonorous qualities of the harpsichord, particularly in the use of left-hand octaves, broken or otherwise. The six suites are an important and significant addition to the literature of the harpsichord.

The music of some minor composers may now be considered. Of these, Christopher Gibbons (1615–1676), the son of Orlando Gibbons, is an interesting figure. As in the case of Locke, who died one year later, most of his surviving keyboard music appears to date from the Restoration epoch. He became organist of Westminster Abbey in 1660, relinquishing the post in favour of Albert Bryan in 1666.[28] His double voluntaries[29] resemble those

---

[27] *A Choice Collection* (1698, devoted entirely to Blow); *A Choice Collection of Ayres* (John Young, 1700; see Table 4); *The Second Book of the Harpsicord Master* (I. Walsh, 1700; see Table 5); modern edition in *SBK*, v. A few miscellaneous pieces by Blow remain unpublished; many, however, in *CP*, i, ii.

[28] See *CEKM*, xviii.   [29] *Ibid.*, Nos. 1, 2, 4.

of Blow, whom he may have taught, rather than those of Locke: they are more extravagant in design than the latter's, though he is probably not to be blamed for the optional extended endings which disfigure the first two of these works in the manuscript of Nicholas Harrison.[30] There is little else extant: two single voluntaries, two short dance movements, and an arrangement of a three-part string fantasia. Christopher Gibbons' true strength, indeed, lies in his ensemble rather than his solo instrumental music.

No other minor composer of the time approached the individuality of Christopher Gibbons. The music of Albert Bryan (d. *ca.* 1670) was evidently popular over a long period: he is still represented (as 'A.B.') in an early eighteenth-century manuscript in the hand of Nicholas Harrison (London, Brit. Mus., Add. 34695, ff. 9v–10). This man, though not himself a composer, perhaps had some connection with Westminster Abbey; the volume contains works by four successive organists of the Abbey: Gibbons, Bryan, Blow and Purcell.

Albert Bryan, with Matthew Locke, T. Prat and John Jackson, was also represented in the third edition (1678) of *Musicks Hand-maid*. The first edition (1663) had already included works by Benjamin Sandley, William Lawes, Benjamin Rogers and Matthew Locke,[31] while amongst the four additional pieces of *ca.* 1668 was one by John Moss. Albert Bryan's pieces are grouped as two suites in A minor, while the new contributions from Locke, some arrangements and some not, are arranged as pairs. Though none of the music added in 1678 can rival the music of William Lawes in the melodic strength, the collection in its final form is one of the richest repositories of mid-seventeenth-century keyboard music.

Melothesia (1673) is hardly of less importance. Apart from Locke himself, the composers represented are William Thatcher

---

[30] London, Brit. Mus., Add. 34695. See above, p. 171. Harrison on the other hand includes interesting details of registration which are probably authentic, including left-hand solos for 'sexquialtera'. See above, p. 158.

[31] See above, p. 155. Four psalm-tunes, laid out for keyboard, included in the editions of 1663 and *ca.* 1668, were omitted from that of 1678 (included in *SBK*, xxviii). Additional music by Bryan and Locke in Oxford, Bod. Lib., Mus. Sch. d. 219.

(whose pieces are unsigned), Christopher Preston, John Roberts, William Gregorie, William Hall, Robert Smith, John Banister, J. Mosse (obviously the John Moss just mentioned) and G. Diesner. Banister (1630–1679) and Smith (*ca.* 1648–1675) were, like Locke himself, in the service of Charles II; evidently the volume was compiled mainly from works by Locke's court-musician friends. 'G. Diesner' was Gerhard Diessener, a German violinist who had settled in London.

A somewhat later generation is represented in The *Second Part of Musick's Hand-maid*: apart from Purcell and Blow, William Turner, [Moses] Snow, Francis Forcer and [Richard] Motley. The music by Forcer is identifiable from a manuscript source; that by Motley is inferred from the title of one piece, 'Motley's Maggot'. It also includes pieces by a member of the Verdier family and G. B. Draghi, an Italian musician settled in London.[32] Arrangements of works by foreigners, especially violinists, often found their way into keyboard manuscripts of the period; the 'Segnier Nichola' of Add. 34695 is obviously Nicola Matteis, the most renowned violinist of his day. But the art of arranging had by now ceased to be creative; like the setting of popular tunes it had largely descended to the level of mere hackwork.

A final generation of minor seventeenth-century composers is represented by the contributors to *A Choice Collection of Ayres* published by John Young in 1700, and *The Second Book of the Harpsicord Master* (Walsh, 1700). Apart from Blow, they include F. Piggott, J. Clarke, J. Barrett and W. Crofts [sic]. Their music, however, with that of several of their contemporaries, will be considered in the following two chapters.

[32] See the notes by Dart in *SBK*, xxviii.

X

The Eighteenth Century: Voluntaries and Fugues for the Organ; The Organ Concerto

The eighteenth-century musical scene presents a quite different aspect from that of the last forty years of the seventeenth century. The spirit of adventure is lost; stylistic development comes almost to a standstill. Quite suddenly a change of practice in music publishing comes about. Collections of pieces by different composers cease to occupy a central position; they are superseded by publications devoted to a single composer. The number of composers whose keyboard works were printed in the eighteenth century is vast; the manuscript collection also ceases to be so significant as a source. The earliest editions to present the work of a single composer were the *Choice Collection* by Purcell (1696) and the similarly entitled work of Blow (1698). They were soon followed by such collections as those of Philip Hart (1702, 1704), Jeremiah Clarke (the *Choice Lessons* published posthumously in 1711) and Anthony Young (1719). The last of the old-style collections was probably *The Second Book of the Ladys Banquet*, published in 1706 by Walsh and Hare; subsequent anthologies depended increasingly on inartistic arrangements and settings of popular tunes. However, anthologies of old organ voluntaries were still published late in the century, and the autographs of individual composers begin to be more plentiful.

It is tempting to relate the artistic complacency of eighteenth-century England to the Hanoverian succession and the prosperity and calm which now succeeded two centuries of civil and religious strife. It used to be the fashion to lay the blame for musical decadence on the broad shoulders of Handel; but great as his influence undoubtedly was, there is no particular evidence that his presence snuffed out any native genius. The best of our own composers survive through a distinctive flavour which is experienced as a dressing to the main Handelian dish: Boyce with his sturdy forthright utterance, Stanley and Arne with their melodic distinction. Maurice Greene, older than these, fell more completely under his sway. However, in the field of keyboard music English composers enjoyed a certain advantage: Handel, though he wrote fugues, wrote no voluntaries on the English pattern; and though he wrote suites, he composed virtually no sonatas for keyboard alone. But he was the inventor of the organ concerto as it was known to the English; and this convenient substitute for the standard Corellian 'concerto of seven parts' (*ripieno a 4, concertino a 3*) took the country by storm. Some composers (e.g. Avison of Newcastle) made their works available in either form.

The development of the organ in England in the eighteenth century has often disappointed the enthusiast of the continental instrument. With no pedal-board and relatively few stops, it was a puny affair beside the monsters of Lüneburg or Haarlem. Nevertheless it had its own quiet charm. There were exceptions, such as the large instruments built by Renatus Harris (Salisbury Cathedral, 1710, etc.) and John Snetzler (St. Margaret's Church, King's Lynn, 1754). Harris proposed a six-manual instrument with pedals for St. Paul's in 1712; but his design was not accepted. The commonest addition to the standard two-manual scheme of great and chair (or choir) organs was the echo or swell. The echo organ had originally been placed in a box to give an effect of distance; when in 1712 the swell device was introduced to England by the Abraham Jordans (father and son) it occasionally formed a fourth manual but more commonly replaced the echo organ.[1] In this way it fulfilled a dual function. It also became the natural repository of imitative stops. A pedal board was added at St. Paul's Cathedral in 1720–1, but it seems to have been a primitive affair and few eighteenth-century organs possessed one. It is not clear under what circumstances a pedal part was included in one of Handel's concertos.[2] The downward compass of the great organ was now regularly extended to F_1;

[1] The introduction of the Swell Organ to England is described in Sumner, *The Organ*, pp. 191–3.
[2] See below, p. 204.

in a few cases it descended to C_1. When in the nineteenth century the pedal board became a more regular feature it was the F_1 compass which became standard. Only with the full force of the Bach revival later in the century was this replaced by C compass in both manuals and pedals.

Printed organ music of the eighteenth century made small demands of the instruments available. The voluntaries of Boyce and Stanley do not require the pedals, and rarely descend lower than C; nor do they specify the crescendo and diminuendo of the swell organ. Though Boyce calls for the 'Eccho or Swell', there is nothing in his *Ten Voluntaries* which demands the use of more than two manuals. Most organ music was published as 'for organ or harpsichord'; and much of it is indeed equally suited to the latter instrument.

The principal forms of solo organ music were the fugue and the voluntary. The latter might incorporate a fugue, but not as a matter of course. We have already seen that certain works of Blow were called fugues, at least by the scribes of the early eighteenth century. By later standards these were very irregular examples of the form; but they may be taken as a starting-point of a tradition. Philip Hart's *Fugues for the Organ or Harpsichord: with Lessons for the Harpsichord* was published in 1704 and contains three fugues and three suites; these were the earliest separate fugues to be published in England.[3] Later publications including separate fugues are those of Roseingrave (1728, 1750), Handel (1735) and Burney.

The voluntary was the only completely indigenous form of solo keyboard music in the eighteenth century. In the preceding chapters we have traced the use of the term from the Mulliner Book to Blow. In the Restoration period it usually took the form of a prelude and fugue; or else of a slow followed by a quick fugue. In the eighteenth century the standard pattern was a slow introduction followed by a lively movement in concerto style. A favourite type employed the cornet stop as if it were a solo instrument, while other, imitative, stops were also used. Not infrequently the concertante movement was replaced by a fugue;

[3] Thus anticipating Roseingrave by twenty-four years. In fact, the first fugue has a (detached) prelude. See below, pp. 192–5.

and even a solitary fugue might on occasion be denominated 'voluntary'.[4] There are also voluntaries of three and four movements, for example by Stanley. The great strength of the form lay in its flexibility.

The stylistic transition between the seventeenth and eighteenth centuries may be examined in the work of a group of composers born during the 1670s: John Barrett (*ca.* 1674–*ca.* 1735), Philip Hart (*ca.* 1676–1749), John Reading (1677–1764) and William Croft (1678–1727). To their names may be added that of John James (d. 1745). Much of their music remained popular until towards the end of the eighteenth century, in spite of its somewhat archaic nature. James and Reading are represented in C. and S. Thompson's *Ten Voluntarys* (1767), and James also in Longman and Broderip's *Ten Select Voluntaries* of *ca.* 1780 (CV3). Croft's voluntaries survive mainly in a late eighteenth-century MS. The main sources of Reading's music, however, are autographs at Dulwich and Manchester, while that of Philip Hart is handed down in contemporary and autograph MSS and a contemporary print.[5]

Barrett and Reading were both pupils of Blow. Barrett was a thoroughly minor composer, but a voluntary of his, a 'cornet' voluntary in C, illustrates the problems of ascription and textual criticism which often occur in music of the period. In the earliest source (London, Brit. Mus., Add. 17852) it is anonymous. The second source is a copy by John Reading (London, Dulwich Coll., MS 92d) attributed to 'Mr. Barratt': here numerous alterations are made and a fugal movement, based loosely on the opening theme, is added. Finally the work was published by Benjamin Goodison as part of the 'complete' works of Henry Purcell, *ca.* 1790. All three versions have been printed in modern times: that of Add. 17852 in *TW*, x, as part of a volume devoted to Purcell; the Dulwich version in *TW*, xxi; and Goodison's edition in Purcell's *Collected Works*, vi. There can be little doubt that the work is by Barrett; but the question is which of the two

---

[4] As in Roseingrave's *Voluntarys and Fugues*.

[5] See Appendix II and Johnstone, *MT* (1967) 1003. A six-movement Voluntary by William Hine (1687–1730) was published in his *Harmonia Sacra Glocestriensis* [1731], ed. *RRMBE*, vi.

manuscript versions is the more authentic. As far as the changes in ornamentation and registration, the addition of left-hand octaves, and even adding and subtracting of short phrases in the Dulwich MS are concerned the changes may well be thought to be largely by Reading, since he regularly edited as well as copied his sources. But it is difficult to say whether the fugal movement (retained by Goodison) is also his work: its written appearance certainly suggests Reading, but it too might have been drastically modified. In any case yet another source, from which Reading made his copy, must once have existed, since some at least of the differences between Add. 17852 and Reading's MS must be regarded as corruptions in the former rather than wanton alterations in the latter.

Reading himself is a much more formidable figure. He was organist of Dulwich College, 1700–1702, and, after a period at Lincoln Cathedral, of several London churches in succession. He also seems to have returned to his old post at Dulwich. He was a teacher of the blind organist John Stanley, many of whose voluntaries he copied, possibly from the composer's own dictation. Indeed he is perhaps as important for the copies he made of works by a whole succession of composers, from Blow to Greene and Stanley, as he is as a composer in his own right. His own music strives to extract as much fullness and grandeur from the organ as the instrument of his day would allow; but it is not free from monotony and even pedantry, as can be seen from a Voluntary in G recently printed (*TW*, xxi). This is the work found in *Ten Voluntarys* (C. and S. Thompson, [1767]), where it is prefixed with a short introductory movement.

Much less is known about John James, a turbulent figure who left only scanty written records of his supposedly extravagant style of playing. There is little individuality about the Voluntary in A minor included in *Ten Voluntarys* (partly reprinted in *OEOM*, iii), while it is not certain which of the works in *Ten Select Voluntaries* is actually his. More interesting, in their very different ways, are the organ works of Philip Hart and William Croft.

The organ music of Hart represents a development of Restoration traditions which in fact turned out to be a dead end. In

many ways the composer was an eccentric who seems to antici-
pate Roseingrave, not least in his penchant for fugue and concern
for fullness of sound. There is often a sense of rhythmic urgency
about his writing. But unlike Roseingrave he preserved an old-
fashioned attitude to ornamentation, which, if Hawkins is to be
believed, even his contemporaries found excessive.[6] These
qualities are all present in his published fugues of 1704. The first
of these, in A major, has, as has been said, a prelude, a simple
arpeggiando affair of a dozen or so bars. The third, in F, exhibits
a fanfare style of fugue subject which was beginning to be
popular:

The second, in C minor, is elegiac in character and is the most
interesting of the set. It will be noticed that every note of the
subject after the first two is provided with an ornament:

The first and third of the set are also in the Nicholas Harrison
manuscript which has been discussed in Chapter IX.[7] The same

6 Cited by Dawes, *PRMA* (1967–8) 63.
7 London, Brit. Mus., 34695. See above, p. 171.

source also preserves a C major fugue similar in character to the F major work (see Ex. 117 above). But by far the most interesting of all the composer's surviving works is the G major prelude and fugue from Add. 32161 (ff. 84v–87r). The part of the manuscript containing this work was originally completely separate from the rest; and it is almost certainly in Hart's own handwriting. It is written on eight pages of manuscript, the outer pages having originally been left blank and the inner pages numbered 1–6. The first page has remained blank, but on the last a later hand has scribbled a fugal sketch of a kind found elsewhere in the manuscript. The work is entitled 'A Lesson for the Organ by Phil: Hart', but it is actually a prelude and fugue. In it his mannerisms are found to excess. The prelude employs arpeggiando passages which are written out in full and marked 'Twice' or 'Thrice'. The opening, transcribed as closely as possible from the manuscript, will illustrate this:

The opening of the fugue will again illustrate his love of ornamentation and his concern for fullness of sound:

The meaning of the sign ⤙ is not clear, since Hart retains the old English signs for shake (≠) and beat (∿). It is possible that it refers to a forefall and beat, formerly written ↗∿. The fugue may be played twice (there are very complex directions for first- and second-time bars) followed by a passage marked 'Adagio to end'. This must be quoted in full:

Ex. 121 Adagio to End — Philip Hart

This splendid work gave promise of many fine things to come: a promise which unhappily remained unfulfilled.

The case of Croft is very different. If the voluntaries attributed to him are genuine, it was he who inaugurated the eighteenth-century tradition. The external evidence is slight. Add. 5336 contains a set of twelve voluntaries anonymously and in a late eighteenth-century hand. In the catalogue of manuscript music at the British Museum by Hughes-Hughes, these works are marked 'said to be by Dr. William Croft'. Whatever the justification for the tradition may be, it is to some extent supported by the style, which is similar to that of the organ solos in Croft's anthems. The scribe has obviously modified the ornament-signs; but his transcription is very clear and competent. The first two works[8] are in two linked sections, 'Slow' and 'faster', in the Restoration tradition. Nos. 4 and 8 are single slow movements; Nos, 5, 6, 7 and 9 are single fugues. The remainder are in two movements in the later manner. A thirteenth work, also in a late eighteenth-century hand, is a slow movement and is ascribed to Croft.[9] Formally, these works are exactly what one would expect of a transitional figure. Stylistically, however, they are far removed in their simple dignity from the frenzied utterances of Philip Hart. Their calm, majestic idiom might be called Handelian, but there is an indefinably English quality about the writing which, admittedly, Handel sometimes came near to achieving. Without recalling any of Purcell's actual organ music, a movement such as the following, from the third voluntary, has a distinctly Purcellian flavour about it:

Ex. 122

[8] Voluntary No. 1 is printed in *OEOM*, i. 4.

[9] London, Brit. Mus., Add. 31814. Croft's authorship of Nos. 7, 9 and 10 of the set of twelve is confirmed by their appearance in John Reading's MSS at Dulwich College (MSS 92a, 92b, 92d) and Manchester (Henry Watson Lib., BRm. 7105. Rf. 31), where they are ascribed to him (information kindly communicated by Mr. Barry Cooper).

The alternation between the trumpet and cremona stops suggests a dialogue between orchestral trumpets and oboes. Whether the effect is sublime or comic depends entirely upon the quality and tuning of the stops themselves. The left-hand solo of the eleventh voluntary is an old device adapted to the simpler rhythmic style of the eighteenth century; the technique, however, was not destined to survive. In the introduction to the final voluntary, however, there is a true Handelian dignity:

Ex. 123   [Croft]

Croft's use of keys is very limited; there is nothing outside a signature of two flats or two sharps. The next important composer of voluntaries, Maurice Greene (*ca.* 1695–1755) was more adventurous. His *Twelve Voluntarys,* published posthumously by J. Bland in about 1780, venture as far afield as F minor (with three flats) and E major. There is the question as to whether these voluntaries are in fact by Boyce. However, they seem different in style from those published under his name: they have more charm and are less academic. Greene's work also appeared in Reading's MSS and in several late eighteenth-century collections: *A Collection of Voluntaries . . . by Dr. Green, Mr. Travers & Several other Eminent Masters* (Longman, *ca.* 1780) and its sequels *Ten Select Voluntaries . . . by Mr. Handel, Dr. Green etc.* and *Ten Select Voluntaries . . . Book IIId* (a fourth book does not refer to Greene on the title-page). There was also *Ten Voluntarys . . . by Dr. Green, Skinner, Stubley, James, Reading, Selby and Kuknan* [sic] published by C. and S. Thompson in 1767. Only in the last of these printed sources, however, is Greene's contribution speci-

fied, and even in this case the first of the two works concerned is
clearly made up of unrelated movements. So it is difficult, if not
impossible, to establish a canon of Greene's voluntaries.[10]

Assuming the twelve voluntaries published by Bland to be
genuine works, it was Greene who established the two-movement
pattern as the norm, and who first applied the concerto style to
the voluntary. The Allegro of the C minor voluntary shows how
well he had assimilated the Italian style:

His delicate sensibility may be illustrated by the opening of the
A major voluntary:

---

[10] See Mann, *MT* (1901) 529 and the edition by P. Williams (addenda to
Bibliography s.v. Boyce). The two voluntaries by Greene in TV printed
TW, xv, Nos. 1–2 (with the mistaken implication that they are from
Greene's own *Twelve Voluntarys*); the first two movements of the first of
these in *EOM*, xviii, as 'Voluntary XIII'.

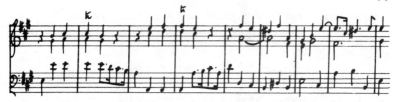

In a more scholastic mood is the fugue of the F minor work, with some passages of extreme chromaticism:

We may next be concerned with William Boyce (1710–1779), as Greene's pupil and putative composer of the latter's *Twelve Voluntarys*. But as has been said, the set of ten published post-humously under his own name (by S. A. and P. Thompson) is of a distinctly more academic nature. There is a return to the more circumscribed key-range of Croft; the style, too, is less varied. Nos. 1, 3, 5 and 6 are trumpet voluntaries; No. 2 uses the 'vox humane' and No. 4 the cornet as solo stops. Nos. 7–10 are pre-ludes and fugues. Nevertheless one should not underestimate the sterling qualities of this music. The deceptively simple introduc-tions nearly all embody a natural rise and fall of melody in the shape of an arch. There is an intellectually satisfying quality about the form of the concertante and fugal movements. In No. 1, for example, the shortened and modified return of the main section conveys the effect of a recapitulation while re-taining scarcely four bars of the original. In the final work the second subject of the 'Double Fuge' is skilfully modified on its second and subsequent appearances to meet the exigencies of the counterpoint; this is fugue prior to its ossification in the school-room:[11]

Ex. 127   Boyce

John Stanley (1713–1786) was another pupil of Greene. Unlike Greene and Boyce he achieved the distinction of having his thirty voluntaries, Opp. 5, 6 and 7, published during his lifetime. Though blind, he seems to have enjoyed the services of a skilled amanuensis and his publications are remarkably free of error. He wrote in all the styles so far discussed, and may well have introduced the three- and four-movement forms. Particularly notable is Op. 5, No. 8 in D minor, a three-movement work in Italian concerto style. A three-manual instrument is really necessary in the first movement: great organ for the tutti passages, marked 'Full Organ'; choir organ for the solos ('Stopt Diapason or Flute') and 'Eccho' organ (or swell) for the accompaniments to the solos, which the former often overlap in pitch. The slow movement is assigned to the swell, and its richly expressive chordal writing would undoubtedly benefit from crescendo and diminuendo:

[11] The voluntaries of Boyce are now published in facsimile by Oxford University Press. An eleventh work appeared in *Ten Select Voluntaries* . . . *Book IIId*, but cannot be identified with certainty. For other editions, see Bibliography, s.v. Boyce.

In the finale, exhilarating tutti-solo contrasts are heard in a fugal context.[12]

Stanley's three sets, though undated in the original editions, have been assigned to the years 1748, 1752 and 1754. Maurice Greene died in 1755. Though the date of composition of Boyce's voluntaries is unknown, it would appear that they are not late works and that the finest achievements in this field were over by 1755.

Of the minor composers belonging to this earlier generation the most important is Thomas Roseingrave (1690–1766). A dictionary of 1827, doubtless recalling contemporary opinion, described his playing as 'harsh and disgusting'.[13] Though he was an eccentric there is nothing unprofessional about his published music. In his fugal writing he often, like Philip Hart, felt the need to fill out the strict contrapuntal texture with extra notes. A 'Voluntary and Fugue' in F minor from his first set (1728) may be taken as representative of his style.[14] The Voluntary, though numbered as a separate work, is in fact an introduction, ending on an imperfect cadence, to the fugue which follows. A short passage from the latter will illustrate his fondness for remote keys:

[12] The three books have been edited in facsimile by Oxford University Press. Passages in C clefs in the original, however, have been changed to G or F clefs. Complete modern edition in *TW*, xxvii–xxix.

[13] Cited by P. Williams, *SBK*, xviii. Another selection is in *PSMS*, ii.

[14] *Ibid.*, No. 1 (= Nos. 2 and 3 of the 1728 edition).

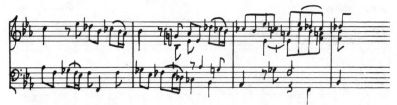

The modulation itself is not particularly daring—it is no further from F minor to A flat minor than from A minor to C minor—but the key of A flat minor is itself remote, and must have sounded intolerable in mean-tone tuning.[15] This, together with such things as the unresolved $^6_4$ in bar 3 of the quotation, no doubt gave rise to the epithet 'disgusting'. The *Six Double Fugues* of 1750 were probably inspired by Handel's *Six Voluntaries or Fugues,* published by Walsh in 1735, two of which are also double fugues.[16] They certainly have a degree of Handelian breadth and are less chromatic than the earlier works.

John Travers (*ca.* 1703–1758) is another interesting figure. His *XII Voluntaries* were published posthumously in 1769, and he was represented in Longman's *A Collection of Voluntaries . . . Book I,* though his contribution to the latter cannot now be identified with certainty. His music is tuneful and decorative, though occasionally an archaic style or massive chordal writing are essayed:[17]

Ex. 130

15 An organ with 'quarter notes' (split keys to distinguish between D sharp and E flat, G sharp and A flat) such as was built for the Temple Church by Bernard Smith in 1668, would have been better equipped to play in F minor.

16 Printed *TW,* xii. These works appear in a manuscript of *ca.* 1720 which also contains versions of movements from the eight suites (*Pièces de Clavecin*) published in that year (London, Brit. Mus., R.M. 20. g. 4). Two of Handel's fugues are found in his *Concerti grossi,* Op. 3, and it is possible that the keyboard versions are the originals. The voluntaries attributed to Handel in CV2, CV4 are spurious (some printed in *TW,* xix). See Johnstone, *op. cit.*

17 *XII Voluntaries,* No. 10. No. 12 is in *TW,* xxii.

Amongst a vast number of later eighteenth-century composers a very few stand out as having some originality. The voluntaries of William Walond (1725–1770) were published *ca.* 1752 (Op. 1) and 1758 (Op. 2), while the only known set by John Bennett (1735–1784) also appeared in 1758. Bennett succeeded Charles Burney as organist of St. Dionis Backchurch in 1752, and was widely known as a virtuoso. His voluntaries are conceived on a large scale, and he had a predilection for running passages shared between the hands. Walond appears to have been the first to specify *crescendo* and *diminuendo* in organ music.[18] Charles Burney himself (1726–1814) as might be expected, represents the more academic approach, while estimable work was also produced by such men as John Alcock (1715–1806) and Thomas Sanders Dupuis (1733–1796).[19] But the majority of the pieces published between 1760 and 1800 alternate between the sentimental and the meretricious. Only with the arrival of the Wesleys, and in particular Samuel (1766–1837) was a genuinely new voice heard in English keyboard music. The organ concertos of his brother Charles Wesley (1757–1834) were composed during the 1770s and will be considered later in this chapter. However, the organ music of Samuel Wesley belongs mainly to the nineteenth century and will be deferred until the final chapter.

The organ concerto was apparently the personal invention of Handel. As is well known, these works were intended as interludes between the acts of his oratorios. Research has not yet allotted each concerto to its particular oratorio. The standard Corellian concerto grosso had been introduced to England in 1715,[20] and Hutchings is undoubtedly right in regarding the

[18] Voluntaries by Bennett in *EOM*, xv; *RRMBE*, vi. Walond: *TW*, i, xx, xxxii; *RRMBE*, vi.

[19] Pieces by Burney in *OEOM*, i, iv; by Alcock in *TW*, xxiii; by Dupuis in *TW*, xxii; *OEOM*, iii, iv. [20] Rinaldi, *Arcangelo Corelli*, Milan, 1953, p. 317.

organ concerto as initially a counterpart to this form.[21] Handel
was happy to write for concertino strings instead when opportunity arose and time permitted, as in the glorious work
intended for 'Alexander's Feast'; and some of the other orchestral
concertos had a similar origin. But an organ concerto was a
convenient alternative, since the solos could be improvised by
Handel himself. Even in their published form many of the concertos still required improvised episodes and even whole movements, which are not to be regarded as 'cadenzas' in the later
sense. It is also true that many of their movements are derived
from earlier works such as the harpsichord suites and recorder
sonatas.[22] Op. 4 was published in 1738 and Op. 7 posthumously
in 1761. A *Second Set*, consisting mostly of arrangements, appeared in 1740, while Arnold brought out a final collection in
1797.[23] Op. 7, No. 1 is unique in having a pedal part. Since these
works were intended for the theatre organ it is unlikely that there
is any connection here with Handel's known familiarity with the
St. Paul's Cathedral organ.[24] Nor is it likely that the movements
concerned emanated from his continental period; the organ
concerto is not known to have existed before the production of
'Esther' in 1732. Somewhere in England (or Ireland) a theatre
organ with pedals almost certainly existed.

Though Handel's concertos were published as for organ or
harpsichord there is no doubt that they were originally intended
for the former instrument.[25] The harpsichord would have been
too weak for the large theatres and halls in which they were
played. But some of his English followers may have meant the
alternative quite seriously, their works being suitable for both

[21] *The Baroque Concerto*, p. 204.

[22] E.g. Op. 4, No. 3/iv from Op. 1, No. 2/iv (Recorder Sonata in G minor),
also utilised for the finale of Op. 7, No. 5; Op. 4, No. 5 from Op. 1, No. 11
(Recorder Sonata in F major); Op. 7, No. 4/iii from Harpsichord Suite No. 3
in D minor, last movement. The *Second Set* is derived mainly from Op. 6.

[23] For modern editions see Bibliography, s.v. Handel. Of the *Second Set*,
only the first two ever had an orchestral accompaniment. For a thorough
examination of all the concertos see Nielsen, *Dansk Aarbog for Musik
Forskning* (1963) 3.

[24] Sumner, *The Organ*, p. 183.

[25] Op. 4, No. 6, however, was originally written for the harp.

large and small halls. There are also a number of works from later in the century which do not mention the organ at all and were intended for the harpsichord (or indeed the pianoforte) in the first instance.

The concertos of Thomas Augustine Arne (1710–1778) enjoyed great popularity, but they were not published until *ca.* 1787 (in parts). They include many movements for solo organ which are amongst his most attractive pieces. The Bath composer Thomas Chilcot (d. 1766) had already published two sets, in 1756 and 1765 respectively. Still earlier, Charles Avison of Newcastle (1709–1770) had published a concerto in 1742, and soon after arranged his string concertos Op. 2 and Op. 4 for organ or harpsichord.[26] Other composers included Philip Hayes (1738–1797) and the prolific William Felton (1715–1769), whose thirty-two concertos appeared between 1744 and 1762. An attractive set of six was published by John Stanley in 1775 (Op. 10). Amongst works intended for harpsichord, pianoforte, or either, we may note *Three concerto's for the harpsichord . . . Opera XV* by Samuel Arnold (1740–1802), published in 1782; *A favorite concerto for the harpsichord or pianoforte . . . Op. 7* by Robert Broderip (1758–1808), published *ca.* 1785; and a work by John Worgan published at about the same time. James Hook, organist of Vauxhall Gardens from 1774 to 1820, published fifteen keyboard concertos.[27]

The most interesting works of this kind are undoubtedly the keyboard concertos of Charles Wesley. Fourteen such works survive, but there is evidence that the original total was at least seventeen and probably eighteen (three sets of six). One autograph score (London, Brit. Mus., Add. 35018) contains full scores of a Concerto in D, originally composed in 1775 but revised in 1780; of a Concerto in E flat described as 'Concerto 5th First Set'; and six concertos forming a 'third set' dated 1778. Another autograph (London, R.C.M. MS 4023), on the other hand, has a 'second set' of six, signed at the end 'C. Wesley April 7th 1776'. The first movement of the first Concerto of this set, written as an afterthought on a separate leaf, is marked '2d

26 See Appendix II.
27 Edwards, *PRMA* (1968–9) 3. See also Appendix II.

opera'. This is probably a mistake, for the works actually printed in parts as 'Opera IId' are the first, third, sixth, fourth and fifth of the third set, followed by the fifth of the first set. This is the publication described in a recent account of the composer's works[28] as 'Op. 2a' and dated approximately 1780. However, a note in Add. 35018, f. 59v, seems to suggest that they were already in print in 1778.[29] Date of publication apart, there is evidence of extreme rapidity of composition. All the surviving works can be placed with confidence in the years 1775 to 1778.

One of the most fascinating aspects of these works is their orchestration. In the printed publication this is described as being for oboes, horns and strings; but this is an over-simplification. Set 1 No. 5 (Op. 2 No. 6) calls for flutes as well as oboes and horns, while Set 3 No. 4 (Op. 2 No. 4) requires 'fagotti solo', indicated in the autograph full score on the viola staff. On the other hand only Set 2 No. 6 (not printed) requires trumpets and drums. But the interest of the orchestration does not lie solely in the instruments employed; a happy device is the mingling of muted violins with pizzicato lower strings and the organ oboe stop:

Ex. 131 Andante — Vn. I & II con sordini — Charles Wesley (Concerto Set 2 No. 4)

[28] *MGG*, s.v. Wesley.
[29] This reads: 'Cha. Wesley London 1778. NB The First, Third, Fourth, Fifth, and Sixth of this Set are in Print, also the Fifth of the 1st Set'.

Even more imaginative is the following variant, with divided violas:

The 'March Pomposo' from the fifth concerto of the first set (Op. 2 No. 6) begins with wind only as follows:

In this movement, which is a set of variations, the third variation is marked 'Cembalo Harp Stop', although in the manuscript
the work is clearly designated as an organ concerto. It is not
impossible that some of these concertos were designed to be
played on a claviorgan. The printed edition describes them as
being for organ or harpsichord, and this is true also of some of
those in Set 2. What is perhaps curious is that none of them are
for pianoforte. Compared with the continental keyboard concerto, they are decidedly old-fashioned works, with their semi-
baroque formal features and their long 'Handelian' solo passages
and even indications for *ad libitum* episodes and movements.
But for idiomatic writing for pianoforte in the context of large-
scale 'symphonic' structure in a British concerto, we have to
wait for the arrival on the scene of John Field; and by that time
the classical style has been by-passed in favour of romanticism.

XI

The Eighteenth Century: Suites and Lessons for the Harpsichord

For the first two or three decades of the century fashions in domestic keyboard instruments remained much as they had in the last forty years of the seventeenth century. Towards 1730, however, double-manual harpsichords were being made by English craftsmen, and examples have survived by Thomas Hitchcock (the younger) and Francis Coston.[1] The normal harpsichord compass was from F_1, but the instrument by Hitchcock, who was primarily a maker of spinets, has the eighteenth-century spinet compass of five octaves chromatic from G_1 (sixty-one keys). The Coston instrument has five octaves chromatic from F_1, but most eighteenth-century harpsichords lacked F_1 # (sixty keys). There are two 8-foot stops and one 4-foot, the upper manual 8-foot being also available on the lower without the assistance of a coupler, an arrangement which became standard on English harpsichords.

From about 1730 English harpsichord making was dominated by two foreigners, Shudi and Kirkman. Burkat Shudi, of Swiss birth, was making harpsichords on his own account from 1729 at the latest. In 1761 he took into partnership John Broadwood, who became the head of the firm on Shudi's retirement in 1771. The normal specification of Shudi's instruments is as shown above, the upper manual 8-foot stop being a lute. A harp stop was generally added after 1760,[2] and from 1765 a 'machine' stop for multiple changes. A venetian-blind swell mechanism

[1] Russell, *The Harpsichord and Clavichord*, pp. 74–5, from whom the following account is largely taken.

[2] Harp effects were possible on earlier instruments by drawing the upper-manual eight-foot and lute, and playing on the lower manual. The former, being playable from the lower manual, will sound, but damped by the dampers of the lute jacks. *Ibid.*, p. 75.

was patented in 1769, operated by foot. A few late instruments had a 5½ octave compass descending to C_1.

The Alsatian Jacob Kirkman set up his own business in 1738. He died in 1792, the firm being taken over by his nephew Abraham, and when the latter died two years later by Abraham's son Joseph. The specifications of his harpsichords are similar to those of Shudi, and later instruments often incorporated the harp stop, the machine stop and the venetian swell.

Between them, Shudi and Kirkman and the firms they founded account for by far the majority of surviving harpsichords made in England between 1730 and 1800; and many of their standard features have been incorporated into modern harpsichord designs. It must be emphasised, however, that their elaboration goes far beyond the requirements of English solo harpsichord music of the period. But it is possible to understand the popularity of these instruments. Something was needed to rival the strength of tone and expressive powers of the organ, and in the later years of the century the pianoforte. These were the harpsichords on which organ voluntaries and even organ concertos could be played. The venetian swell provided a counterpart both to the swell organ and to the pianoforte. With their bright and deep tone they could command attention even in large halls. Nevertheless even this noble instrument eventually succumbed to the change in musical fashions which was responsible for the pianoforte.

Most English harpsichord music could be played quite adequately on the spinet. The firm of Hitchcock included Thomas the elder, a spinet of whom is dated 1660; Thomas the younger (a harpsichord by whom has already been described) and John, who died in 1774. In the eighteenth-century instruments the short octave to G_1 is replaced by a fully chromatic bass and the total compass extended to five octaves. This is musically more useful than the standard harpsichord compass, and it may be noted that it is exactly what is required for the performance of Scarlatti's mature sonatas, which became extremely popular in England. Several of them require top $f'''\#$ and g'''.

The chamber organ continued in popularity throughout the eighteenth century.[3] In 1720 the Duke of Chandos possessed at

[3] Wilson, M., *The English Chamber Organ.*

Cannons a three-manual chamber organ with eighteen stops.[4] Claviorgans (combined harpsichords and organs) continued to be made, and an interesting one by Kirkman and Snetzler has survived.[5]

The clavichord seems not to have been made in England in the eighteenth century, but instruments were occasionally imported from Germany, including some from the Hass workshop in Hamburg. On the other hand pianofortes were made from the late 1760s. They were destined to oust the harpsichord, but not until after a prolonged battle lasting some thirty years. Haydn directed his London symphonies from the pianoforte in 1791–2 and 1794–5. His last three pianoforte sonatas, moreover, were written in London in 1794–5 and dedicated to the London performer Therese Jansen (later Bartolozzi). They require the compass F_1 (including also G_1 flat) to a''', while the first of them, in C major, has two passages marked 'pp open Pedal'. Here the dampers are temporarily lifted while the harmonies change, creating a blurred effect. It must be remembered that the sustaining power of the early pianoforte was limited, and that Beethoven found it possible to mark the whole of the first movement of his Sonata in C sharp minor, Op. 27 No. 2 'senza sordini'. The dampers on early instruments were operated by stop handles rather than by pedals.

John Burton's *Ten Sonatas for the Harpsichord, Organ or Pianoforte* were published in 1766, while the instrument is first mentioned alone in some title-pages of the following decade. But a true pianoforte style is hardly to be found in British music prior to the work of Pinto and Field (see Chapter XII).

The production of solo keyboard music other than for organ is very uneven during the eighteenth century. During the first twenty years composers continued to cultivate the suite, which developed little from the Purcellian model. In 1720 Handel's first set of suites was published by Walsh. These not very mature works found few imitators, and the English seem to have been intimidated by the Handelian virtuosity. Nevertheless his influence is present, though in a general sense, in the most

4 Russell, *op. cit.*, p. 75.
5 *Ibid.*, p. 83.

TABLE 6. *Contents of* 'The Third Book of the Harpsicord Master'
(*1702*)

No.[1]	Title and Ascription	No.[1]	Title and Ascription
1	The Kings March by Mr. Clark (D major)	11	Minuett (A major)
2	Minuett by Mr. Clark (D major)	12	Minuet by Mr. Barrett (C minor)
3	A Trip to Case-horten by Mr. Clark (D major)	13	Song tune by Mr. Crofts (G minor)
4	Round O Minuett by Mr. Clark (F major)	14	Aire by Mr. Crofts (G minor)
5	A Farewell by Mr. Clark (F minor)	15	Scotch tune by Mr. Crofts (G major)
6	Aire by Mr. Clark (F minor)	16	Minuet (G minor)
7	Hornpipe by Mr. Clark (F minor)	17	Aire by Mr. Crofts (D major)
8	Maggett by Mr. Wood (E minor)	18	Scotch Aire (G major)
9	Gavott by Mr. Clark (F minor)	19	The English Paspy (G major)
		20	Round O (G major)
10	The Pilgrim by Mr. Barrett (A major)	21	Minuett Madam Subligny (G minor)
		22	Jigg (G minor)
		23	Aire Slow (A minor)
		24	Round O (A minor)

[1] Not in source.

TABLE 7. *Contents of* 'The Ladys Banquet' (*1704*)

No.[1]	Title and Ascription	Page
1	A new Cebell by Mr. Ier. Clarke (D major)	2
2	A new Scotch Tune by Mr. Ier Clarke (E flat major)	3
3	Mdm. Subligny's Iigg by Mr. Ier. Clarke (A major)	4
4	Minuett by Mr. Ier. Clarke (F major)	5
5	A trip to Berry by Mr. Ier Clarke (F major)	6
6	Prince Eugenes March by Mr. Ier. Clarke (D major)	7
7	King James Farewell by Mr. Ier Clarke (F major)	8
8	Cebell by Mr. King (G major)	9

Table 7 (*contd.*)

No.[1]	Title and Ascription	Page
9	A paspie by Mr. King (G major)	10–11
10	The Duke of Ormonds March by Mr. Croft (D major)	12
11	Trumpet Tune by Mr. Croft (D major)	13
12	Scotch tune in the Funeral by Mr. Croft (F major)	14
13	Air by Mr. Croft (F major)	15
14	Iigg by Mr. Croft (F major)	16
15	Saraband by Mr. Barrett (D minor)	17
16	Almand by Mr Barrett (D minor)	18–19
17	An Air (D minor)	19
18	Corrant by Mr. Barrett (D minor)	20
19	Iigg by Mr. Barrett (D minor)	21
20	Almand by Mr. Weldon (F major)	22
21	Corrant by Mr. Weldon (F major)	23
22	Minuet by Mr. Weldon (F major)[2]	24
23	Almand by Mr. Courtiville (G major)	26
24	Courant (G major)	26–27
25	Sarabrand by Mr. Courtiville (G major)	27

[1] Not in source.

[2] Incomplete (or a piece missing), page 27 having been printed again instead of page 25.

TABLE 8. *Contents of* 'The Second Book of The Ladys Banquet'
(*1706*)

No.[1]	Title and Ascription	Page
1	The Marlborough (C major)	1
2	The Royall (F major)	2
3	The Spanheim (A minor)	3
4	Minuett Round O (C major)	3
5	Aymable Vainqueur (F major)	4
6	Du Ruels Dutch Scipper (D major)	5
7	Minuet (A major)[2]	6
8	New Minuett (A major)	6

Table 8 (*contd.*)

No.[1]	Title and Ascription	Page
9	Baloons Iigg (F minor)	7
10	Bath Minuett (B flat major)	8
11	Minuett (C minor)	8
12	Gavott (C minor)	9
13	Minuett (G minor)	9
14	Iigg (G minor)	10
15	Tunbridge Minuett (G minor)	10
16	Minuett Round O (G major)	11
17	Hornpipe (C major)	11
	This following Sett by Mr. Barret[3]	
18	Allmand (D major)	12
19	Aire (D major)	13
20	Iigg (D major)	13
21	Gavott Round O (D major)	14
22	Minuett (D major)	14
	This following Set by Mr. H. Purcell[4]	
23	Aire (D minor)	15
24	Aire (D minor)	15
25	Iigg (G minor)	16

[1] Not in source. Nos. 1–17 were repeated in LE3 in a different order.
[2] Not in table of contents.
[3] This title not in table of contents.
[4] This title not in table of contents. These 3 pieces printed in *SBK*, xxii.

TABLE 9. *Contents of* 'The Ladys Entertainment' (*1708*)

No.[1]	Title and Ascription	Page
1	A Prelude (G minor)	1
2	Can you leave Ranging	2
3	Ever merry gay and Ayry	3
4	Never let your Heart	4
5	What shou'd Allarme me[2]	4
6	Tocata del Signr. Amadori (G major)	5

Table 9 (*contd.*)

[1] Not in source.
[2] Not the same version as LE2, No. 13.

TABLE 10. *Contents of* 'The 2d Book of the Ladys Entertainment'
(*1708*)

No.[1]	Title and Ascription	Page
	a set of lessons for the Harpsichord composed by the late Mr. Henr. Hall of Hereford (D minor)[3]	
7	Allmand	9
8	Corrant	10
9	Gavot	11
10	Minuet	12
11	Jigg	12
12	Tocata	13
13	What should allarm me	14
14	Gavot (F major)	15
15	Saraband (F major)[4]	15
16	Allmand ⎫ by Mr. Richardson of Winton (F major)	16
17	Saraband ⎭	
18	Tocata by Mr. D. Purcell	17
19	Strike me Fate	18
20	A while tho Conquest	19
21	Pleasure calls	20
22	Since in vain	21
23	In vain is delay	22
24	Gently treat my sorrow	24

[1] Not in source.
[2] *Il Trionfo di Camilla,* by G. or M. A. Bononcini. Not from the opera by Leo, as *RISM* seems to assume.
[3] Ending with the 'Tocata', No. 12 (or perhaps the 'Jigg', No. 11).
[4] Thus in index, but 'Minuet' on p. 15.

important native product of the mid-century, the eight sonatas of Thomas Augustine Arne, which were advertised in 1756. After that, little of significance appeared until the end of the century. More interesting than the numerous second-rate works for keyboard alone are those which included *ad libitum* string parts, resulting in what are in effect primitive violin sonatas, piano trios and even piano quartets.

In 1697 Walsh advertised a volume entitled *The Harpsicord Master*, but no copy survives. The Royal College of Music, however, possesses the second and third books, published in 1700 and 1702 respectively. Also in 1700 appeared *A Choice Collection of Ayres,* published by John Young. Between them these volumes preserve a repertory of suites and miscellaneous pieces by Blow, Courteville, Clarke, Barrett, Croft and Piggott. The 'other masters' referred to in the 1702 title-page are anonymous except for a 'Mr. Wood'. Even this *Third Book* already evinces a deterioration in style, which is carried a stage further in the two books of *The Ladies Banquet* (1704 and 1706). Here the craze for theatrical novelty eclipses the suite as a serious form, which must henceforth be studied in the individual publications of Philip Hart (1704), Jeremiah Clarke (1711) and Anthony Young (1719).[6]

Clarke himself does not appear to best advantage in the collections of 1700 and 1702. His famous 'Prince of Denmark's March', still widely known in perverted form as a 'Trumpet Voluntary' for organ, appears both in *A Choice Collection of Ayres* and in *The Second Book of the Harpsicord Master*. While its original conception as a harpsichord or spinet piece in 'Round O' form is now generally known to the scholarly world,[7] it is less well known that it is the third movement of a set of pieces in D major of which the first two are 'The Emperour of Germanys March' and 'The Serenade', which precede it in each of the two publications mentioned. Though an early owner of *A Choice Collection of Ayres* was moved to bestow on 'The Serenade' the epithet 'remarkable', the whole cannot be said to do full justice to Clarke as a composer; it does, however, exhibit a charming gift for melody. The same comments could be made of a suite in C consisting of 'A Trumpett Minuett', 'A March' and 'An Ayre', which also appears in both collections.

Apart from Blow, who has already been discussed, it is Piggott, Barrett, Courtivill and Croft who appear as suite-writers in these collections. The thoroughly anglicised violin-virtuoso Courtivill (originally Courteville) provides an Almand, Corrant

---

[6] For contents of printed collections, see Tables 3–10. See also Appendix II. Music by Croft in *CP*, iii, iv (12 suites); by Clarke in *CP*, v; by Piggott, Barrett and others in *CP*, vi, vii.

[7] Cudworth, *MT* (1953) 401. 'Round O' = rondo, including simple ternary movements.

and Aire in C for *The Second Book of the Harpsicord Master*. To the same volume Barrett contributes a seven-movement suite in B minor, the last three movements separated from the first four by two pieces in A major. These two also prove to be by Barrett, since they are the last two of a four-movement 'Set of Ayers' by him in *A Choice Collection*. The third of these four, a 'Sarabrand', shows Barrett, like Clarke, moving away from the conventional figuration associated with such movements:

Ex. 134 Sarabrand — John Barrett

The fourth movement, 'The St. Catherine' (in *The Second Book of the Harpsicord Master* called 'The Catherine a Country Dance') was dismissed by that critic who found Clarke's 'Serenade' 'remarkable' as 'Airy tautology':

Ex. 135 The St. Catherine — John Barrett

Piggott also composed a seven-movement suite (*A Choice Collection*) but he was not so adventurous stylistically as Barrett. His Prelude is hardly an advance on Locke, while the eighteenth-century pundit who found the Almand 'near to Handel' was sadly astray. Though his seven movements are uninterrupted he places his 'Iigg' fifth (in Barrett this movement is last) and follows it with a March and Minuet.

Croft was a finer composer than any of these: and his serious mood is conveyed to admirable effect in the two 'sets' in *A Choice Collection*, in C minor and E minor respectively. The first of these has come down to us in a slightly different form in *The Second Book of the Harpsicord Master*. The following table sets out the relationship between the two:

Choice Collection	Second Book
Almand	= Almand
Sarabrand	
Corant	= [Corant]
[Aire]	= Aire
	[Minuet]

It would seem justifiable to reconstruct a five-movement suite out of the two versions. The Sarabrand deserves quotation in full: it is a remarkable instance of profound feeling compressed into a little space:

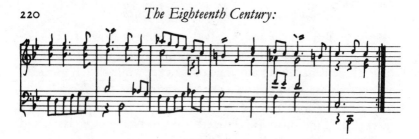

The annoying syncopated mannerisms of the earlier generation are completely superseded. The movement called 'Aire' is in reality a rather serious hornpipe, as the rhythm of the opening shows:

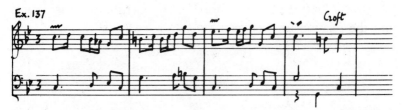

The suites of Philip Hart, published in 1704 with three of his fugues (see above, p. 190) are disappointingly conventional compared with his organ music. The three suites, in C major, A minor and A major respectively, each have three movements. In addition, there is a D minor Ground of no very great originality.

The *Choice Lessons* of Jeremiah Clarke, on the other hand, show a side of his personality hardly evident in the collections of 1700 and 1702. Published in 1711, four years after his suicide, they represent his own personal choice of compositions as finally revised by him for publication (if Charles King's title-page is to be trusted). This rare and elegant volume is also a fine example of the engraver's art. Numerous blank pages obviate the necessity of page-turning during a movement.[8] Of its six suites, only the fifth, in seven movements, is a slight disappointment; a purely haphazard collection of pieces follows the third movement, 'A Iigg'. But the general level is astonishingly high. The very first piece, 'A Ground' in G major, has a sober dignity. Two quota-

[8] Blank pages also occur, apparently for this purpose, in the second and third books of *The Harpsicord Master*.

tions will illustrate the range of his art. From the Almand of the fourth suite, in C minor, the beginning of the second half, though conventional enough on the surface, is a singularly eloquent presentation of a commonplace sequence of modulations:

At the other end of the scale the following 'Iigg' in A major illustrates a straightforward rhythm and a modern use of imitation and motivic development:

On this showing, Clarke emerges as the most seriously under-estimated *petit-maître* of his generation. But his suites were already unfashionable when they were finally published. Only Anthony Young, whose *Suits of Lessons* were published in 1719, seems to have resuscitated the genre in its pre-Handelian form.

Handel's *Suites de Pièces pour le clavecin* appeared in 1720, London, 'Printed for the Author'. While Handel's style in general was enormously influential, the eight suites of this collection did not themselves exert a strong influence on English keyboard music. Their very personal fusion of French and Italian elements could not be reconciled with the traditional English style. A subsequent volume, published without authority by Walsh in 1733, was even less representative of the composer's true powers at the time of publication. In the same year five pieces were published in Amsterdam, and a few more survive in manuscript.[9]

The direct influence of Handel's suites may be seen in the works of such minor composers as Thomas Chilcot, whose *Six Suites of Lessons* are supposed to have been published in 1734.[10] One may make such obvious direct comparisons as the following:

Ex. 140(a)

---

[9] Chrysander's edition of Handel's harpsichord works is still the standard one (see Bibliography; reprinted by Gregg Press, 1965); the important material of London, Brit. Mus., R.M. 20. g. 4 (see above, Chapter X, footnote 16) has never been collated, but a few miscellaneous pieces, not all of them authentic, were included in Chrysander's vol. xlviii. See, however, Bibliography (addenda s.v. Handel).   [10] Two suites in *PSMS*, xxii.

The contribution of Maurice Greene has been seriously underestimated owing to the lack of modern editions. His first publication of suites was the collection entitled *A Choice of Lessons*, in a pirated edition by Daniel Wright (1733). The contents of this were re-pirated by Walsh in the first 19 pages of *The Lady's Banquet 2d Book*, published in the same year.[11] In 1750 John Johnson published *A Collection of Lessons for the Harpsichord* with the full co-operation of the composer. Walsh's *A Collection of Lessons . . . 2d Book* is largely a reprint of *The Lady's Banquet 2d Book*. Apart from these works and others preserved in minor sources, he published a keyboard arrangement of his *Six Overtures in Seven Parts, ca.* 1745.

Greene strongly repudiated Wright's publication, and it is easy to see why this should be so. In its four complete suites and four separate pieces there is little evidence of real mastery of composition. The traditional idiom is uneasily wedded to that of Italian opera, resulting in a curiously shortwinded melodic style, as in the following 'Allmand' from the C minor Suite:

11 See Johnstone, *MT* (1967) 36.

The 1750 collection is a very different matter. Johnstone in the article cited has drawn attention to the very clear influence of Domenico Scarlatti, some of whose sonatas were published in London in 1739, and many more of which appeared in England during the rest of the century.[12] But quite apart from this there is a new command of form and material, and a wholly personal synthesis of styles. In the twelve suites or sonatas into which the individual lessons may be grouped (the original publication affords no assistance here) dance-titles are largely abandoned, even though the idioms which they denote are still often present. The following untitled, gigue-like movement illustrates the enormous distance travelled since the composition of Ex. 141:

Ex. 142

Greene

12 See Appendix II, s.v. Scarlatti, Roseingrave. Four suites by Roseingrave himself in *PSMS*, ii.

Another important publication of the mid-century was the collection of eight sonatas by Thomas Augustine Arne. The title-page bears no date, but the work was advertised as 'new music' in 1756.[13] As with Greene the pervading influence is now Italian, including Scarlatti; but in place of virtuosity there is an emphasis on melodic grace. There is also at times what can only be described as a Neapolitan flavour, possibly derived from such works as 'Zipolis Lessons', which are advertised on the Arne title-page. This can be seen in for example the B flat minor episode in the finale of the first Sonata, or in the following passage from the fourth Sonata:

Ex. 143

T. A. Arne

---

[13] Facsimile edition in *SBK*, xxvii.

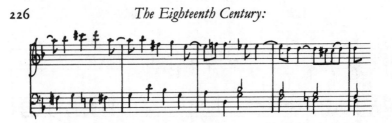

On the other hand it is impossible to deny the Englishness of such forthright melodies as the 'Gavotta' from the fifth Sonata or the Presto from the eighth:

In addition to works originally composed for keyboard the performer of this period could choose from a wide variety of pieces for a solo instrument and *basso continuo*, such as John Stanley's *Solos,* Op. 1 and Op. 4, which are described on their title-pages as being for 'German flute, Violin or Harpsicord'. The music is written on two staves with figured bass, and is easily adapted to solo keyboard performance. Indeed the copies of these works in London, Brit. Mus., show clear indications of having been used for this purpose.[14]

By 1750 the spinet had virtually disappeared from title-pages as an alternative to harpsichord, though the instrument continued to be made. Before long the choice was to be between the harpsichord and the pianoforte, and a more grandiose style cultivated. Composers began to introduce *ad libitum* string parts into their sonatas. Avison's Opp. 5, 7, and 8, published re-

[14] E.g. keyboard fingering, chords. Modern edition of Op. 1 to be published by Oxford University Press.

spectively in 1756, 1760 and 1764, each consist of six sonatas with 'accompaniments' for two violins and violoncello. This combination proved to be unfashionable and the majority of such works call for the violin only or the violin and violoncello. These string parts were not always as totally unnecessary as one might suppose, and occasionally one comes across the word 'obbligato' on a title-page, as in Thomas Attwood's Trios for violin, violoncello and pianoforte, Op. 1 (in Op. 2, for the same instruments, the string parts are 'ad libitum'.)

By the end of the century London was flooded with continental exponents of keyboard art, and with the music of those who did not actually settle here. To name only those who did, J. C. Bach (who arrived in 1759), Dussek, Hummel, Clementi and Cramer were the most important. We have already referred to Haydn and his last three sonatas: the influence of Mozart was still stronger, and not only on his pupil Thomas Attwood. Even the Wesleys scarcely provide an original note in this genre. Charles Wesley's *Three sonatas for the harpsichord*, Op. 4 (*ca.* 1790) include violin cues in spite of the title-page. In fact they seem also to require a violoncello in places where the left-hand bass is defective as it stands. Publishers were sometimes over-anxious to make such works readily available and the composers were not always sufficiently strong-willed to prevent them from appearing in distorted form. Stylistically these sonatas are scarcely an advance on J. C. Bach, and show nothing of the mastery and originality of the organ concertos.

Samuel Wesley was more prolific but hardly more advanced than his elder brother. His *Two Sonatas for the Piano Forte or Harpsichord; with an Accompanyment for a Violin* (Op. 2) are chiefly remarkable for their date; the British Museum copy is signed by its first owner with the date 1786, when the composer was only twenty. The *Three Sonatas for the Piano Forte* (Op. 3) are only marginally more interesting and may be only slightly later; but they dispense with the violin. The *Eight Sonatas,* printed without opus number, have been assigned to 1780,[15] but this may very well be too early: 1790 is more likely. The style here is noticeably more brilliant than in the previous two sets. In 1800

[15] *MGG*, s.v. Wesley.

was printed his Opus 5: *Four Sonatas and Two Duets for the Piano Forte*. The general impression in all of these works is of a rather pallid galant style, redeemed by an attractive sense of pianoforte colour.

About 1802 Field published in Paris his early set of three sonatas, Op. 1, and in adopting a Hummellian brilliance transformed British keyboard style. Though he was not the individualist that he later became in his nocturnes, his entire output has a certain unity in that it belongs to that curious pianistic world that is at once post-Mozartian and pre-Chopinesque and yet almost totally evades the spirit of Beethoven and Schubert; in this respect he belongs in varying degrees with the already-mentioned Dussek, Hummel, Clementi (his teacher) and Cramer who were his London contemporaries. An essentially nineteenth-century composer, his work is intimately bound up with the further development of the pianoforte and the final collapse of the harpsichord.

XII

New Horizons

The nineteenth century saw the general acceptance of the piano-
forte and of the pedal organ; but whereas the former was already
in common use by the beginning of the century the latter took
far longer to achieve recognition. This was largely due to the
innate conservatism of English organists, for there is no doubt
that Smith, Harris and Snetzler would have been capable of
building pedal-boards on the continental model had they been
required. In the first half of the nineteenth century progress was
impaired by the great variety of manual compass in use. Long
and short octaves to G_1 and F_1 were common. The earliest pedal-
boards were simply duplications of the lowest octave or so of this
compass in the form of 'pull-downs'. Later, when independent
pedal-pipes were introduced, it was often thought necessary to
extend the manual compass only to G or F: a retrograde step,
if anything. Only the most ambitious instruments possessed
the full manual compass with independent pedal-stops of '8-
foot' and '16-foot' tone. It was for such an instrument that
the finest organ music of S. S. Wesley (1810–1876) was conceived; and it is clear that even he could not necessarily rely on
'16-foot' stops. Only when the lower manual compass was
finally standardised at C was real progress possible. Samuel
Wesley, the great pioneer for the appreciation of J. S. Bach in
this country, was obliged to arrange the organ music of his hero
in the form of keyboard duets before it could be performed.[1]

Other developments in organ building in the early nineteenth
century included the use of manual couplers; the increased
insistence on orchestral timbres and the decline of emphasis on
'upper-work'; the diminishing importance of the choir organ in

[1] On the introduction of the pedal-board to England see Sumner, *The
Organ*, pp. 181–90.

favour of the swell; and the earliest experiments in pneumatic action.[2] All these factors were to influence subsequent organ-building for the worse.

The earliest composer to write a pedal part in solo organ music was probably William Russell (1777–1813), whose first set of *Twelve Voluntaries* (1804) already requires pedals.[3] Their function is merely to help out where impossible manual stretches are involved, and 16-foot tone is not implied. In much the same way Samuel Wesley wrote for pedals in the 'Full Voluntary' attached to his *Twelve* (recte thirteen) *short pieces*.[4] This primitive pedal-function, which would be supplied quite adequately by a coupler or pull-down attachment, lasted incredibly long in English organ music: at least until the publication of S. S. Wesley's *A Second Set of Three Pieces for a Chamber Organ* some time between 1867 and 1876.[5] On the other hand it is clear from other works of this composer intended for church organ, that 16-foot tone was sometimes available, as has been said, in connection with the F_1 compass in both manuals and pedals.

As far as style is concerned, the early nineteenth century begins to exhibit a deterioration only partially halted by Samuel Wesley and a few kindred spirits such as Thomas Adams (1785–1858). In Samuel Wesley's case the great strength of much of his music arises from the influence of J. S. Bach, combined with his own individual feeling for melody and harmony. Where the Bachian element is absent, as it is from many of his 'short pieces' and 'introductory movements', the result is apt to be sentimental or tuneful in a facile manner. Other composers, such as Charles Wesley and Matthew Camidge (1774–1844) relied on models which had been popular half a century earlier, chiefly Handel and Corelli. Camidge's concertos, published *ca.* 1815, were composed for organ solo without orchestra, and are very similar in plan to the four-movement voluntaries of Charles Wesley (published separately *ca.* 1815): prelude, fugue, slow movement, and march or similar genre-piece.[6]

---

2 Sumner, *The Organ*, p. 337.

3 See Clutton and Niland, *The British Organ*, p. 132.

4 Modern edition in *TW*, v.   5 See *TW*, xxiv.

6 Voluntaries by Charles Wesley in *TW*, v, xxiv; Concerto No. 2 in G minor by Camidge in *EOM*, xxii.

The extremes of English organ style in the early nineteenth century may be illustrated in two publications of the period: the *Six fugues* by Thomas Adams, and *Three voluntaries* by Samuel Webbe the younger (*ca.* 1770–1843). Adams, paring his contribution down to the essentials, writes the words 'Introduction ad libitum', followed in each case by a fugue on an original and inventive subject. Webbe on the other hand writes sonata-form allegros, pianistic rather than organistic in spite of an occasional held note for organ pedal. Here are extracts from Adams' third Fugue, in C minor, and from Webbe's third Voluntary:

Ex. 145 (a)

In spite of these excellent works the period is dominated for
the organist by Samuel Wesley himself, composer of the splendid
but little-known nine *Voluntaries . . . Op. 6 (ca.* 1800) and several
duets, amongst them the masterly work in three movements
dated 24 May 1812. And it is Samuel Wesley who provides a
fitting epilogue in the rather pathetic little fugue on a subject by
Mendelssohn dated 9 September 1837, one month before
Wesley's death.[7] Almost all that was of value between that time
and the renaissance heralded by Parry and Stanford was provided
by his natural son S. S. Wesley.

In the field of keyboard music outside the church, the decline in
taste was more marked. The transition from harpsichord to
pianoforte in England has been well told by Russell.[8] The great
early master of the latter instrument was John Field (1782–1849),
of whom 'it could be claimed, with much justice, that he was the
first composer for the piano in whose style no trace of harpsichord
influence remains'.[9] His nocturnes, long admired, have recently
been the subject of intensive study.[10] Almost contemporary with
Field was the short-lived George Frederick Pinto (1785–1806).
In 1803 he published *Two Grand Sonatas, For the Piano Forte . . .
Op. 3.* The first of these has been republished,[11] and shows considerable originality. The key is E flat minor, and there is much
harmonic daring. Unlike the sonatas of Field's Op. 1 it has a
slow movement, and is considerably more intense in expression
throughout. All these works make full use of the extended range
and perfected sustaining-pedal mechanism of the latest instruments.

[7] Printed *TW*, xiv.   [8] *The Harpsichord and Clavichord*, pp. 119–21.
[9] *MB*, xvii, p. xiii.   [10] Piggott, *PRMA* (1968–9) 55.
[11] *SBK*, xx.

It is in the solo concerto that the pianoforte and organ repertory finally meet and are in some ways comparable. Fragments of
three early harpsichord concertos by S. Wesley survive, though
they are not so labelled in the manuscript. Since the latter is said
to date from 1774–5, when the composer was only eight or nine,
these sketches may be dismissed as unimportant.[12] There remain
three mature works for organ and orchestra. These are in D
major (1800), B flat major (1813) and C major (? 1815). The first
work incorporates a Bach fugue: No. 5 from *Das Wohltemperirte
Klavier*, Book I. The other two exist only in the orchestral parts:
it is not even certain that the second work is for organ. The third
incorporates the song 'Rule Britannia' in the finale. With such
materials only superficial comments are possible: they are very
fully scored, down to trombones and timpani; and the writing is
full and contrapuntal even to the extent of pedantry. They
would seem to lack the very genuine charm of his numerous
violin concertos.[13]

If these works are the final manifestations of an obsolete form,
Field's pianoforte concertos look to the future. Yet there are
some points of contact with the traditional English organ
concerto, even as practised in the 1770s by Charles Wesley. To
begin with there is the manner of publication: in separate parts
with a solo part that is continuous from beginning to end.[14]
From Wesley's autograph full scores we know that the organ was
intended to play in most of the tutti's; and even the printed part
generally marks the exceptions with the words 'senza organo'.
For Field we have no autograph full scores; and the printed solo
parts are not explicit. Divergences between the pianoforte and
orchestral parts in the tutti's seem to indicate that in orchestral
performance the pianoforte did not double; Field's own annotations to the printed solo parts seem to refer to performance
by the pianoforte alone, a contingency foreseen by virtually every
publisher of English organ concertos in the eighteenth century.

[12] London, Brit. Mus., Add. 34998, ff. 50r-52v; 53r-54v; f. 61.
[13] London, Brit. Mus., Add. 35008, 35009.
[14] The parts of all seven concertos were published by Breitkopf und
Härtel, Leipzig. I have examined only the first three, published in *MB*, xvii.
No. 5 is subtitled 'L'Incendie par l'orage'.

Another point of contact is the use of folk-songs in slow movements: compare for example Charles Wesley's *Rondeau* 'Birks of Endermay' from his early D major concerto (see above, p. 205), with Field's 'Within a mile of Edinburgh town' from his first concerto. Both involve the use of fairly elaborate variation technique. Note also the occasional opportunity for improvising a slow movement (Wesley, second concerto, third set, and Field, third concerto), but conversely no cadenzas. Finally both men were, in their different ways, masters of orchestral writing in this context.

In a less superficial sense, of course, Field inhabits a different world. His first concerto, published in St. Petersburg in 1814, appears to be the work played by the composer at the Haymarket theatre in 1799, when he was aged seventeen. Only in the disappointingly early conclusion of the finale is there any hint of immaturity: a fault rectified to excess in the second and third concertos. The second movement, the variations just referred to, presents a wealth of ornamental detail in the florid solo part. The first movement is a real *tour de force* of construction within a broadly classical frame. Here the curtailing of the recapitulation achieves a dramatic effect. After a lengthy orchestral exposition, ending in the tonic but with a second subject in the dominant, the pianoforte enters with new material. When the dominant is reached once more the soloist is content with a broad paraphrase of the second subject. The development opens with a grand gesture:

Modulating to C minor, the music stays there for some time until it veers round to E flat major for the soloist's version of the second subject. From there the music is practically identical with the solo exposition, and there is a short coda.

It is salutory to recall that, although these works are in a sense more modern than Beethoven's concertos in that their keyboard style foreshadows that of Chopin, they are a good deal less modern than those of the mature Mozart in that they can be played straight through on the solo instrument without much loss. The pianoforte may be silent, but it never seems to accompany an orchestral theme, as so often in Mozart and of course Beethoven himself. Nevertheless John Field, who emigrated to Russia and died in Moscow, is a composer of great significance in the history of music. Of him it can truly be said that he was the last composer from the British Isles to have influenced the subsequent course of the art in Europe; and as a master of the keyboard in composition and in performance he fittingly concludes our study.

APPENDIX I

Sources of English Solo Keyboard Music

ARRANGEMENT

1 MSS (in order: Town, Library, Shelf-mark)

    A Before 1500
    B 1500–1660
    C 1660–1800

2 PRINTED

    A Collections in Chronological Order
    B Individual Composers. This section is incorporated into Appendix II
       (Part 2, 1660–1800)

1

A

Town	Library	Manuscript	Mod. Edn.[1]
London	Brit. Mus.	Add. 28550 (Robertsbridge Codex, *ca.* 1325)	*CEKM*, i; facs. in *EEH*, i.

B

Town	Library	Manuscript	Mod. Edn.
Berlin	Staatsbib.	Lynar A1 and 2* (Weckmann)[2] 40316³* (see *MB*, xix. 225)	
Cambridge	Fitz. Mus.	52. d. 25 (owned by Bull; ?copied by Tisdale)	*SBK*, xxiv
		32. g. 29 (Tregian)	*FWVB*
	Univ. Lib.	Anne Cromwell's Book (Photographic copy only)	

[1] Brackets indicate an incomplete edition of the source.

[2] Lynar B1–10 contain no music by English composers. See Dickinson, *MR* (1956) 97.

[3] Photographic copy in Harvard University, Isham Mem. Lib. Partial edition in *AMO*, x.

* Continental MSS containing English music.

Town	Library	Manuscript	Mod. Edn.
		Dd. 4. 22	
Dublin	Trinity Coll.	Marsh's Lib., D. 3. 30 (Dublin Virginal MS)	*DVM*
Edinburgh	Nat. Lib.	Panmure 8 ('Jean Campbell')	(*SBK*, xv)
		9 ('Clement Matchett', 1612)	(*SBK*, xv)
		10 ('Duncan Burnett')	(*SBK*, xv)
Huntingdon	Cromwell Mus.	Anne Cromwell's Book (see also Cambridge)	
Liège	Univ. Lib.	MS 153, *olim* 888 (*Liber Fratrum Cruciferorum*)[4]*	
London	Brit. Mus.	R.M. 23. l. 4 (Cosyn, 1620)	
		24. d. 3 (Forster, 1624)	
		R.A. 56† (*ca.* 1530)	
		58 (*ca.* 1530)	*EKM*, i
		Add. 5465† ('Fayrfax Book', *ca.* 1540)	
		10337 (Elizabeth Rogers, 1656)	(*EKM*, v)
		15233† (*ca.* 1540)	
		23623* (Messaus, 1629)	
		29485* (Suzanne van Soldt, 1599)[5]	*MMN*, iii
		29996† (*ca.* 1548, *ca.* 1555 and 17th cent.)	
		30485	
		30486 (Byrd and Anon. only)	(*EKM*, iii)
		30513† (Thomas Mulliner, *ca.* 1550–75)	*MB*, i
		31392 (Byrd only) and lute music	
		31403 (1st sect., written by Edward Bevin)	
		36661 (Thomas Tunstall)	
	R.C.M.	2093 (see also Section C)	
New York	Pub. Lib.	Drexel 5469 (Henry Loosemore)	

[4] Ed. Guilmant, *AMO*, x. It contains two Fantasias by P. Philips and one by 'Brouno' (William Brown).

[5] A companion volume (London, Brit. Mus., Add. 29486) apparently contains no English music (see Sweelinck, *Werken*, i, p. xlii).

* Continental MSS containing English music.
† Contains English liturgical organ music.

Town	Library	Manuscript	Mod. Edn.
		5611 (Thomas Heardson)	
		5612	
Nottingham	Univ. Lib.	'Lord Middleton's Lute Book'	
Oxford	Bod. Lib.	Mus. d. 143 (*ca.* 1380, but with 4 leaves of keyboard mus. See Dart, *ML* (1954) 99)	
		Mus. Sch. c. 93* (early part, written by Thomas Tomkins and associates)	
	Brasenose Coll.	Fragment bearing pencil number 156*	
	Ch. Ch.	MS 49 (devoted to Lugge)	
		89 (Catholic organ music; copied and in large part composed by Richard Deering?)	
		92	
		371*	
		431	
		436 (includes Hexachord by Ferrabosco)	
		437	
		1003 ('Morgan his Book')	
		1034A*	
		1113	
		1142A	
		1207	
		1236 (William Ellis: virginal music)	
Paris	Bib. Nat.	Fonds du Cons., Rés. 1122 (formerly 18547) (Tomkins)	
		Rés. 1185* (formerly 18548) (Bull/Cosyn)6	
		1186 (formerly 18546) (Creighton)	
		1186bisII (formerly 18570)	
Uppsala	Univ. Lib.	Instr. mus. hs. 408 (*olim* 108)† (Gustav Düben, 1641)	
Vienna	Nat. Bib.	17771† (in tablature)	
Wimborne	Minster Lib.	MS without shelf-mark (*ca.* 1635–1640)	

6 Bound up with Paris, Bib. Nat., fonds du Cons., Rés. 1184 (Cosyn's copy of *Parthenia*).

* Contains English liturgical organ music.
† Continental MSS containing English music.

Town	Library	Manuscript	Mod. Edn.
Privately owned		*My Ladye Nevells Booke*	MLNB

'IB' (see *MB*, xx)
'Priscilla Bunbury's Book'   (*PBVB*)
'Robinson Bible' (see Dart, *English Historical Review* (1964) 777)

Lost		MS of Vincentius de la Faille† (transcr. by van den Borren)	

MS belonging to W. H. Cummings (? in Cosyn's hand)
Pepusch MS 18, Vol. I† (written by Messaus. See *MB*, xiv. 160)

C

Town	Library	Manuscript	Mod. Edn.
Brussels	Bib. du Cons.	MS 15418 (Elizabeth Edgeworth. See *ML* (1969) 470)	
Cambridge	Fitz. Mus.	MS 30. f. 21 (106)	
		32. f. 14 (149)	
		52. b. 7* (653)	
Edinburgh	Nat. Lib.	Inglis 94, MS 3343 (1695. See *ML* (1969) 278–89)	
Glasgow	Euing Lib.	R. d. 54 (*ca.* 1730)	
		R. d. 62 (*ca.* 1790)	
London	Brit. Mus.	R.M. 21. d. 8	

Egerton 2485*
     2959 (late 17th cent.)
     2970
Harley 7340* (one of Tudway's church mus. vols.)
Add. 5336 (Croft, late 18th cent.)
     14335 (*ca.* 1768–1799) (S. Webbe)
     14340 (1788—autograph S. Wesley)
     14343 (see *EOM*, xix)
     14344
     16155 (2nd half 18th cent: John Garth)
     17850
     17852 (before 1712; owned by Thomas Brignell)
     17853 (1694)
     22099* (early 18th cent.)

* MS contains at least one pre-Restoration piece.
† Continental MSS containing English music.

Town	Library	Manuscript	Mod. Edn.
		27753 (1789—autograph T. S. Dupuis)	
		30382	
		30392 (1791—fugues by Crotch)	
		30932 (early 18th cent.)	
		31403* (2nd section, *ca.* 1700)	
		31446 (George Holmes, 1698)	
		31465 (Nicholas Harrison, early 18th cent.)	
		31467 (music by Greene, copied 1735)	
		31468 (*ca.* 1700, Will Davis)	
		31814 (late 18th cent., hand of R. J. S. Stevens)	
		32161 (autograph of Philip Hart)	
		34267	
		34609 (2nd half of 18th cent.)	
		34695 (Nicholas Harrison, early 18th cent.)	
		34996 (18th cent. Pieces by S. Wesley)	
		34998 (pieces by S. Wesley)	
		35007–8	
		35009 (organ concertos by S. Wesley)	
		35018 (organ concertos by C. Wesley)	
		35024–5	
		35039 (1770–1780, S. Wesley)	
		35040	
		37027 (*ca.* 1780)	
		37074 (*ca.* 1727). Pieces by Robert Creyghton the younger	
		38188	
		39549	
		39569 (William Babel, 1702)	
		39957 (Burney)	
		40139	
		41205	
		47846	

* MS contains at least one pre-Restoration piece.

Town	Library	Manuscript	Mod. Edn.
		52363 (Elizabeth Barrett, 1704)	
		Leaves at end of printed books Hirsch III. 472 and K. i. c. 57	
	Dulwich Coll. Lib.	MSS 92a, 92b, 92d (*olim* 1, 2, 4) and others	
	R.C.M.	MS 694	
		734–5	
		810–25	
		1018	
		1039	
		1056	
		1057 (John Alcock, 1763)	
		1120	
		2093 (see also Section B)	
		4018	
		4023 (concertos by C. Wesley)	
	R.C.O.	MS without shelf-mark	
Manchester	Henry Watson Lib.	MS BRm. 7105. Rf. 31	
New York	Pub. Lib.	Drexel 5609* (written by Hawkins, late 18th cent.)	
		Drexel 5611 (later additions thereof)	
		Music Reserve +MN	
Oxford	Bod. Lib.	Mus. d. 82 (W. Hayes, *ca.* 1750)	
		Mus. Sch. c. 93 (later part)	
		d. 219 (Albert Bryan)	
		e. 397 (begun 1747)	
		e. 399 (Elizabeth Nodes, 1681)	
		f. 575* (William Jenkins, 1673)	
	Ch. Ch.	MS 15	
		46 (late 17th cent.)	
		47* (late 17th cent.)	
		378*	
		1003* (see also section B)	
		1142	
		1175*	
		1176*	
		1177* (belonged to 'R. Goodson')	
		1178	

7 Copies of Purcell's *Choice Collection* (1696).

* MS contains at least one pre-Restoration piece.

Town	Library	Manuscript	Mod. Edn.
		1179 (1685–1690: belonged to George Lluellyn)	
		1236* (see also Section B)	
Paris	Bib. Nat.	Fonds du Cons., Rés. 1186bisI (formerly 18570) (*ca.* 1680–1705)	
Tenbury	St. Michael's Coll.	MSS 752, 784, 1131 (mid-18th-cent.)	
		MS 1508 (Babel, 1701; cf. London, Brit. Mus., Add. MS 39569)	
Private		A 17th-cent. MS, formerly the property of Thurston Dart	*(CM)*
		Lady Leans MSS 1, 2, 6 (18th cent.)	
		The former MS r. 1 of the Nanki Music Library (see McLean, *MT* (1963) 702 and *EOM*, xxiii)	*(EOM*, xxiii)
		MS containing voluntaries by Greene (published by Bland, *ca.* 1780), with a note in the hand of J. S. Smith ascribing them to Boyce. See Mann, *MT* (1901) 529, and the edition cited opposite	ed. P. Williams

2

A⁸

Symbol	Title and Editions	Mod. Edn.
P	*Parthenia* (1612?, 1613?, 1646, 1651, 1655)⁹	*SBK*, xix
PI	*Parthenia In-Violata* (1625?)	*PI*
MH/1	*Musicks Hand-maide* (J. Playford, 1663). No copy survives	*SBK*, xxviii
MH/2	*Musicks Hand-maide* (J. Playford, *ca.* 1668). Reprint of MH/1 with original title-page dated 1663, but with four new pieces	*SBK*, xxviii

⁸ After 1700 this list omits publications devoted solely to transcriptions, or settings of popular songs. For present locations, see *BUCEM*. Place of publication London unless otherwise stated.

⁹ See *SBK*, xix, for further bibliographical discussion.

Symbol	Title and Edition	Mod. Edn.
MH/3	*Musicks Hand-maid* (J. Playford, 1678). Reprint of MH/2 with additions, but without four psalm-tunes	*SBK*, xxviii
M	*Melothesia: or certain general rules for playing upon a continued-bass. With a choice collection of lessons for the harpsichord and organ . . . All carefully reviewed by M. Locke . . . The first part* (J. Carr, 1673)	(*SBK*, vi, *SBK*, vii, *PSMS*, xvi, *TW*, vi)
2MH/1	*The Second Part of Musick's Hand-maid* (H. Playford, 1689)	*SBK*, x
2MH/2	*A Choice Collection of Lessons* (H. Playford, 1705). Reprint of 2MH/1	*SBK*, x
HM	*The Harpsicord Master* (I. Walsh, [1697]). No copy survives[10]	
2HM	*The Second Book of the Harpsicord Master* (I. Walsh, 1700)[11]	
CC	*A Choice Collection of Ayres* (John Young, 1700)	
CL	*A Collection of Lessons and Aires for the Harpsichord or Spinnett compos'd by Mr. J. Eccles, Mr. D. Purcell and others* (I. Walsh and I. Hare, [1702])	*CP*, vi. 9–23
3HM	*The Third Book of the Harpsicord Master* (I. Walsh and I. Hare, 1702). Books 4–13 (4HM–13HM) contain transcriptions only. See *BUCEM*	
LB	*The Ladys Banquet* (J. Walsh, 1704)	
2LB	*The Second Book of the Ladys Banquet* (I. Walsh and I. Hare, 1706). 3LB (1720) was probably identical with LB3. See Smith, *Bibliography*, i	
LE	*The Ladys Entertainment or Banquet of Musick* (I. Walsh, I. Hare and P. Randall, [1708])	
2LE	*The 2d Book of the Ladys Entertainment* (I. Walsh, I. Hare and P. Randall, [1708]). Books 3–5 contain transcriptions only. See *BUCEM*	
MM1–7	*Mercurius Musicus* (7 nos., I. Walsh and I. Hare, 1708–1709). More were printed	
HMI(1)	*The Harpsicord Master Improved* (Pippard, 1711)	
SHSL	*Suits of Harpsichord and Spinnet Lessons* (ed. W. Babell. R. Meares, *ca.* 1715)	
SCL	*Suits of the most celebrated Lessons* (ed. W. Babell. I. Walsh and I. Hare, [1717]). Re-issued *ca.* 1718, and twice more, *ca.* 1730	
HMI(2)	*The Harpsicord Master Improved* (Daniel Wright and John Young, [1718])	

[10] Probably contained a copy of the Purcell 'Instructions' for ornamentation. See *SBK*, xxii.

[11] See *MT* (1965) 127; *SBK*, v. 17.

Symbol	Title and Edition	Mod. Edn.
LB1	*The Lady's Banquet, 1st Book* (I. Walsh, [1730]).	
LB2	*The Lady's Banquet, 2d Book* (I. Walsh, 1733). In large part a reprint of M. Greene's *A Choice Book of Lessons* (D. Wright, [1733]). Books 3–6 (LB3–LB6) contain transcriptions only. See *BUCEM*	
HSM	*The Harpsichord or Spinnet Miscellany* (ed. and pub. R. Bremner, Edinburgh, [1761]). Another issue: London, *ca.* 1765. Various publications entitled *The Harpsichord Miscellany* contain only transcriptions. See *BUCEM*	
TV	*Ten Voluntarys . . . by Dr. Green, Skinner, Stubley, James, Reading, Selby and Kuknan* [=Kühnau] (C. and S. Thompson, [1767])	
SS	*Six Sonattas for the Harpsichord. Composed by Arnold, Galuppi and Mazzinghi* (C. and S. Thompson, *ca.* 1770)	
SV	*Six Voluntaries for the Harpsichord or Organ by different Masters, never before printed, selected by E. Kendall* (Longman, Lukey and Co., *ca.* 1775)	
PH	*Playing the Harpsichord . . . with choice lessons . . .* (Longman, Lukey and Co., *ca.* 1775). Further editions by Longman and Broderip (*ca.* 1780) and J. Dale (*ca.* 1785)	
CV1	*A Collection of Voluntaries for the Organ or Harpsichord Composed by Dr. Green, Mr. Travers and Several other Eminent Masters* (Longman, Lukey and Co., *ca.* 1777 [or 1771 ?])	
CV2	*Ten Select Voluntaries . . . Composed by Mr. Handel, Dr. Green &c., Book II* (Longman and Broderip, 1780)[12]	
CV3	*Ten Select Voluntaries . . . by Orlando* [recte Christopher] *Gibbons, Blow, Purcell, Doctr. Green, Doctr. Boyce, Mr. Jams., Martin Smith, Organst. of Gloucestr. & J. Stafford Smith, Book IIId* (Longman and Broderip, *ca.* 1780)	
CV4	*Twelve Voluntaries and Fugues for the Organ or Harpsichord with Rules for Tuning by the celebrated Mr. Handel. Book IV* (Longman and Broderip, *ca.* 1780)	
TwV	*Twelve voluntaries for the organ or harpsichord . . .* (J. Carr, *ca.* 1780)	

[12] Broderip joined the firm of Longman and Lukey in 1778 and Lukey left in 1779.

Symbol	*Title and Editions*	*Mod. Edn.*
CSEL	*A Collection of Six Easy Lessons* . . . (P. Hodgson, *ca.* 1780)	
MM	*Musical Miscellanies* (songs and pianoforte pieces. T. Williams, 1784)	
SCP	*Select Concert Pieces* [R. Bremner, 1785]. 8 nos., No. 4 lost	
HP	*The Harpsichord Preceptor . . . II. Thirty . . . Lessons* (S. A. and P. Thompson, *ca.* 1785)	
SC	*Storace's Collection of Original Harpsichord Music* (2 vols. Birchall and Andrews, for S. Storace, [1787–1789]). Another edition printed for the editor and sold by Hugh Andrews, *ca.* 1790	
NA	*A New Assistant for the Piano Forte, or Harpsichord, Containing . . . Twelve . . . Lessons for Beginers* (*ca.* 1790)	
PeL1–4	*Periodical Lessons* (4 nos., J. Bland, *ca.* 1790)	
BC	*Bland's Collection of Sonatas, Lessons . . . by The Most Esteem'd Composers* (4 vols., 48 nos. J. Bland, *ca.* 1790–1794). Re-issued [1790–1794], *ca.* 1792–1797, and by Rt. Birchall, *ca.* 1800. See also Appendix II, Pt. 2, s.v. Linley	
LT	*The Leaves of Terpsichore . . .* (C. Wheatstone, *ca.* 1795)	
PrL1–2	*Progressive Lessons . . .* (2 Books, R. Birchall, *ca.* 1795)	
LBC	*Longman and Broderip's Collection of Original Music for the Grand and Small Piano Forte* (10 nos., Longman and Broderip, *ca.* 1795)	
PM1–16	*The Piano-Forte Magazine* (16 vols., Harrison and Co., [1797–1802])	

Anthologies of continental music include especially the following:

Voluntarys and fugues (Walsh, Randall and Hare, [1710]).

A second collection of toccates, vollentarys and fugues (Walsh and Hare, [1719])

A collection of lessons for the harpsichord (3 vols., J. Walsh, [1761–1764])

A collection of lessons for the harpsichord (Thompson and Sons, [1762])

Six lessons for the harpsichord (Welcker, *ca.* 1770)

APPENDIX II

List of Composers

Part 1: 1500–1660

Part 2: 1660–1800

Composers whose dates overlap the two periods are cross-referenced, the position of the main entry being determined by the date of the main sources. An asterisk indicates that a composer is not listed in *Grove's Dictionary of Music and Musicians* (5th edn. 1954, including *Supplement* 1961). In such cases, and where *Grove* is inaccurate or incomplete, alternative sources of biographical information are mentioned; only information not otherwise readily available is recorded here. Where possible, works and sources are indicated by references to a standard edition; otherside full details are provided. For works of reference cited only by the author's name, see Bibliography. Add. = London, Brit. Mus., Add. MSS; Ch. Ch. = Oxford, Christ Church, Musical MSS.

PART 1

1500–1660

This part includes composers whose music was transcribed for keyboard, and continental composers whose music appears in English sources. References to Cambridge, Fitz. Mus., MS 32. g. 29 are given through the modern edn., *FWVB*.

ALWOOD (ALLWOOD), Richard (b. ?, d. ?), probably active *ca.* 1550–1570. 5 pieces in Add. 30513 (mod. edn. in *MB*, i); 2 pieces in Add. 30485 (mod. edn. in *EEOM*).

*AMBROSE, John (b. ?, d. ?), clerk at King's Coll., Cambridge, 1481–2? Untitled piece in Ch. Ch. 1034, f. 1. The only other recorded piece by a man of this name, not for keyboard, is a wordless canon in London, Brit. Mus., Roy. App. 58, f. 16v.

APRYS (APPRYS, APRYCE, RYSE; in *Grove* s.v. Rhys), Philip (b. ?, d. ?). See also Baillie, *ML* (1955) 55. Organ Mass and 2 other works in Add. 29996. Mod. edn. of the Mass in *EECM*, x, and *Altenglische Orgelmusik*; of the other 2 pieces in *EECM*, vi.

ASTON, Hugh (b. ?, d. ?). Not Archdeacon of York (d. 1522) or Canon of St. Stephen's, Westminster (d. 1523). B. Mus., 1510 (*TCM*, x, p. xiv); *magister choristarum*, Newarke Coll., Leicester, 1525–1548. Still alive in 1549. (Harrison, *Music in Medieval Britain*, 29–30). 'A Hornepype' for keyboard in London, Brit. Mus., Roy. App. 58, f. 40v; he may also have composed the 2 following pieces: 'My lady Careys dompe' (f. 44v) and 'The short mesure off my lady Wynkfyld's rownde' (f. 45v).

AVERE: see Burton.

BANISTER, John (1630–1679): see Part 2.

BARRE, Pierre de la: see La Barre.

BEVIN, Edward (=Elway Bevin, *ca.* 1550–1637 or later?). In *Grove* s.v. Bevin, Elway. Pulver mentions that he was alive in 1637. Pieces in Add. 31403, the first part of which may be in his hand. Includes 'Graces in play', followed by the same 'exprest in notes' (f. 5; see Dolmetch, Interpretation, p. 387). The pieces are ascribed to Edward, except the canon 4 in 2 on f. 21 ('Elway Bevin'). Also a Fancy in Add. 36661, f. 59.

*BICKERLL (b. ?, d. ?). Nothing is known of his life. Pavan in Add. 30485, f. 41.

BLITHEMAN (BLYTHEMAN), William (d. 1591). 11 (possibly 12) pieces in Add. 30513 (mod. edn. in *MB*, i). Of these *Gloria tibi Trinitas* (II) also in Cambridge, Fitz. Mus., 32. g. 29, p. 91 (mod. edn. in *FWVB*, No. 50) and New York, Pub. Lib., Drexel 5612, p. 168. Also '3 parts', Add. 31403, f. 9.

*BROWN (BROUNO, BRUNO), William, *alias* JEANNETON (b. ?, d. ?), late 16th- and early 17th-century composer working in Catholic Netherlands. See Curtis, *The Keyboard Music of Sweelinck*, 32–33; Dart, *ML* (1971) 27; *Grove* s.v. 'English Musicians Abroad'. Keyboard works in Berlin, Staatsbib., 40316 (*olim* 191); Ch. Ch. 89; Liège, Univ. Lib., 153 (*olim* 888; mod. edn. in *AMO*, x).

BRYAN (BRYNE), Albert (Albertus) (*ca.* 1621–*ca.* 1670): see Part 2.

BULL, John (*ca.* 1563–1628). For biography see also *MB*, xiv. Complete keyboard works and details of sources in *MB*, xiv, xix.

*BURNETT, Duncan (b. ?, d. ?), Scottish 16th–17th-century musician. Pavan in Edinburgh, Nat. Lib., MS Panmure 10, which he owned (mod. edn. in *SBK*, xv, No. 8).

BURTON (BURNET), Avery (Davy, David; also known as AVERE) (b. ?, d. 1542 or later). *Te Deum* for organ in Add. 29996, f. 22v (mod. edn. in *EECM*, vi).

BYRD, William (*ca.* 1543–1623). For biography see also Fellowes, *William Byrd*. Complete keyboard works and details of sources in *MB*, xxvii, xxviii; for other mod. edns. see Bibliography, s.v. Byrd.

*C., S. (b. ?, d. ?), identity unknown. Composed piece for keyboard, 'The Countess of Portland's Delight', Ch. Ch. 92.

CACCINI, Giulio (*ca.* 1545–1618), Italian composer. His madrigal, *Amarilli*, set by Peter Philips (*FWVB*, No. 82).

CARLETON, Nicholas (Nycholas) (b. ?, d. ?). Nothing is known of his life. *Grove* has only a single entry under this name, confusing this and the following composer. 2 pieces in Add. 30513 (mod. edn. in *MB*, i).

*CARLETON, Nicholas (d. 1630). For biography see *Two Elizabethan Keyboard Duets*, ed. F. Dawes. 4 pieces in Add. 29996: the first, a duet, ed. Dawes, *ibid.*; the other 3, of which one is merely the lower half of an incomplete duet, in *EKM*, iv.

CHAMBONNIÈRES, Jacques Champion de (*ca.* 1602–*ca.* 1672): see Part 2. His father was a friend of Bull, but none of his music was copied into English sources. See *MGG*; Dart, *ML* (1959) 279.

COPERARIO (COOPER), John (*ca.* 1575–1626). 'A maske' set by Giles Farnaby in *FWVB*, No. 209. 18th-century arrangements in London, Brit. Mus., Egerton 2485.

COSYN, Benjamin (*ca.* 1570–1652 or later). The index to Paris, Bib. Nat., fonds du Cons. Rés. 1185, which is in his hand, is dated 1652. Many pieces in his holograph collection, London, Brit. Mus., R.M. 24. l. 4 (some in *Twenty-five pieces . . . from . . . Cosyn's Virginal Book,* ed. Fuller-Maitland and Barclay Squire); some possibly in Ch. Ch. 1113, ascribed to 'B.C.' (3 in *EOM*, xiv). Pieces also in the lost MS belonging to W. H. Cummings (see *MT* (1903) 780).

COXSUN, Robert (b. ?, d. ?). Nothing is known of his life. 2 pieces in Add. 29996 (mod. edn. in *EECM*, x).

CREYGHTON (or CREIGHTON), Robert (1593–1672). Professor of Greek at Cambridge, etc. See *Grove* s.v. Creighton, Robert, his son (entry in Part 2). Probably compiler of Paris, Bib. Nat., fonds du Cons., Rés. 1186, which includes several compositions signed 'R. Cr.', some dated 1635, 1636 or 1638.

DEERING, Richard (d. 1630). Composed the bulk of Ch. Ch. 89 (anon.)?

DOWLAND, John (1562–1626). Settings of his 'Lachrymae' Pavan by an anonymous composer (Add. 30485, f. 71v), Byrd, Cosyn, Giles Farnaby, Morley, Randall (q.v.); of 'Piper's Galliard' by Bull (mod. edn. in *MB*); of 'Frog Galliard' by Hall and Wilbye (q.v.); and anon. settings of 'Can she excuse my wrongs' (*FWVB*, No. 188) and an Alman (Oxford, Bod. Lib., Mus. d. 143, f. 6v).

DU FAULT (DUFAULT) (b. ?, d. ?), see Part 2.

EDWARDS, Richard (*ca.* 1522–1566). Arrangements of 3 part-songs (only one assigned to him, but the other two assumed to be his from his authorship of the words) in Add. 30513 (mod. edn. in *MB*, i).

*ELLIS, William (*ca.* 1620–1674). Biography in Pulver. A keyboard piece by 'W.E.' in Ch. Ch. 1113 is commonly assigned to him, on the grounds that he wrote this MS. Comparison with Ch. Ch. 1236, parts of which he certainly wrote, makes this very doubtful. The latter includes 13 pieces by him.

*ENGLITT, = INGLOT(T) (q.v.)? Boyd, *Elizabethan Music and Musical Criticism,* however, indexes him as 'Englitt, C.'. One piece ascribed to 'Englitt' in London, Brit. Mus., R.M. 24. d. 3.

FACY (FACEY, etc.), Hugh (b. ?, d. ?). 16th–17th-century composer. See *Grove, Supplement.* 11 pieces in New York, Pub. Lib., Drexel 5611; one piece in *ibid.*, Drexel 5612; 3 pieces (two also in Drexel 5611) in Add. 36661.

FARNABY, Giles (*ca.* 1566–*ca.* 1640). For biography see also *MB*, xxiv. Complete keyboard works and details of sources, *ibid*. All but one also in *FWVB*.

FARNABY, Richard (b. *ca.* 1594), son of preceding. Biography and keyboard works (4 pieces) in *MB*, xxiv; all also in *FWVB*.

FARRANT, Richard (d. 1581). 2 pieces in Add. 30513 (mod. edn. in *MB*, i).

FERRABOSCO, Alfonso (II) (*ca.* 1575–1628), English composer of Italian parentage, son of Alfonso Ferrabosco (I). No original keyboard music, but arrangement of his works in Add. 29996, 30485; Ch. Ch. 436.

FER(R)ABOSCO, John (1626–1682), son of preceding. One suite in Ch. Ch. 1236.

FRESCOBALDI, Girolamo (1583–1643), Italian composer. Many keyboard works copied into Ch. Ch. 1113.

FROBERGER, Johann Jacob (1616–1667): see Part 2.

*GALEAZZO, presumably an Italian composer. A 'Praeludium' in *FWVB*, No. 99.

GIBBONS, Christopher (1615–1676): see Part 2.

GIBBONS, Edward (1568–*ca.* 1650). One piece, a prelude to an anthem, in London, Brit. Mus., Harley 7340, f. 193v. Mod. edn. in *Old English Organ Music*, xx, ed. J. E. West (Novello).

GIBBONS, Orlando (1583–1625), brother of preceding. Complete keyboard works and details of sources in *MB*, xx.

GIBBS, R(ichard) (b. ?, d. ?), organist of Norwich Cathedral, 1635. 'Allmaine' and 'Corant' in Ch. Ch. 1177.

GREGORIE, William (d. 1663): see Part 2.

*HALL, Robert (b. ?, d. ?), 16th–17th-century composer. 5 pieces in 'Priscilla Bunbury's Book' (mod. edn. of 2 in *PBVB*).

HARDING, James (Jeames HARDEN) (*ca.* 1560–1626). Accurate biography in *MGG*. 2 fantasias, possibly arrangements, in Add. 30485; setting by Byrd of a 'Gagliarda' in *FWVB*, No. 122. Galiard by 'Mr. James' in Berlin, Staatsbib., 40316 (also 2 pieces by 'James' in the former Berlin MS 167: see Eitner).

HEATH, John (b. ?, d. ?), 16th-century composer. Contributed a Morning and Communion Service to Day's *Certaine Notes*, 1560 (also partly in Oxford, Bod. Lib., Mus. Sch. e 420–22, *ca.* 1548). ? = 'Hethe the singing man' at St Mary-at-Hill, London, 1555: Baillie, *ML* (1955) 55. Probably the composer of a 'Christe qui lux' for keyboard in Add. 30513, f. 102v, ascribed to 'Heath' (mod. edn. in *MB*, i).

HEYBOURNE, Ferdinando: see Richardson, Ferdinando.

HEYWOOD, John (*ca.* 1514–1587). Virginalist to Henry VIII and Mary. On her death fled to Malines, where he probably died. He witnessed Thomas Mulliner's ownership of Add. 30513. No keyboard music survives; but see above, p. 117.

HINGSTON, John (d. 1683): see Part 2.

*HODGES (b. ?, d. ?). Mentioned in Morley, *Plain and Easy Introduction*, p. 177, as master of descanting upon plainsong. Became organist of Hereford Cathedral, 1581; he was still there in 1582 when Bull was appointed joint organist on 24 December (*MB*, xiv, p. xxi). West (*Cathedral Organists*), refers to him as 'John Hodge'. It is possible that Morley was referring to an older composer. No music survives.

HOLMES, John (d. 1602). Not, as Arkwright, etc., subsequently organist of Salisbury. 'Fantazia' for keyboard in Ch. Ch. 1113; Pavin in Cambridge, Fitz. Mus., 52. d. 25, f. 96v (mod. edn. in *SBK*, xxiv).

HOLMES, Thomas (d. 1638), son of preceding. 'Saraband' in Ch. Ch. 92; also? a piece called 'Puddinge' by 'T.H.'.

HOOPER, Edmund (*ca.* 1553–1621). 2 pieces for keyboard in *FWVB*, Nos. 222, 228.

INGLOT(T) (? = ENGLITT; formerly misread as JUGLOTT), William (1554–1621). Two pieces in *FWVB*, Nos. 250, 251; untitled piece by 'Englitt' in London, Brit. Mus., R.M. 24. d. 3.

IVES (YVES), Simon (1600–1662). Two pieces in London, Brit. Mus., R.M. 23. l. 4, by 'Yves', 'sett forth by B. Cosyn'.

* JEANNETON: see Brown.

JENKINS, John (1592–1678): see Part 2.

JEWETT, Randall (*ca.* 1603–1675). Three pieces in 'Priscilla Bunbury's Book'; mod. edn. of 2 in *PBVB*.

JOHNSON, Edward (b. ?, d. ?). His relation to the other Johnsons, if any, is unknown. 'Johnson's Medley' (*FWVB*, No. 243) is a lute piece set by Byrd and Randall (q.v.). His Pavan and Galliard, 'Delight' (*FWVB*, Nos. 277–8) was set by (?) Kinloch and Byrd (q.v.), but the lute sources ascribe it variously to Robert Johnson, John Johnson, or simply 'Johnson'.

JOHNSON, John (d. 1594). Arrangement of 'The Flat Pavan' by Giles Farnaby (q.v.). An anonymous arrangement in Add. 36661, f. 56.

JOHNSON, Robert (I) (*ca.* 1485–*ca.* 1560). No known relation with John, or Robert (II). 3 pieces (all arranged) in Add. 30513 (mod. edn. in *MB*, i).

JOHNSON, Robert (II) (*ca.* 1580–*ca.* 1633), son of John Johnson. 2 (? original) pieces in *FWVB*, Nos. 145–6. A pavan set by Farnaby (q.v.), and anonymously in Cambridge, Fitz. Mus., 52. d. 25 (mod. edn. in *SBK*, xxiv, No. 19). An alman set by Farnaby in *FWVB*, No. 147. Two arrangements in Add. 36661, and 3 pieces in Ch. Ch. 1113 (one also in *FWVB*).

*KENNEDY, John (b. ?, d. ?), 16th–17th-century composer. Corant in Berlin, Staatsbib., 40316.

*KIDERMINSTER, El. Possibly the composer's name of *FWVB*, No. 23 ('Praeludium').

*KINLOCH, William (b. ?, d. ?), Scottish 16th–17th-century composer. 5 pieces (and possibly others) from Edinburgh, Nat. Lib., MS Panmure 10 (mod. edn. of 3 in *SBK*, xv); Pavan and Galliard by 'Kinloughe' in Add. 30485, ff. 22, 23.

*KYRTON (b. ?, d. ?), early 16th-century composer. Nothing is known of his life. *Miserere* for keyboard in Add. 29996, ff. 6, 7v. (2 copies: mod. edn. in *EECM*, vi, No. 18).

*LA BARRE, Pierre de (also BARE, BEARE, etc., in English sources) (1592–1656), French composer. Biography in *MGG*. Arkwright quotes Eitner incorrectly in giving the date of death as 1678. Pieces in Add. 10337;

Ch. Ch. 1177, 1236; New York, Pub. Lib., Drexel 5611; some pieces also in Berlin, Staatsbib., Lynar A1, which contains much English music. Mod. edn. of pieces from Ch. Ch. 1177 in *L'Organiste liturgique*, xviii (1958) pp. 27–9, ed. J. Bonfils.

LASSO, Orlando di (1532–1594), Flemish composer. Transcriptions of *Susanne un jour* in Edinburgh, Nat. Lib., MS Panmure 10, Add. 30485, f. 51v, and by Philips, who also arranged other works (see Philips).

LAWES, William (1602–1645). Two keyboard suites in MH; one also in Ch. Ch. 1003 (in full) and Ch. Ch. 1236 (2 movements only). Suite from Paris, Rés. 1185 in *Trois Masques à la Cour de Charles Ier d'Angleterre,* ed. M. Lefkowitz, Paris, 1970, p. 316.

LOCKE, Matthew (*ca.* 1622–1677): see Part 2.

LOOSEMORE (? Henry, d. 1670). 'Courant' in Ch. Ch. 1236.

LOWE, Edward (*ca.* 1610–1682): see Part 2.

LUGGE, John (*ca.* 1587–*ca.* 1647). 9 plainsong settings, 1 hexachord, 3 voluntaries for double organ in Ch. Ch. 49 (autograph); 'Mr Luggs Jigg' in Ch. Ch. 431; 2 'Toys' in Paris, Bib. Nat., fonds du Cons. Rés. 1186. The 3 Voluntaries ed. S. Jeans and J. Steele; Toys and Jigg ed. ditto (see Bibliography).

*MARCHANT, John (b. ?, d. ?), 16th–17th-century composer. Pavan in Cambridge, Fitz. Mus., 52. d. 25 (mod. edn. in *SBK*, xxiv); 'Allemanda' in *FWVB*, No. 187; 'The Marchant's Dream' in London, Brit. Mus., R.M. 24. d. 3, p. 170 (in table of contents 'Marchant's Dreame'); Pavan and Galliard in Add. 30485, ff. 20v, 21r.

MARENZIO, Luca (1553–1599), Italian composer. His *Tirsi* arranged by P. Philips (q.v.).

*MERCURE (b. ?, d. ?), 17th-century French composer: see Arkwright. Pieces in Add. 10337, Ch. Ch. 1236.

MICO, Richard (d. before 1665). 2 18th-century arrangements of pavans for viols in London, Brit. Mus., Egerton 2485.

MORLEY, Thomas (1557–? 1602). See also *MGG*. He was *magister puerorum* at Norwich Cathedral, 1583–1587 (*ML*, xlii. 97). Complete keyboard works in *SBK*, xii, xiii. Pavan and Galliard for strings arr. by Richardson (q.v.). 'La volta', arr. Byrd, in *FWVB*, No. 159.

*MULLINER, Thomas (b. ?, d. ?). *Grove* has a long article on the 'Mulliner Book' (Add. 30513; mod. edn. in *MB*, i), compiled by Mulliner. No original keyboard works by him are known. In 1563 he was *modulator organorum* at Corpus Christi College, Oxford. For arrangements assumed to be his work, see Edwards, Johnson (Robert I), Mundy (William), Newman, Shepherd, Tallis, Taverner, Tye, White.

MUNDY, John (*ca.* 1550–*ca.* 1630). Five pieces in *FWVB*.

MUNDY, William (d. ? 1591), father of preceding. 'Tres partes in una', arranged from his antiphon *Exsurge Christe,* in Add. 30513, f. 114v (mod. edn. in *MB*, i).

*NAU: see Noue.

*NEWMAN (b. ?, d. ?), 16th-century composer. Two pieces in Add. 30513 (mod. edn. in *MB*, i), both arranged from lute works (see Lumsden,

Anthology). The 'Newman's Pavan' arranged by Randall (q.v.) may be by a different composer.

*Noue. 'Perhaps Stephen or Simon Nau, both of whom were Musicians to Charles I' (Arkwright). 'Corant' in Ch. Ch. 1236.

Oldfield, Thomas (b. ?, d. ?). Nothing is known of his life. A 'Praeludium' is in *FWVB*, No. 49.

*Ostermayre, John (b. ?, d. ?), Flemish composer? Details of life unknown. 'Galiarda' in *FWVB*, No. 260.

Parsons, Robert (d. 1570). His *In nomine* a 5 arranged by Byrd (q.v.) and anon. in Add. 29996.

Peerson, Martin (*ca.* 1572–1650). 4 pieces in *FWVB*.

Philips, Peter (1561–1628). See esp. *MGG, Grove Supplement*. 19 pieces in *FWVB*, Nos. 70–88 (6 also in Berlin, Staatsbib., Lynar A1); 5 pieces in Berlin, Staatsbib., MS 40316 (2 also in *FWVB*, Lynar A1); 2 pieces in Liège, Univ. Lib., MS 153 (1 is a variant of Striggio's *Chi fara* in *FWVB*; mod. edn. in *AMO*, x); 5 pieces in Uppsala, Univ. Lib., MS 408 (2 also in *FWVB*); 1 piece, probably an arrangement, in Ch. Ch. 89.

Phillips, Arthur (1605–1695). 'Ground' in Add. 29996. Possibly by Thomas Tomkins; but this ascription, found only in the index, is doubtful. Mod. edns. in *EKM*, iv, and *MB*, v (ascribed to Tomkins).

Pichi (Picchi), Giovanni (b. ?, d. ?). In *Grove* s.v. Picchi. Italian 16th–17th-century composer. A 'Toccata' in *FWVB*, No. 95.

Pilkington, Francis (d. 1638). A setting of 'My choice is made, and I desire no change' by Robert Hall (q.v.), mod. edn. in *PBVB*, No. 16.

Portman, Richard (d. *ca.* 1655). 'Sarabrand' in Ch. Ch. 1177; Double Voluntary in Wimborne, Minster Lib., MS without shelf-mark.

Preston, Thomas (b. ?, d. ?), 16th-century composer. ? organist and *informator*, Magdalen Coll., Oxford, 1543; organist of Windsor, 1558–9. Harrison, *Music in Medieval Britain*, p. 192; Fellowes, *Windsor Organists*. 17 pieces in Add. 29996, all liturgical (1 in *EECM*, vi; 15 in *EECM*, x).

Price, Robert (b. ?, d. ?), see Part 2.

Randall, William (d. ? 1640). See *Grove Supplement*. Three arrangements, of works by (Edward) Johnson, 'Newman' and Dowland (q.v.) in Cambridge, Fitz. Mus., MS 52. d. 25 (mod. edn. in *SBK*, xxiv).

Redford, John (d. 1547). About 45 pieces, all but one liturgical, in Add. 15233, 29996, 30513; Ch. Ch. 371, 1034; and Oxford, Bod. Lib., Mus. Sch. c.93. Mod. edns. in *MB*, i; *EECM*, vi, x.

*Renold (b. ?, d. ?). Identity unknown. 1 piece in Add. 30485, f. 42.

Richardson, Ferdinando (= Sir Ferdinando Heybourne) (d. 1618). Pavan and Galliard, each with variation, in *FWVB*, Nos. 4–7 (also in Add. 30485, f. 75v); a second pair, each with variation, in *FWVB*, Nos. 27–30; Alman in Add. 30485, f. 77v; Pavan and Galliard by Thomas Morley, 'set by Mr. Heybourne', in Cambridge, Fitz. Mus., MS 52. d. 25 (mod. edns. in *SBK*, xiii, xxiv).

*Roberts, John (b. ?, d. ?): see Part 2.

Rogers, Benjamin (1614–1698): see Part 2.

Rosseter, Philip (1568–1623): see Farnaby (*FWVB*, No. 283).

Rossi, Michele Angelo (*ca.* 1600–*ca.* 1660), Italian composer, pupil of Frescobaldi. A Toccata which may be by him is attributed to H. Purcell in Add. 31446 and 34695.

Ryse: see Aprys.

*S., M. Not a composer, but an abbreviation ('M.S.') for 'Mal Sims', *FWVB*, No. 16. *Cf. FWVB*, No. 281, by G. Farnaby.

Shelby (Selby), William (d. ? 1570). According to West, *Cathedral Organists*, he died in 1570. 2 liturgical pieces in Add. 30513 (mod. edn. in *MB*, i).

Shepherd (Sheppard), John (*ca.* 1520–? 1563). 8 pieces in Add. 30513, probably all arrangements (mod. edn. in *MB*, i).

*Soncino, Emanuell (b. ?, d. ?), Italian composer? Prelude dated 1633 in Add. 31403, f. 5v. Also a piece called 'Cromotica' (*sic*) in Add. 36661, f. 65.

*Stone, John (b. ?, d. ?): see Part 2.

*Strengthfeild, Thomas (b. ?, d. ?), mid-17th-century composer. Nothing is known of his life. 4 suites, 3 in 2 movements and 1 in 3, in Add. 10337.

Striggio, Alessandro, the elder (*ca.* 1535–*ca.* 1595). His madrigal *Chi farà fed' al ciel* set twice by Philips (q.v.). For the original source of this work (only the first 65 bars are extant) see Grove; mod. edn. in *AMO*, x.

Strogers, Nicholas: see Strowgers.

Strowger, E. (b. ?, d. ?), early 16th-century composer. Only a single piece for keyboard (*Miserere*, Add. 29996, f. 6v: mod. edn. in *EECM*, vi) can be attributed to him.

Strowgers (Strogers), Nicholas (b. ?, d. ?). 3 (probably 4) pieces in Ch. Ch. 371 (1 ed. in *Altenglische Orgelmusik*); Fantasia in *FWVB*, No. 89.

Sweelinck, Jan Pieterszoon (1562–1621), Dutch composer. 4 pieces in *FWVB* (1 also in Ch. Ch. 1113, also 1003, ending only). Mod. edns. in Sweelinck, *Werken*, i, and *The Instrumental Works*, i.

Tallis, Thomas (*ca.* 1505–1585). About 23 pieces in Ch. Ch. 371, 1034; Add. 30513 (including 6 arrangements: mod. edn. in MB, i); *FWVB*, Nos. 109, 110 (2 settings of *Felix namque*, the 2nd also in London, Brit. Mus., R.M. 23. l. 4, R.M. 24. d. 3, Add. 30485 and 31403); Add. 30485, 31403. All except the arrangements in Tallis, *Complete Keyboard Works*.

Taverner, John (*ca.* 1490–1545). The *In nomine* from his Mass *Gloria tibi Trinitas* is arranged for keyboard in Add. 30513 (mod. edn. in *MB*, i) and, ornamented, in Ch. Ch. 371 (mod. edn. in *Altenglische Orgelmusik*). The *Agnus Dei* from his 'Western Wind' Mass (bars 1–20, voices 1 and 3 only) is found in keyboard score in London, Brit. Mus., Roy. App. 56, f. 17v. A piece, the source of which cannot be traced, is printed in *EEOM*.

*Taylere (b. ?, d. ?), 16th-century composer, ? John Taylor, 'master of the singing children of the hospital of St. Mary's, Woolnoth, in 1557, and between 1561–1568, master of "the children of the grammar schoole in the colledge of Westminster" ' (*DVM*, p. xi). He was also organist of Westminster Abbey. Composed a Pavan (and doubtless the following Galliard) in *DVM*, Nos. 3, (4).

Thorne, John (d. 1573). In 1540 he was at St. Mary-at-Hill: see Baillie, *ML* (1955) 55. Probably became Minster organist, York, where he died. *Exsultabunt sancti* in Add. 29996, f. 37v (mod. edn. in *EECM*, x).

*Tisdale (Tisdall), William (b. ?, d. ?), 16th-century musician. Complete keyboard works in *SBK*, xiv. 2 pieces from Cambridge, Fitz. Mus., MS 52. d. 25, also in *SBK*, xxiv.

Tomkins, John (*ca.* 1586–1638). 'John come kiss me now' (variations) in Add. 29996, f. 205v (mod. edn. in *EKM*, iv).

Tomkins, Thomas (1572–1656), half-brother of preceding. For biography see also Stevens, *Thomas Tomkins*. Complete keyboard works in *MB*, v, with details of sources.

Tregian, Francis (*ca.* 1574–1619). Copyist of *FWVB*. No. 105, 'Heaven and Earth' is ascribed to 'Fre.' Nos. 61 and 93 are settings of works of his by Byrd and No. 80, and presumably also 81, settings by Philips. No. 214 is 'Mrs. Katherin Tregian's Paven', by William Tisdall.

*Tresure, Jonas (? d. before 1660). ? French composer. 5 pieces in Ch. Ch. 1236.

Tye, Christopher (*ca.* 1500–1572). 2 arrangements, in Ch. Ch. 371 and Add. 30513 (mod. edn. in *MB*, i).

Warrock (Warwick), Thomas (b. ?, d. ?). In *Grove* s.v. Warwick. Bull's assistant as organist of Hereford Cathedral, 1586–1589 (*MB*, xiv, p. xxi). 2 pieces in *FWVB*, Nos. 97–8 (*Grove* mistakenly attributes these to his son, d. 1660).

Weelkes, Thomas (*ca.* 1575–1623). Two voluntaries (the first anon.) and a pavan in New York, MS Drexel 5612; galliard in Add. 30485. For mod. edn. see Bibliography (Addenda).

White (Whyte), Robert (d. 1574). 'Ut re mi fa soul la' in Ch. Ch. 371 (mod. edn. in *Altenglische Orgelmusik*); *In nomine* in Add. 30513 (mod. edn. in *MB*, i).

Wilbye, John (1574–1638). A setting by him of Dowland's 'Frog Gallliard' is in Edinburgh, Nat. Lib., Panmure 9 (mod. edn. in *SBK*, ix, No. 10).

Wilder, Philip van (d. ? 1557). Netherlands composer resident in England. An anon. setting of 'Je file' in Nottingham, Univ. Lib., 'Lord Middleton's Lute Book', f. 91v.

*Wodson (b. ?, d. ?). Probably not Thomas Woodson, and certainly not Leonard Woodson (see below). *Miserere* in Ch. Ch. 371.

Woodson, Leonard (d. 1641). 'Mall Sims' in Berlin, Staatsbib., Lynar A1, p. 290.

Woodson, Thomas (d. ? 1605). 'Forty Wayes of 2 pts. in one', Add. 29996, f. 184v. These are canonic settings of *Miserere*. Only 20 are written down. Thomas Tomkins wrote in the MS: 'the rest of these wayes are prickt in my morleys Introduction'; but they are not to be found in his copy of Morley now in Oxford, Magdalen College Library.

*Wynslate (Wynslade), Richard (d. ? 1573). Singer at St. Mary-at-Hill, 1537–8; master of the choristers, Winchester Cathedral, 1540–1572 or 1573. *Lucem tuam* in Add. 29996, f. 19v (mod. edn. in *EECM*, vi, No. 9).

Yves: see Ives, Simon.

PART 2

1660–1800

In this part reference to transcriptions is generally omitted after 1700. References to sets or variations and rondos on popular tunes, as to other ephemeral material, are given only in abbreviated form. Continental composers are mentioned when there is evidence of a substantial contribution in English sources, even when the sources do not appear in Appendix I. Information about a composer's output is given in the following order: printed editions devoted to his music in chronological order (place of publication London unless otherwise stated); printed collections containing his work (referred to by symbol: see List of Abbreviations, p. xix); MSS containing his work; modern editions (see also Bibliography). For locations of printed sources, see *BUCEM*. Keyboard concertos are included; also works for solo keyboard with accompanying parts if specially so designated; also works for harp if the pianoforte is named as an alternative. Works written on two staves but intended primarily for a solo instrument with *continuo* are not included. Documentation on composers who died after 1800 is continued until their death, even though again such sources do not appear in Appendix I. Composers born after 1780 are not listed.

ABEL, Karl Friedrich (1723–1787), German composer, resident in London 1759–1783 and from 1785, where many of his keyboard works were published. In BC. 4 sonatas in Add. 14335.

*ABINGTON, William (b. ?, d. ?), late 18th-century composer. *Six favorite canzonets for the piano forte, with an accompaniment for the violin . . . Op. 1* (for the Author, *ca.* 1790).

ALCOCK, John (1715–1806). *Six suites of easy lessons* . . . (for the Author, 1741); *Six suites of easy lessons* . . . (Reading: for the Author, [1742]); *Ten voluntaries for the organ or harpsichord* . . . *Book I* (C. and S. Thompson, [1774]); *Twelve divertimentis for the guitar, harpsichord or piano forte . . . Book 2nd* (John Rutherford, *ca.* 1775); *A favorite lesson for the harpsichord or forte piano* (G. Gardom, *ca.* 1775). Mod. edns. in *OEOM*, i, ii; see also Bibliography.

ALCOCK, John (*ca.* 1740–1791), son of preceding. *The Chace, a favorite lesson for the harpsichord or piano forte* (C. and S. Thompson, *ca.* 1770); *A favorite rondo for the harpsichord or piano forte* (C. [and] S. T[hompson], *ca.* 1770); *Eight easy voluntaries for the organ* (Longman, Lukey and Co., *ca.* 1775). Mod. edn. in *OEOM*, iii.

AMADORI, Giuseppe (b. ?, d. ?), early 18th-century Italian composer, never resident in England. 'Tocata' in LE. Music in *A second collection* . . . (Walsh, [1719]).

AMOS, G. B. (full name and dates unknown). *No. 1 of a set of sonatas in a pleasing and familiar stile for the piano forte or harp* (for the Author, *ca.* 1800).

*ANGKISTRO, G. (b. ?, d. ?). *A grand sonata, for the harpsichord or piano forte, with an accompaniment for a violin & violoncello* (Preston, *ca.* 1785).

ANONYMOUS. For collections including works by several anonymous composers see Appendix I, Part 2. Authors identified only by their initials are dealt with alphabetically according to the final initial. Also the following: *Eighteen preludes or short fuges for the organ or harpsichord proper for interludes to psalm tunes* (C. and S. Thompson, *ca.* 1770); *New Music for the piano forte or harpsichord composed by a Gentleman* (Edinburgh: James Johnson, *ca.* 1785); *The Bastile, a favourite sonata for the harpsichord or piano forte* (Preston and Son, *ca.* 1789); *A favourite lesson for the harpsichord by a celebrated author* (*ca.* 1790); *Six sonatinas for the harpsichord or piano forte by a pupil of Giuseppe Haydn* (G. Goulding, *ca.* 1790); *Twice 2 is 4. The Multiplication Table, adapted for juvenile improvement as a lesson for the piano forte* (Preston and Son, *ca.* 1790); *Music made Easy . . . being a complete book of instructions . . . to which are added eight progressive lessons . . .* (1798); *Nelson's Victory. A Sonata for the piano forte. Inscribed to his Lordship by the Author* (Longman and Broderip, [1798]); *Four new German Waltzes for the piano forte* (for the Author, *ca.* 1800). Also numerous works of an ephemeral nature.

ARNE, Thomas Augustine (1710–1778). *VIII Sonatas or lessons for the harpsichord* (Walsh, [1756]); *Six favourite concertos, for the organ, harpsichord, or piano forte* (Harrison and Co., *ca.* 1787). MSS include Add. 39957; Tenbury, St. Michael's Coll., MS 752. Mod. edns. in *OEOM*, i, iii; see also Bibliography.

ARNOLD, Samuel (1740–1802). *A favourite lesson . . .* (Welcker, [1768]); *Eight lessons . . . Opera VII* (Welcker, *ca.* 1770. Another edn: Longman and Broderip, *ca.* 1785); *Six overtures . . . Opera VIII* (Welcker, *ca.* 1775); *A second sett of eight lessons . . . Opera X* (Welcker, [1775]. Another edn: Longman and Broderip, *ca.* 1778); *Twelve minuets . . .* (Welcker, *ca.* 1775); *A third sett of eight sonatas . . . with an accompaniment for a violin . . . Opera XI* (J. Blundell, *ca.* 1780. Another edn: Longman and Broderip, *ca.* 1785); *A set of progressive lessons . . . Opera XII* (2 books, Welcker, *ca.* 1777–1779. Another edn. of Book I: Longman and Broderip, *ca.* 1785, bound with Book II of the original edn. Eitner gives *Leçons progressives pour clavier*, Op. 12, Broderip, n.d.); *Three concerto's for the harpsichord . . . Opera XV* (to be had at the Author's house, [1782]); *Three grand sonatas . . . Opera XXIII* (for the Author, [1783]). Eitner mentions 8 sonatas by 'Arnold' without first name. Sonatas in SS. MSS: London, R.C.M., 735; Add. 14335, 35024, 35040.

ARRESTI, Floriano (*ca.* 1650–1719), Italian composer. In *A second collection . . .* (Walsh, [1719]).

ASHLEY, John James (1772–1815). *Three sonatas for the piano forte. With an accompaniment for the violin . . . Op. 1ma* (for the Author, *ca.* 1790).

ATTWOOD, Thomas (1765–1838). *Three sonatas . . . with accompanyments for a violin and violoncello ad libitum . . . Op. II*ᵃ (Longman and Broderip, *ca.* 1788. Another edn.: F. Linley, *ca.* 1798); *Easy progressive lessons . . .* (Longman and Broderip, *ca.* 1795). Eitner lists in addition: *The Salzburg Waltz* (1816); *A short introduction to the pianoforte* (n.d.). Sonata (with violoncello) in SC2.

AVISON, Charles (1709–1770). *Two concerto's, the first for an organ or harpsichord, in eight parts . . .* (Newcastle; Joseph Barber, 1742); *Six sonatas for the harpsichord with accompanyments for two violins and violoncello . . . Opera quinta*

(John Johnson, 1756); *Six sonatas, with accompanyments* [as above] . . . *Opera settima* (Newcastle: for the Author, 1760. Another edn.: R. Bremner, *ca.* 1765. Another edn.: Preston and Son, *ca.* 1793); *Six sonatas, for the harpsichord, with accompanyments* as above . . . *Opera ottava* (for the Author, 1764. Another edn.: for the Author, *ca.* 1768). The string concertos, opp. 2, 4 and 9 were published in arrangements for keyboard and strings.

AYLWARD, Theodore (1730–1801). *Six Lessons for the harpsichord, organ or piano forte* . . . *Opera prima* (for the Author, [1784]). Lesson in Add. 35025.

BABB, Samuel (b. ?, d. ?), 18th-century composer and publisher. *Six sonatas for the piano forte or harpsichord with an accompanyment for a violin ad libitum* . . . *Op. 1* (for the Author, *ca.* 1770).

BABELL, William (*ca.* 1690–1723), editor and arranger. He edited SHSL, LE3–4, and made many operatic transcriptions, especially of Handel. See Bibliography s.v. Handel, ed. Chrysander, *Works*, xlviii.

BACH, Johann Christian (1735–1782), German composer, resident in England from 1762, where much of his keyboard music was published (including music in BC and *Six Lessons*, Welcker). C. P. E. Bach (1714–1788), J. C. F. Bach (1732–1795) and W. F. E. Bach (1759–1845) were also published in London. Music by J. S. Bach (1685–1750), C. P. E. Bach and W. F. Bach (1710–1784) exists in English MSS before 1800.

BANISTER, John (1630–1679). One piece in M; Saraband in Ch. Ch. 1003; 'Banister's Tune' in Oxford, Bod. Lib., Mus. Sch. d. 219. Mod. edn. of piece in M in *PSMS*, xvi.

BAPTIST: see Draghi; Lully.

*BARBER, Robert (of Newcastle; b. ?, d. ?). *Six sonatas for piano forte or harpsichord with an accompaniment for a violin and violoncello* . . . *Opera prima* (for the Author, *ca.* 1775); *A favourite sonata for the piano forte or harpsichord with accompanyment for a violin and a violoncello* (Longman and Broderip, *ca.* 1780).

*BARBIERI, C. (b. ?, d. ?), Italian composer. See *BUCEM*; also in LT.

BARRETT, John (*ca.* 1674–*ca.* 1735). Pieces in CC, 2HM, 3HM, LB, 2LB. MSS: Add. 17853, 22099, 47846, 52363; Ch. Ch. 46. London, Dulwich Coll., Reading MSS (incl. voluntary elsewhere ascribed to H. Purcell). Suite in A from CC in *CP*, vii, with 1 other piece; Voluntary in *TW*, xxi.

*BARTHÉLEMON, Celia Maria, later Mrs. C. M. Henslowe (b. ?, d. ?), daughter of François Hippolyte Barthélemon (1741–1808), who published keyboard music in London after his arrival there in 1765. *Three sonatas* . . . *Opera Prima* (Vauxhall: for the Author, [1791]); *Two sonatas* . . . *with accompaniments* . . . *Opera seconda* [1792]; *Sonata* . . . *Op. 3* (J. Bland, *ca.* 1794); *A Sonata* . . . *with an accompaniment for a violin* . . . *Op. IV* (for the Authoress, *ca.* 1795); *The Capture of the Cape of Good Hope* . . . *concluding with a song and chorus* (L. Lavenu, [1795]).

BARTHÉLEMON, Mrs. Maria (formerly Mary Young, *ca.* 1749–1799), mother of preceding. *Six sonatas* . . . *with an accompaniment for the violin* (for the Authoress, [1776]).

BASSANI, Giovanni Battista (*ca.* 1657–1716), Italian composer. In *Voluntarys and fugues* . . . (Walsh, [1710]).

BATIS: see Draghi.

BATTISHILL, Jonathan (1738–1801). His work appeared in a few 19th-century collections (see Eitner). Of these, Novello's *Cathedral Voluntaries* (1831, wrongly dated 1731 by Eitner; also in MS Add. 31120) consists of transcriptions from sacred vocal works. One piece in *OEOM*, i, ii.

BAUMGARTEN, Karl Friedrich (*ca.* 1740–1824), German composer, settled in England *ca.* 1758. Many publications in England; MSS include London, R.C.M., 735, 1150–1.

BECKWITH, John Christmas (1750–1809). *Six voluntaries for the organ, harpsichord, etc.* (for the Author, 1780); *A favorite sonata* . . . [Op. 3] (Longman and Broderip, *ca.* 1795); *A favorite concerto* . . . *with accompanyments* [Op. 4 according to Eitner] (Longman and Boderip, *ca.* 1795).

BEETHOVEN, Ludwig van (1770–1827). A few minor keyboard works were published in England before 1800.

BELLAMY, Richard (d. 1813). *Two sonatas for the piano-forte or harpsichord adapted for the use of schools* (Longman and Broderip, 1789).

BENDA, Georg (1722–1795), Bohemian, German composer. Lesson in *Six Lessons* (Welcker, *ca.* 1770).

*BENNETT, John (*ca.* 1735–1784). For biography see *RRMBE*, vi. *Ten voluntaries for the organ or harpsichord* (for the Author, *ca.* 1758). Mod. edn. of 6 in *RRMBE,* vi; voluntaries and extracts in *OEOM*, i–iv; see also Bibliography.

*BENSON, Thomas (b. ?, d. ?). One piece in Add. 17853.

BERG, Georg(e) (b. ?, d. ?), German 18th-century composer settled in London. 7 keyboard publications there listed in *BUCEM*, Eitner. Nos. 4, 2, 5 and 3 of *Ten Voluntaries*, Op. 2 (or Op. 8?) in Add. 14335.

*BEWLAY, Henry (b. ?, d. ?). *Three sonatas* . . . *with an accompaniment for a violin or German flute ad libitum* (for the Author, *ca.* 1794); *Twelve easy and familiar lessons* . . . . *Op.* 2nd (Culliford, Rolfe and Barrow, *ca.* 1795).

BILLINGTON, Mrs. Elizabeth, née Weichsell (1765 or 1768–1818). *Three lessons* . . . *by Elizabeth Weichsell, a child eight years of age* (Welcker, *ca.* 1773 or 1776); *Six Sonatas* . . . *composed by Elizabeth Weichsel in the eleventh year of her age. Opera 2da* (for the Author, [1776 or 1779]). NB: *BUCEM* gives the date of these publications as *ca.* 1775 and 1778 respectively. *Grove* prefers the earlier date of birth.

BILLINGTON, Thomas (*ca.* 1754–1832). *A fourth set of twelve love canzonets* . . . *to which is added a sonata* . . . *Opera X* (for the Author, [1784]). The 6 sonatas Op. 6 have an 'obbligato accompaniment'; other keyboard works are arrangements of Cramer and Boccherini.

BLAKE, Benjamin (1761–1827). *Six sonatas for the piano forte with an accompaniment for a violin* . . . *Opera 4* (for the Author, [1794]); *Nine divertimentis, for the piano forte, with an accompaniment for a violin ad libitum. Op. 5* (for the Author, *ca.* 1795).

BLEWITT, Jonas (d. 1805). *Ten voluntaries for the organ or harpsichord* . . . *Op. 2* (for the Author, *ca.* 1780); *A complete treatise on the organ, to which is added a set of explanatory voluntaries* . . . *Op. 4* (Longman and Broderip, *ca.* 1795); *Ten voluntaries or pieces for the organ* . . . *Opera V* (Culliford, Rolfe and Barrow, [1796]); *Twelve easy and familiar movements for the organ . . . Opera 6th* (for the Author, *ca.* 1797).

BLOW, John (1649–1708). *A choice collection of lessons for the harpsichord, spinnet, &c. containing four setts . . .* (Henry Playford, [1698]. Another edn: I. Walsh and I. Hare, [1704]). Pieces in 2MH, CC, 2HM; an unidentified work in CV3. MSS include London, Brit. Mus., Egerton 2959; Add. 22099, 31403, 31465, 31446, 31468, 31814, 34695, 52363; R.C.M. 2093; Ch. Ch. 47, 1003, 1176–7, 1179; *ibid.*, Dulwich Coll., MSS 92a, b, d; Brussels, Bib. du Cons., MS 15418; Cambridge, Fitz. Mus., MS 653; Edinburgh, Nat. Lib., Inglis 94 MS 3343; Paris, Bib. Nat., fonds du Cons., Rés. 1186 bis I. Mod. edn. of 2HM in *SBK*, x; see also Bibliography. Many pieces in *CP*, i, ii, some not otherwise published, and in *Old English Composers*.

BOWMAN, Henry (b. ?, d. ?), 17th–18th-century composer. Short piece in Add. 30382.

BOYCE, William (1711–1779). *Ten voluntaries for the organ or harpsichord* (S.A. and P. Thompson, *ca.* 1785). An unidentified work in CV3. See also Greene, Maurice. Voluntaries in *OEOM*, i-iv; see also Bibliography.

*BOYTON, William (b. ?, d. ?). *A second concerto for harpsichord or organ with accompaniments . . .* (Longman, Lukey and Co., *ca.* 1775). Both his concertos are apparently extant. See Cudworth, *The Score* (1953) 59.

*BREWSTER, Henry (b. ?, d. ?). *A set of lessons for the harpsichord or piano forte . . . Op. iv* (for the Author, *ca.* 1785).

*BRIGNELL, Thomas (b. ?, d. ?). Owner of Add. 17852 in 1712, possibly the composer of its first piece.

BRODERIP, Robert (1758–1808), of Bristol. See *MT* (1970) 1220. Related to Francis Broderip, the publisher? *Eight voluntary's for the harpsichord or piano forte . . . Op. V* (Longman and Broderip, *ca.* 1785); *A favorite concerto for the harpsichord or the piano forte . . . Op. 7* (Longman and Broderip, *ca.* 1785); *Plain and easy instructions for young performers on the piano forte or harpsichord, to which are added twelve progressive lessons* (Longman and Broderip, *ca.* 1788); *Four sonatas . . . with an accompagniment for a violin* (Longman and Broderip, *ca.* 1790). Eitner refers to 8 voluntaries, Op. 1.

*BROOKS, James (b. ?, d. ?). *Favourite sonata . . . with a violin accompt.* ([Bland and Weller, *ca.* 1795]); *A sonata for the piano forte . . . with an accompaniment for the violin* (Bland and Weller, *ca.* 1800).

BRYAN, Albertus (Albert BRYNE, BRIAN) (d. *ca.* 1670). 2 suites in MH/3. Pieces in Add. 34695 (as 'A.B.'); Ch. Ch. 1177, 1236; Oxford, Bod. Lib., Mus. Sch. d. 219.

*BURBRIDGE, R. (b. ?, d. ?). *A first sett of three favorite rondos for the forte-piano . . . Op. 1* (W. Cope, [1796]); *Sally in our Alley with variations . . .* (W. Hodsall, *ca.* 1800).

*BURGESS, Henry, the elder (b. ?, d. ?). A collection of lessons for the harpsichord (John Johnson, *ca.* 1740).

*BURGESS, Henry, the younger (b. ?, d. ?). *Six concertos, for the organ and harpsichord* (J. Walsh, *ca.* 1740); *Six concertos for the harpsichord or organ* (I. Walsh, *ca.* 1745).

BURNEY, Charles (1726–1814). *VI cornet pieces with an introduction for the diapasons, and a fugue* (I. Walsh, [1751]); *Six sonatas for the harpsichord* (for the Author, [1761]. Another edn.: for the Author, [1766]); *Two sonatas for the harpsichord and forte piano with accompaniments for a violin and violoncello* (R. Bremner, *ca.* 1770); a second set of the same (R. Bremner, *ca.* 1770, but according to *Grove* 1772); *Four sonatas or duets for two performers on one piano forte or harpsichord* (for the Author, 1777); *A second set of four sonatas or duets* (for the Author [1778]); *Sonate à trois mains, for harpsichord* (R. Bremner, *ca.* 1780); *Preludes, fugues and interludes for the organ, Book I* (for the Author, *ca.* 1790; *Grove*: 1787); *A favourite rondo* (*ca.* 1801); *A second rondo* (*ca.* 1805); mod. edns. in *OEOM*, i, iv.

*Burney, Charles Rousseau (b. ?, d. ?). *Four sonatas for the harpsichord or piano-forte, with an accompanyment for a violin and a duet for two performers on one instrument* (for the Author, [1781]); *Two sonatas for the harpsichord or piano-forte; and a duet for two performers on one instrument . . . Opera II* (for the Author, [1786]); *Air with variations for the piano forte* (*ca.* 1795).

Burton, John (1730–1782). *Ten sonatas for the harpsichord, organ or piano forte* (for the Author, [1766]. Another ed: Welcker, *ca.* 1770. Numerous selections were also published); *Six sonatas for the piano forte, harpsichord or organ with an accompaniment for the violin . . . Opera seconda* (for the Author, *ca.* 1770). Various minor publications are listed by Eitner. Various works in Add. 16155, including the whole of Op. 2. Concerto in A (Cambridge, Fitz. Mus., MS 30 f. 21) and 5 keyboard pieces (*ibid.*, MS 32. f. 14). *Grove* refers to 4 keyboard concertos.

Busby, Thomas (1755–1838). *Six sonatas for the harpsichord or piano forte . . . Opera 1* (for the Author, *ca.* 1785; also in PM7, No. 5).

Butler, Thomas Hamley (1755–1823). Many sets of variations and rondos on popular tunes. Music anonymously in BC.

*Byron, William Lord (1669–1736). Pieces in Add. 22099, 47846.

Callcot, John Wall (1766–1821). *Six sonatinos . . . with an accompanyment for a violin . . . Op. III* (P. Hawthorn, *ca.* 1786). Also many ephemeral works.

Camidge, John (1735–1803). *Six easy lessons for the harpsichord* (York: for the Author, [1764]. Another edn: Welcker, *ca.* 1770). Nos. 1, 2 and 6 of the above in Add. 14335.

Camidge, Matthew (1758–1844), son of preceding. *Three sonatas . . . with accompaniments for a violin & violoncello . . . Op. 5* (Preston and Son, *ca.* 1790). Another edn: *ca.* 1796); *Instructions for the piano forte or harpsichord, and eight sonatinas, with an accompaniment for a violin . . . to which is added useful preludes* (for the Author, *ca.* 1795); *A first and second sett of easy preludes* (for the Author, *ca.* 1795); *Ten easy sonatas . . . with an accompaniment for a violin* (for the Author, *ca.* 1796); *A favourite sonata for the piano forte or harp, with an accompaniment for a violin or flute . . . Op. 8* (for the Author, *ca.* 1800); *A favorite sonata . . . Op. 9* (Bland and Weller, *ca.* 1800); *Six concertos for the organ or grand piano forte* [without orchestra] *. . . Op. 13* (Preston, *ca.* 1815). Concerto movements in *OEOM*, i, iii; see Bibliography.

*Carbonelli, E. (b. ?, d. ?), 18th-century Italian (?) composer. In Tenbury, St. Michael's Coll., MS 752.

Carey, Henry (*ca.* 1687–1743). In HMI(2)

CARNABY, William (1772–1839). *A favorite sonata for the piano-forte* (for the Author, *ca.* 1800). Many minor keyboard works were printed.

CARTER, Charles Thomas (*ca.* 1735–1804). *Six lessons for the harpsichord or forte piano* (Welcker, [1770]); *Six sonatas for the harpsichord or piano forte with an accompanyment for a violin and violoncello* . . . *Opera IIId* (Napier, [1774]); *Social powers, with variations* (G. Smart, *ca.* 1775); *Twelve familiar sonatinas* . . . *Opera VI* (Smart, *ca.* 1780); *Sonata for the piano forte* . . . *Opera 26* (for the Composer, *ca.* 1800); *Fugues and full pieces* [for organ]. *Book the first. Opera 37* (A. Hamilton, *ca.* 1800). Eitner mentions several other minor works, printed and MS; Cudworth (*The Score* (1953) 59) mentions a concerto.

*CASSON, John (b. ?, d. ?). *Eight favourite airs with variations for the pianoforte or harpsichord* (for the Author, *ca.* 1794). Also variations on 'God save the King', 'Rule Britannia' and 'The Cottage Maid' (Pleyel).

*CESARINI, Carlo Franceso (b. ?, d. ?), 18th-century Italian (?) composer. Keyboard music published in England.

*CHALON, John (b. ?, d. ?). *Six sonatinas* . . . *Opera terza* (for the Author, [1765]. Another edn: Harrison, Cluse and Co., *ca.* 1797. Also in PM12); *Six sonates* . . . *accompagnées* [sic] *d'un violon et d'un violoncelle* . . . *Œuvre quatrième* (for the Author, *ca.* 1770). Also sets of variations, including one in PM7.

CHAMBONNIÈRES, Jacques Champion de (1602–*ca.* 1672), French composer. Corant by 'Sambonier' in Ch. Ch. 1236.

*CHAPMAN, R. (b. ?, d. ?), 18th-century composer (see Eitner). In BC.

*CHIAVA, P.D. (b. ?, d. ?), Italian composer. In *Voluntarys and Fugues* (Walsh, [1710]).

CHILCOT, Thomas (d. 1766). *Six suites of lessons for the harpsichord or spinet* (W. Smith, [1734]); *Six concertos for the harpsichord* . . . (John Johnson, 1756); *Six concertos for the harpsichord* . . . *Opera secunda* (Bath: for the Author, 1765).

CHILD, William (1606–1697). 'Preludium' in London, R.C.M., MS 2093.

*CHURCHILL, William (b. ?, d. ?). *A favorite sonata for the harpsichord or piano forte, with an accompanyment for a violin* (W. Campbell, *ca.* 1785); *Ten progressive lessons for the piano forte or harpsichord* . . . *Opera 5* (R. Birchall, *ca.* 1790); *Three sonatas for the grand or square piano forte* . . . *with an accompaniment for the violin* . . . *Op. IV* (Lewis, Houston and Hyde, *ca.* 1795).

CIMAROSA, Domenico (1749–1801), Italian composer. In BC.

CLAGGET, Walter (*ca.* 1741–1798). *A favourite overture for the harpsichord* . . . (C. and S. Thompson, *ca.* 1770).

CLARK(E), Jeremiah (b. ?, d. ?), 18th-century composer. *Six sonatas for the harpsichord or piano forte with accompanyments for two violins & violoncello* . . . *Opera terza* (for the Author, *ca.* 1775).

*CLARK, Stephen (b. ?, d. ?). *Six sonatas for the harpsichord or piano-forte with an accompanyment for the violin* . . . *Opera I* (Edinburgh: for the Author, *ca.* 1790); *Six easy lessons, for the harpsichord* . . . *Opera II* (Edinburgh: N. Stewart, *ca.* 1790); *Two sonatas* . . . *in which are introduced favorite Scotch airs* . . . *Op. 3d* (Edinburgh: for the Author, *ca.* 1795).

CLARKE, Jeremiah (1673 or 1674–1707). *Choice lessons for the harpsichord or spinnett* . . . (Charles King, Jn. Young, Jn. Hare, 1711). Pieces in CC, 2HM,

3HM, LB. MSS include Add. 17853, 22099, 31465, 31467, 47846, 52363: Ch. Ch. 46; Tenbury, St. Michael's Coll., MS 1508. Five suites from *Choice lessons* in *CP*, v.

CLARKE, afterwards CLARKE-WHITFIELD, John (1770–1836). *Three sonatas for the piano forte or harpsichord* . . . *Op. 1* (for the Author, ca. 1789). *Grand sonata for the harp or piano-forte* (Oxford: H. Hardy, ca. 1794). Many keyboard arrangements (Eitner).

*CLARKE, William (b. ?, d. ?). *Three sonatas, for the piano forte, with an accompaniment for the violin* . . . *Op. 1* (Preston, ca. 1799).

CLEMENTI, Muzio (1752–1832), lived in England intermittently from 1766. Many keyboard publications in London; Pieces in SC; MSS in London, Brit. Mus. and R.C.M.

COGAN, Philip (1748–1833). *A favourite lesson and rondo* . . . (Dublin: Anne Lee, ca. 1780); *Mr. Cogan's capital sonata* . . . (Dublin: Anne Lee, ca. 1780. Another edn: ditto. Another edn: Dublin: John Lee, ca. 1785); *Mr. Cogan's celebrated variations to Push about the Jorum* (Dublin: Anne Lee, ca. 1780. Another edn: Dublin, John Lee, ca. 1795); *Six sonatas* . . . (Wm. Napier, 1782); *Cogans favourite rondo* (Dublin: John Lee, ca. 1785); *Three favorite sonatas* . . . *Op. IV* (Longman and Broderip, ca. 1790); *A concerto for the piano forte* . . . *Op. 5* (Edinburgh: Corri and Sutherland, ca. 1790); *A favorite concerto* . . . *Opera 6* (Longman and Broderip, ca. 1790); *Three sonatas* . . . *Op. 7* (Longman and Broderip, ca. 1795. Another edn: ditto); *Three sonatas* . . . *Op. 8* (for the Author, ca. 1800); *Sonata* (1817). MSS include London, R.C.M., 735, 1150.

*COLEMAN, Mark (b. ?, d. ?), mid-17th-century composer. Related (?) to Charles Coleman (d. 1664). 'Corant' for harpsichord in Ch. Ch. 1236.

COLONNA, Giovanni Paolo (1637–1695), Italian composer. In *Voluntarys and Fugues* . . . (Walsh, [1710]).

*CONINGWORTH, Richard (b. ?, d. ?). *Three sonatas, for the piano-forte* . . . *and an accompaniment (ad libitum) for a flute or violin* . . . *Op. 1* (Goulding, Phipps and D'Almaine, ca. 1800).

COOKE, Benjamin (1734–1793). *Fugues and other pieces for the organ* (R. Birchall, ca. 1795). Keyboard works, including a Concerto in D, in London, R.C.M., MSS 810, 814, 816, 817, 820, 823, 824.

*COOKE, Henry (b. ?, d. ?), son (?) of preceding. Keyboard works in London, R.C.M., MS 825.

*COOKE, Matthew (b. ?, d. ?). *A sett of six lessons for the harpsichord or piano forte* . . . (for the Author, ca. 1780. Another edn: J. Bland, ca. 1785).

*COPE, W. P. R. (b. ?, d. ?). *Sonata for the piano forte or harpsichord* . . . *Op. 2* (for the Author, ca. 1795); and a few ephemeral works.

*CORBETT, P. (b. ?, d. ?). *A first set of three sonatas* . . . *Opera I°* (Dublin: for the Author, ca. 1780).

CORELLI, Arcangelo (1653–1713). His music was widely circulated in England and often played in keyboard arrangements, e.g. in HSM. MSS containing such arrangements include: Add. 14335, 17853, 22099, 31403, 31814, 35040; London, R.C.M., MS 1056; R.C.O., MS without shelf-mark; Tenbury, St. Michael's Coll., MS 752.

CORRI, Domenico (1746–1825), Italian composer who settled in Edinburgh in 1771 and moved to London *ca.* 1790. Many solo keyboard publications.

CORRI, Natale, (1765–1822), brother of preceding. See *BUCEM*.

*COSTELLOW, Thomas (b. ?, d. ?). *A favourite lesson for the harpsichord* (Straight and Skillern, *ca.* 1775).

COURTEVILLE, Raphael (d. *ca.* 1735). Pieces in 2HM, LB. MSS include Add. 17853, 22099, 34695, 52363.

*COYLE, Miles (b. ?, d. ?). *Six lessons for the harpsichord or piano forte* . . . (John Preston, *ca.* 1785).

CRAMER, Johann Baptist (1771–1858). Born in Mannheim, but brought to England when a year old. Lived and worked in London with extensive travels abroad. Wrote 7 piano concertos, 105 sonatas, numerous variations, rondos, fantasias etc., and 84 studies and '16 nouvelles études'.

CRAMER, Wilhelm (1745–1799), father of preceding. Settled in England 1772. See *BUCEM*.

CREYGHTON, Robert (*ca.* 1639–1734), son of Robert Creyghton (see Part 1). 2 pieces by 'R.C.' in Add. 37074, in his hand.

CROFT, William (1678–1727). Pieces in 2HM, CC, 3HM, LB. MSS include London, Brit. Mus., Egerton 2959; Add. 5336 (anon.), 17853, 22099, 31465, 31467, 31468, 31814, 40139, 52363; Dulwich Coll., MSS 92a, b, d. Voluntary No. 1 in *OEOM*, i. Many pieces in *CP*, iii, iv.

CROTCH, William (1775–1847). *Three sonatas* . . . (J. Bland, *ca.* 1794); *Prelude and Air for the piano forte* (R. Birchall, *ca.* 1800); with John Crotch, three numbers of *Familiar Airs* (for the Authors, *ca.* 1800); *A concerto for the organ* (*ca.* 1805); *Fugue for the organ or piano forte, composed on a subject of T. Muffat's* (1806); *Divertimento No. 1* (*ca.* 1825); *March and Waltz for two performers on the piano forte* (1833); *Fugues for the organ or piano forte* . . . (12 nos., 1835–1837). MSS include Add. 30392, 32587, 35026. Cudworth (*The Score* (1953) 59) refers to three concertos.

*CROUTCH, (Frederick) William (b. ?, d. ?). Not to be confused with F(reder-ick) W. N(icholls) Crouch, a later composer. *Six sonatas or lessons* . . . *Opera primo* (for the Author, *ca.* 1775); *Three sonatas* . . . *Op. IV* (for the Author, *ca.* 1785; *Six sonatas* . . . *with an accompanyment for a German flute or violin* . . . *Op. 6* (for the Author, *ca.* 1789); *Six sonatas* . . . *Op. 7th* (Preston and Son, [1792]); *Divertimento for the piano forte* . . . *Op. 10* (for the Author, *ca.* 1800).

DALE, James (b. ?, d. ?). *Musical compositions* [for pianoforte] *Op. 2* (for the Author, *ca.* 1800).

DALE, Joseph (1750–1821). Brother (?) of preceding, music-publisher. Published and arranged a large amount of pianoforte music as well as composing many ephemeral works; also *Six sonatas and a fantasia cromatica* . . . *Opera 2da*; 2 concertos, Opp. 4, 5; two sets of 3 sonatas, Opp. 6, 8; 2 sets of duets, Opp. 7, 10, and *Thirty organ pieces*, Op. 11, all published by his own firm till *ca.* 1800.

DALE, William (d. ? 1827), son (?) of preceding. *Six sonatas for the harpsichord or piano-forte, with accompaniment* . . . *Opera seconda* (for the Author, 1783).

DANBY, John (1757–1798). *La guida della musica instrumentale, or the rudiments of the forte piano and harpsichord;* . . . *to which are subjoined, eight progressive lessons constructed on . . . familiar airs. To conclude with a lesson for two performers on one forte piano . . . Op. 5* (G. Smart, *ca.* 1790).

DANCE, William (1755–1840). *Six lessons . . . Opera prima* (J. Blundell, *ca.*1780); *Six lessons . . . with an accompaniment for a violin . . . Opera seconda* (J. Blundell, [1782]); *Three lessons . . . and eight preludes . . . Opera terza* (J. Dale, *ca.* 1800); Sonata, Op. 4; *God save the King . . . with new variations . . .* (L. Lavenu, 1800); *Preludes . . . in various keys* (L. Lavenu, 1800. Partly reprinted without title-page, *ca.* 1800); *Fantasia for the piano forte* (1811).

DAVAUX, Jean Baptiste (*ca.* 1732–1822), French composer. In BC.

*DAVIS, Bartholomew (b. ?, d. ?). *Six easy lessons for the harpsichord . . . Opera primo* (for the Author, *ca.* 1775).

*DAVIS, Will(iam) (b. ?, d. ?), Gentleman of Chapel Royal from 23 May 1685 (Rimbault). Copyist of Add. 31468 (*ca.* 1700), and composer of a four-movement suite in it.

*DAY, John (b. ?, d. ?). *A favorite sonata . . . Op. 1* (Longman and Broderip, [1789]).

DEANE, Thomas (b. ?, d. ?), D. Mus., Oxford, 1731. 2 pieces in Add. 31467.

*DENMAN, Henry (b. ?, d. ?). *Three sonatas . . . Opera primo* (for the Author, *ca.* 1780); *Three sonatas . . . Opera 2* (for the Author, *ca.* 1792); *Three sonatas . . . Opera IV* (for the Author, *ca.* 1794); *Two grand marches . . .* (A. Bland and Weller, *ca.* 1795); *A favorite sonata . . .* (Longman and Broderip, *ca.* 1795).

DEZÈDE(s), Nicolas (*ca.* 1745–1792), French composer. In BC.

DIBDIN, Charles (1745–1814). *Six lessons for the harpsichord, or piano forte* (Longman, Lukey and Co., *ca.* 1772). Also 3 sonatas arranged from songs in *Wags and Oddities* (for the Author, *ca.* 1790, 3 nos.). Single movements in Add. 30950–1, 30953–4.

*DIESNER (DISINEER), Gerhard (b. ?, d. ?), German composer and violinist resident in England. Pieces in M. MSS: Add. 22099, Ch. Ch. 1177 (piece from the latter in *CP*, vi).

*DIETZ, Joseph (b. ?, d. ?), German composer. *BUCEM* lists several works published in London.

*DIETTENHOFER, Joseph (b. ?, d. ?), German composer. Two sets of sonatas published in London.

DIEUPART, Charles (d. 1740), French composer. Settled in London in 1700 and published there: *Select lessons for the harpsichord or spinnett as allemands sarabands corants gavots minuets and jiggs* (I. Walsh and I. Hare, [1705]). Music in Add. 52363.

*DINSLEY, William (b. ?, d. ?). *Three sonatas for the piano forte or harpsichord* (for the Author, [1796]).

DISINEER: see Diesner.

DITTERSDORF, Karl Ditters von (1739–1799), Austrian composer. In BC.

DRAGHI, Giovanni Battista (b. *ca.* 1640), Italian composer. Lived in London *ca.* 1667–*ca.* 1706. He published there: *Six select sutes* [sic] *of leszons for the harpsichord . . .* (I. Walsh, I. Hare and P. Randall, [1707]. Another issue: I. Walsh and I. Hare, [1707]). One piece (anon.) in 2HM. MSS: Add. 22099,

52363; Ch. Ch. 1177 (suite by 'Batis'); Edinburgh, Nat. Lib., Inglis 94, MS 3343 (by 'Senu Baptist' and 'Senior Baptist').

*Du Faut (Dufaut, Dufault, Dufaux) (b. ?, d. ?), French 17th-century composer of lute music. See *MGG*, Arkwright, Eitner. Corant for keyboard in Ch. Ch. 1236.

*Duncombe, William (b. ?, d. ?). *First book of progressive lessons* . . . (J. Bland, *ca*. 1785); *A second book of twelve progressive lessons* . . . (J. Bland, *ca*. 1785); *The favorite air of God save the King, with variations for two performers on one piano forte or harpsichord* (Kensington: for the Author, *ca*. 1790).

*Du Phly (1715–1789), French composer. See *BUCEM*, *MGG*, Eitner.

Dupuis, Thomas Sanders (1733–1796). *Six concerto's for the organ, or harpsichord* (*ca*. 1760); *Six* [Cudworth '5'] *concertos* . . . *Opera prima* (for the Author, *ca*. 1795 [2nd edn?]); *Sonatas for the harpsichord, organ or piano forte, with an accompanyment for a violin* . . . *Opera seconda* (for the author, [1768]); *Six familiar lessons* . . . *Opera terza* (Welcker, *ca*. 1775); *Eight easy lessons* . . . *Opera quarta* (Welcker, *ca*. 1775); *God save the King, with variations* . . . (G. Smart, *ca*. 1780); *Six sonatas for the piano forte or harpsichord with an accompanyment for a violin* . . . *Op. VI* (for the Author, [1788]. Another edn: Longman and Broderip, *ca*. 1790); *Pieces for the organ or harpsichord* . . . *Op. VIII* (Preston and Son, [1794: 2nd edn?]); *A second set of pieces* . . . *Op. X* (J. Dale, *ca*. 1792); *Nine voluntaries for the organ* . . . (C. Wheatstone, *ca*. 1800). Music in BC. MS: Add. 27753 (autograph). Mod. edns. in *OEOM*, ii, iii; see also Bibliography.

Dussek, Jan Ladislav (1760–1812), Bohemian composer. Lived in London 1790–1800. Married in 1792 the daughter of Domenico Corri (q.v.). Much of his keyboard music was published in London. Pianoforte music was also published by Veronica Elizabeth Dussek (afterwards Cianchettini) and Sophia Giustina Dussek (afterwards Dussek Moralt). See *BUCEM*.

Ebdon, Thomas (1738–1811). *Six sonata's* . . . *with accompaniments for two violins and a violoncello* (Welcker, *ca*. 1765).

*Eberhard, Gotthilf Anton (b. ?, d. ?), 18th-century German composer. Resident in London? Not in *MGG* or Eitner, though the latter has two Eberhards without Christian names. See *BUCEM*.

Eccles, John (1668–1735). Pieces in CL. MSS include Add. 22099, 40139. Contents of CL, and piece from Add. 22099, in *CP*, vi.

Edelmann, Johann Friedrich (1749–1794), Alsatian composer. Much keyboard music published in London (see *BUCEM*). In BC.

*Edwards (? Thomas, b. ?, d. ?—see Eitner). *Six concerto's for the organ or harpsichord*. With instrumental parts (for the Author, *ca*. 1760).

Eichner, Ernst (1740–1777). German composer, travelled to London. See *BUCEM*.

Ellis, William (d. 1674): see Part 1.

*Essex, Margaret (b. ?, d. ?). *Three sonatas for the piano forte* . . . *with an accompaniment for a violin ad libitum* . . . *Op. 1st* (for the Composer, *ca*. 1795).

*Essex, Timothy (*ca*. 1765–1847). Biography in Eitner. *A grand military sonata* . . . *Op. 4th* (for the Author, *ca*. 1800); *Eight lessons and four sonatinas on a peculiar plan* . . . *Op. 6* (for the Composer, *ca*. 1800).

*EVANCE, William (b. ?, d. ?). *Six sonatas for the piano forte or harpsichord with an accompanyment for a violin and violoncello* (Welcker, *ca.* 1775); *A favorite concerto, for the harpsichord or piano forte, with accompanyments* (Longman and Broderip, *ca.* 1785).

*EVANS, Charles (b. ?, d. ?), organist at Ludlow. *A favorite sonata* (2 nos., I. Fentum, *ca.* 1775). Also 6 sonatas Op. 3 with violin *obbligato*.

*FANTINI (b. ?, d. ?), Italian composer? See *BUCEM*.

FARINEL, Michel (b. 1649). French composer. 'Farranellas Ground' in London, R.C.M., MS 2093, is a keyboard version of the *folia* in a very simple arrangement.

FELTON, William (1715–1769). *Six concerto's for the organ or harpsichord with instrumental parts Op. 1* (John Johnson, [1744]. Another issue, *ca.* 1745). *Six concerto's for the organ or harpsichord with instrumental parts. . . Opera seconda* (J. Johnson, [1747]). *Eight suits of easy lessons for the harpsichord. Opera terza* (John Johnson, [1752]). *Six concerto's for the organ or harpsichord, with instrumental parts . . . Opera quarta* (J. Johnson, [1752]). *Six concerto's for organ or harpsichord, with instrumental parts . . . Opera quinta* (John Johnson, *ca.* 1755); *Eight suits of easy lessons for the harpsicord . . . Vol. II. Opera sesta* (John Johnson, [1757]); *Six concerto's for the organ or harpsichord, with instrumental parts . . . Opera settima* (J. Johnson, *ca.* 1760. Re-issued as *Eight concerto's . . . Opera settima*, John Johnson, [1762]). Various pieces in Add. 34267, 35025.

FERRABOSCO, John (1626–1682): see Part 1.

FERRARI, Giacomo Gotifredo (or Jacopo Goffredo) (1763–1842), Italian composer, settled in London from 1792. See *BUCEM*, Eitner.

FESTING, Michael Christian (1680–1752). German, later English, composer. In Tenbury, St. Michael's Coll., MS 784, as 'Festin'.

FINGER, Gottfried (or Godfrey) (*ca.* 1660–after 1723), Moravian composer, resident in England *ca.* 1685–ca. 1703. 'A solo' (probably an arrangement) in Add. 34695.

FISCHER, Johann Caspar Ferdinand (*ca.* 1665–1746), German composer. Pieces in Brussels, Bib. du Cons., MS 15418.

FLACKTON, William (1709–1793). *Six overtures adapted for the harpsichord or piano forte . . . Opera III* (for the Author, [1771]). *Grove* refers to 'harpsichord lessons' also.

*FONTANA, Fabrizio (d. 1695), Italian composer. See *MGG*. 'Tocata' in LE2. Also pieces in *A second collection . . .* (Walsh, [1719]).

FORCER, Francis (*ca.* 1650–1705). Piece in 2MH (anon.), from one of two suites by him in Add. 31403; also music in Add. 52363.

*FREAKE, John (John George FREEKE or FREKE) (1688–1756). See Eitner. *XII solos for a harpsichord . . .* [Op. I] (W. Smith, [1747]). *Six solos for a violin, or lessons for a harpsichord . . . Opera quarta* [1753].

*FREYSTAEDLER (FREYSTÄDTLER), Franz Jakob (1768–1841), Austrian composer, see *MGG*. In BC.

FRICK, Philipp Joseph (1740–1798). German composer, settled in London from 1780. See *BUCEM*.

FROBERGER, Johann Jacob (1616–1667), German composer. Pieces in *A second collection* . . . (Walsh, [1719]). MSS: Brussels, Bib. du Cons., MS 15418; London, Brit. Mus., Egerton 2959.

*FROUD (b. ?, d. ?), early 18th-cent. English (?) composer. London, Dulwich Coll., MS 92.

*FURTADO, A. Charles (b. ?, d. ?). *A famillar sonatina for the piano-forte* (for the Author, *ca.* 1797); *Three sonatas, for the harpsichord or piano-forte* (for the Author, *ca.* 1797).

GALUPPI, Baldassare (1706–1785), Italian composer. Resident in London 1741–1743, where much of his keyboard music was published. Represented in SS.

*GAMBARINI, Elisabetta de (b. ?, d. ?), 18th-century Italian (?) composer. See *BUCEM*, Eitner.

GARTH, John (1722–1810). *Six sonata's for the harpsichord, piano forte and organ; with accompanyments for two violins, and a violoncello* . . . *Opera seconda* (R. Bremner, 1768. 3 further English and 1 Amsterdam edns. followed); *Six voluntarys for the organ, piano forte or harpsichord* . . . *Opera terza* (Welcker, [1771]); *A second sett of six sonata's* . . . *with accompanyments for two violins and a violoncello. Opera IV* (Welcker, [1772]. A third set, Op. 5 ?); *A fourth set of six sonatas* . . . *Opera VI* (John Welcker, *ca.* 1778); *A fifth set of six sonatas* . . . *Opera VII* (Robson, [1782]). MSS: Add. 14335; Op. 3, Nos. 2, 3 in Add. 16155.

*GARTINI (b. ?, d. ?), Italian composer. See *BUCEM*.

*GEARY, T. A. (b. ?, d. ?). In BC.

GELINEK (Jelinek), Joseph (1758–1825), Bohemian composer. In BC.

GEMINIANI, Francesco (1687–1762), Italian composer. Resident in England (later Dublin) from 1714. In LB2. *Pièces de Clavecin* [1743] copied into Add. 16155. Other MSS: Add. 31814, 39957; Cambridge, Fitz. Mus., 30. f. 21; Tenbury, St. Michael's Coll., 752, 784.

GIARDINI, Felice (1716–1796). Italian composer. Lived in London, *ca.* 1750–1784, 1790. For keyboard works published there see *BUCEM*.

GIBBONS, Christopher (1615–1676). Complete keyboard works in *CEKM*, xviii. Sources include CV3 (a work misattributed to Orlando Gibbons); MSS Add. 31468, Ch. Ch. 15, 47, 1003, 1176, 1179.

GILLIER ('the younger', b. ?, d. ?). *Eight sonatas for two violins, a violoncello &c., and one concerto for the harpsichord* (J. Johnson, [1756]. The concerto is missing from the only extant copy, Brit. Mus.); *Six setts of lessons for the harpsichord. Opera seconda* (John Johnson, [1757]); *Eight sonatas or lessons for the harpsichord* . . . *Opera terza* (for the Author, [1759]).

GIORDANI, Tommaso (1730–1806), Italian composer. Lived in England and Ireland from 1733. See *BUCEM* . In BC.

*GIORGI, Giuseppe or Gioseffo (*ca.* 1777–after 1834), Italian composer. See Eitner, *BUCEM*.

GIORNOVICHI, Giovanni Mane (1740–1804), Italian composer. Lived in England 1791–1796. See *BUCEM*.

*GIULIANI, Francesco (b. *ca.* 1760), Italian composer. See Eitner. 6 sonatas Op. 6 appeared in PM5, No. 4 (1798). See *BUCEM*. A Giovanni Francesco

Giuliani published: *Tre concerti per cimbalo a piena orchestra . . . Opera 4* (J. Cooper, *ca.* 1790).

*GLADWIN, Thomas (b. ?, d. ?). *Eight lessons for the harpsichord or organ, three of which have an accompaniment for a violin* (for the Author, *ca.* 1750. Another edn: Welcker, *ca.* 1770). Gavot from a concerto arranged as a song *Greenwood Hall* (Cudworth, *The Score* (1953) 59). MSS include London, R.C.O., MS without shelf-mark.

GLUCK, Christoph Willibald (1714–1787), German composer. In BC.

GOODSON, Richard (1655–1718), or his son (d. 1741). In Add. 22099.

*GOODWIN, Starling (b. ?, d. ?), organist of St. Mary Magdalen, Bermondsey, in 1740s (Johnstone, *MT* (1967) 1003). *Twelve voluntarys for the organ or harpsichord . . . Book I* (C. and S. Thompson, *ca.* 1770); *A favorite lesson for the harpsichord* (C. and S. Thompson, *ca.* 1773); *The complete organist's pocket companion, containing a choice collection of psalm-tunes with their givings-out, and interludes* (C. and S. Thompson, *ca.* 1775); *Twelve voluntarys . . . Book II* (C. and S. Thompson, *ca.* 1776). London, R.C.O., MS without shelf-mark. Mod. edns. in *OEOM,* i, iii, iv.

*GOODWIN, William (b. ?, d. ?). *A favourite lesson for the harpsichord, or piano forte . . .* (3 nos., C. and S. Thompson, *ca.* 1775); *Twelve voluntaries for the organ or harpsichord* (C. and S. Thompson, 1776). Mod edns. in *OEOM,* ii.

*GORTON, William (b. ?, d. ?), 18th-century composer. See Eitner. 4 pieces in Add. 17850 (autograph).

*GRAEFF, Johann Georg (b. ?, d. ?), 18th-century German composer. Resident in England? See *BUCEM* for keyboard music published in London.

GRAF, Friedrich Hartmann (1727–1795), German composer. In London, 1783–*ca.* 1790. See *BUCEM*.

GRAUN, Carl Heinrich (1704–1759), German composer. Lesson in *Six lessons for the harpsichord* (Welcker, *ca.* 1770).

*GRAY, Thomas Brabazon (b. ?, d. ?). *A lesson for the harpsichord or piano forte with an accompaniment for the violin or German flute* (T. Skillern, *ca.* 1780).

*GREEN, G. (b. ?, d. ?). *Six voluntarys for the organ, piano forte or harpsichord* (Longman, Lukey and Co., *ca.* 1775).

GREENE, MAURICE (1695–1755). *A choice book of lessons* (D. Wright, [1733]. Reprinted as LB2, pp. 1–19, and as *A collection of lessons for the harpsichord . . . 2d Book* (Walsh, [? 1758]); *Six overtures for the harpsichord or spinnet . . .* (I. Walsh, *ca.* 1745, arranged from *Six overtures in seven parts*); *A collection of lessons for the harpsichord* (John Johnson, [1750]); *A favorite lesson* (Thompson and Son, [1758]. Three movements of 4th suite in *A choice book of lessons*); *Twelve voluntarys for the organ or harpsichord* (J. Bland, *ca.* 1780). '3 Sonatas by Dr. Green' advertised on title page of above. Printed collections: TV, CV1–3. MSS: Add. 14335, 31467; London, R.C.M., MSS 1057, 1120; R.C.O., MS without shelf-mark; Dulwich Coll., MSS 92a, b, d; Tenbury, St. Michael's Coll., MS 752; New York, Pub. Lib., Music Reserve +MN. Mod. edns. in *OEOM,* iii, iv; see also Bibliography.

GREGORIE, William (d. 1663). 2 suites in M. The first in *PSMS,* xvi.

*GRIFFES, Charles (b. ?, d. ?). *A favourite march* (J. P[reston], *ca.* 1790); *A favorite sonata for the piano forte* (Preston and Son, *ca.* 1795).

GUEST, George (1771–1831). *Sixteen pieces or voluntaries for the organ* . . . *Op. 3* (for the Author, *ca.* 1795); *Four fugues for the organ* . . . *Op. 13* (Preston and son, n.d.).

GUEST (afterwards Miles), Jane Mary (b. ?, d. ?). *Six sonatas* . . . *Opera prima* (*ca.* 1783. Also in an edition with a French title [Eitner]).

GUGLIELMI, Pietro Alessandro (1728–1804), Italian composer, for a time resident in London, where he published keyboard music. See *BUCEM*.

GUNN, Barnabas (1680–1753). *Six setts of lessons for the harpsichord* (for John Johnson, [1750]). A B. Gunn is represented in Tenbury, St. Michael's Coll., MS 752.

GYROWETZ, Adalbert (1763–1850), Bohemian composer, in London 1789–1792. See *BUCEM* for keyboard music published there.

HAIGH, Thomas (1769–1808). *Six concertos for the harpsichord or piano forte* . . . *Opera I* (for the Author, *ca.* 1785); *Twelve preludes* . . . (R. Birchall, *ca.* 1796); *Three easy duetts* . . . *Op. 7* (Preston and Son, *ca.* 1800). Also 32 sonatas and numerous rondos, etc., on popular songs. See *BUCEM* for full details.

HALL, Henry, the elder (*ca.* 1655–1707), of Hereford. Suite in LE2; MS: Add. 22099.

HALL, William (d. 1700). 1 piece in M. In *PSMS*, xvi.

*HALL (b. ?, d. ?), identity uncertain, but probably later than the two preceding. In London, R.C.O., MS without shelf-mark.

*HAMILTON, Henry (b. ?, d. ?). *Four airs for the harpsichord, piano forte and organ* (Leeds: for the Author, *ca.* 1800).

HÄNDEL, Georg Friedrich, later George Frideric HANDEL (1685–1759), German composer. Lived in England 1710 and from 1712 until his death except for short visits abroad in 1716–1717 and 1719. His most important keyboard publications were the *Suites de pièces pour le clavecin* . . . *Premier volume* (for the Author, [1720]) and 3 sets of organ concertos (Op. 4, a *Second set* . . ., and Op. 7). For others, down to the end of the 18th century, see *BUCEM*. Arrangements in SHSL, SCL, etc. Spurious works in CV2, CV4. MSS include London, Brit. Mus., R.M. 20. g. 12 and 20 g. 14: see W. Barclay Squire, *Catalogue of the King's Music Library*, i, part 1, A, s.v. 'Instrumental' (pp. 40–7). Also many other MSS in London, Brit. Mus., Dulwich Coll., R.C.M. and R.C.O. (MS without shelf-mark), Cambridge, Fitz. Mus., and Tenbury, St. Michael's Coll. See Bibliography.

*HARDIN, Elizabeth (b. ?, d. ?). *Six lessons for the harpsichord* (for the Author, *ca.* 1770).

*HARDY, Henry (b. ?, d. ?). *Twelve waltzes* . . . *for the pianoforte or harp* (Oxford: for Henry Hardy, *ca.* 1800).

*HARDY, Joseph (b. ?, d. ?). *A favorite lesson for the harpsichord* (Straight and Skillern, *ca.* 1775); *Caprice pour le clavecin ou pianoforte* . . . *Ouvre* [sic] *55* (Longman and Broderip, *ca.* 1793).

*HARGRAVE, Henry (b. ?, d. ?), 18th-century composer. 5 bassoon concertos arranged for keyboard (see *BUCEM*).

HART, Philip (*ca.* 1676–1749). *A choice set of lessons for the harpsichord or spinet* (1702, lost); *Fugues for the organ or harpsichord with lessons for the harpsichord* (for the Author, [1704]). MSS: Add. 31465, 32161, 34695; Edinburgh, Nat. Lib., Inglis 94 MS 3343.

HASSE, Johann Adolph (1699–1783), German composer. Visited London *ca.* 1738–9, where some of his keyboard music was published (see *BUCEM*). 1 lesson in *Six lessons* (Welcker, *ca.* 1770). MSS include Tenbury, St. Michael's Coll., MSS 752, 784.

HAWDO(W)N, Matthias (d. 1787). *Two concertos for the harpsichord, organ or piano forte* (Longman, Lukey and Co., *ca.* 1775); *Six conversation sonatas for the harpsichord or piano forte with accompanyments for two violins and a violoncello . . . Opera seconda* (Longman, Lukey and Broderip, *ca.* 1778); *Two concertos for the organ, or harpsichord . . .* [Op. 3?] (Longman and Broderip, *ca.* 1780); *A first sett of six sonatas spirituale or voluntarys . . . Op. IV* (Preston, *ca.* 1780).

HAYDN, Franz Joseph (1732–1809), Austrian composer. Visited London 1790–1792 and 1794–1795. He wrote his last 3 pianoforte sonatas (Breitkopf und Härtel, Nos. 50–2) during or in preparation for his second visit, dedicating two of them to the English pianist Therese Jansen-Bartolozzi. No. 52 in E flat was published as *A new grand sonata for the piano forte composed expressly for Mrs. Bartolozzi. Op. 78* (Longman, Clementi and Co., *ca.* 1800; originally Vienna: Artaria, 1798). For other English edns. of his keyboard music see *BUCEM*. Also music in BC.

HAYES, Philip (1738–1797). *Six concertos . . . for the organ, harpsichord or forte piano; to which is added a harpsichord sonata . . .* (for the Author, 1769); *Six sonatas for the harpsichord or piano forte with an accompaniment for a violin . . . Opera II* (Welcker, [1774]). Piece from a concerto in *OEOM*, ii.

HAYES, William (1705–1777), father of preceding. 2 organ concertos in Oxford, Bod. Lib., MS Mus. d. 82.

*HEATON, Isaac (b. ?, d. ?). *Six sonatas for the harpsichord with an accompanyment for a violin. Opera prima* (1766); *Six sonatas* [as above]. *Opera seconda* (1766).

HELLENDAAL, Pieter (1721–1799), Dutch composer. Settled in England 1752. See *BUCEM* for keyboard publications in England.

HENSLOWE, Celia Maria: See Barthélemon, C.M.

*HERING, John Frederic (b. ?, d. ?). *Three Sonatas for the piano forte or harpsichord with accompaniments for a violin and violoncello* (for the Author, [1790]).

*HERON, Henry (b. ?, d. ?). *Ten voluntaries for the organ or harpsichord* (for the Author, *ca.* 1760). *Ibid., Opera prima* (C. and S. Thompson, *ca.* 1765: another issue of the same work). Voluntary in Add. 35040. Mod. edns. in *OEOM*, i, ii, iv.

HERSCHEL, Friedrich Wilhelm (1738–1822). The publications of the famous astronomer include: *Sei sonate per il cembalo, cogli accompagnamenti di violino e violoncello che di* [sic] *possono sonare anche sole* (Bath, 1769).

*HEWITT, John (b. ?, d. ?). *Six favorite French airs, with variations for the piano forte . . . Op. III* (to be had of the Author, *ca.* 1795).

HINE, William (1687–1730). *Harmonia Sacra Glocestriensis, or select anthems . . . together with a voluntary for the organ . . .* [1731]. A slow movement in Add. 31814. Mod. edn. of the voluntary in *RRMBE*, vi, No. 10; 3 movements separately in *OEOM*, iii, iv.

HINGSTON, John (d. 1683). 'Voluntarie' for organ in Ch. Ch. 47 and 1176.

*HOEBERECHTS, John Lewis (b. ?, d. ?), 18th-century composer. See Eitner. Published numerous sonatas and overtures for keyboard, mostly with violin accompaniment *ad libitum*. See *BUCEM*.

*HOFFMAN, Miss J. (b. ?, d. ?), late 18th-century composer. Two publications of keyboard duets. See *BUCEM*.

*HOFFMANN, J. A. (b. ?, d. ?), late 18th-century composer. Two publications of sonatas for harp or pianoforte. See *BUCEM*.

HOFFMEISTER, Franz Anton (1754–1812), German composer. Pieces in SC, BC.

HOLDER, Joseph William (1765–1832). *Six sonatas for the piano forte or harpsichord with an accompaniment for violin . . . Op. 2* (Longman and Broderip, *ca.* 1785).

HOLMES, George (d. 1721). Probably copyist of Add. 31446 and composer of some of its anonymous pieces. Music by 'Holmes' in Add. 17853 and 31465.

HOOK, James (1746–1827). Hook's keyboard publications are too numerous to list individually. *BUCEM* lists 13 concertos, Opp. 5, 55 and an unnumbered set (Welcker, [1774]); *Six conversation pieces . . . Opera XL (ca.* 1785); 24 divertimenti, Opp. 25, 33; 5 duets, Opp. 44, 82, 84; 6 lessons and an overture; 53 sonatas, including Opp. 10, 16, 17, 30, 54, 77, 78, 84, 92, and 6 sonatas in PM4; 2 sets of 12 'sonatinos', the second Op. 13; the *Guida di musica . . . Op. 37* (J. Preston, *ca.* 1785), with its *second part . . . Op. 7;* (Preston and Son, [1794]. Another edn: Edinburgh, N. and H. Stewart and Co., *ca.* 1796); and the *New Guida di Musica . . . Op. 81* (Bland and Weller, [1796]). Cudworth (*The Score* (1953) 60) adds: 2 Vauxhall Concertos.

HORN, Karl Friedrich (1762–1830), German composer. Resident in London from 1782. See *BUCEM*.

*HORN, Ferdinand (b. ?, d. ?), German composer? See *BUCEM*.

*HOWARD, William (b. ?, d. ?). *Six sonatas for the piano-forte or harpsichord, with an accompaniment for a violin . . . Opera 1ᵐᵉ* (J. Preston, 1782). *Six sonatinos . . . with an accompaniment for the violin . . .* (Longman and Broderip, [1789]).

*HOWELL, Thomas (b. ?, d. ?). *Air, composed and varied for the piano-forte . . .* (Bristol: for the Author, *ca.* 1800).

HOWGILL, William (b. ?, d. ?). *Inglewood Hunt a favorite sonata . . .* (for the Author, *ca.* 1795); *Whitehaven Hunt, a sonata . . .* (Preston and Son, *ca.* 1795); *An original anthem & two voluntaries for the organ or piano forte . . .* (for the Author, *ca.* 1800); *A duett, for the organ & grand pianoforte . . .* (Preston, *ca.* 1800); *A sonata for the harpsichord, or pianoforte* (Preston and Son, *ca.* 1800); *Four voluntaries* (n.d., but probably after 1800).

HÜLLMANDEL, Nicolas Joseph (1751–1823), Alsatian composer. Pieces in SC.

*HUMBLE, Maximilian (b. ?, d. ?). *A sonata and an overture for the piano forte . . .* (for the Author, *ca.* 1785).

HUMMEL, Johann Nepomuk (1778-1837), Hungarian composer. Visited Great Britain, 1788–1792, during which time and later some of his early compositions were published in London. He returned to London on various occasions in later life. See *BUCEM*, Eitner, *MGG*. Also various MSS in London, Brit. Mus. (Hughes-Hughes, *Catalogue*).

HUMPHRIES, J. S. (b. ?, d. ?). Or ? John Humphries (1707–1730). See Eitner. Keyboard music in Tenbury, St. Michael's Coll., MS 752.

*JACKSON, Dr. George (b. ?, d. ?). *A favorite sonata for the harpsichord, or piano forte* . . . *Op. 4* (for the Author, *ca.* 1795).

*JACKSON, James (b. ?, d. ?). *Six voluntaries for the organ or harpsichord* . . . (for the Author, *ca.* 1775).

JACKSON, John (d. 1688). 'A Simphony by Mr. John Jackson' (from an anthem or masque?) in MH/2.

JACKSON, Thomas (*ca.* 1715–1781). *A favourite lesson for the harpsichord* . . . (Longman, Lukey and Broderip, *ca.* 1778).

JACKSON, William (1730–1803), of Exeter. *Six sonatas for the harpsichord accompanied with a violin* (John Johnson, [1760]); *A favorite sonata for the harpsichord and pianoforte* . . . *Op. 4* (Longman and Broderip [2nd edn?], *ca.* 1790); *Eight sonatas for the harpsichord accompanied with two violins, a tenor and bass* . . . *Opera X* (Longman and Broderip, 1773).

JAMES, John (d. 1745). Voluntaries in SV, TV, CV3. MSS: Add. 31814, 34609, 35040; London, R.C.O., MS without shelf-mark; Dulwich Coll., MSS 92a, d; Manchester, Henry Watson Lib., MS BRm. 7105. Rf. 31; Lady Jeans MSS; Mod. edns: *OEOM*, iii (= TV, No. 4, without middle movement); see also Bibliography.

JANIEWICZ, Felix: see Yaniewicz.

*JANSEN, Charles (b. ?, d. ?). *Eighteen favorite minuets for the piano forte* . . . *Book I* (for L. Jansen, *ca.* 1795). See also next entry.

*JANSEN, Louis (b. ?, d. ?). *Three sonatas for the piano forte* . . . *Op. 1* (for the Author, [1793]); *Three sonatas for the piano forte with an accompaniment for a violin ad libitum* . . . *Op. 2* (for the Author, *ca.* 1795). Eitner gives Jansen, Louis Charles (*ca.* 1774–1840), b. Aachen, d. London, and mentions a sonata, Op. 5, published in Leipzig and Berlin.

JARVIS, Samuel (d. *ca.* 1785). *Six lessons for the harpsichord or forte-piano* . . . *Opera seconda* (H. Thorowgood, [1769]).

JAY, John George Henry (1770–1849). *A phantasia and two sonatas for the piano-forte* (for the Author, *ca.* 1800).

JELINEK: see Gelinek.

JENKINS, John (1592–1678). Composer of 'Mr. Jnckings his Belles', Ch. Ch. 1175?

JONES, Edward (1752–1824). Various minor works for pianoforte, etc. See *BUCEM*.

*JONES, Griffith (b. ?, d. ?). *The Complete Instructor for the harpsichord or pianoforte* . . . *together with* . . . *some original pieces by G. Jones* (Geo. Goulding, *ca.* 1800).

JONES, John (1728–1796). *Eight setts of lessons for the harpsichord* . . . (for the Author, 1754); *Lessons for the harpsichord* . . . (2 vols., for the Author, 1761).

JONES, Richard (b. ?, d. ?). *Suits or setts of lessons for the harpsichord or spinnet* . . . (I. Walsh, [1732]). In LB1.

JONES, William (1726–1800). *Ten church pieces for the organ* . . . (2 bks., for the Author, [1789]); *Ten church pieces* . . . *Opera II* (2 bks., for the Author. [1789]).

*Jukes, (b. ?, d. ?). Add. 22099.

Just, Johann August (b. *ca.* 1750), German composer. Probably resident for a time in London, where various keyboard works were published. See *BUCEM.*

*Justice, Richard (b. ?, d. ?). *Six sets of lessons for the harpsichord* (John Johnson, *ca.* 1753).

*Kambra, Karl (b. ?, d. ?), 18th-century German (?) composer. Presumably resident in England. Numerous minor pianoforte works. See *BUCEM.*

Kauer, Ferdinand (1751–1831). Austrian composer. In BC.

Keeble, John (1711–1786). *Select pieces for the organ* ... (2 bks., for the Author, [1777–8]); *Selected pieces for the organ* ... (4 bks., Longman and Broderip, [1778]–*ca.* 1780. Another issue: Broderip and Wilkinson, *ca.* 1800). With Jacob Kirkman: *Forty interludes to be played between the verses of the psalms: twenty five* ... *by Mr. J. Keeble, & fifteen by Mr. J. Kirkman* ... (Birchall and Andrews, *ca.* 1787). Mod. edns. in *OEOM,* i, ii.

*Kelly, Charles (b. ?, d. ?). *Two sonatas for the piano forte* ... (for the Author, *ca.* 1800).

Kelway, Joseph (d. ? 1782). *Six sonatas for the harpsichord* ... ([1764]. Another issue: Welcker, *ca.* 1770). 2 sonatas, etc., in Cambridge, Fitz. Mus., MS 30. f. 21.

Kerll, Johann Caspar von (1627–1693), German composer. In *A second collection* ... (Walsh, [1719]). London, Dulwich Coll., MS 92.

*Kilmanseck (b. ?, d. ?). In LB1.

*King, J. (b. ?, d. ?), organist of Wellington. *A favorite lesson for the piano forte or harpsichord* (for the Author, *ca.* 1795).

King, Matthew Peter (1733–1823). *Six sonatas for the piano forte or harpsichord, with an accompaniment for a violin* ... *Op. prima* (for the Author, *ca.* 1785); *Three sonatas* [as above] *Op. 2* (for the Author, *ca.* 1790); *Six sonatinas for the piano forte or harpsichord* ... *Op. 4* (H. Andrews, 1789); *Cape St. Vincent. A grand sonata for the piano forte, with accompaniments for a violin and violoncello* ... *Op. 8* (Longman and Broderip, [1797]); *A grand duett for two performers on the piano forte* ... *Op. 8* [sic] (Longman and Broderip, *ca.* 1797); *The coronation, a grand sonata sinfonia for the pianoforte* (1820).

King, Robert (d. after 1728). MSS include London, Brit. Mus., Egerton 2959; Ch. Ch. 46 (as 'R.K.'). In LB. One piece in *CP,* vi.

Kirkman, Jacob (1710–1792), Alsatian composer and instrument-maker. Settled in England in the early 1730s. See *BUCEM;* also s.v. Keeble.

Kirnberger, Johann Philipp (1721–1783), German composer. One lesson in *Six lessons for the harpsichord* (Welcker, *ca.* 1770).

*Kirshaw, George (b. ?, d. ?). *Six sonatas or lessons for the harpsichord* ... *Op. 1me* (J. Longman and Co., 1769).

Kloeffler, Johann Friedrich (1725–1790), German composer. Visited London 1783. See *BUCEM.*

Koczwara: see Kotzwara.

*Koeber, J.L. (b. ?, d. ?), possibly the 18th-century German oboe virtuoso mentioned by Eitner. *An easy sonata for the piano forte* ... (for the Author, *ca.* 1797).

KOLLMAN, August Friedrich Christoph (*ca.* 1756–1829), German composer. Settled in England *ca.* 1784. See *BUCEM*.

KOTZWARA, Franz (KOCŽWARA, František) (d. 1791), Bohemian composer. Settled in England *ca.* 1785. Composed the 'Battle of Prague', etc. See *BUCEM*. Also music in BC.

KOŽELUCH, Leopold (1752–1818), Bohemian composer. He does not appear to have visited England but numerous keyboard works of his were published in London. See *BUCEM*. Music in SC.

*KREUSSER, Peter Anton (b. 1772), German composer. For biography see Eitner; for keyboard works published in London see *BUCEM*.

*KRIFT, William B. de (b. *ca.* 1765), Canadian composer. For biography see Eitner. *Siege of Quebec, a sonata for the harpsichord or piano-forte with accompaniments for violin, violoncello & tympano ad libitum* (J. Bland, *ca.* 1792). Also music in BC, 3rd edn. See also *BUCEM*, s.v. Kotzwara.

KRUMPHOL(T)Z, Johann Baptist (1745–1790), Bohemian composer and harpist. He did not settle in London, but numerous works for harp and keyboard by him were published there. See *BUCEM*. Music in SC.

KÜHNAU, Johann Christoph (1735–1805), German composer. A work of his was included in TV under the name 'Kuknan'.

KUNZEN, Adolph Carl (1720–1781), German composer. Paid several visits to London. See *BUCEM*. Also in *A collection of lessons* . . . (Thompson and Sons, [1762]).

*LANG, J.C. (b. ?, d. ?), 18th-century Bohemian (?) composer. See *BUCEM* for music published in England.

*LANG, Johann Georg (1724-before 1800), Bohemian composer, related to preceding? See Eitner, *MGG, BUCEM*.

LANGDON, Richard (1729–1803). *Six sonatas for the harpsichord . . . Opera terza* (C. and S. Thompson, [1765]).

*LARKIN, (b. ?, d. ?), 18th-century composer. Music in London, R.C.O., MS without shelf-mark.

LATES, Charles (d. *ca.* 1810). *A favorite sonata for the piano-forte or harpsichord* . . . (for the Author, *ca.* 1800).

*LATOUR, T. (b. ?, d. ?). 7 sonatas in 3 books, Opp. 1–3 (all Bland and Weller, [1797]; also various rondos and overtures (see *BUCEM*).

LATROBE, Christian Ignatius (1757–1836). *Three sonatas for the piano forte . . . Op. III* (for the Author, *ca.* 1790).

LE BRUN, Franzeska (née DANZI) (1756–1791), German singer and composer. Visited London 1779–1781, where keyboard music by her was published. See *BUCEM*.

LECLAIR (? Jean Marie 'l'aîné', 1697–1764), French composer. In Tenbury, St. Michael's Coll., MS 784.

*LEE, Peter (b. ?, d. ?). *Six progressive lessons* . . . (Wandsworth: for the Author, *ca.* 1785); *Three sonatas . . . Op. 2d* (for the Author, *ca.* 1786). Also more ephemeral works (see *BUCEM*).

*LEONE, Benedetto (b. ?, d. ?), Italian composer? No entries in Eitner or *MGG*. See *BUCEM*.

LINLEY, Francis (1771–1800). No relation to the following. 1 sonata in BC.

Grove mentions organ music and an organ tutor. Short organ piece in
OEOM, ii.

LINLEY, Thomas, the elder (1733–1795). Allegretto from a sonata in Add.
35024.

LOCKE, Matthew (*ca.* 1622–1677). Suites and voluntaries in M. MSS include
Add. 22099, 31465; Ch. Ch. 1177; Oxford, Bod. Lib., Mus. Sch. d. 219;
New York, Pub. Lib., Drexel 5611. See Harding, *Thematic Catalogue.*
Mod. edn. in *SBK*, vi, vii; see also Bibliography.

*LOCKHART, Charles (b. ?, d. ?). *Six sonatas for the harpsichord ... Opera primo*
(for the Author, *ca.* 1772); *A favorite sonata for the harpsichord or forte-piano*
(W. Cope, *ca.* 1795).

LOEILLET, Jean Baptiste (1680–1730), Flemish composer. Settled in London
by 1705. Sets of keyboard pieces by him were published in London *ca.*
1715 and *ca.* 1725 (see *BUCEM*).

LOMBARDINI, Maddalena Laura, afterwards M. L. Sirmen or Syrmen (b. ?,
1735), Italian violinist and composer. Visited London in 1771 and 1772. 12
concertos by her, arranged for keyboard by Giordani (q.v.), were published
in London (see *BUCEM*).

LONG, Samuel (b. ?, d. ?). *Four lessons and two voluntarys for the harpsichord or*
organ (for the Widow, *ca.* 1770). Voluntary in Add. 14335.

LOOSEMORE, Henry (d. 1670): see Part 1.

*LOOTENS, W. (b. ?, d. ?), Dutch composer? No entries in Eitner or *MGG*.
Six divertimentos for the piano forte (Broderip and Wilkinson, *ca.* 1799).

*LORD, John (b. ?, d. ?). *Two sonatas for the piano forte, with an accompaniment*
for a violin ... to which is annexed a favorite selected sonata (for the Author, *ca.*
1792).

LULLY, Jean-Baptiste (originally Giovanni Battista) (1632–1687), French
composer of Italian birth and parentage. Pieces in HSM; and in
Edinburgh, Nat. Lib., Inglis 94, MS 3343, by 'French Baptist' and 'Baptist
Lully of France'.

*LUTHER, John Christian (b. ?, d. ?). *Eight sonatas for the harpsichord or piano*
forte ... (for the Author, [1775]); *A set of easy familiar introductory lessons ...*
(for the Author, *ca.* 1780); *Two sonatas for the harpsichord or piano-forte ...*
(for the Author, *ca.* 1785); *A sonata with variations to the favorite French air*
Ah: vous dirai ... Op. IV (J. Bland, *ca.* 1790).

*LYNEHAM, James, the younger (b. ?, d. ?). *Lesson for the harpsichord or piano*
forte ... (I. Fentum, *ca.* 1780).

M., J. *A set of easy lessons for the harpsichord ... Opera trentesima prima* (J. Hill,
1766. Preface signed 'J.M.').

*MAASMAN, Alexander (b. ?, d. ?). See Eitner. *A compleat suite of lessons for*
the harpsicord ... (I. Walsh and I. Hare, *ca.* 1715).

*MACDONALD, John (b. ?, d. ?). See Eitner. *Nine minuets for the Harpsichord*
or piano forte (Dundee, *ca.* 1800).

*MAC KERRELL, John (b. ?, d. ?). *Three sonatas for the harpsichord or piano forte*
... Opera Prima (for the Author, *ca.* 1785); *A familiar introduction to the first*
principles of music, to which is added twenty-four progressive lessons ... Opera IId
(for the Author, *ca.* 1800).

*MALME, George (b. ?, d. ?). *A sett of practical essays for the harpsichord or piano forte . . . Op. II* (to be had at the Author's, *ca.* 1790); *A sett of practical essays* . . . (Westminster: for the Author, *ca.* 1795).

*MANTEL, John Christian (b. ?, d. ?), organist of South Benfleet in Essex (Eitner). *Six setts of lessons for the harpsichord or organ . . . Opera prima* (Wm. Smith, *ca.* 1750); *Six concerto's for the organ or harpsichord . . . Op. III* (for the Author, [1752]).

MARSH, John (1752–1828). *An overture & six pieces for the organ* (Preston, [1791]); *Eighteen voluntaries for the organ . . . to which is prefix'd an explanation of the . . . stops . . . with a few thoughts on style, extempore playing* (Preston and Son, [1791]); *An overture and eight sonatinas . . . with accompaniments for a violin and violoncello . . .* (for the Author, *ca.* 1795); *Twenty voluntaries for the the organ . . . second sett* (T. Preston, *ca.* 1795).

MARTINI, Giovanni Battista (1706–1784), Italian composer and theorist. Music in BC and in Tenbury, St. Michael's Coll., MSS 752, 784, by 'Martini'. The index to the Tenbury catalogue, however, lists the composer as 'Martini, G. san', i.e. Giuseppe Sammartini (*ca.* 1693–*ca.* 1750), who lived in London from 1727 as an oboist. Sonata in Cambridge, Fitz. Mus., MS 30. f. 21.

MARTINI, Jean Paul Egide (Johann Paul Aegidius Schwartzendorf) (1741–1816), German composer. Music in the 3rd (*ca.* 1800) edn. of BC.

*MASI, Girolamo (b. ?, d. ?), late 18th-century Italian composer. See *BUCEM* for keyboard music published in England.

MATTEIS, Nicola (b. ?, d. ?), Italian violinist and composer, resident in England from 1672. His son, Nicholas, d. *ca.* 1749. 'Segnier Nichola's Trumpett', arranged from a violin piece, in Add. 34695; also in Add. 22099.

*MAURER, Georg(e), (b. ?, d. ?), German composer. See Eitner. 2 sets of sonatas, Opp. 1, 2 (see *BUCEM*).

MAYNARD, John (b. ?, d. ?), 16th–17th-century composer. Voluntary in London, R.C.M., MS 2093.

MAZZINGHI, Joseph (1765–1844), English composer of Corsican stock. See Eitner, *MGG*. He composed a substantial amount of keyboard music, including numerous sonatas (see *BUCEM*). Also in SS.

ME(T)ZGER, Karl Theodor (b. 1774), German flautist and composer. In BC.

MILES, Jane Mary: see Guest, Jane Mary.

MILLER, Edward (1731–1807). *Six sonatas for the harpsichord; with an accompaniment to three of them, for a violin, or German flute* (for the Author, *ca.* 1760. Another edn: Welcker, *ca.* 1765); *Institutes of Music, or easy instructions for the harpsichord . . . to which are added . . . lessons for practice* (Longman and Broderip, [1771]); *Sixteen easy voluntaries for the organ . . . Opera IX* (Longman and Broderip, *ca.* 1790).

*MOLENAER, C. R. (b. ?, d. ?), German or Flemish composer? Two sets of 6 sonatas with violin accompaniment published in London, *ca.* 1780 and *ca.* 1795 respectively (see *BUCEM*).

*MOLLER (or MÖLLER), J. C. (b. ?, d. ?), 18th-century German composer. See Eitner (biography) and *BUCEM* (keyboard music published in London).

*MONARI, Probably Bartolomeo (b. ?, d. ?), 17th-century Italian composer. In *Voluntarys and fugues* . . . (Walsh, [1710]).

MONRO(E), George (d. ? 1731). Music in London, R.C.O., MS without shelf-mark.

MOOREHEAD, John (d. 1804), Irish composer. In London, R.C.M., MS 735.

MOSS(E), John (b. ?, d. ?), 17th-century composer. One piece in MH and a suite in M. Mod. edns. in *SBK*, xxviii, and *PSMS*, xvi, respectively.

*MOTLEY, Richard (b. ?, d. ?), 17th-century composer, presumed author of 'Motleys Maggot' in 2MH. Mod. edn. in *SBK*, x. For evidence of the full name, see *BUCEM*.

MOULDS, John (b. ?, d. ?). *Three favorite sonatas for the harpsichord or piano forte with an accompanyment for a violin*. Op. X (G. Goulding, [1788]). Music in LT.

MOZART, Wolfgang Amadeus (1756-1791). Mozart visited London as a child in 1764-5. Later much of his keyboard music was published there (see *BUCEM*). Also pieces in SC.

MUDGE, (b. ?, d. ?), 18th-century composer. No. 6 of *Six concertos in seven parts* . . . (I. Walsh, [1749]) is for solo organ or harpsichord.

*MULLY, J. (b. ?, d. ?). *Six sonatas for the piano or harpsichord with an accompaniment for a violin* . . . (Longman and Broderip, *ca.* 1780); *Six sonatas* . . . *Opera 2* (Longman and Broderip, *ca.* 1790); *A favorite sonata for the piano forte or harpsichord* (Longman and Broderip, *ca.* 1790).

MYSLIVEČEK, Josef (1737-1781), Bohemian composer. Many of his keyboard works were published in London (see *BUCEM*).

NARES, James (1715-1783). *Eight setts of lessons for the harpsichord* . . . (for the Author, 1747. Another edn.: J. Johnson, 1757); [5] *lessons for the harpsichord with a sonata in score* . . . *Opera II* (for the Author, *ca.* 1759); *Six fugues with introductory voluntary's for the organ or harpsichord* (Welcker, [1772]); *Il principio; or a regular introduction to playing on the harpsichord or organ* (n.d.).

NAUMANN, John Gottlieb (1741-1801), German composer. Music in BC.

*NICOLAI, Valentin(o) (d. *ca.* 1800), German (or Italian?) composer, resident in England? See Eitner, *MGG*, *BUCEM*.

NIELSON, Lawrence Cornelius (b. ?, d. ?), *Three sonatas, for the harpsichord or piano forte* (Preston, *ca.* 1785). Also more ephemeral music.

*ORPIN, T. (b. ?, d. ?). Cudworth (*The Score* (1953) 60) mentions a Concerto in D, 1st movement only extant.

OVEREND, Marmaduke (d. 1790). *Lessons for the harpsichord or piano forte. No. 1* (Messrs. Thompson's, *ca.* 1780).

PAISIBLE, James the younger (b. ?, d. ?), son of James Paisible, who was resident in England from *ca.* 1670. See *MGG*. Lesson with variations by 'Mr. Paisible of Southampton' in Add. 34609.

PAISIELLO, Giovanni (1740-1816), Italian composer. Keyboard music published in London, around the time of the production of his opera *La Laconda* in London, 1791. See *BUCEM*.

PARADIES (or PARADISI), Pietro Domenico (1707-1791), Italian composer, resident in London 1747-1750. See *BUCEM* for keyboard music published there. Autograph pieces in Cambridge, Fitz. Mus., MS 30. f. 21.

PARK(E), Maria Hester (1775–1822). *Two sonatas for the piano forte or harpsichord* . . . *Op. IV* (for the Author, *ca.* 1794); *A concerto, for the piano-forte or harpsichord* . . . *Op. VI* (Rt. Birchall, *ca.* 1795. Another issue: for the Author, *ca.* 1795); *A sonata for the piano forte* . . . *Op. VII* (for the Author, *ca.* 1796).

*PARK, Miss M. F. (b. ?, d. ?). Eitner lists this composer as 'Parke, Miss M . . .'. *Three grand sonatas for the piano forte* . . . *Op. 1ma* (for the Author, [1799]). Eitner adds: *Two grand sonatas* . . . *Op. 3* (n.d.).

*PARSONS, John (b. ?, d. ?). *The elements of Music with progressive practical lessons for the harpsichord or piano forte* . . . (published by the Author, *ca.* 1800).

PASQUINI, Bernardo (1637–1710), Italian composer. Music in *A second collection* . . . (Walsh, [1719]). 8 pieces as later additions to Add. 36661.

*PELLEGRINI, Ferdinando (b. ?, d. ?), of Naples. See Eitner, *MGG, BUCEM* (keyboard music published in London).

PEPUSCH, John Christopher (1667–1752), English composer of German birth, resident in England from *ca.* 1700. Pieces in Add. 31467, 35040; London, R.C.O., MS without shelf-mark. He owned several early MSS, now lost except for Add. 23623 (see Appendix I, 1, B.)

PERGOLESI, Giovanni Battista (1710–1736), Italian composer. 2 books of 'harpsichord lessons' were published by Longman, 1771 and 1778: see *BUCEM.*

PESCETTI, Giovanni Battista (*ca.* 1704–*ca.* 1766), Italian composer. Music in Tenbury, St. Michael's Coll., MS 784.

PHILLIPS, Arthur (1605–1695): see Part 1.

*PHILPOT, Stephen (b. ?, d. ?). *Six capital lessons for the harpsichord or piano forte* . . . (J. Bland, *ca.* 1780).

PICHL, Wenzel (1741–1804), Austrian composer of Czech origin. See *BUCEM* for keyboard music published in London.

PIGGOTT, Francis (d. 1704). Suite in CC; 2 pieces in Ch. Ch. 46, one also in CC; music in Add. 52363. Suite from CC and 1 other piece in *CP*, vii.

PIOZZI, Gabriele (1740–1809), Italian composer. Lived in England from 1781, where keyboard music by him was published: see *BUCEM.*

*PLATTS, James (b. ?, d. ?). *A favorite lesson for the harpsichord or piano forte* . . . *Sonata I* [–II] (2 nos. Printed . . . by the Author, [1793]). Also more ephemeral works: see *BUCEM.*

PLEYEL, Ignaz Joseph (1757–1831), Austrian composer. In London, 1791–2, where a large amount of his keyboard music was published: see *BUCEM.* Also in BC.

POGLIETTI, Alessandro (d. 1683), Italian composer. Music in *A second collection* . . . (Walsh, [1719]).

POLAROLI (or Pollarolo), Carlo Francesco (1653–1722), Italian composer. Music in *Voluntarys and fugues* . . . (Walsh, [1710]).

*PRAT (b. ?, d. ?), 17th-century composer. 2 pieces in MH/3. Mod. edn. in *SBK*, xxviii.

PRELLEUR, Peter (b. ?, d. ?), 18th-century English composer of French extraction. *The Modern Music Master. VI. The harpsichord illustrated and improv'd* . . . *with suits of lessons* . . . (published anonymously. Engrav'd,

Printed and Sold at the Printing Office in Bow Church-Yard, [1730]. Reprinted as *The compleat tutor for the harpsichord or spinnet,* with different music: Peter Thompson, *ca.* 1755. Another edn: C. and S. Thompson, *ca.* 1770. Facsimile edn. by A. H. King in *Documenta Musicologica,* Erste Reihe . . . xxvii, 1965). Some single movements anonymously in CV1. MS: London, R.C.O., MS without shelf-mark.

*PRESTON, Christopher (b. ?, d. ?), 17th-century composer. Suite and 2 pieces in M. Mod. edn. of the suite in *PSMS,* xvi.

*PRICE, Robert (b. ?, d. ?), 17th-century composer. 1 piece in Ch. Ch. 1236.

PRING, Jacob Cubitt (1771–1799). *Six progressive sonatinas . . . Book 1st* (for the Author, *ca.* 1795); *Easy progressive lessons . . .* (Upper Clapton: for the Author, *ca.* 1798); *Ally Croaker, with variations, for the piano forte* (Low Layton: for the Author, *ca.* 1798). Music in BC.

PURCELL, Daniel (*ca.* 1660–1717), pieces in CL, LE2. Psalm-tunes with interludes in HMI (also a similar publication, I. Walsh, *ca.* 1731). Contents of CL in *CP,* vi.

PURCELL, Henry (1659–1695). *A choice collection of lessons for the harpsichord or spinnet* (Henry Playford, 1696. 2nd edn. [1697] lost. 3rd edn: Westminster, 1699, re-issued *ca.* 1700). Pieces in 2MH, 2LB, CV3. For MSS consult Zimmerman, *Catalogue;* also Add. 52363 and Edinburgh, Nat. Lib., Inglis 94, MS 3343. The edns. by H. Ferguson (*SBK,* xxi, xxii) and H. McLean (see Bibliography) comprise a virtually complete edn. of the keyboard works. The edn. by Squire and Hopkins (Purcell Society, vi) is superseded, though it includes some spurious material which is of intrinsic interest. See also Barrett; Rossi (in Part 1).

QUINTIN BUÉE, A. (b. ?, d. ?), English composer? *Three sonatas for the piano forte, the third for two performers on one instrument* (for the Author, *ca.* 1797).

*RADIGER, Anton (b. ?, d. ?), German composer resident in England. See Eitner; *BUCEM.*

RAMEAU, Jean-Philippe (1683–1764), French composer. Some of his harpsichord music was published in London: see *BUCEM.*

RAUZZINI, Venanzio (1746–1810), Italian castrato and composer. Keyboard music by him was published in London (see *BUCEM*). Also music in BC.

*RAYMOND, S. (b. ?, d. ?). *Three sonatas for the harpsichord or piano forte* (G. Smart, [1788]).

READING, John (1677–1764). Voluntary in TV. MSS include London, Dulwich Coll., MSS 92a, b, d; R.C.O., MS without shelf-mark; Manchester, Henry Watson Lib., MS BRm. 7105. Rf. 31.

REICHARDT, Johann Friedrich (1752–1814), German composer. Visited England 1785. Keyboard concertos published in London *ca.* 1780 (see *BUCEM*).

REINAGLE, Alexander (1756–1809). *Twenty four short and easy pieces . . . for the piano forte or harpsichord . . . Op. 1st* (J. Bland, *ca.* 1780); *A collection of the favourite Scots tunes with variations for the harpsichord . . .* (for the Author, *ca.* 1782. Another edn: London and Glasgow: J. Aird, *ca.* 1782); *Six sonatas for the piano-forte or harpsichord with an accompaniment for a violin* (for the Author, [1783]).

RELFE, John (1763–*ca.* 1837). *Two duetts for the harpsichord* . . . *Op. III* (for the Author, [1786]); *A set of twelve miscellaneous lessons* . . . *some composed by J. Relfe. Opera IV* (Longman and Broderip, 1786); *An overture and song for the harpsichord or piano forte with accompanyments* (for the Author, [1786]); *A set of grand lessons* . . . (for the Author, [1786]); *A select set of airs for the harpsichord or piano-forte* . . . (G. Goulding, [1787]); *Lessons, songs and duetts for the piano forte* . . . (Longman and Broderip, *ca.* 1790); *A second set of six progressive sonatas* (G. Goulding, *ca.* 1790); *Six divertimentos for the piano forte Op. 8* (for the Author, *ca.* 1800).

REUTTER, George (1656–1738), Austrian composer. One piece in Brussels, Bib. du Cons., MS 15418.

*RHODES, John (b. ?, d. ?). *Lessons, adapted for juvenile performers on the piano forte, or harpsichord* . . . (for the Author, *ca.* 1800).

RICHARDSON, Vaughan (d. 1729). 2 pieces by 'Mr. Richardson of Winton' (i.e. Winchester) in LE2.

RICHARDSON, William (d. *ca.* 1732). *Lessons for the harpsichord or spinet* . . . (for the Author, 1708).

RICHTER, Franz Xaver (1709–1789), Austro-Moravian composer. A good deal of his keyboard music was published in London (see *BUCEM*).

*ROBERTS, John (b. ?, d. ?), 17th-century composer. Suite in M. MSS: Ch. Ch. 1003, 1177, 1236. The suite from M in *PSMS*, xvi.

ROBINSON, John (1682–1762). The 'Prelude, Trio and Fugue' in B flat ascribed to him by B. Cooke in London, R.C.M., MS 814 is, at least in part, by J. S. Bach (mod. edn. in *EOM*, xii). Voluntary in Jeans MS 6, ed. *EOM*, xxiv.

ROESER, Valentin (1735–after 1782), German composer. Keyboard music by him was published in London (see *BUCEM*).

ROGERS, Benjamin (1614–1698). Pieces in MH. MSS include London, Brit. Mus., R.M. 21. d. 8; R.C.M., MSS 820, 2093; New York, Pub. Lib., Drexel 5611; Ch. Ch. 1236. Pieces from MH in *SBK*, xxviii; see also Bibliography. Piece from Ch. Ch. 1236 in *CP*, vi.

*ROLLI, Giovanni or John (b. ?, d. ?), Italian composer. See Eitner. Lessons of his were published in London, 1733 (see *BUCEM*).

ROSEINGRAVE, Thomas (1690–1766). *Eight suits of lessons for the harpsichord or spinnet* . . . (I. Walsh and Joseph Hare, [1728]. Another issue: I. Walsh, *ca.* 1731); *Voluntarys and fugues made on purpose for the organ or harpsichord* . . . (I. Walsh and Joseph Hare, [1728]. Another issue: I. Walsh, *ca.* 1731. Another edn: D. Wright, *ca.* 1734); *Six double fugues for the organ or harpsi-cord* . . . (I. Walsh, [1750]); *A celebrated concerto for the harpsichord* . . . (C. and S. Thompson, *ca.* 1770). MSS include Cambridge, Fitz. Mus., 30. f. 21; London, R.C.M., MS 1057; R.C.O., MS without shelf-mark. Roseingrave was also an editor of D. Scarlatti (q.v.). Mod. edns: 1 voluntary in *OEOM*, ii; see also Bibliography.

ROSETTI, A(madeo) (b. ?, d. ?), 18th-century Neapolitan composer. See Eitner. 4 sonatas published in London, *ca.* 1795 (see *BUCEM*).

ROSETTI, Francesco Antonio (Rös(s)LER, Franz Anton) (1746 or *ca.* 1750–1792), Bohemian composer. In *Grove* s.v. Rössler; *MGG* s.v. Rösler;

BUCEM, Eitner s.v. Rosetti. 6 sonatas published in London, *ca.* 1782 (see *BUCEM*). Also in BC (or the preceding?).

Ross, John (1764–1837). Numerous variations, dances, and sonatas based on Scottish and Irish songs. See *BUCEM*.

Rössler, Franz Anton: see Rosetti, Francesco Antonio.

Rush, George (d. *ca.* 178₃). *Six easy lessons for the harpsichord* . . . (John Cox, 1759); *A sett of sonatas for the harpsichord with an accompanyment for the violin* (Welcker, [1766]. This edn. also includes his first concerto. Reprinted (?) as *Six sonates* . . . *Œuvre troisième,* at La Haye: B. Hummel, *ca.* 1770); *A second sett of sonatas* . . . *Opera V* (Welcker, *ca.* 1770); *A first concerto for the harpsichord* . . . (for the Author, *ca.* 1770. Another edn: Welcker, *ca.* 1773. Another edn: *The favorite concerto* . . . *No. 1,* Longman and Broderip, *ca.* 1783. See also *A sett of sonatas* above); *A second concerto* . . . (Welcker, [1773]. Another edn: Welcker, *ca.* 1773); *A third concerto* . . . (Welcker, [1773]); *A fourth concerto* . . . (S. and A. Thompson, *ca.* 1778).

*Russel, D. (b. ?, d. ?). *A favorite lesson for the harpsichord* (*ca.* 1765).

Russell, William (1777–1813). *Twelve voluntaries for the organ or pianoforte* (Clementi, 1804); *Twelve voluntaries* . . . *Bk. II* (Clementi, 1812). For mod. edns. of these voluntaries, see *MGG*.

S., A. Two duettinos for two performers on one piano forte (for the Author, [1796]).

Sacchini, Antonio Maria Gasparo (1730–1786), Italian composer. Resident in England 1772–1782. Keyboard music by him published in London (see *BUCEM*).

*Saizoi, P. (b. ?, d. ?). *A lesson for the harpsd. with an accompt. for a G. flute and violin* . . . (*ca.* 1770); *Six sonatas for the harpsichord or piano forte, with an accompanyment for a German flute or violin and violoncello* (for the Author, *ca.* 1770).

Salomon, Johann Peter (1745–1815), German composer. Resident in England from 1781. Keyboard works copied by S. Wesley in London, R.C.M., MS 4021.

Sambonier: see Chambonnières.

Sammartini (San Martini), Giovanni Battista (1698–1775), Italian composer. Keyboard music published in London (see *BUCEM*, s.v. San Martini).

Sammartini (San Martini), Giuseppe (*ca.* 1693–*ca.* 1750), brother of preceding. Lived in London from 1727, where keyboard music of his was published (see *BUCEM* s.v. San Martini). See also Martini, G. B.

*Sampieri, Nicola (b. ?, d. ?), Italian composer resident in England? Some keyboard music published in London (see *BUCEM*).

*Sandell, Edmund (b. ?, d. ?). *Six pieces, for the piano forte* . . . (for the Author, *ca.* 1800).

*Sandley, Ben(jamin) (b. ?, d. ?), 17th-century composer. 1 piece (or the complete suite to which it belongs) in MH Mod. edn. in *SBK,* xxviii.

Sandoni, Pietro Giuseppe (*ca.* 1680–1748), Italian composer. In London 1719–1728, 1734–1737 (see *MGG*). Keyboard music published there (see *BUCEM*).

San Martini, Giovanni Battista and Giuseppe: see Sammartini.

SARTI, Giuseppe (1729–1802), Italian composer. Some of his keyboard music was published in London (see *BUCEM*).

SAVAGE, Jane (b. ?, d. ?). *Six easy lessons for the harpsichord or pianoforte* . . . *Opera 2nd* (for the Author, [1783]); *Six rondos* . . . *Opera III* (for the Author, *ca.* 1790); *A favourite duett for two performers, on one piano forte or harpsichord. Opera VI* (for the Author, *ca.* 1790); *God save the King. Adapted as a double lesson* . . . *Opera 8th* (for the Author, *ca.* 1790).

*SAYER, (b. ?, d. ?). Cudworth (*The Score* (1953) 60) mentions 2 keyboard concertos, present whereabouts unknown.

SCARLATTI, Domenico (1685–1757). The *Essercizi per gravicembalo* were apparently published in 1739 in London (30 sonatas; facsimile edn. by Gregg Press, 1967). There followed many edns. of his music in London, the most distinguished of his editors being T. Roseingrave (q.v.). See *BUCEM*. Also MS copies in London, R.C.M., MSS 824, 1120, etc.

SCHETKY, Johann Georg Christoff (1740–1824), German composer. Settled in Edinburgh. Keyboard music published there and in London (see *BUCEM*).

*SCHMID, Giovanni A. (b. ?, d. ?), German composer. See Eitner, s.v. Schmidt, Johann Adam. 2 keyboard publications in London (see *BUCEM*).

SCHMIDT, Theodore: see Smith, Theodore.

SCHOBERT, Johann (1720–1767), German composer. Much keyboard music published in London (see *BUCEM*).

*SCHROEDER, H. B. (or J. B.) (b. ?, d. ?), English composer of German stock? *Ten sonatas for the piano forte or harpsichord with an accompanyment for a violin* . . . *Opera I* (Longman and Broderip, *ca.* 1790). *A favorite sonata* . . . (for the Author, *ca.* 1795); *The Chace or Royal Windsor Hunt. A favorite grand sonata* . . . (for the Author, *ca.* 1795).

SCHROETER, Johann Samuel (*ca.* 1752–1788), German composer. Settled in London in 1772, where many of his keyboard works were published (see *BUCEM*). Music in SC.

*SCHUMANN, Friedrich Theodor (b. ?, d. ?), German composer resident in England? Many keyboard works published in London (see *BUCEM*).

SCHUSTER (? Joseph, 1748–1812), German composer. In BC.

SCHWINDL, Friedrich (1737–1786), Dutch composer. Visited London 1765. Sonatas Op. 8 published there *ca.* 1776 (see *BUCEM*).

*SCOULER, Alexander (b. ?, d. ?). *A favourite lesson for the harpsichord or forte piano* (Welcker, *ca.* 1775); *Lesson for the harpsichord or piano forte* (No. 3) . . . (J. Preston, *ca.* 1776. A 2nd lesson has obviously been lost); *Six sonatas for the harpsichord or piano-forte, with an accompaniment for a violin* . . . *Op. II* (J. Preston, [1783]).

*SEDO (SEEDO, SIDOW, SYDOW) (*ca.* 1690–1745), German composer, in England from the early 18th cent., but d. in Potsdam. See *MGG* s.v. Seedo. London, Dulwich Coll., MS 92.

*SELBY, William (b. ?, d. ?), organist of St. Sepulchre, London, *ca.* 1767 (Eitner, after Pohl). 1 voluntary in TV. See also *Oxford Companion to Music*.

*SEYBOLD, S. Philip (b. ?, d. ?). His 'keyboard' music is evidently intended primarily for the harp. See *BUCEM*.

*SHARP, Francis (b. ?, d. ?). *Six sonatas for the harpsichord or piano forte, three with an accompanyment for the violin* (Welcker, *ca.* 1775); *Six sonatas . . . with accompanyments for the violin (or flute) & violincello* [sic] *. . . Opera the fifth* (for the Author, *ca.* 1785); *New Guida di Musica, being a complete book of instructions for beginners on the piano forte . . . Op. 6* (Preston and Son, [1797]).

*SHAW, Thomas (b. ?, d. ?), violinist (see Eitner). *Three sonatas for the piano forte or harpsichord* (Longman and Broderip, [1787]); *A second sett of three sonatas . . . Opera IV* (S.A. and P. Thompson, [1790]). Eitner mentions 3 sonatas, Op. 13, but does not mention Op. 4.

*SHEELES, John (b. ?, d. ?). See Eitner. *Suites of lessons for the harpsichord or spinnet* (Wm. Smith. M. Rawlins and I. Barret, *ca.* 1725).

SHIELD, William (1748-1829). *The Union Volunteers. March, troop & quick step . . . for the piano forte or harp* (for the Author, *ca.* 1800).

*SIMONELLI, Matteo (? 1618-1696), Italian composer (see *MGG*). 'Tocata' in LE.

SIRMEN (SYRMEN): see Lombardini.

*SKINNER, Benjamin (b. ?, d. ?). *Six solos for a German flute violin or harpsicord, to which are added some pieces designed as lessons for the harpsicord* (Richard Bride, *ca.* 1770). Voluntary in TV.

*SMETHERGELL, William (b. ?, d. ?). See Eitner, *MGG*. *Six lessons for the harpsichord, or forte piano . . . Opera I.* (Henry Thorowgood, *ca.* 1770); *Six concertos for the harpsichord or piano forte . . .* (for the Author, *ca.* 1775); *A favorite concerto for the harpsichord or piano forte . . .* (Longman and Broderip, [1784]); *Six lessons for the harpsichord or piano forte* (Longman and Broderip, *ca.* 1785).

*SMITH, Clement (b. ?, d. ?). *Sonata capricciosa for the piano forte or harpsichord* (for the Author, [1791]); *The Frog and Mouse. An old air arranged as a rondo for the piano forte* (for the Author, *ca.* 1795).

SMITH, John Christopher (1712-1795), English composer of German birth, Handel's copyist. Several collections of lessons and sonatas (see *BUCEM*); MSS include London, R.C.M., MS 1018; Tenbury, St. Michael's Coll., MS 784 (surname only).

SMITH, John Stafford (1750-1836). 3 voluntaries in CV3. A prelude and fugue in J. Pittman, *A series of progressive studies*, ii. For his work as an editor see Bibliography, addenda.

*SMITH, Martin (b. ?, d. ?), father of preceding. 1 voluntary in CV3. See *Grove* under preceding.

SMITH, Robert (*ca.* 1648-1675). 3 pieces in M. 2 pieces in Ch. Ch. 1003. Pieces from M in *PSMS*, xvi.

*SMITH (or SCHMIDT), Theodor(e) (b. ?, d. ?), German composer. Lived for a time in London (see *MGG*), where he published numerous concertos, duets, sonatas, etc. for keyboard (see *BUCEM*). MSS include Add. 14335 ('T. Smith').

*SMITHS, D. A. L. (b. ?, d. ?). *Six sonatas for the piano forte or harpsichord . . .* (Preston and Son, *ca.* 1790).

*Snow, John (b. ?, d. ?). Not Eitner, 'Snow, J . . .'. *Variations for the harpsichord to a minuet of Corelli's, the gavot in Otho, and the old Highland Laddie . . .* (J. Johnson, *ca.* 1760).

Snow, Moses (d. 1702). 2 pieces by 'Snow' in 2MH. Mod. edn. in *SBK*, x.

Solér, Antonio (1729–1783), Spanish composer, pupil of D. Scarlatti. His *XXVII Sonatas para clave* were published by Robert Birchall, *ca.* 1795 (see *BUCEM*).

*Southbrook, William E. (b. ?, d. ?). *Six sonnets and six sonatinas . . .* (Knightsbridge: for the Author, 1797); *Second set of six sonnets and three sonatinas . . .* (for the Author, *ca.* 1799).

*Southwell, F. W. (b. ?, d. ?). *A concerto for the piano forte . . . Op. IV* (Dublin: for the Author, *ca.* 1795).

Spencer, G. (b. ?, d. ?), 18th-century composer. In Add. 40139.

Staes, Ferdinand Philippe Joseph (1748–1809), Netherlands composer. A number of his keyboard works were published in London (see *BUCEM*). Music in BC.

Stamitz, Carl (1745–1801), German composer of Bohemian parentage. Keyboard music by him published in London (see *BUCEM*). Music by 'Stamitz' in BC is probably by him.

Stamitz, Johann (1717–1757), Bohemian composer, father of preceding. Some keyboard works (especially concertos) published in London. See *BUCEM*.

Stanley, John (1713–1786). *Six concertos set for the harpsicord or organ* (arranged from his string concertos, Op. 2. I Walsh, *ca.* 1745. Another issue: H. Wright, *ca.* 1795); *Ten voluntarys for the organ or harpsicord . . . Opera quinta* (John Johnson, [1748]. Another issue: John Johnson, *ca.* 1750. Another edn.: C. and S. Thompson, *ca.* 1770); *Ten voluntarys . . . Opera sesta* (John Johnson, [1752]. Another edn: C. and S. Thompson, *ca.* 1765); *Ten voluntaries . . . Opera settima* (John Johnson, [1754]. Another edn: C. and S. Thompson, *ca.* 1765); *Six concertos for the organ, harpsichord or forte piano . . . Opera X* (for the Author, 1775. Another issue, Harrison and Co., *ca.* 1785). Music in TwV. MSS include Add. 14335, 31814, 35025, 35040; London, R.C.M., MS 1056; R.C.O., MS without shelf-mark; Dulwich Coll., MSS 92a, b; Manchester, Henry Watson Lib., MS BRm. 7105. Rf. 31. Pieces in *OEOM*, ii, iv; see also Bibliography.

*Steemson, Miss (b. ?, d. ?), organist at Lancaster. Piece in Add. 37027.

Steibelt, Daniel Gottlieb (1765–1823), German composer. Resident in London 1796–1799, where many of his keyboard works were published (see *BUCEM*).

Sterkel, Johann Franz Xaver (1750–1817), German composer. Many of his keyboard works were published in London (see *BUCEM*).

Stevens, Richard John Samuel (1757–1837). *Three sonatas for the harpsichord or piano-forte with an accompaniment for a violin . . . Opera prima* (for the Author, *ca.* 1786). Pieces in Add. 31814 (autograph) and 31822.

*Stone, John (b. ?, d. ?), 17th-century composer. 'Hye Landers March' in Ch. Ch. 1175.

STORACE, Stephen (1763–1796). *Three sonatas for the harpsichord or piano-forte, with accompaniments* (H. Andrews, *ca.* 1785); *Three sonatas, for the piano-forte with accompaniments for a violin & violoncello . . . and the celebrated air 'Cara Donne' with variations* (Preston and Son, *ca.* 1790); *Six easy and progressive sonatinas* . . . (for the Author, [1790]). Two sonatas in SC.

*STUBLEY, Simon (b. ?, d. ?), 18th-century composer. 2 voluntaries in TV.

*SUETT, Richard (b. ?, d. ?). *Three sonatas for the piano forte or harpsichord with an accompaniment for a violin or a flute* . . . (for the Author, *ca.* 1791).

*SYMONDS, Henry (d. 1730). See Eitner. *Six sets of lessons for the harpsichord* (William Smith, *ca.* 1734).

SYRMEN: see Lombardini.

*T., C. I. L. *Sonatinas for the piano forte . . . inscribed to Dr. Burney* (F. Bland, *ca.* 1785).

TAYLOR, Raynor (1747–1825), of Chelmsford. Emigrated to America in 1792. See *MGG. Divertimento for harpsichord or pianoforte, Op. 1* (Longman, Lukey and Broderip, *ca.* 1775); *Fye! nay prithee John . . . with variations* . . . (Longman, Lukey and Broderip, *ca.* 1775); *Martini's favorite minuet, with variations* . . . (Longman, Lukey and Broderip, *ca.* 1775); *Six sonatas for the harpsicord, or, piano forte with an accompaniment for a violin . . . Opera seconda* (Longman and Broderip, *ca.* 1780); *Lessons* in C and F (Longman and Broderip, *ca.* 1780); also a *Lesson* published Philadelphia, 1795.

TENDUCCI, Giusto Ferdinando (b. *ca.* 1736), Italian castrato soprano and composer. Settled in London from 1758, visiting Dublin (1756–1768), and Edinburgh (1768–91). Keyboard music by him was published in all three capitals (see *BUCEM*).

*THATCHER, William (d. 1678), Irish composer who settled in London (see Eitner, following Hawkins). Several pieces in M (Unsigned: see Locke's Preface). Some in *PSMS*, xvi.

*THOMSON, John (b. ?, d. ?). *Three sonatas for the harpsd. or piano-forte, with an accompanyment for a violin . . . Op. Imo* (Edinburgh: Corri and Sutherland, *ca.* 1785).

*THOMSON, William (b. ?, d. ?), of Leominster. Not the William Thomson mentioned in Eitner, *MGG. Six easy lessons for the harpsichord* (Welcker, *ca.* 1775).

*THORLEY, Thomas (b. ?, d. ?). *Ten voluntary's for the organ or harpsichord. Perform'd at the Cathedral Norwich* (J. Bland, *ca.* 1780). 1 movement in *OEOM*, ii.

*THORNOWITZ, Henry (b. ?, d. ?), 17th-century composer. 5 pieces in Ch. Ch. 1142.

*TINDAL, William (b. ?, d. ?). *Three sonatas for the piano forte or harpsichord accompanied by one violin . . . Opera 3* (H. Wright, *ca.* 1790).

TOMICH, Francesco (František Vaclav TOMEŠ) (1759–after 1796), Bohemian composer. Some keyboard music published in London (see *BUCEM*).

*TOURS, Jacob (*ca.* 1759–1811), Dutch composer, (see Eitner). 2 keyboard publications in London (see *BUCEM*).

TRAVERS, John (*ca.* 1703–1758). *XII Voluntaries for the organ or harpsichord* . . .

(C. and S. Thompson, [1769]). Music in CV1 (unidentified: not identical with any of the above). Mod. edns: *OEOM*, i, ii, iv, including extracts from CV1 supposed to be by Travers. See also Bibliography.

*TREMAIN, Thomas (b. ?, d. ?). *Six sonatas, for the harpsichord or forte-piano, with an accompaniment for the violin . . . Opera IV* (Longman and Broderip, *ca.* 1785); *Six sonatas spirituale or voluntarys for the organ or harpsichord . . . Op. VIII* (Preston and Son, *ca.* 1800. According to Eitner, Op. 7).

*TURNER, Elizabeth (b. ?, d. ?). *A collection of songs . . . with six lessons for the harpsichord* (for the Author, [1756]).

TURNER, William (1651–1740). 1 piece in 2MH. Modern edn. in *SBK*, x, and *CP*, vii.

URBANI, Pietro (1749–1816), Italian composer. Settled in London before 1781, and afterwards in Scotland, where his keyboard music, mostly ephemeral, was published (see *BUCEM*).

VAŇHAL, Jan (1739–1813). Bohemian composer. Some keyboard music published in London (see *BUCEM* s.v. Wanhal). Music in SC, BC.

*VALENTINE, Ann (b. ?, d. ?). *Ten sonatas for the piano forte or harpsichord with an accompaniment for the violin or German-flute . . . Opera prima* (for the Author, *ca.* 1798).

VENTO, Mattia (1735–1776), Italian composer. Settled in London in 1763, where many keyboard works by him were published (see *BUCEM*). Music in BC.

VINCENT, Thomas, the younger (*ca.* 1720–1783). *A sett of familiar lessons for the harpsichord . . . Opera 2da* (for the Author, [1755]).

VIOTTI, Giovanni Battista (1755–1824), Italian composer. Settled in London in 1792. Various keyboard works, mostly arranged from string works, were published in London (see *BUCEM*).

WAGENSEIL, Georg Christoph (1715–1777), Austrian composer. Much of his keyboard music was published in London (see *BUCEM*). Lesson in *Six lessons for the harpsichord* (Welcker, *ca.* 1770).

WAINWRIGHT, Robert (1748–1782). *Six sonatas for the harpsichord or piano forte, with an accompaniment for a violin . . . Opera 1* (for the Author, [1774]). The 6 *Quintettos* for harpsichord, 2 violins, violoncello and bass are listed by Cudworth, *The Score* (1953) 60.

*WAKEFIELD, W. (b. ?, d. ?). *Four sonatas for the piano forte or harpsichord with an accompaniment, for a violin* (for the Author, *ca.* 1800).

WALOND, William (1725–1770). [6] *Voluntaries for the organ or harpsichord . . . Opera I* (J. Johnson, *ca.* 1755); *Ten voluntaries for the organ or harpsichord . . . Opera II* (J. Johnson, 1758). MSS: Add. 14335 (Op. 1, No. 2); Add. 35040. Pieces in *OEOM*, i, iii, iv.

*WALSH, Henry (b. ?, d. ?). *Six sonatas for the harpsichord* (for the Author, *ca.* 1778); *The Heavy Hours, with variations for the harpsichord or piano forte* (P. Evans, *ca.* 1780).

*WALSINGHAM (b. ?, d. ?). *A gavot, with variations for the piano forte* (Longman and Broderip, 1797).

WANHAL(L): see Vaňhal.

WEBBE, Samuel (1740–1816). *Six sonatas for the piano forte or harpsichord* (Welcker, *ca.* 1780). Pieces in Add. 14335 (2 signed 'S.W.' and others anonymous: see Hughes-Hughes, *MGG*).

WEBBE, Samuel (*ca.* 1770–1843), son of preceding. *Four sonatas for the harp*[sichord?] (Longman, Clementi and Co., [1799]; *Duett for two performers on the piano forte* (R. Birchall, *ca.* 1800). Compositions published after 1800 include: *A sonata for the harp or pianoforte with the violin ad libitum* (1811); *Duet for harp and piano* (1813); *Three voluntaries, for the organ, or piano forte* (Clementi, Banger, Collard, Davis and Collard, 1820); *Preludes for the pianoforte* (1825); *Funeral March in honour of Beethoven* (1828); for complete list see *MGG*, which also refers to harpsichord variations in MS, without specifying which.

WEICHSELL, Charles (*ca.* 1765–?). Pieces in Add. 29295.

WEICHSELL, Elizabeth: see Billington.

WELDON, John (1676–1736). 2 pieces in LB. Pieces in Add. 22099, 31467, 52363.

*WENNINGTON, William (b. ?, d. ?). *Two short progressive lessons for the piano forte, and a ground, with variations thereon* (for the Author, *ca.* 1798); *Five short progressive lessons* [etc. as above] (for Mr. Astor, *ca.* 1799).

*WENTWORTH, G. (b. ?, d. ?). Minuet in London, R.C.M., MS 694.

*WERNER, Daniel (b. ?, d. ?). *Six easy lessons for the harpsichord* (for the Author, *ca.* 1760).

*WERNER, Francis (b. ?, d. ?). Numerous dance publications 'for harp, harpsichord or violin' in 1780s (see *BUCEM*).

WESLEY, Charles (1757–1834). *Six concertos for the organ or harpsichord . . . Opera IId* (for the Author, [1781]); *Three sonatas for the harpsichord . . . Op. 4* (*ca.* 1790); *God save the King, with new variations for the organ or harpsichord . . .* (for the Author, [1799]); *Voluntary* [Nos. 1–6] *for the organ or piano forte . . .* (Bland and Weller, *ca.* 1815). MSS: Add. 35018 (8 organ concertos, including the 6 of Op. 2); London, R.C.M., MSS 4023 (6 organ concertos), 4024. Concerto movement in *OEOM*, i.

WESLEY, Samuel (1766–1837), brother of preceding. *Eight sonatas for the harpsichord or piano forte* (for the Author, *ca.* 1780); *Two sonatas for the piano forte or harpsichord; with an accompanyment for a violin . . . Op. 2* (for the Author, *ca.* 1786); *Three sonatas for the piano forte . . . Op. 3* (for the Author, [1789]); *Twelve sonatinas . . . Op. 4* (for the Author, *ca.* 1799); *Four sonatas and two duets for the piano forte . . . Op. 5* (L. Lavenu, 1800); *A favorite rondo, for the piano forte* (L. Lavenu, *ca.* 1800); *A Voluntary for the organ . . . Op. 6* (9 nos: 1–6 printed and sold by W. Hodsall; 7–9 by Rt. Birchall: n.d., *ca.* 1800?); *Sonata* (for pianoforte: R. Birchall, 1808); *Twelve* [recte 13] *short pieces for the organ with a full voluntary added* (Clementi, 1815); *Six introductory movements for the organ . . .* (Clementi, Collard and Collard, *ca.* 1825); *Six organ voluntaries, composed for the use of young organists . . . Op. 36* (J. Dean, [1836]); also two duet publications (Hodsall and Lonsdale respectively, both without date), and a single voluntary (Hodsall, n.d.). For posthumous publications, see *MGG*. MSS include Add. 14340, 14343–4, 31239, 31764, 34089, 34996, 34998, 35005–8, 35009 (3 organ concertos), 35025, 35038–9;

London, R.C.M., MSS 640, 1039, 1151, 4018, 4021-2, 4025, 4028-9, 4038. Mod. edns. include pieces in *OEOM*, ii, iv; see also Bibliography, and lists in *MGG* s.v. *Werke* and *Ausgaben*.

W(H)ICHELLO, Abiell (d. *ca.* 1745). *Lessons, for the harpsichord, or spinett* . . . (for the Author, [1707]. Another edn: for the Author, *ca.* 1707).

*WHITE, John (b. ?, d. ?), early 18th-century composer. In Add. 52363.

WILLIAMSON, T. G. (b. ?, d. ?). *Six favorite sonatinas for the piano-forte* . . . *Op. 1* (for the Author, *ca.* 1798).

*WILLSON, Joseph (b. ?, d. ?). *A favorite sonata for the piano forte or harpsichord* . . . (W. Cope, *ca.* 1798).

*WILLTON, Charles Henry (b. ?, d. ?). *A set of eighteen lessons for the piano forte or harpsichord* . . . *Opera V* (Liverpool: J. B. Pye, *ca.* 1795).

*WINTERSALL, Robert (b. ?, d. ?), 17th-century composer. Many pieces in Ch. Ch. 1175.

*WISE, Samuel (b. ?, d. ?). *Six lessons for the harpsichord* (for the Author, *ca.* 1765); *Six concertos for the organ or harpsichord* (for the Author, *ca.* 1770).

WOLF (? Ernst Wilhelm, 1735-1792), German composer, represented in BC.

*WOOD (b. ?, d. ?), early 18th-century composer. 1 piece in 3HM.

*WOOD, Charles (b. ?, d. ?). *A favorite duetto for two performers on the piano forte or harpsichord* . . . (for the Author, *ca.* 1790); *A favorite lesson for the harpsichord or piano forte* (for the Author, *ca.* 1790); *Three sonatas for the piano forte or harpsichord with an accompaniment for a violin* . . . *Op. 2d* (for the Author, *ca.* 1790). Eitner mentions a Daniel J. Wood as having composed organ music.

*WORGAN, James, the younger (b. ?, d. ?). Tentatively identified in *MGG* with John Worgan, son (?) of the following, b. 1770. *A favorite carillon sonata* . . . *Opera prima* (for the Author, *ca.* 1795). Also more ephemeral publications (see *BUCEM*).

WORGAN, John (1724-1790), father or uncle of preceding? *Six sonatas for the harpsichord* (for the Author, 1769); *Pieces for the harpsichord* . . . (for the Author, *ca.* 1780); *A new concerto for the harpsichord* . . . (for the Author, 1785); *Organ pieces by the late Dr. Worgan never before published* (Fentum, *ca.* 1795); *Select organ pieces by the late Doctr. Worgan* . . . (3 nos., for I. Worgan, *ca.* 1795). MSS: London, R.C.O., MS without shelf-mark.

WRIGHT, Thomas (1763-1829). *A concerto, for the harpsichord or piano forte* . . . (for the Author, *ca.* 1795).

*XALON, J. (b. ?, d. ?), foreign composer? He published *Six sonatas for the harpsichord or piano forte* . . . *Opera IV* (for the Author, [1780]).

YANIEWICZ (JANIEWICZ), Felix (1764-1848). Polish violinist and composer (see *BUCEM*).

YATES, William (b. ?, d. ?). *Six easy sonatas for the harpsichord* . . . *Opera III* (C. and S. Thompson, *ca.* 1770).

YOUNG, Anthony (*ca.* 1685-after 1739). *Suits of lessons for the harpsicord or spinnet* . . . (I. Walsh and I. Hare, [1719]).

YOUNG, Mary: see Barthélemon.

ZIANI, Petro Andrea (*ca.* 1620–1684), Italian composer. Music in *Voluntarys and Fugues* (Walsh, [1710]).

ZIPOLI, Domenico (1688–1726), Italian composer. The contents of his *Sonate d'intavolatura* were published in London by Walsh in 2 volumes dated respectively 1725 and 1731 (see *BUCEM*).

Bibliography

1. *Editions of music*

ALCOCK, John [the elder], *Four Voluntaries*, ed. Peter Marr (*TW*, xxiii), London, 1961.

Altenglische Orgelmusik, ed. Denis Stevens, Kassel and Basel: Bärenreiter, 1953.

ANDREWS, Hilda, ed., see *My Ladye Nevells Booke*.

ANONYMOUS, *Voluntaries in A minor and G minor*, ed. Walter Emery (*EOM*, xvii), London, 1961 (= CV2, Nos. 8, 9).

—— *Voluntary in D minor for Double Organ*, ed. Watkins Shaw (*EOM*, iv), London, 1960 (= Add. 31446, ff. 16–17v).

An Anthology of English Lute Music, ed. David Lumsden, London, 1954.

Archives des Maîtres de l'Orgue, see separate entry under *Liber Fratrum Cruciferorum* (*AMO*, x).

ARNE, Thomas, *Eight Keyboard Sonatas*, ed. Gwilym Beechey and Thurston Dart (*SBK*, xxvii), London, 1969 (facs.).

ASTON, Hugh, see *Early Keyboard Music*.

Balli Antichi Veneziani per cembalo, ed. Knud Jeppesen, Copenhagen: Wilhelm Hansen, 1962.

BARRETT, see *Three Voluntaries*.

BEECHEY, Gwilym, ed., see Chilcot, Thomas; *Ten Eighteenth-Century Voluntaries*.

—— and DART, Thurston, edd., see Arne, Thomas.

BENNETT, John, *Voluntaries IX and X*, ed. H. Diack Johnstone (*EOM*, xv), London, 1966.

—— see *Ten Eighteenth-Century Voluntaries*.

BLOW, John, *Complete Organ Works*, ed. Watkins Shaw, London: Schott & Co. Ltd., 1958.

—— *Six Suites*, ed. Howard Ferguson (*SBK*, v), London, 1965.

—— see *Contemporaries of Purcell*; *Old English Composers*; *Three Voluntaries*.

BOSTON, John L., see *Priscilla Bunbury's Virginal Book*.

BOYCE, William, *Four Voluntaries From 'Ten Voluntaries for Organ or Harpsichord'* (Nos. 1, 4, 8, 9), ed. Gordon Phillips (*TW*, xxvi), London, 1966.

—— see *Voluntaries by Stanley, Walond and Boyce*.

BROWN, Alan, ed., see Byrd, William; *Tisdale's Virginal Book*.

BULL, John, *Keyboard Music: I*, ed. John Steele and Francis Cameron (*MB*, xiv), London, 1960 (2nd. rev. edn. 1967).

—— *Keyboard Music: II*, ed. Thurston Dart (*MB*, xix), London, 1963.

—— *Ten Pieces*, ed. John Steele and Francis Cameron (*SBK*, viii), London, 1960 (=*MB*, xiv, Nos. 5, 20, 16, 17, 15, 32, 39, 40, 41, 54).

—— see *Parthenia*.

BYRD, William, *The Collected Keyboard Works,* ed. Edmund H. Fellowes (*The Collected Works of William Byrd,* xviii-xx), London: Stainer and Bell Ltd., 1950.

—— *Fifteen Pieces,* ed. Thurston Dart (*SBK,* iv), London, 1956 (2nd rev. edn. 1969).

—— *Forty-five Pieces for Keyboard Instruments,* ed. Stephen D. Tuttle, Paris: Editions de l'Oiseaux-lyre, 1939.

—— *Keyboard Music: I,* ed. Alan Brown (*MB,* xxvii), London, 1969.

—— *Keyboard Music: II,* ed. Alan Brown (*MB,* xxviii), London, 1971.

—— *Prelude, Fantasia, Miserere (1) and (2), Gloria tibi Trinitas, Ut re mee fa sol la, Veni Creator Spiritus (1) and (2),* ed. Philip Ledger (*TW,* viii), London, 1968.

—— see *My Ladye Nevells Booke.*

—— see *Parthenia.*

CALDWELL, John, ed., see *Early Tudor Organ Music I.*

CAMIDGE, Matthew, *Concerto No. 2 in G minor,* ed. Francis Jackson (*EOM,* xxii), London, 1966.

CAPIROLA, Meser Vincenzo, *Compositione,* ed. Otto Gombosi, Neuilly-sur-Seine: Société de Musique d'Autrefois, 1955.

CHILCOT, Thomas, *Two Suites for Harpsichord,* ed. Gwilym Beechey (*PSMS,* xxii), Pennsylvania University Park and London, 1969.

CHRYSANDER, Fr., ed., see Handel.

Clavichord Music of the Seventeenth Century, ed. Thurston Dart (*CM*), London: Stainer and Bell Ltd., 1960 (2nd rec. edn. 1964).

Clement Matchett's Virginal Book (1612), ed. Thurston Dart (*SBK,* ix), London, 1957.

The Contemporaries of Purcell (CP), ed. J. A. Fuller-Maitland, London: Chester, n.d. (7 vols.). The composers are Barrett, Blow, Clark, Coleman, Croft, Diesner, Eccles, King, Piggott, D. Purcell, Rogers and Turner.

Corpus of Early Keyboard Music, see separate entry under Gibbons, Christopher (*CEKM,* xviii).

COSYN, Benjamin, *Three Voluntaries,* ed. John Steele (*EOM,* xiv), London, 1959 (Oxford, Christ Church, MS 1113, Nos. 56, 62, 73, all ascribed to 'B.C.'). See also *Twenty-five pieces for keyed instruments.*

CURTIS, Alan, ed., see *Dutch Keyboard Music.*

DART, Thurston, ed., see Bull, John; Byrd, William; *Clavichord Music of the Seventeenth Century*; *Clement Matchett's Virginal Book*; Farnaby, Giles; *Fitzwilliam Virginal Book*; Gibbons, Orlando; Locke, Matthew; Morley, Thomas; *Musick's Hand-Maid*; *Parthenia*; *Parthenia In-Violata*; *The Second Part of Musick's Hand-Maid.*

DAVISON, Archibald T., and APEL, Willi, edd., see *Historical Anthology of Music.*

DAWES, Frank, ed., see *Early Keyboard Music*; *Two Elizabethan Keyboard Duets.*

The Dublin Virginal Manuscript, ed. John Ward (*DVM*), Wellesley College, 1954 (2nd rev. edn. 1964).

DUPUIS, Thomas S., see *Three Voluntaries of the Later 18th Century.*

Dutch Keyboard Music of the 16th and 17th Centuries, ed. Alan Curtis (*MMN*, iii), Amsterdam, 1961. Includes complete edn. of Add. 29498.

Early English Church Music, see separate entries under *Early Tudor Organ Music I* and *II* (*EECM*, vi, x).

Early English Harmony, ed. H. E. Wooldridge (*EEH*, i, facs.), London: Bernard Quaritch, 1897.

Early English Organ Music, ed. Margaret Glyn (*EEOM*), London: Plainsong and Mediaeval Music Society, 1939.

Early Keyboard Music, ed. Frank Dawes (*EKM*, 5 vols.), London: Schott and Co. Ltd., 1951. Vol. i, *Ten pieces by Hugh Aston and others* [London, Brit. Mus., Roy. App. 58]; ii, *Twelve pieces from Mulliner's Book* [Brit. Mus., Add. MS 30513]; iii, *Seven Virginal Pieces from B.M. Add. 30486*; iv, *Pieces from the Tomkins Manuscript* [Brit. Mus., Add. MS 29996]; v, *Fifteen Pieces from Elizabeth Rogers's Virginal Book* [Brit. Mus., Add. MS 10337].

Early Organ Music (*EOM*, Novello), see separate entries under Anonymous (iv, xvii); Bennet, John (xv); Blow, John (xxiv); Camidge, Matthew (xx); Cosyn, Benjamin (xiv); Greene, Maurice (xviii); Robinson, John (xxiv); Rogers, Benjamin (xi); Stanley, John (viii, ix); Wesley, Samuel (iii, x, xix).

Early Scottish Keyboard Music, ed. Kenneth Elliott (*SBK*, xv), London, 1958.

Early Tudor Organ Music I: Music for the Office, ed. John Caldwell (*EECM*, vi), London, 1966.

Early Tudor Organ Music II: Music for the Mass, ed. Denis Stevens (*EECM*, x), London, 1969.

ELLIOTT, Kenneth, ed., see *Early Scottish Keyboard Music*.

EMERY, Walter, ed., see Anonymous; Greene, Maurice; Wesley, Samuel.

FARNABY, Giles, *Seventeen Pieces*, ed. Thurston Dart (*SBK*, xi), London, 1957 (2nd rev. edn. 1968).

—— and Richard, *Keyboard Music*, ed. Richard Marlow (*MB*, xxiv), London, 1965.

FELLOWES, Edmund H., ed., see Byrd, William.

FERGUSON, Howard, ed., see Blow, John; *Early English Keyboard Music*; Purcell, Henry.

FIELD, John, *Piano Concertos 1–3*, ed. Frank Merrick (*MB*, xvii), London, 1961.

The Fitzwilliam Virginal Book, ed. J. A. Fuller-Maitland and W. Barclay Squire (*FWVB*, 2 vols.) Leipzig: Breitkopf und Härtel, 1899 (reprints by Broude Bros. and Dover Publications, New York, n.d.).

The Fitzwilliam Virginal Book, Twenty-four Pieces, ed. Thurston Dart (*SBK*, xvi), London, 1964.

GIBBONS, Christopher, *Keyboard Compositions*, ed. Clare G. Rayner (*CEKM*, xviii), American Institute of Musicology, 1967.

GIBBONS, Orlando, *Eight Keyboard Pieces*, ed. Gerald Hendrie (*SBK*, xxvi, = *MB*, xx, Nos. 17–19, 21, 26, 30, 32, 33], London, n.d.

—— *A Fancy for a double Orgaine; A Voluntary in A minor; Fantazia of Foure Parts from Parthenia*, ed. Gordon Phillips (*TW*, ix), London, 1957.

—— *Keyboard Music*, ed. Gerald Hendrie (*MB*, xx), London, 1962 (2nd rev. edn. 1967).

—— *Nine Organ Pieces*, ed. Gerald Hendrie (*SBK*, xxv, = *MB*, xx, Nos. 1–3, 10, 11, 7, 49, 5, 6), London, 1962 (2nd rev. edn. 1967).

—— *A Selection of Short Dances*, ed. Margaret Glyn (*SBK*, xvii), London, 1925 (2nd rev. edn. by Thurston Dart, 1960).

—— see *Parthenia*.

GLYN, Margaret, ed., see *Early English Organ Music*; Gibbons, Orlando; Weelkes, Thomas.

GOMBOSI, Otto, ed., see Capirola, Meser Vincenzo.

GREENE, Maurice, *Four Voluntaries for Organ or Harpsichord*, ed. Francis Routh (*TW*, xv), London 1960 (Nos. 1–2 = TV, Nos. 1, 10; the other two are from Greene's *Twelve Voluntarys* [1780], Nos. 7, 8).

—— *Three Voluntaries for Organ or Harpsichord*, ed. Gordon Phillips (*TW*, iv), London, 1958 (= *Twelve Voluntarys* [1780] Nos. 2, 6, 11).

—— *Voluntary XIII*, ed. Walter Emery (*EOM*, xviii), London, 1961 (= TV, No. 1, first 2 movements; complete in 4 movements in *TW*, xv, No. 1).

GUILMANT, A., ed., see *Liber Fratrum Cruciferorum*.

HANDEL, G. F., *Concerto for Organ in F major*, ed. Gordon Phillips (*TW*, xxxiii), London, 1962. The continuous organ part of the 1st concerto in Walsh's *Second Set*.

—— *Four Voluntaries for the Organ or Harpsichord*, ed. Francis Routh (*TW*, xix), London, 1961. These works, from CV4, are spurious.

—— *A Miscellaneous Collection of Instrumental Music*, ed. Fr. Chrysander (*The Works of George Frederic Handel*, xlviii), Leipzig, 1894. Facsimile reprint by Gregg Press Ltd., 1965. Includes organ concertos in MS, from Walsh's *Second set* and Arnold's edn., solo keyboard music from MSS, and contemporary transcriptions, especially from SCL.

—— *Pièces pour le Clavecin*, ed. Fr. Chrysander (*The Works of George Frederic Handel*, ii), Leipzig, 1859. Contains all the solo keyboard music published in Handel's lifetime, with some additions.

—— *Six Fugues or Voluntarys*, ed. Gordon Phillips (*TW*, xii), London, 1960.

—— *Twelve Organ Concerti*, ed. Fr. Chrysander (*The Works of George Frederic Handel*, xxviii), Leipzig, 1868. Facsimile reprint by Gregg Press Ltd., 1965. Opp. 4 and 7 in score.

HEARTZ, Daniel, ed., see *Preludes, Chansons and Dances for Lute*.

HENDRIE, Gerald, ed., see Gibbons, Orlando.

HINE, William, see *Ten Eighteenth-Century Voluntaries*.

Historical Anthology of Music, ed. Archibald T. Davison and Willi Apel (*HAM*, 2 vols.), Cambridge, Massachusetts, 1954.

Intabolatura Nova di Balli (Venice, 1551), ed. William Oxenbury and Thurston Dart (*SBK*, xxiii), London, 1965.

JACKSON, Francis, ed., see Camidge, Matthew.

JEANS, Susi, ed., see Robinson, John; Rogers, Benjamin.

—— and Steele, John, edd., see Lugge, John.

JEPPESEN, Knud, ed., see *Balli*.

JOHNSTONE, H. Diack, ed., see Bennett, John; Stanley, John.

KEEBLE, John, see *Three Voluntaries of the Later 18th Century*.

KOOIKER, Anthony, ed., see *Melothesia*.

LEDGER, Philip, ed., see Byrd, William.

LEONHARDT, Gustav, Annegarn Alfons and Noske, Frits, see Sweelinck.

Liber Fratrum Cruciferorum, ed. A. Guilmant (*AMO*, x), 1909–11.

LOCKE, Matthew, *Keyboard Suites*, ed. Thurston Dart (*SBK*, vi), London.

—— *Organ Voluntaries*, ed. Thurston Dart (*SBK*, vii), London, 1957.

—— *Seven Pieces (Voluntaries) from "Melothesia" (1673)*, ed. Gordon Phillips (*TW*, vi), London, 1957.

LUGGE, John, *Three Voluntaries*, ed. Susi Jeans and John Steele, London: Novello and Co., Ltd., 1956.

LUMSDEN, David, ed., see *An Anthology of English Lute Music*.

MCLEAN, Hugh, ed., see Blow, John; Purcell, Henry.

MAITLAND, J. A. Fuller-, ed., see *The Contemporaries of Purcell*.

—— , and Squire, W. Barclay, edd., see *The Fitzwilliam Virginal Book*; *Twenty-five pieces for keyed instruments*.

MARLOW, Richard, ed., see Farnaby, Giles and Richard.

MARR, Peter, ed., see Alcock, John.

Melothesia, Keyboard Suites, ed. Anthony Kooiker (*PSMS*, xvi), Pennsylvania University Park and London, 1968.

MERRICK, Frank, ed., see Field, John.

Monumenta Musica Neerlandica (*MMN*), see *Dutch Keyboard Music* (*MMN*, iii).

MORLEY, Thomas, *Keyboard Works*, ed. Thurston Dart (*SBK*, xii, xiii), London, 1959 (2nd rev. edn. 1964).

The Mulliner Book, ed. Denis Stevens (*MB*, i), London, 1951 (2nd rev. edn. 1954).

The Mulliner Book, Eleven Pieces, ed. Denis Stevens (*SBK*, iii), London, 1951 (=*MB*, i, Nos. 13–15, 18, 1, 9, 116, 113, 51, 81, 96).

The Mulliner Book, see also *Early Keyboard Music*.

Musica Britannica (*MB*, Stainer and Bell), see separate entries under Bull, John (xiv, xix); Byrd, William (xxvii, xxviii); Farnaby, Giles and Richard (xxiv); Field, John (xvii); Gibbons, Orlando (xx); *The Mulliner Book* (i); Tomkins, Thomas (v).

Musick's Hand-Maid, ed. Thurston Dart (*SBK*, xxviii), London, 1969.

My Ladye Nevells Booke (music by William Byrd), ed. Hilda Andrews (*MLNB*), London: J. Curwen & Sons, 1926 (reprints by Broude Bros. and Dover Publications, New York, n.d.).

Nederlandse Klaviermuziek, see *Dutch Keyboard Music*.

Old English Organ Music for Manuals, ed. C. H. Trevor (*OEOM*, 4 vols.), London: Oxford University Press, 1966.

OXENBURY, William, and Dart, Thurston, edd., see *Intabolatura Nova di Balli*.

Parthenia (Byrd, Bull and Gibbons), ed. Thurston Dart (*SBK*, xix), London, 1960 (2nd rev. edn. 1962).

Parthenia In-Violata, ed. Thurston Dart, New York: C. F. Peters Corporation, 1961.

The Penn State Music Series (*PSMS*, Pennsylvania University Press), see separate entries under Chilcott, Thomas (xxii); *Melothesia* (xvi); Roseingrave, Thomas (ii).

PFATTEICHER, C. F., ed., see Part 2 (Books and Articles). *

PHILLIPS, Gordon, ed., see Boyce, William; Gibbons, Orlando; Greene, Maurice; Handel, G. F.; Locke, Matthew; Purcell, Henry; Stanley, John; *Three Voluntaries; Voluntaries by Stanley, Walond and Boyce*; Walond, William; Wesley, Samuel; The Wesleys.

PINTO, George Frederick, *Sonata in E flat minor*, ed. Nicholas Temperley (*SBK*, xx), London, 1963.

Preludes, Chansons and Dances for Lute Published by Pierre Attaingnant, Paris (1529–1530), ed. Daniel Heartz, Neuilly-sur-Seine: Société de Musique d'Autrefois, 1964.

Priscilla Bunbury's Virginal Book, Sixteen Pieces, ed. John L. Boston (*PBVB*), London: Stainer and Bell Ltd., 1962.

PURCELL, Henry, *Eight Suites*, ed. Howard Ferguson (*SBK*, xxi), London, 1964.

—— *Miscellaneous Keyboard Pieces*, ed. Howard Ferguson (*SBK*, xxii), London, 1964.

—— *The Organ Works*, ed. Hugh McLean, London: Novello and Co. Ltd., 1957 (2nd rev. edn. 1967).

—— *Three Voluntaries*, ed. Gordon Phillips (*TW*, x), London, 1961.

RAMSEY, Basil, ed., see Wesley, Samuel.

RAYNER, Clare G., ed., see Gibbons, Christopher.

READING, John, see *Three Voluntaries*.

Recent Researches in Music of the Baroque Era, see separate entry under *The Eighteenth-Century Voluntaries* (*RRMBE*, vi).

ROBINSON, John, *Voluntary in A minor*, ed. Susi Jeans (*EOM*, xxiv), London, 1966.

ROGERS, Benjamin, *Voluntary for the Organ*, ed. Susi Jeans (*EOM*, xi), London, 1962.

ROSEINGRAVE, Thomas, *Compositions for Organ and Harpsichord*, ed. Denis Stevens (*PSMS*, ii), Pennsylvania University Park and London, 1964.

—— *Ten Organ Pieces*, ed. Peter Williams (*SBK*, xviii), London, 1961.

ROUTH, Francis, ed., see Greene, Maurice; Handel, G. F.

The Second Part of Musick's Hand-Maid, ed. Thurston Dart (*SBK*, x), London, 1958 (2nd rev. edn. 1962).

SEIFFERT, Max, ed., see Sweelinck.

SHAW, Watkins, ed., see Anonymous; Blow, John.

Stainer and Bell, Keyboard Music Series (*SBK*), see separate entries under Arne, Thomas (xxvii); Blow, John (v); Bull, John (viii); Byrd, William (iv); *Clement Matchett's Virginal Book* (ix); *Early Scottish Keyboard Music* (xv); Farnaby, Giles (xi); *Fitzwilliam Virginal Book* (xvi); Gibbons, Orlando (xvii, xxv, xxvi); *Intabolatura Nova di Balli* (xxiii); Locke, Matthew (vi, vii); Morley, Thomas (xii, xiii); *Mulliner Book* (iii); *Musick's Hand-maid* (xxviii); *Parthenia* (xix); Pinto, George Frederick (xx); Purcell, Henry (xxi, xxii); Roseingrave, Thomas (xviii); *The Second Part of Musick's Hand-Maid* (x); *Tisdale's Virginal Book* (xxiv); Tisdall, William (xiv); Tomkins, Thomas (i, ii).

STANLEY, John, *Thirty Organ Voluntaries, Op. 5–7*, ed. Gordon Phillips (*TW*, xxvii–xxix), London, 1967.

—— *Three Voluntaries from Opera Quinta*, ed. Gordon Phillips (*TW*, xi), London, 1959.

—— *Twelve Diapason Movements from the Voluntaries*, ed. Gordon Phillips (*TW*, xxxiv), London, 1966.

—— *Voluntaries for the Organ*, ed. Denis Vaughan (facs.), London, Oxford University Press, 1957.

—— *Voluntary in A minor* (Op. 6, No. 2), ed. H. Diack Johnstone (*EOM*, ix), London, 1959.

—— *Voluntary in G minor* (Op. 6, No. 3), ed. H. Diack Johnstone (*EOM*, viii), London, 1959.

—— see *Voluntaries by Stanley, Walond and Boyce*.

STEELE, John, ed., see Cosyn, Benjamin.

—— and CAMERON, Francis, edd., see Bull, John.

STEVENS, Denis, ed., see *Altenglische Orgelmusik*; *Early Tudor Organ Music II*; *The Mulliner Book*; Roseingrave, Thomas; Tallis, Thomas; Tomkins, Thomas.

SWEELINCK, J. P., *The Instrumental Works*, ed. Gustav Leonhardt, Alfons Annegarn and Frits Noske (Sweelinck, *Opera Omnia*, i), Amsterdam, 1968 (3 fascicles).

—— *Werken voor Orgel en Clavecimbel*, ed. Max Seiffert (*Werken van Jan Pieterszn Sweelinck*, i), Amsterdam, 1943. Supplement, ed. Alfons Annegarn, Amsterdam, 1958.

TALLIS, Thomas, *Complete Keyboard Works*, ed. Denis Stevens, New York, London and Frankfurt: Peters Edition and Hinrichsen Edition, 1953.

—— *Four Pieces from the Mulliner Book*, ed. Denis Stevens (*TW*, iii, = Tallis, *Complete Keyboard Works*, Nos. 15, 11, 14, 7), London, 1953.

—— *Three Organ Hymn Verses and Four Antiphons*, ed. Denis Stevens (*TW*, ii, = Tallis, *Complete Keyboard Works*, Nos. 16, 17, 12, 10, 1–3), London, 1953.

Tallis to Wesley (*TW*, Hinrichsen Edition), see separate entries under Alcock, John (xxiii); Boyce, William (xxvi); Byrd, William (viii); Gibbons, Orlando (ix); Greene, Maurice (iv, xv); Handel, G. F. (xii, xix, xxxiii); Locke, Matthew (vi); Purcell, Henry (x); Stanley, John (xi, xxvii–xxix, xxiv); Tallis, Thomas (ii, iii); *Three Voluntaries* (xxi); *Three Voluntaries of the Later Eighteenth Century* (xxii); *Voluntaries by Stanley, Walond and Boyce* (i); Walond, William (xx, xxxii); Wesley, Samuel (vii, xiv, xviii); *The Wesleys* (v, xxiv).

TEMPERLEY, Nicholas, ed., see Pinto, George Frederick.

Ten Eighteenth-Century Voluntaries (by Bennett, Walond and Hine), ed. Gwilym Beechey (*RRMBE*, vi), Madison: A-R Editions Inc., 1969.

Three Voluntaries (by Blow, Barrett and Reading), ed. Gordon Phillips (*TW*, xxi), London, 1962.

Three Voluntaries of the Later 18th Century (by Travers, Keeble and Dupuis), ed. Peter F. Williams (*TW*, xxii), London, 1961.

Tisdale's Virginal Book, ed. Alan Brown (*SBK*, xxiv), London, 1966.

Tisdall, William, *Complete Keyboard Works*, ed. Howard Ferguson (*SBK*, xiv), London, 1958.

Tomkins, Thomas, *Fifteen Dances*, ed. Stephen D. Tuttle (*SBK*, ii, = *MB*, v, Nos. 67, 41, 42, 59, 47–53, 65, 54, 55, 57), London, 1965.

—— *Keyboard Music*, ed. Stephen D. Tuttle (*MB*, v), London, 1955 (2nd rev. edn. 1964).

—— *Nine Organ Pieces*, ed. Stephen D. Tuttle (*SBK*, i, = *MB*, v, Nos. 23–31), London, 1955.

—— *Three Hitherto Unpublished Voluntaries*, ed. Denis Stevens (*TW*, xvii), London, 1959 (included in *MB*, v, 2nd edn.).

Travers, John, see *Three Voluntaries of the Later 18th Century*.

Trevor, C. H., ed., see *Old English Organ Music*.

Tuttle, Stephen D., ed., see Byrd, William; Tomkins, Thomas.

Twenty-five pieces for keyed instruments from Cosyn's Virginal Book, ed. J. A. Fuller-Maitland and W. Barclay Squire, London: Chester, 1923. The composers included are Bull, Byrd, Cosyn, O. Gibbons and anon.

Two Elizabethan Keyboard Duets, ed. Frank Dawes, London, Schott and Co. Ltd., 1949.

Vaughan, Denis, ed., see Stanley, John.

Voluntaries by Stanley, Walond and Boyce, ed. Gordon Phillips (*TW*, i), London, 1956.

Walond, William, *Three Cornet Voluntaries*, ed. Gordon Phillips (*TW*, xx), London, 1961.

—— *Three Voluntaries*, ed. Gordon Phillips (*TW*, xxxii), London, 1962.

—— see *Ten Eighteenth-Century Voluntaries*.

—— see *Voluntaries by Stanley, Walond and Boyce*.

Ward, John, ed., see *The Dublin Virginal Manuscript*.

Wesley, Charles, see *The Wesleys*.

Wesley, Samuel, *Air and Gavotte*, ed. Gordon Phillips (*TW*, xviii, = *TW*, vii, Nos. 8 and 9), London, 1957.

—— *Duet for Organ*, ed. Walter Emery (*EOM*, xix), London, 1964.

—— *Organ Fugue* in *Samuel Wesley and Dr. Mendelssohn*, ed. Gordon Phillips (*TW*, xiv), London, 1962.

—— *Twelve Short Pieces*, ed. Gordon Phillips (*TW*, vii), London, 1957.

—— *Two Short Pieces in A minor*, ed. Basil Ramsey (*EOM*, x, = *Twelve Short Pieces*, Nos. 6 and 7), London, 1961.

—— *Two Short Pieces in F: 'Air' and 'Gavotte'*, ed. Basil Ramsey (*EOM*, iii, = *Twelve Short Pieces*, No. 8 and 9), London, 1961.

The Wesleys, Set 1 (3 pieces, one each by C., S. and S. S. Wesley), ed. Gordon Phillips (*TW*, v), London, 1960.

The Wesleys, Set 2 (4 pieces, 1 each by C. and S. S. Wesley, two by S. Wesley), ed. Gordon Phillips (*TW*, xxiv), London, 1961.

Williams, Peter, ed., see Boyce, William; Roseingrave, Thomas; *Three Voluntaries of the Later Eighteenth Century*.

Wooldridge, H. E., ed., see *Early English Harmony*.

2. *Books and articles*

APEL, Willi, 'Early History of the Organ', *Speculum*, xxiii (1948), 191.

—— *The Notation of Polyphonic Music 900–1600*, 5th edn., Cambridge, Mass., 1961.

ARKWRIGHT, G. E. P., *Catalogue of Music in the library of Christ Church, Oxford*, London, 1915–1923 (2 vols.).

ATKINS, Sir Ivor, *The Early Occupants of the Office of Organist and Master of the Choristers of the Cathedral Church of . . . Worcester* (cited as *Worcester Organists*), London: *Worcestershire Historical Society*, 1918.

BAILLIE, Hugh, 'A London Church in Early Tudor Times', *ML*, xxxvi (1955), 55.

BEECHEY, Gwilym, 'A New Source of Seventeenth-Century Keyboard Music', *ML*, l (1969), 278. See also letter from Watkins Shaw on p. 555.

BERGSAGEL, John, 'An Introduction to Ludford', *Musica Disciplina*, xiv (1960), 105.

BORREN, Charles van den, *Les Origines de la Musique de Clavier en Angleterre*, Brussels, 1912. English translation by J. E. Matthew, *The Sources of Keyboard Music in England*, London, 1913.

BOSTON, John L., 'Priscilla Bunbury's Virginal Book', *ML*, xxxvi (1955), 365.

BOYD, M. C., *Elizabethan Music and Musical Criticism*, 2nd edn., 2nd printing, Philadelphia, 1967.

The British Union-Catalogue of Early Music, ed. Edith B. Schnapper, London, 1957 (2 vols.).

BROWN, Alan, ' "My Lady Nevell's Book" as a Source of Byrd's Keyboard Music', *PRMA*, xcv (1968–1969), 29.

BURNEY, Charles, *A General History of Music*, 2nd edn., London, 1789 (4 vols.).

BUKOFZER, Manfred, *Studies in Medieval and Renaissance Music*, New York, 1950.

CALDWELL, John, 'Duddyngton's Organ: Another Opinion', *MT*, cviii (1967), 254.

—— 'Keyboard Plainsong Settings in England, 1500–1660', *Musica Disciplina*, xix (1965), 129.

—— 'The Pitch of Early Tudor Organ Music', *ML*, li (1970), 156.

CLUTTON, Cecil, and NILAND, Austin, *The British Organ*, London, 1963.

CUDWORTH, C. L., 'The English Organ Concerto', *The Score*, viii (September 1953), 51.

—— 'Some new Facts About the Trumpet Voluntary', *MT*, xciv (1953), 401.

CURTIS, Alan, *Sweelinck's Keyboard Music*, Leiden and London, 1969.

DART, Thurston, 'An Early Seventeenth-Century Book of English Organ Music for the Roman Rite', *ML*, lii (1971), 27.

—— 'Elizabeth Edgeworth's Keyboard Book', *ML*, l (1969), 470.

—— 'John Bull's "Chapel" ', *ML*, xl (1959), 279.

—— 'A New Source of Early English Organ Music', *ML*, xxxv (1954), 201.

—— 'Notes on a Bible of Evesham Abbey (ii): a Note on the Music', *English Historical Review*, lxxix (1964), 777.

——'Notes on a Bible of Evesham Abbey (ii): a Note on the Music', *English Historical Review*, lxxix (1964), 777.

——'The Organ-Book of the Crutched Friars of Liège', in *Revue Belge de Musicologie*', xvii (1963), 21.

DAWES, Frank, 'The Music of Philip Hart (*ca.* 1676–1749)', *PRMA*, xciv (1967–8), 63.

——'Nicholas Carlton and the Earliest Keyboard Duet', *MT*, xcii (1951), 542.

A Description or Briefe Declaration, see *Rites of Durham*.

DICKINSON, A. E. F., 'A forgotten Collection: A Survey of the Weckmann Books', *MR*, xvii (1956), 97.

DUCKLES, Vincent, 'The "Curious" Art of John Wilson (1595–1674): An Introduction to His Songs and Lute Music', *JAMS*, vii, (1954), 93.

EDWARDS, Owain, 'English String Concertos before 1800', *PRMA*, xcv (1968–9), 1.

EITNER, Robert, *Biographisch-Bibliographisches Quellen-Lexicon*, Leipzig, 1900–1904 (10 vols.).

FELLOWES, E. H., *The Catalogue of Manuscripts in the Library of St. Michael's College, Tenbury*, Paris, 1934.

——*Organists and Masters of the Choristers of St. George's Chapel in Windsor Castle* (cited as *Windsor Organists*), London, [1939].

——*William Byrd*, 2nd edn., London and New York, 1948.

FERGUSON, Howard, 'Repeats and Final Bars in the Fitzwilliam Virginal Book', *ML*, xliii (1962), 345.

FLOOD, W. H. Grattan, *Early Tudor Composers, 1485–1555*, London and Freeport, N.Y., 1925.

FOWLER, J. T., see *Rites of Durham*.

GALPIN, Francis W., *Old English Instruments of Music*, 3rd edn, London, 1932; 4th edn., New York, 1965.

GOMBOSI, Otto, 'About Dance and Dance Music in the Late Middle Ages', *MQ*, xxvii (1941), 289.

GREER, David, ' "What if a day"—an Examination of the Words and Music', *ML*, xliii (1962), 304.

Grove's Dictionary of Music and Musicians, 5th edn., ed. Eric Blom, London and New York, 1954 (9 vols.), and *Supplement*, 1961. Note especially articles 'Virginal Music, Collections of' and 'English Musicians Abroad', as well as on individual composers.

HANDSCHIN, Jacques, 'Über Estampie und Sequenz', *Acta Musicologica*, x (1938), 29.

HARLEY, John, 'Ornaments in English Keyboard Music of the Seventeenth and Early Eighteenth Centuries', *MR*, xxxi (1970), 177.

HARMAN, R. Alec, ed., see Morley.

HARRISON, F. Ll., 'Faburden in Practice', *Music Disciplina*, xvi (1962), 11.

——*Music in Medieval Britain*, London, 1958.

HAWKINS, Sir John, *A General History of the Science and Practice of Music*, London, 1776 (5 vols.); New York [1853] (2 vols.).

HAYES, Gerald, 'Musical Instruments', *NOHM*, iii, 466.

HEARTZ, Daniel, 'The Basse Dance, Its Evolution circa 1450–1550', in *Annales Musicologiques,* vi (1958–1963), 287–340.

HOPKINS, Edward J., and RIMBAULT, Edward F., *The Organ, Its History and Construction,* 3rd edn., London, 1870. The first part of this work, 'The History of the Organ', is by E. F. Rimbault.

HUGHES, Dom Anselm, *Medieval Polyphony in the Bodleian Library,* Oxford, 1951.

HUGHES-HUGHES, Augustus, *Catalogue of Manuscript Music in the British Museum,* 3 vols., London, 1906–1909. See also Willetts, *Handlist.*

HUTCHINGS, Arthur, *The Baroque Concerto,* London and New York, 1961.

JOHNSTONE, H. Diack, 'Greene and the Lady's Banquet', *MT,* cviii (1967), 36.

——'An Unknown Book of Organ Voluntaries', *MT,* cviii (1967), 1003.

LAFONTAINE, Henry Cart de, *The King's Musick,* London and New York [1909].

LEFKOWITZ, Murray, *William Lawes,* London, 1960.

LE HURAY, Peter, *Music and the Reformation in England, 1549–1660,* London and New York 1967.

LOWINSKY, Edward E., 'English Organ Music of the Renaissance', *MQ,* xxxix (1953), 373, 528.

LUMSDEN, David, *The Sources of English Lute Music (1540–1620),* unpublished dissertation, Cambridge, 1957 (3 vols.).

MAITLAND, J. A. Fuller-, and MANN, A. H., *Catalogue of the Music in the Fitzwilliam Museum, Cambridge,* London, 1893.

MASLEN, B. J., 'The Earliest English Organ Pedals', *MT,* ci (1960), 578. See also subsequent correspondence on pp. 717 ff., and in cii (1961), 107 ff.

MELLERS, Wilfrid, 'John Bull and English Keyboard Music', *MQ,* xl (1954), 364, 548.

MILLER, HUGH M., 'The Earliest Keyboard Duets', *MQ,* xxix (1943), 438.

——'Forty Wayes of 2 Pts. in One of Tho[mas] Woodson', *JAMS,* viii (1955), 14.

——'*Fulgens Praeclara*: A Unique Keyboard Setting of a Plainsong Sequence', *JAMS,* ii (1949), 97.

——'John Bull's Organ Works', *ML,* xxviii (1947), 25.

——'Pretty Wayes: For Young Beginners To Looke On', *MQ,* xxxiii (1947), 543.

——'Sixteenth-Century English Faburden Compositions for Keyboard', *MQ,* xxvi (1940), 50.

MORLEY, Thomas, *A Plain and Easy Introduction to Practical Music,* ed. R. Alec Harman, London and New York, 1952.

Die Musik in Geschichte und Gegenwart (MGG), ed. F. Blume, Kassel and New York, 1949– (14 vols. to date).

NEIGHBOUR, Oliver, 'New Consort Music by Byrd', *MT,* cviii (1967), 506.

NIELSEN, Niels Karl, 'Handel's Organ Concertos Reconsidered', *Dansk Aarbog for Musik Forskning,* 1963, 3.

PANUM, Hortense, *The Stringed Instruments of the Middle Ages,* English edn. by Jeffrey Pulver, London, n.d.; American edn., New York, 1970.

PARRISH, Carl, *The Notation of Medieval Music,* New York, 1957.

PERROT, Jean, *L'Orgue de ses origines hellénistiques à la fin du xiiie siècle*, Paris, 1965.

PFATTEICHER, C. F., *John Redford*, Kassel, 1934.

PIGGOTT, Patrick, 'John Field and the Nocturne', *PRMA*, xcv (1968-9), 55.

PHOL, C. F., *Mozart und Haydn in London*, Vienna, 1867 (2 vols.); New York, 1970 (1 vol.).

PULVER, Jeffrey, *A Biographical Dictionary of Old English Music*, London and New York, 1927; 2nd edn., New York, 1969.

RASTALL, Richard, 'Benjamin Rogers (1614–1698): Some Notes on his Instrumental Music', *ML*, xlvi (1965), 237.

REESE, Gustave, *Music in the Middle Ages*, New York, 1940.

——*Music in the Renaissance*, New York, 1954; rev. edn., 1959.

Répertoire International des Sources Musicales (RISM), vol. B II: *Recueils Imprimés, XVIIIe Siècle*, ed. François Lesure, Munich and Duisburg, 1964.

RIMBAULT, Edward F., 'The History of the Organ'. See Hopkins, Edward J., *The Organ*.

——*The Old Cheque-Book, or Book of Remembrance, of the Chapel Royal, from 1561–1744*, London: Camden Society, 1872; 2nd edn., New York, 1966.

Rites of Durham, ed. J. T. Fowler, London: Surtees Society, 1903 (originally published 1842).

ROKSETH, Yvonne, 'The Instrumental Music of the Middle Ages and Early Sixteenth Century', *NOHM*, iii. 406.

ROSE, Gloria, 'Purcell, Michelangelo Rossi and J. S. Bach: Problems of Authorship', *Acta Musicologica*, xl (1968), 203.

RUSSELL, Raymond, *The Harpsichord and Clavichord*, London, 1959.

SACHS, Curt, 'Die Musikinstrumente der Minneregel', *Sammelbande der IMG*, xiv (1912–13), 484.

SHAW, Watkins, 'William Byrd of Lincoln', *ML*, xlviii (1967), 52.

SMITH, W. C., *A Bibliography of . . . John Walsh, 1695–1720*, London and New York, 1948.

——*Handel: A Descriptive Catalogue of the Early Editions*, 2nd edn., Oxford and New York, 1970.

SQUIRE, W. Barclay, *Catalogue of Printed Music in the Library of the Royal College of Music, London*, London and Leipzig, 1909.

——*Catalogue of Printed Music Published between 1487 and 1800 and now in the British Museum*, London and Leipzig, 1912 (2 vols.).

——*Catalogue of the King's Music Library*, London, 1927–1929 (3 vols.).

STEELE, H. J., *English Organs and Organ Music from 1500 to 1650*, unpublished dissertation, Cambridge, 1958 (2 vols.).

STERNFELD, F. W., 'Ophelia's Version of the Walsingham Song', *ML*, xlv (1964), 108.

STEVENS, Denis, 'Further Light on *Fulgens Praeclara*', *JAMS*, ix (1956), 1.

——'The Keyboard Music of Thomas Tallis', *MT*, xciii (1952), 303.

——*The Mulliner Book: A Commentary*, London, 1952.

——'Thomas Preston's Organ Mass', *ML*, xxxix (1958), 29.

——*Thomas Tomkins*, London, 1957; New York, 1966.

——'A Unique Tudor Organ Mass', *Musica Disciplina*, vi (1952), 167.

STEVENS, John, *Music and Poetry in the Early Tudor Court*, London and New York, 1961.

SUMNER, William Leslie, *The Organ, its Evolution, Principles of Construction and Use*, 3rd edn., London, 1962.

TROWELL, Brian, 'Faburden and Fauxbourdon', *Musica Disciplina*, xiii (1959), 43.

WALKER, Ernest, *A History of Music in England*, 3rd edn., rev. by J. A. Westrup, Oxford and New York, 1952.

WARD, John, 'The "Dolfull Dumps" ', *JAMS*, iv (1951), 111.

——'The Lute Music of MS Royal Appendix 58', *JAMS*, xii (1960), 117.

——'Music for *A Handfull of pleasant delites*', *JAMS*, x (1957), 151.

WEST, John E., *Cathedral Organists Past and Present*, 2nd edn., London, 1921.

WESTRUP, J. A., *Purcell*, 5th edn., London and New York, 1965.

WILLETS, Pamela J., *Handlist of Music Manuscripts Acquired by the British Museum 1908–1967*, London, 1970.

WILLIAMS, Peter F., 'Some interesting Organ Terms: I, Diapason', *MT*, cvi (1965), 463.

WILSON, Michael, *The English Chamber Organ*, Oxford, and Columbia, S.C., 1968.

YOUNG, William, 'Keyboard Music to 1600', *Musica Disciplina*, xvi (1962), 115 and xvii (1963), 163.

ADDENDA

1. *Editions of music*

ARNE, T. A., *Concerto V für Orgel*, ed. A. de Klerk, Kassel: Nagels Verlag, 1962 (*Nagels Musik-Archiv*, No. 210).

BLOW, John, *Two Voluntaries from the Nanki Manuscript*, ed. H. McLean (*EOM*, xxiii), London, 1971.

BOYCE, William, or GREENE, Maurice, *Twelve Voluntaries for Organ or Harpsichord*, ed. Peter Williams, New York: Galaxy Music Corporation, 1969.

Early English Keyboard Music, ed. Howard Ferguson, London: Oxford University Press, 1971 (2 vols.).

HÄNDEL, G. F., *Klavierwerke*, ed. Rudolf Steglich, Peter Northway and Terence Best, Kassel and Basel: Bärenreiter-Verlag, 1955–70 (*Hallische Handel-Ausgabe*, IV: i, v, vi).

—— *Orgelkonzerte* Op. 4, ed. Karl Matthaei, Kassel and Basel: Bärenreiter-Verlag, 1956 (*ibid.*, IV: ii).

JAMES, John, '*Echo*' *Voluntary in D major for the organ*, ed. Kenneth Simpson, London: Hinrichsen, 1941.

—— See *A Series of Progressive Studies*.

LAWES, William, *Trois Masques à la Cour de Charles Ier d'Angleterre*, ed. Murray Lefkowitz, Paris: Éditions du Centre National de la Recherche Scientifique 1970.

Musica Antiqua, ed. J. S. Smith, London, 1812 (2 vols.).

Old English Composers for the Virginals and Harpsichord . . . selected from the works of William Byrd, John Bull, Orlando Gibbons, John Blow, Henry Purcell and Thomas Aug. Arne, ed. Ernst Pauer, 2nd edn., London: Augener, 1879 (various reprints, especially of Blow, *Popular Pieces*).

Old English Organ Music, ed. J. E. West, London: Novello, 1904–11 (36 vols.).

A Series of Progressive Studies, ed. J. Pittman, London: Chappell, 1882 (12 vols: includes works by James, J. S. Smith).

STANLEY, John, *Concerto in C minor* [Op. 10 No. 4; organ part with instrumental cues], ed. P. le Huray, London: Oxford University Press, 1967.

WEELKES, Thomas, *Pieces for Keyed Instruments*, ed. Margaret Glyn, London: Stainer and Bell, 1924.

WESLEY, Charles, *Concerto No. 4 in C* [from Op. 2], ed. Gerald Finzi, London: Hinrichsen, 1956.

2. *Books and articles*

APEL, Willi, *Geschichte der Orgel und Klaviermusik bis 1700*, Kassel etc., 1967

BROWN, Beulah, *The Harpsichord Music of Handel's Younger English Contemporaries: A Reassessment*, unpublished dissertation, Manchester, 1965–6.

BROWN, David, *Thomas Weelkes: A Biographical and Critical Study*, London, 1969.

COOPER, Barry, 'Albertus Bryne's Keyboard Music', *MT,* cxiii (1972), 142.

DART, Thurston, 'New Sources of Virginal Music', *ML*, xxxv (1954), 93.

DAWE, Donovan, 'New Light on William Boyce', *MT,* cix (1968), 802.

DICKINSON, A. E. F. ,'John Bull's Fugal Style', *Monthly Musical Record*, lxxiv (1954), 228.

GLYN, Margaret, *About Elizabethan Virginal Music and its Composers*, London, 1924.

HARDING, Rosamund E. M., *A Thematic Catalogue of the Works of Matthew Locke*, Oxford,1971.

McLEAN, Hugh, 'Blow and Purcell in Japan', *MT*, civ (1963), 702.

SMITH, William C., and HUMPHRIES, Charles, *A Bibliography of the Musical Works Published by the Firm of John Walsh during the years 1721–1766*,London, 1968.

WILLIAMS, Peter, *English Organ Music and the English Organ under the First Four Georges*, unpublished dissertation, Cambridge, 1962–3.

WILSON, John, 'John Stanley: Some Opus Numbers and Editions', *ML*, xxxix (1958), 359.

ZIMMERMAN, Franklin B., *Henry Purcell, 1659–1695: An Analytical Catalogue of his Music*, London and New York, 1963.

Index

A CATALOGUE OF
SELECTED DOVER BOOKS
IN ALL FIELDS OF INTEREST

A CATALOGUE OF SELECTED DOVER BOOKS IN ALL FIELDS OF INTEREST

CELESTIAL OBJECTS FOR COMMON TELESCOPES, T. W. Webb. The most used book in amateur astronomy: inestimable aid for locating and identifying nearly 4,000 celestial objects. Edited, updated by Margaret W. Mayall. 77 illustrations. Total of 645pp. 5⅜ x 8½.
20917-2, 20918-0 Pa., Two-vol. set $10.00

HISTORICAL STUDIES IN THE LANGUAGE OF CHEMISTRY, M. P. Crosland. The important part language has played in the development of chemistry from the symbolism of alchemy to the adoption of systematic nomenclature in 1892. ". . . wholeheartedly recommended,"—Science. 15 illustrations. 416pp. of text. 5⅝ x 8¼. 63702-6 Pa. $7.50

BURNHAM'S CELESTIAL HANDBOOK, Robert Burnham, Jr. Thorough, readable guide to the stars beyond our solar system. Exhaustive treatment, fully illustrated. Breakdown is alphabetical by constellation: Andromeda to Cetus in Vol. 1; Chamaeleon to Orion in Vol. 2; and Pavo to Vulpecula in Vol. 3. Hundreds of illustrations. Total of about 2000pp. 6⅛ x 9¼.
23567-X, 23568-8, 23673-0 Pa., Three-vol. set $32.85

THEORY OF WING SECTIONS: INCLUDING A SUMMARY OF AIRFOIL DATA, Ira H. Abbott and A. E. von Doenhoff. Concise compilation of subatomic aerodynamic characteristics of modern NASA wing sections, plus description of theory. 350pp. of tables. 693pp. 5⅜ x 8½.
60586-8 Pa. $9.95

DE RE METALLICA, Georgius Agricola. Translated by Herbert C. Hoover and Lou H. Hoover. The famous Hoover translation of greatest treatise on technological chemistry, engineering, geology, mining of early modern times (1556). All 289 original woodcuts. 638pp. 6¾ x 11.
60006-8 Clothbd. $19.95

THE ORIGIN OF CONTINENTS AND OCEANS, Alfred Wegener. One of the most influential, most controversial books in science, the classic statement for continental drift. Full 1966 translation of Wegener's final (1929) version. 64 illustrations. 246pp. 5⅜ x 8½.(EBE)61708-4 Pa. $5.00

THE PRINCIPLES OF PSYCHOLOGY, William James. Famous long course complete, unabridged. Stream of thought, time perception, memory, experimental methods; great work decades ahead of its time. Still valid, useful; read in many classes. 94 figures. Total of 1391pp. 5⅜ x 8½.
20381-6, 20382-4 Pa., Two-vol. set $19.90

YUCATAN BEFORE AND AFTER THE CONQUEST, Diego de Landa. First English translation of basic book in Maya studies, the only significant account of Yucatan written in the early post-Conquest era. Translated by distinguished Maya scholar William Gates. Appendices, introduction, 4 maps and over 120 illustrations added by translator. 162pp. 5⅜ x 8½.
23622-6 Pa. $3.50

THE MALAY ARCHIPELAGO, Alfred R. Wallace. Spirited travel account by one of founders of modern biology. Touches on zoology, botany, ethnography, geography, and geology. 62 illustrations, maps. 515pp. 5⅜ x 8½.
20187-2 Pa. $6.95

THE DISCOVERY OF THE TOMB OF TUTANKHAMEN, Howard Carter, A. C. Mace. Accompany Carter in the thrill of discovery, as ruined passage suddenly reveals unique, untouched, fabulously rich tomb. Fascinating account, with 106 illustrations. New introduction by J. M. White. Total of 382pp. 5⅜ x 8½. (Available in U.S. only)   23500-9 Pa. $5.50

THE WORLD'S GREATEST SPEECHES, edited by Lewis Copeland and Lawrence W. Lamm. Vast collection of 278 speeches from Greeks up to present. Powerful and effective models; unique look at history. Revised to 1970. Indices. 842pp. 5⅜ x 8½.   20468-5 Pa. $9.95

THE 100 GREATEST ADVERTISEMENTS, Julian Watkins. The priceless ingredient; His master's voice; 99 44/100% pure; over 100 others. How they were written, their impact, etc. Remarkable record. 130 illustrations. 233pp. 7⅞ x 10 3/5.   20540-1 Pa. $6.95

CRUICKSHANK PRINTS FOR HAND COLORING, George Cruickshank. 18 illustrations, one side of a page, on fine-quality paper suitable for watercolors. Caricatures of people in society (c. 1820) full of trenchant wit. Very large format. 32pp. 11 x 16.   23684-6 Pa. $6.00

THIRTY-TWO COLOR POSTCARDS OF TWENTIETH-CENTURY AMERICAN ART, Whitney Museum of American Art. Reproduced in full color in postcard form are 31 art works and one shot of the museum. Calder, Hopper, Rauschenberg, others. Detachable. 16pp. 8¼ x 11.
23629-3 Pa. $3.50

MUSIC OF THE SPHERES: THE MATERIAL UNIVERSE FROM ATOM TO QUASAR SIMPLY EXPLAINED, Guy Murchie. Planets, stars, geology, atoms, radiation, relativity, quantum theory, light, antimatter, similar topics. 319 figures. 664pp. 5⅜ x 8½.
21809-0, 21810-4 Pa., Two-vol. set $11.00

EINSTEIN'S THEORY OF RELATIVITY, Max Born. Finest semi-technical account; covers Einstein, Lorentz, Minkowski, and others, with much detail, much explanation of ideas and math not readily available elsewhere on this level. For student, non-specialist. 376pp. 5⅜ x 8½.
60769-0 Pa. $5.00

THE SENSE OF BEAUTY, George Santayana. Masterfully written discussion of nature of beauty, materials of beauty, form, expression; art, literature, social sciences all involved. 168pp. 5⅜ x 8½. 20238-0 Pa. $3.50

ON THE IMPROVEMENT OF THE UNDERSTANDING, Benedict Spinoza. Also contains *Ethics, Correspondence,* all in excellent R. Elwes translation. Basic works on entry to philosophy, pantheism, exchange of ideas with great contemporaries. 402pp. 5⅜ x 8½. 20250-X Pa. $5.95

THE TRAGIC SENSE OF LIFE, Miguel de Unamuno. Acknowledged masterpiece of existential literature, one of most important books of 20th century. Introduction by Madariaga. 367pp. 5⅜ x 8½.
20257-7 Pa. $6.00

THE GUIDE FOR THE PERPLEXED, Moses Maimonides. Great classic of medieval Judaism attempts to reconcile revealed religion (Pentateuch, commentaries) with Aristotelian philosophy. Important historically, still relevant in problems. Unabridged Friedlander translation. Total of 473pp. 5⅜ x 8½. 20351-4 Pa. $6.95

THE I CHING (THE BOOK OF CHANGES), translated by James Legge. Complete translation of basic text plus appendices by Confucius, and Chinese commentary of most penetrating divination manual ever prepared. Indispensable to study of early Oriental civilizations, to modern inquiring reader. 448pp. 5⅜ x 8½. 21062-6 Pa. $6.00

THE EGYPTIAN BOOK OF THE DEAD, E. A. Wallis Budge. Complete reproduction of Ani's papyrus, finest ever found. Full hieroglyphic text, interlinear transliteration, word for word translation, smooth translation. Basic work, for Egyptology, for modern study of psychic matters. Total of 533pp. 6½ x 9¼. (USCO) 21866-X Pa. $8.50

THE GODS OF THE EGYPTIANS, E. A. Wallis Budge. Never excelled for richness, fullness: all gods, goddesses, demons, mythical figures of Ancient Egypt; their legends, rites, incarnations, variations, powers, etc. Many hieroglyphic texts cited. Over 225 illustrations, plus 6 color plates. Total of 988pp. 6⅛ x 9¼. (EBE)
22055-9, 22056-7 Pa., Two-vol. set $20.00

THE STANDARD BOOK OF QUILT MAKING AND COLLECTING, Marguerite Ickis. Full information, full-sized patterns for making 46 traditional quilts, also 150 other patterns. Quilted cloths, lame, satin quilts, etc. 483 illustrations. 273pp. 6⅞ x 9⅝. 20582-7 Pa. $5.95

CORAL GARDENS AND THEIR MAGIC, Bronsilaw Malinowski. Classic study of the methods of tilling the soil and of agricultural rites in the Trobriand Islands of Melanesia. Author is one of the most important figures in the field of modern social anthropology. 143 illustrations. Indexes. Total of 911pp. of text. 5⅝ x 8¼. (Available in U.S. only)
23597-1 Pa. $12.95

THE PHILOSOPHY OF HISTORY, Georg W. Hegel. Great classic of Western thought develops concept that history is not chance but a rational process, the evolution of freedom. 457pp. 5⅜ x 8½. 20112-0 Pa. $6.50

LANGUAGE, TRUTH AND LOGIC, Alfred J. Ayer. Famous, clear introduction to Vienna, Cambridge schools of Logical Positivism. Role of philosophy, elimination of metaphysics, nature of analysis, etc. 160pp. 5⅜ x 8½. (USCO) 20010-8 Pa. $2.75

A PREFACE TO LOGIC, Morris R. Cohen. Great City College teacher in renowned, easily followed exposition of formal logic, probability, values, logic and world order and similar topics; no previous background needed. 209pp. 5⅜ x 8½. 23517-3 Pa. $4.95

REASON AND NATURE, Morris R. Cohen. Brilliant analysis of reason and its multitudinous ramifications by charismatic teacher. Interdisciplinary, synthesizing work widely praised when it first appeared in 1931. Second (1953) edition. Indexes. 496pp. 5⅜ x 8½. 23633-1 Pa. $7.50

AN ESSAY CONCERNING HUMAN UNDERSTANDING, John Locke. The only complete edition of enormously important classic, with authoritative editorial material by A. C. Fraser. Total of 1176pp. 5⅜ x 8½.
20530-4, 20531-2 Pa., Two-vol. set $17.90

HANDBOOK OF MATHEMATICAL FUNCTIONS WITH FORMULAS, GRAPHS, AND MATHEMATICAL TABLES, edited by Milton Abramowitz and Irene A. Stegun. Vast compendium: 29 sets of tables, some to as high as 20 places. 1,046pp. 8 x 10½. 61272-4 Pa. $19.95

MATHEMATICS FOR THE PHYSICAL SCIENCES, Herbert S. Wilf. Highly acclaimed work offers clear presentations of vector spaces and matrices, orthogonal functions, roots of polynomial equations, conformal mapping, calculus of variations, etc. Knowledge of theory of functions of real and complex variables is assumed. Exercises and solutions. Index. 284pp. 5⅝ x 8¼. 63635-6 Pa. $5.00

THE PRINCIPLE OF RELATIVITY, Albert Einstein et al. Eleven most important original papers on special and general theories. Seven by Einstein, two by Lorentz, one each by Minkowski and Weyl. All translated, unabridged. 216pp. 5⅜ x 8½. 60081-5 Pa. $3.50

THERMODYNAMICS, Enrico Fermi. A classic of modern science. Clear, organized treatment of systems, first and second laws, entropy, thermodynamic potentials, gaseous reactions, dilute solutions, entropy constant. No math beyond calculus required. Problems. 160pp. 5⅜ x 8½.
60361-X Pa. $4.00

ELEMENTARY MECHANICS OF FLUIDS, Hunter Rouse. Classic undergraduate text widely considered to be far better than many later books. Ranges from fluid velocity and acceleration to role of compressibility in fluid motion. Numerous examples, questions, problems. 224 illustrations. 376pp. 5⅝ x 8¼. 63699-2 Pa. $7.00

THE AMERICAN SENATOR, Anthony Trollope. Little known, long unavailable Trollope novel on a grand scale. Here are humorous comment on American vs. English culture, and stunning portrayal of a heroine/villainess. Superb evocation of Victorian village life. 561pp. 5⅜ x 8½.
23801-6 Pa. $7.95

WAS IT MURDER? James Hilton. The author of *Lost Horizon* and *Goodbye, Mr. Chips* wrote one detective novel (under a pen-name) which was quickly forgotten and virtually lost, even at the height of Hilton's fame. This edition brings it back—a finely crafted public school puzzle resplendent with Hilton's stylish atmosphere. A thoroughly English thriller by the creator of Shangri-la. 252pp. 5⅜ x 8. (Available in U.S. only)
23774-5 Pa. $3.00

CENTRAL PARK: A PHOTOGRAPHIC GUIDE, Victor Laredo and Henry Hope Reed. 121 superb photographs show dramatic views of Central Park: Bethesda Fountain, Cleopatra's Needle, Sheep Meadow, the Blockhouse, plus people engaged in many park activities: ice skating, bike riding, etc. Captions by former Curator of Central Park, Henry Hope Reed, provide historical view, changes, etc. Also photos of N.Y. landmarks on park's periphery. 96pp. 8½ x 11. 23750-8 Pa. $4.95

NANTUCKET IN THE NINETEENTH CENTURY, Clay Lancaster. 180 rare photographs, stereographs, maps, drawings and floor plans recreate unique American island society. Authentic scenes of shipwreck, lighthouses, streets, homes are arranged in geographic sequence to provide walking-tour guide to old Nantucket existing today. Introduction, captions. 160pp. 8⅞ x 11¾. 23747-8 Pa. $7.95

STONE AND MAN: A PHOTOGRAPHIC EXPLORATION, Andreas Feininger. 106 photographs by *Life* photographer Feininger portray man's deep passion for stone through the ages. Stonehenge-like megaliths, fortified towns, sculpted marble and crumbling tenements show textures, beauties, fascination. 128pp. 9¼ x 10¾. 23756-7 Pa. $6.95

CIRCLES, A MATHEMATICAL VIEW, D. Pedoe. Fundamental aspects of college geometry, non-Euclidean geometry, and other branches of mathematics: representing circle by point. Poincare model, isoperimetric property, etc. Stimulating recreational reading. 66 figures. 96pp. 5⅝ x 8¼.
63698-4 Pa. $3.50

THE DISCOVERY OF NEPTUNE, Morton Grosser. Dramatic scientific history of the investigations leading up to the actual discovery of the eighth planet of our solar system. Lucid, well-researched book by well-known historian of science. 172pp. 5⅜ x 8½. 23726-5 Pa. $3.95

THE DEVIL'S DICTIONARY. Ambrose Bierce. Barbed, bitter, brilliant witticisms in the form of a dictionary. Best, most ferocious satire America has produced. 145pp. 5⅜ x 8½. 20487-1 Pa. $2.50

THE ART OF THE CINEMATOGRAPHER, Leonard Maltin. Survey of American cinematography history and anecdotal interviews with 5 masters— Arthur Miller, Hal Mohr, Hal Rosson, Lucien Ballard, and Conrad Hall. Very large selection of behind-the-scenes production photos. 105 photographs. Filmographies. Index. Originally *Behind the Camera*. 144pp. 8¼ x 11. 23686-2 Pa. $5.00

THE COMPLETE NONSENSE OF EDWARD LEAR, Edward Lear. All nonsense limericks, zany alphabets, Owl and Pussycat, songs, nonsense botany, etc., illustrated by Lear. Total of 321pp. 5⅜ x 8½. (Available in U.S. only) 20167-8 Pa. $4.50

INGENIOUS MATHEMATICAL PROBLEMS AND METHODS, Louis A. Graham. Sophisticated material from Graham *Dial*, applied and pure; stresses solution methods. Logic, number theory, networks, inversions, etc. 237pp. 5⅜ x 8½. 20545-2 Pa. $4.95

BEST MATHEMATICAL PUZZLES OF SAM LOYD, edited by Martin Gardner. Bizarre, original, whimsical puzzles by America's greatest puzzler. From fabulously rare *Cyclopedia*, including famous 14-15 puzzles, the Horse of a Different Color, 115 more. Elementary math. 150 illustrations. 167pp. 5⅜ x 8½. 20498-7 Pa. $3.50

THE BASIS OF COMBINATION IN CHESS, J. du Mont. Easy-to-follow, instructive book on elements of combination play, with chapters on each piece and every powerful combination team—two knights, bishop and knight, rook and bishop, etc. 250 diagrams. 218pp. 5⅜ x 8½. (Available in U.S. only) 23644-7 Pa. $4.50

MODERN CHESS STRATEGY, Ludek Pachman. The use of the queen, the active king, exchanges, pawn play, the center, weak squares, etc. Section on rook alone worth price of the book. Stress on the moderns. Often considered the most important book on strategy. 314pp. 5⅜ x 8½. 20290-9 Pa. $5.00

LASKER'S MANUAL OF CHESS, Dr. Emanuel Lasker. Great world champion offers very thorough coverage of all aspects of chess. Combinations, position play, openings, end game, aesthetics of chess, philosophy of struggle, much more. Filled with analyzed games. 390pp. 5⅜ x 8½. 20640-8 Pa. $5.95

500 MASTER GAMES OF CHESS, S. Tartakower, J. du Mont. Vast collection of great chess games from 1798-1938, with much material nowhere else readily available. Fully annotated, arranged by opening for easier study. 664pp. 5⅜ x 8½. 23208-5 Pa. $8.50

A GUIDE TO CHESS ENDINGS, Dr. Max Euwe, David Hooper. One of the finest modern works on chess endings. Thorough analysis of the most frequently encountered endings by former world champion. 331 examples, each with diagram. 248pp. 5⅜ x 8½. 23332-4 Pa. $3.95

THE COMPLETE BOOK OF DOLL MAKING AND COLLECTING, Catherine Christopher. Instructions, patterns for dozens of dolls, from rag doll on up to elaborate, historically accurate figures. Mould faces, sew clothing, make doll houses, etc. Also collecting information. Many illustrations. 288pp. 6 x 9. 22066-4 Pa. $4.95

THE DAGUERREOTYPE IN AMERICA, Beaumont Newhall. Wonderful portraits, 1850's townscapes, landscapes; full text plus 104 photographs. The basic book. Enlarged 1976 edition. 272pp. 8¼ x 11¼. 23322-7 Pa. $7.95

CRAFTSMAN HOMES, Gustav Stickley. 296 architectural drawings, floor plans, and photographs illustrate 40 different kinds of "Mission-style" homes from The Craftsman (1901-16), voice of American style of simplicity and organic harmony. Thorough coverage of Craftsman idea in text and picture, now collector's item. 224pp. 8⅛ x 11. 23791-5 Pa. $6.50

PEWTER-WORKING: INSTRUCTIONS AND PROJECTS, Burl N. Osborn. & Gordon O. Wilber. Introduction to pewter-working for amateur craftsman. History and characteristics of pewter; tools, materials, step-by-step instructions. Photos, line drawings, diagrams. Total of 160pp. 7⅞ x 10¾. 23786-9 Pa. $4.50

THE GREAT CHICAGO FIRE, edited by David Lowe. 10 dramatic, eyewitness accounts of the 1871 disaster, including one of the aftermath and rebuilding, plus 70 contemporary photographs and illustrations of the ruins—courthouse, Palmer House, Great Central Depot, etc. Introduction by David Lowe. 87pp. 8¼ x 11. 23771-0 Pa. $4.95

SILHOUETTES: A PICTORIAL ARCHIVE OF VARIED ILLUSTRATIONS, edited by Carol Belanger Grafton. Over 600 silhouettes from the 18th to 20th centuries include profiles and full figures of men and women, children, birds and animals, groups and scenes, nature, ships, an alphabet. Dozens of uses for commercial artists and craftspeople. 144pp. 8⅜ x 11¼. 23781-8 Pa. $4.50

ANIMALS: 1,419 COPYRIGHT-FREE ILLUSTRATIONS OF MAMMALS, BIRDS, FISH, INSECTS, ETC., edited by Jim Harter. Clear wood engravings present, in extremely lifelike poses, over 1,000 species of animals. One of the most extensive copyright-free pictorial sourcebooks of its kind. Captions. Index. 284pp. 9 x 12. 23766-4 Pa. $8.95

INDIAN DESIGNS FROM ANCIENT ECUADOR, Frederick W. Shaffer. 282 original designs by pre-Columbian Indians of Ecuador (500-1500 A.D.). Designs include people, mammals, birds, reptiles, fish, plants, heads, geometric designs. Use as is or alter for advertising, textiles, leathercraft, etc. Introduction. 95pp. 8¾ x 11¼. 23764-8 Pa. $4.95

SZIGETI ON THE VIOLIN, Joseph Szigeti. Genial, loosely structured tour by premier violinist, featuring a pleasant mixture of reminiscenes, insights into great music and musicians, innumerable tips for practicing violinists. 385 musical passages. 256pp. 5⅝ x 8¼. 23763-X Pa. $5.00

TONE POEMS, SERIES II: TILL EULENSPIEGELS LUSTIGE STREICHE, ALSO SPRACH ZARATHUSTRA, AND EIN HELDEN-LEBEN, Richard Strauss. Three important orchestral works, including very popular *Till Eulenspiegel's Marry Pranks,* reproduced in full score from original editions. Study score. 315pp. 9⅜ x 12¼. (Available in U.S. only)
23755-9 Pa. $9.95

TONE POEMS, SERIES I: DON JUAN, TOD UND VERKLARUNG AND DON QUIXOTE, Richard Strauss. Three of the most often performed and recorded works in entire orchestral repertoire, reproduced in full score from original editions. Study score. 286pp. 9⅜ x 12¼. (Available in U.S. only)
23754-0 Pa. $9.95

11 LATE STRING QUARTETS, Franz Joseph Haydn. The form which Haydn defined and "brought to perfection." (*Grove's*). 11 string quartets in complete score, his last and his best. The first in a projected series of the complete Haydn string quartets. Reliable modern Eulenberg edition, otherwise difficult to obtain. 320pp. 8⅜ x 11¼. (Available in U.S. only)
23753-2 Pa. $8.95

FOURTH, FIFTH AND SIXTH SYMPHONIES IN FULL SCORE, Peter Ilyitch Tchaikovsky. Complete orchestral scores of Symphony No. 4 in F Minor, Op. 36; Symphony No. 5 in E Minor, Op. 64; Symphony No. 6 in B Minor, "Pathetique," Op. 74. Bretikopf & Hartel eds. Study score. 480pp. 9⅜ x 12¼. 23861-X Pa. $12.95

THE MARRIAGE OF FIGARO: COMPLETE SCORE, Wolfgang A. Mozart. Finest comic opera ever written. Full score, not to be confused with piano renderings. Peters edition. Study score. 448pp. 9⅜ x 12¼. (Available in U.S. only) 23751-6 Pa. $13.95

"IMAGE" ON THE ART AND EVOLUTION OF THE FILM, edited by Marshall Deutelbaum. Pioneering book brings together for first time 38 groundbreaking articles on early silent films from *Image* and 263 illustrations newly shot from rare prints in the collection of the International Museum of Photography. A landmark work. Index. 256pp. 8¼ x 11.
23777-X Pa. $8.95

AROUND-THE-WORLD COOKY BOOK, Lois Lintner Sumption and Marguerite Lintner Ashbrook. 373 cooky and frosting recipes from 28 countries (America, Austria, China, Russia, Italy, etc.) include Viennese kisses, rice wafers, London strips, lady fingers, hony, sugar spice, maple cookies, etc. Clear instructions. All tested. 38 drawings. 182pp. 5⅜ x 8.
23802-4 Pa. $2.75

THE ART NOUVEAU STYLE, edited by Roberta Waddell. 579 rare photographs, not available elsewhere, of works in jewelry, metalwork, glass, ceramics, textiles, architecture and furniture by 175 artists—Mucha, Seguy, Lalique, Tiffany, Gaudin, Hohlwein, Saarinen, and many others. 288pp. 8⅜ x 11¼. 23515-7 Pa. $8.95

THE CURVES OF LIFE, Theodore A. Cook. Examination of shells, leaves, horns, human body, art, etc., in *"the* classic reference on how the golden ratio applies to spirals and helices in nature . . . . "—Martin Gardner. 426 illustrations. Total of 512pp. 5⅜ x 8½.   23701-X Pa. **$6.95**

AN ILLUSTRATED FLORA OF THE NORTHERN UNITED STATES AND CANADA, Nathaniel L. Britton, Addison Brown. Encyclopedic work covers 4666 species, ferns on up. Everything. Full botanical information, illustration for each. This earlier edition is preferred by many to more recent revisions. 1913 edition. Over 4000 illustrations, total of 2087pp. 6⅛ x 9¼.   22642-5, 22643-3, 22644-1 Pa., Three-vol. set **$28.50**

MANUAL OF THE GRASSES OF THE UNITED STATES, A. S. Hitchcock, U.S. Dept. of Agriculture. The basic study of American grasses, both indigenous and escapes, cultivated and wild. Over 1400 species. Full descriptions, information. Over 1100 maps, illustrations. Total of 1051pp. 5⅜ x 8½.   22717-0, 22718-9 Pa., Two-vol. set **$17.00**

THE CACTACEAE,, Nathaniel L. Britton, John N. Rose. Exhaustive, definitive. Every cactus in the world. Full botanical descriptions. Thorough statement of nomenclatures, habitat, detailed finding keys. The one book needed by every cactus enthusiast. Over 1275 illustrations. Total of 1080pp. 8 x 10¼.   21191-6, 21192-4 Clothbd., Two-vol. set **$50.00**

AMERICAN MEDICINAL PLANTS, Charles F. Millspaugh. Full descriptions, 180 plants covered: history; physical description; methods of preparation with all chemical constituents extracted; all claimed curative or adverse effects. 180 full-page plates. Classification table. 804pp. 6½ x 9¼.
23034-1 Pa. **$13.95**

A MODERN HERBAL, Margaret Grieve. Much the fullest, most exact, most useful compilation of herbal material. Gigantic alphabetical encyclopedia, from aconite to zedoary, gives botanical information, medical properties, folklore, economic uses, and much else. Indispensable to serious reader. 161 illustrations. 888pp. 6½ x 9¼. (Available in U.S. only)
22798-7, 22799-5 Pa., Two-vol. set **$15.00**

THE HERBAL or GENERAL HISTORY OF PLANTS, John Gerard. The 1633 edition revised and enlarged by Thomas Johnson. Containing almost 2850 plant descriptions and 2705 superb illustrations, Gerard's *Herbal* is a monumental work, the book all modern English herbals are derived from, the one herbal every serious enthusiast should have in its entirety. Original editions are worth perhaps $750. 1678pp. 8½ x 12¼.
23147-X Clothbd. **$75.00**

MANUAL OF THE TREES OF NORTH AMERICA, Charles S. Sargent. The basic survey of every native tree and tree-like shrub, 717 species in all. Extremely full descriptions, information on habitat, growth, locales, economics, etc. Necessary to every serious tree lover. Over 100 finding keys. 783 illustrations. Total of 986pp. 5⅜ x 8½.
20277-1, 20278-X Pa., Two-vol. set **$12.00**

GREAT NEWS PHOTOS AND THE STORIES BEHIND THEM, John Faber. Dramatic volume of 140 great news photos, 1855 through 1976, and revealing stories behind them, with both historical and technical information. Hindenburg disaster, shooting of Oswald, nomination of Jimmy Carter, etc. 160pp. 8¼ x 11. 23667-6 Pa. $6.00

CRUICKSHANK'S PHOTOGRAPHS OF BIRDS OF AMERICA, Allan D. Cruickshank. Great ornithologist, photographer presents 177 closeups, groupings, panoramas, flightings, etc., of about 150 different birds. Expanded *Wings in the Wilderness*. Introduction by Helen G. Cruickshank. 191pp. 8¼ x 11. 23497-5 Pa. $7.95

AMERICAN WILDLIFE AND PLANTS, A. C. Martin, et al. Describes food habits of more than 1000 species of mammals, birds, fish. Special treatment of important food plants. Over 300 illustrations. 500pp. 5⅜ x 8½. 20793-5 Pa. $6.50

THE PEOPLE CALLED SHAKERS, Edward D. Andrews. Lifetime of research, definitive study of Shakers: origins, beliefs, practices, dances, social organization, furniture and crafts, impact on 19th-century USA, present heritage. Indispensable to student of American history, collector. 33 illustrations. 351pp. 5⅜ x 8½. 21081-2 Pa. $5.50

OLD NEW YORK IN EARLY PHOTOGRAPHS, Mary Black. New York City as it was in 1853-1901, through 196 wonderful photographs from N.-Y. Historical Society. Great Blizzard, Lincoln's funeral procession, great buildings. 228pp. 9 x 12. 22907-6 Pa. $9.95

MR. LINCOLN'S CAMERA MAN: MATHEW BRADY, Roy Meredith. Over 300 Brady photos reproduced directly from original negatives, photos. Jackson, Webster, Grant, Lee, Carnegie, Barnum; Lincoln; Battle Smoke, Death of Rebel Sniper, Atlanta Just After Capture. Lively commentary. 368pp. 8⅜ x 11¼. 23021-X Pa. $11.95

TRAVELS OF WILLIAM BARTRAM, William Bartram. From 1773-8, Bartram explored Northern Florida, Georgia, Carolinas, and reported on wild life, plants, Indians, early settlers. Basic account for period, entertaining reading. Edited by Mark Van Doren. 13 illustrations. 141pp. 5⅜ x 8½. 20013-2 Pa. $6.00

THE GENTLEMAN AND CABINET MAKER'S DIRECTOR, Thomas Chippendale. Full reprint, 1762 style book, most influential of all time; chairs, tables, sofas, mirrors, cabinets, etc. 200 plates, plus 24 photographs of surviving pieces. 249pp. 9⅞ x 12¾. 21601-2 Pa. $8.95

AMERICAN CARRIAGES, SLEIGHS, SULKIES AND CARTS, edited by Don H. Berkebile. 168 Victorian illustrations from catalogues, trade journals, fully captioned. Useful for artists. Author is Assoc. Curator, Div. of Transportation of Smithsonian Institution. 168pp. 8½ x 9½. 23328-6 Pa. $6.50

SECOND PIATIGORSKY CUP, edited by Isaac Kashdan. One of the greatest tournament books ever produced in the English language. All 90 games of the 1966 tournament, annotated by players, most annotated by both players. Features Petrosian, Spassky, Fischer, Larsen, six others. 228pp. 5⅜ x 8½.   23572-6 Pa. $3.50

ENCYCLOPEDIA OF CARD TRICKS, revised and edited by Jean Hugard. How to perform over 600 card tricks, devised by the world's greatest magicians: impromptus, spelling tricks, key cards, using special packs, much, much more. Additional chapter on card technique. 66 illustrations. 402pp. 5⅜ x 8½. (Available in U.S. only)   21252-1 Pa. **$5.95**

MAGIC: STAGE ILLUSIONS, SPECIAL EFFECTS AND TRICK PHOTOGRAPHY, Albert A. Hopkins, Henry R. Evans. One of the great classics; fullest, most authorative explanation of vanishing lady, levitations, scores of other great stage effects. Also small magic, automata, stunts. 446 illustrations. 556pp. 5⅜ x 8½.   23344-8 Pa. $6.95

THE SECRETS OF HOUDINI, J. C. Cannell. Classic study of Houdini's incredible magic, exposing closely-kept professional secrets and revealing, in general terms, the whole art of stage magic. 67 illustrations. 279pp. 5⅜ x 8½.   22913-0 Pa. **$5.95**

HOFFMANN'S MODERN MAGIC, Professor Hoffmann. One of the best, and best-known, magicians' manuals of the past century. Hundreds of tricks from card tricks and simple sleight of hand to elaborate illusions involving construction of complicated machinery. 332 illustrations. 563pp. 5⅜ x 8½.   23623-4 Pa. $6.95

THOMAS NAST'S CHRISTMAS DRAWINGS, Thomas Nast. Almost all Christmas drawings by creator of image of Santa Claus as we know it, and one of America's foremost illustrators and political cartoonists. 66 illustrations. 3 illustrations in color on covers. 96pp. 8⅜ x 11¼.
23660-9 Pa. $3.50

FRENCH COUNTRY COOKING FOR AMERICANS, Louis Diat. 500 easy-to-make, authentic provincial recipes compiled by former head chef at New York's Fitz-Carlton Hotel: onion soup, lamb stew, potato pie, more. 309pp. 5⅜ x 8½.   23665-X Pa. $3.95

SAUCES, FRENCH AND FAMOUS, Louis Diat. Complete book gives over 200 specific recipes: bechamel, Bordelaise, hollandaise, Cumberland, apricot, etc. Author was one of this century's finest chefs, originator of vichyssoise and many other dishes. Index. 156pp. 5⅜ x 8.
23663-3 Pa. **$2.95**

TOLL HOUSE TRIED AND TRUE RECIPES, Ruth Graves Wakefield. Authentic recipes from the famous Mass. restaurant: popovers, veal and ham loaf, Toll House baked beans, chocolate cake crumb pudding, much more. Many helpful hints. Nearly 700 recipes. Index. 376pp. 5⅜ x 8½.
23560-2 Pa. **$4.95**

ILLUSTRATED GUIDE TO SHAKER FURNITURE, Robert Meader. Director, Shaker Museum, Old Chatham, presents up-to-date coverage of all furniture and appurtenances, with much on local styles not available elsewhere. 235 photos. 146pp. 9 x 12.   22819-3 Pa. $6.95

COOKING WITH BEER, Carole Fahy. Beer has as superb an effect on food as wine, and at fraction of cost. Over 250 recipes for appetizers, soups, main dishes, desserts, breads, etc. Index. 144pp. 5⅜ x 8½. (Available in U.S. only)   23661-7 Pa. $3.00

STEWS AND RAGOUTS, Kay Shaw Nelson. This international cookbook offers wide range of 108 recipes perfect for everyday, special occasions, meals-in-themselves, main dishes. Economical, nutritious, easy-to-prepare: goulash, Irish stew, boeuf bourguignon, etc. Index. 134pp. 5⅜ x 8½.   23662-5 Pa. $3.95

DELICIOUS MAIN COURSE DISHES, Marian Tracy. Main courses are the most important part of any meal. These 200 nutritious, economical recipes from around the world make every meal a delight. "I . . . have found it so useful in my own household,"—N.Y. Times. Index. 219pp. 5⅜ x 8½.   23664-1 Pa. $3.95

FIVE ACRES AND INDEPENDENCE, Maurice G. Kains. Great back-to-the-land classic explains basics of self-sufficient farming: economics, plants, crops, animals, orchards, soils, land selection, host of other necessary things. Do not confuse with skimpy faddist literature; Kains was one of America's greatest agriculturalists. 95 illustrations. 397pp. 5⅜ x 8½.   20974-1 Pa. $4.95

A PRACTICAL GUIDE FOR THE BEGINNING FARMER, Herbert Jacobs. Basic, extremely useful first book for anyone thinking about moving to the country and starting a farm. Simpler than Kains, with greater emphasis on country living in general. 246pp. 5⅜ x 8½.   23675-7 Pa. $3.95

PAPERMAKING, Dard Hunter. Definitive book on the subject by the foremost authority in the field. Chapters dealing with every aspect of history of craft in every part of the world. Over 320 illustrations. 2nd, revised and enlarged (1947) edition. 672pp. 5⅜ x 8½.   23619-6 Pa. $8.95

THE ART DECO STYLE, edited by Theodore Menten. Furniture, jewelry, metalwork, ceramics, fabrics, lighting fixtures, interior decors, exteriors, graphics from pure French sources. Best sampling around. Over 400 photographs. 183pp. 8⅜ x 11¼.   22824-X Pa. $6.95

ACKERMANN'S COSTUME PLATES, Rudolph Ackermann. Selection of 96 plates from the Repository of Arts, best published source of costume for English fashion during the early 19th century. 12 plates also in color. Captions, glossary and introduction by editor Stella Blum. Total of 120pp. 8⅜ x 11¼.   23690-0 Pa. $5.00

THE ANATOMY OF THE HORSE, George Stubbs. Often considered the great masterpiece of animal anatomy. Full reproduction of 1766 edition, plus prospectus; original text and modernized text. 36 plates. Introduction by Eleanor Garvey. 121pp. 11 x 14¾. 23402-9 Pa. **$8.95**

BRIDGMAN'S LIFE DRAWING, George B. Bridgman. More than 500 illustrative drawings and text teach you to abstract the body into its major masses, use light and shade, proportion; as well as specific areas of anatomy, of which Bridgman is master. 192pp. 6½ x 9¼. (Available in U.S. only) 22710-3 Pa. **$4.50**

ART NOUVEAU DESIGNS IN COLOR, Alphonse Mucha, Maurice Verneuil, Georges Auriol. Full-color reproduction of *Combinaisons ornementales* (c. 1900) by Art Nouveau masters. Floral, animal, geometric, interlacings, swashes—borders, frames, spots—all incredibly beautiful. 60 plates, hundreds of designs. 9⅜ x 8-1/16. 22885-1 Pa. **$4.50**

FULL-COLOR FLORAL DESIGNS IN THE ART NOUVEAU STYLE, E. A. Seguy. 166 motifs, on 40 plates, from *Les fleurs et leurs applications decoratives* (1902): borders, circular designs, repeats, allovers, "spots." All in authentic Art Nouveau colors. 48pp. 9⅜ x 12¼.
23439-8 Pa. **$6.00**

A DIDEROT PICTORIAL ENCYCLOPEDIA OF TRADES AND IN-DUSTRY, edited by Charles C. Gillispie. 485 most interesting plates from the great French Encyclopedia of the 18th century show hundreds of working figures, artifacts, process, land and cityscapes; glassmaking, paper-making, metal extraction, construction, weaving, making furniture, clothing, wigs, dozens of other activities. Plates fully explained. 920pp. 9 x 12.
22284-5, 22285-3 Clothbd., Two-vol. set **$50.00**

HANDBOOK OF EARLY ADVERTISING ART, Clarence P. Hornung. Largest collection of copyright-free early and antique advertising art ever compiled. Over 6,000 illustrations, from Franklin's time to the 1890's for special effects, novelty. Valuable source, almost inexhaustible.
Pictorial Volume. Agriculture, the zodiac, animals, autos, birds, Christmas, fire engines, flowers, trees, musical instruments, ships, games and sports, much more. Arranged by subject matter and use. 237 plates. 288pp. 9 x 12.
20122-8 Clothbd. **$15.95**

Typographical Volume. Roman and Gothic faces ranging from 10 point to 300 point, "Barnum," German and Old English faces, script, logotypes, scrolls and flourishes, 1115 ornamental initials, 67 complete alphabets, more. 310 plates. 320pp. 9 x 12. 20123-6 Clothbd. **$16.95**

CALLIGRAPHY (CALLIGRAPHIA LATINA), J. G. Schwandner. High point of 18th-century ornamental calligraphy. Very ornate initials, scrolls, borders, cherubs, birds, lettered examples. 172pp. 9 x 13.
20475-8 Pa. **$7.95**

CATALOGUE OF DOVER BOOKS

GEOMETRY, RELATIVITY AND THE FOURTH DIMENSION, Rudolf Rucker. Exposition of fourth dimension, means of visualization, concepts of relativity as Flatland characters continue adventures. Popular, easily followed yet accurate, profound. 141 illustrations. 133pp. 5⅜ x 8½.
23400-2 Pa. $2.75

THE ORIGIN OF LIFE, A. I. Oparin. Modern classic in biochemistry, the first rigorous examination of possible evolution of life from nitrocarbon compounds. Non-technical, easily followed. Total of 295pp. 5⅜ x 8½.
60213-3 Pa. $5.95

PLANETS, STARS AND GALAXIES, A. E. Fanning. Comprehensive introductory survey: the sun, solar system, stars, galaxies, universe, cosmology; quasars, radio stars, etc. 24pp. of photographs. 189pp. 5⅜ x 8½. (Available in U.S. only)
21680-2 Pa. $3.75

THE THIRTEEN BOOKS OF EUCLID'S ELEMENTS, translated with introduction and commentary by Sir Thomas L. Heath. Definitive edition. Textual and linguistic notes, mathematical analysis, 2500 years of critical commentary. Do not confuse with abridged school editions. Total of 1414pp. 5⅜ x 8½.   60088-2, 60089-0, 60090-4 Pa., Three-vol. set $19.50

Prices subject to change without notice.

Available at your book dealer or write for free catalogue to Dept. GI, Dover Publications, Inc., 31 East 2nd St. Mineola., N.Y. 11501. Dover publishes more than 175 books each year on science, elementary and advanced mathematics, biology, music, art, literary history, social sciences and other areas.